EMERGING MARKET PORTFOLIOS

Diversification and Hedging Strategies

MICHAEL G. PAPAIOANNOU
International Monetary Fund

GEORGE TSETSEKOS
Drexel University

IRWIN
Professional Publishing®

Chicago • London • Singapore

Library of Congress Cataloging-in-Publication Data

Papaioannou, Michael G.
    Emerging market portfolios : diversification and hedging strategies / Michael Papaioannou, George Tsetsekos.
    p. cm.
    Includes bibliographical references and index.
    ISBN 0-7863-0337-9
    1. Capital market—Developing countries. 2. Futures market—Developing countries. 3. Bond market—Developing countries.
4. Commodity exchanges—Developing countries. I. Tsetsekos, George. II. Title.
HG5993.P36 1997
332.67′3′091724—dc21   96–44032

Printed in the United States of America
1 2 3 4 5 6 7 8 9 0 D O 3 2 1 0 9 8 7 6

ABOUT THE EDITORS

Dr. Michael G. Papaioannou

Michael G. Papaioannou is a Senior Economist with the International Monetary Fund (IMF). He holds a permanent appointment with the Treasurer's Department of the IMF. His responsibilities include policy assessment and analysis of foreign exchange and global capital market development. He is involved in research on the role of synthetic currencies, derivative products, and hedging in the management of central bank reserves.

Dr. Papaioannou served as an Advisor to the Governing Board of the Bank of Greece, in the interest of the IMF, from 1993–1995. His tasks included assessment of the foreign exchange exposure of Greece's external liabilities, evaluation of debt servicing options, establishment of borrowing strategies and monitoring of international and domestic financial markets. He was also involved in the design and development of the secondary market for government securities and the derivatives market in Greece.

Prior to joining the IMF, Dr. Papaioannou served as a member of the Wharton Econometric Forecasting Associates (WEFA) group in various capacities of increasing responsibility. He was the Director of Foreign Exchange Services (1986–1988), Vice President of International Financial Markets (1988–1989), and Senior Vice President of International Financial Services (1989–1990). As a Senior Vice President, Dr. Papaioannou directed the activities for analyses and forecasts of the foreign exchange and financial services and oversaw the developments in global financial markets and institutions.

Dr. Papaioannou's publications include articles in academic journals such as the *Journal of Investing,* the *Open Economies Review, Finance and Development,* the *IMF Staff Papers,* the *Journal of Optimization Theory and Applications,* and the *International Journal of Adaptive Control and Signaling Processing,* as well as numerous articles in other professional journals. He has conducted several seminars on foreign exchange forecasting and currency hedging and has been invited as a speaker to professional associations, university lecture series, and conferences. In addition, Dr. Papaioannou has served as a member of the Finance faculty of Temple University, where he taught international finance courses.

Dr. Papaioannou holds a Ph.D. in Economics from the University of Pennsylvania (1986), an M.A. in Economics from Georgetown University, and a B.A. in Economics from the University of Athens.

Dr. George Tsetsekos

George Tsetsekos is Professor of Finance and Associate Department Head of the Finance Department in the College of Business Administration at Drexel University. Currently, Dr. Tsetsekos serves as the Director of The Risk Management Institute. The Institute was formed to offer educational programs and advisory services to interested clients from financial engineering to the use of futures, options, and swaps.

Dr. Tsetsekos' research interests cover the areas of emerging capital markets, risk management, and corporate restructuring. He is the author of numerous articles, monographs, and book reviews and has organized special panel discussion sessions on international finance and corporate finance. He has lectured and conducted seminars in the area of capital markets, served as a member of the program committee of several academic finance associations and is an ad-hoc referee for several academic journals.

Dr. Tsetsekos has been involved in various specialized consulting assignments in corporate finance. In 1989–90, he served as an advisor to the Greek government for the restructuring, planning, and evaluation of a $1.2 billion privatization program of State Owned Enterprises.

Dr. Tsetsekos' publications include articles that have appeared in *The Journal of Financial Economics,* the *Journal of Banking and Finance, Financial Management, Financial Review, The Journal of Portfolio Management,* the *Journal of International Business Studies,* and *The Journal of International Financial Management and Accounting.*

Prior to joining the Finance department at Drexel University in 1988, Dr. Tsetsekos served as an Assistant Professor of Finance at The American University (1985–1988). He holds a Ph.D. in Finance from The University of Tennessee (1986), an M.B.A. in Finance, and a B.S. in Electrical and Mechanical Engineering.

PREFACE

The objective of this book is to develop a framework for effective portfolio management in emerging capital markets. Based on recent academic research, we focus on six distinct features of emerging markets. *First,* we analyze the structural characteristics of emerging capital markets, which determine the breath and depth of their pattern of development over time. Structural features provide opportunities for risk diversification and hedging, but they also may cause problems in active portfolio management.

Second, we discuss the benefits to investors of portfolio allocations when assets from emerging country economies are part of the investor's opportunity set. When commodities are introduced, risk management in emerging countries becomes critical; portfolio allocations are improved when the commodities are included along with equities.

Third, we provide insight regarding the correlation characteristics in emerging markets by focusing on Latin American markets and extrapolating the observed empirical evidence on the broad class of emerging capital markets. The volatility transmission of return distribution across markets and the extent of integration with the developed capital markets dictate diversification benefits. Often the investment horizon within which portfolio flows are allocated plays a role in the correlation patterns of returns in emerging markets. The cointegration of emerging markets provides insights into matters of market efficiency and market segmentation.

Fourth, we focus on asset and derivatives pricing in emerging markets by examining the empirical evidence from a two-factor asset pricing model, which includes emerging equity as a distinct asset class.

Fifth, we discuss derivatives in emerging markets and the hedging of portfolio investment flows in an economy with a soft currency by taking up the case of the Taiwan market.

Sixth, we consider the central role played by regulation, especially in countries with developing economies. Foreign portfolio flows and the use of derivatives may influence the channels of monetary policy in a developing country economy.

To be effective, portfolio management and investment flows in emerging capital should take into account the above six critical parameters.

BRIEF CONTENTS

CONTENTS

Chapter 3

A Survey and Synthesis of Problems and Opportunities in Emerging Capital Markets   39
Brian Bruce and William Reichenstein

PART III

PORTFOLIO ALLOCATION ISSUES IN EMERGING MARKETS

PART VI

DERIVATIVE INSTRUMENTS AND HEDGING IN EMERGING CAPITAL MARKETS

Chapter 11

Derivatives in Emerging Markets   215
Lawrence K. Duke

Chapter 12

Cross-Hedging Currency Investment Flows in an Emerging Market   231
Chung-Hua Shen and Lee-Rong Wang

PART

I

BACKGROUND AND ORIENTATION

1

EMERGING CAPITAL MARKETS AND PORTFOLIO MANAGEMENT

Michael Papaioannou, *International Monetary Fund*
George P. Tsetsekos, *Drexel University*

There is no more celebrated topic in international economics and international finance research than emerging capital markets. There is fascination with extraordinary abnormal returns, and, perhaps, fear of shifts in risk exposure, but above all, there is intellectual curiosity about the architecture of the emerging markets, the convergence of these markets toward developed markets, and the extent to which there are sustainable benefits from diversification from investing in emerging market economies. Portfolio management practices have recognized the significance of emerging capital markets and modern allocation schemes have included emerging markets as an asset class. However, for portfolio management to be effective, it is necessary to recognize several unique features of emerging capital markets:

- Emerging markets are structurally different from their domestic counterparts.
- Capital allocation schemes, which include an emerging equity component or exposure to an emerging country economy, offer persistent diversification benefits.

- The correlation structure and volatility linkages make these markets partially segmented with inefficiency characteristics, thus providing opportunities for arbitrage profits.
- Asset pricing for international institutional investors offers a high level of accuracy in evaluating portfolio exposures only when there is an explicit consideration of a two-factor model with assets from emerging and developed capital markets.
- The availability of derivative instruments allows portfolio flows in emerging capital markets to be hedged; moreover, new techniques allow hedging to be effective for investments in countries with weak or soft currencies.
- Derivative activity in emerging capital markets may influence the monetary policy of an emerging country.

Emerging security markets are expected to have different characteristics from their counterparts in industrialized nations simply because their origin is more recent. The structural features of emerging capital markets encompass both the architecture of the market and the country's institutional infrastructure, which comprises a broad legal framework that recognizes property rights, disclosure requirements, and accounting practices conforming to international standards. However, supervision and regulation of these markets may be inadequate or even absent.

The structural features of the market dictate the extent of *resource allocation* in these markets for portfolio investments and diversification. The intrinsic characteristics of emerging markets bring opportunities for expanding the investment set and allow for the development of vehicles for exposure in these markets. The new asset class of securities traded in emerging capital markets offers a process that ensures optimum portfolio allocations. In addition, if one considers commodities as an asset class, especially for the countries with commodity production, the portfolio allocation should consider the risk management of commodities markets. Financial risk management tools are used to enhance returns in portfolio diversification when commodities are introduced—in addition to equities—as an asset class.

Two characteristic features of emerging capital markets are volatility and integration with other markets. Correlations in emerging capital markets may provide several hints about the benefits to be derived from diversification. The transmission of volatility across emerging markets and their linkages with the developed markets offer a contrast for several other markets. The extent of integration of the markets or the lack of segmentation will dictate possible benefits from diversification.

In emerging markets, the pricing of assets and hedging instruments may be different than that of the developed markets. After introducing the two classes of assets, the pricing of emerging markets' equities takes a new twist. Recent developments in stochastic volatility offer a broad range of new techniques in pricing derivatives.

In recent years we have witnessed the introduction of several new instruments for hedging and the availability of hedging instruments in developing country economies. Hedging techniques are especially important when portfolio investment flows move to an emerging country economy that is experiencing a soft and volatile local currency.

Regulation has contributed to the development of the financial infrastructure within which emerging markets have developed and flourished. The impact of derivatives markets on one aspect of monetary policy is especially notable.

By focusing on each of the above dimensions, this book develops a positive framework for effective portfolio management in emerging capital markets. The following is a discussion of the approach we have taken to present recent research for each of these dimensions.

STRUCTURAL FEATURES IN EMERGING MARKETS

Emerging capital markets are quite dissimilar from those in developed nations. Differentiating elements include, among others, the information-based features that make the emerging markets not fully efficient, the institutional infrastructure, which includes market entry and exit regulations, and the investment tax structure.

The evolution of emerging markets, described by Papaioannou and Duke in Chapter 2, takes into account the idiosyncrasies of the markets and follows several distinct phases. In the first phase, markets are developed based on liberalization policies implemented by the authorities. Markets gradually gain the confidence of domestic investors and become more widely accepted as an investment alternative to traditional bank deposits. In the second phase, because the equity market now has some degree of credibility, pressures abroad for greater accessibility and at home for cheaper capital funding lead to a loosening of regulations in the domestic capital market. In the third phase, new issues of stocks and corporate bonds can be absorbed easily by the investment public and the volume of trade increases rapidly; thus, the increased trading activity produces more effective intermediation. The market then has the potential to be fully integrated with the developed markets or to be closely integrated with the other emerging capital markets.

Although in the process of emerging market development there is the possibility of a speculative bubble (i.e., above normal "positively autocorrelated" returns, which turn negative when the bubble bursts), there are several opportunities available to investors in those markets. These opportunities, discussed by Bruce and Reichenstein in Chapter 3, stem from extraordinary market-adjusted returns and the economic diversification of resources. Problems associated with the process of developing the market are present as well. These involve the impact of macroeconomic forces in the general economic environment, volatility, political risks, information risks, costs, access to those markets, the repatriation of capital, fiduciary constraints, financial risk, liquidity, and regulations.

PORTFOLIO ALLOCATION IN EMERGING CAPITAL MARKETS

Global diversification depends on the correlations among countries. Increased cross-border investments and improved communications technology may be increasing the correlations among developed markets. Empirical data confirms this speculation. In Chapter 4, Speidell and Sappenfield report that correlation coefficients for emerging markets increased particularly during the fourth quarter of 1987 and the third quarter of 1990. Their conclusions suggest that portfolio allocations in emerging markets provided diversification benefits during these periods; these benefits are expected to be increasingly important in the future.

Portfolio allocations also may include exposure to commodities. Although several emerging country economies rely on export revenues from those commodities, it appears that emerging country economies could benefit from improved commodity risk management. In Chapter 5, Claessens and Varangis argue that historically, the performance of other risk management instruments, mainly commodity stabilization funds and commodity agreements, has not been satisfactory. Developing countries have made little use of existing commodity exchanges and the experience with commodity exchanges in developing countries has not been encouraging. The main impediments to the use of market-based risk management tools in developing countries have been: policy-induced distortions, restrictive legal, regulatory, and institutional structures, poor creditworthiness, and lack of awareness and misconceptions about the role of hedging instruments in the public sector. Establishing a domestic commodity futures exchange requires several preconditions that in most cases are hard to find in emerging market countries. For those several important commodities for which futures contracts do not exist and for which futures contracts may not be viable, the establishment of local forward markets may prove to be an effective instrument for price discovery and risk sharing.

ISSUES OF VOLATILITY AND CO-INTEGRATION IN EMERGING CAPITAL MARKETS

Government constraints, investors' perceptions, and imperfections often cause markets to become segmented. A national market in an emerging country economy can be efficient and yet segmented in an international context. In an efficient national market, security prices may accurately reflect information available to the investors who participate in that market. However, if the market is segmented, foreign investors would not be participants. Therefore, in a portfolio context it becomes critical to examine the extent of integration of emerging markets with other developed markets and the degree of co-movement of returns of emerging markets with other markets, as well.

Ratner, in Chapter 6, examines the issue of correlations of returns in several emerging markets. More specifically, he analyzes the correlation structure between the United States and the four largest Latin American equity markets: Argentina, Brazil, Chile, and Mexico. Several causality tests are used to examine whether U.S. equity prices cause changes to occur in the stock prices of those markets. Significant causation implies that equity prices in one market may be used to predict changes in other emerging markets. The results indicate that unidimensional, bidirectional, and contemporaneous adjustments generally do not exist among these markets. These findings suggest that investments in Latin American equities provide measurable risk reductions in a diversified international portfolio.

The analysis of correlations and causality tests helps clarify the role of emerging capital markets in portfolio diversification. Another issue related to diversification is the extent of the integration of markets in terms of volatilities. More specifically, the extent of intraregional and interregional stock market linkages in emerging markets provides additional insights into the transmission of price movements among developed and developing markets and allows an accurate assessment of the benefits of portfolio diversification. Aggarwal and Leal, in Chapter 7, examine these issues for six Asian and four Latin American countries by focusing their attention on linkages with U.S., Japan, and four major Morgan Stanley market indexes: the World Index, the Emerging Markets Index, the Far East Index, and the Latin American Index. The empirical analysis uses a sample of daily returns for these markets covering a twelve year period, 1982–1993. Results indicate that emerging markets, particularly those of Latin America, are extremely volatile with high standard deviations.

Most markets exhibit significant skewness, kurtosis, and autocorrelation. Daily correlations between the emerging markets themselves and with other major markets are increasing over time but continue to be fairly low. During periods of large market movements in the U.S., the correlations are found to be even higher. The practical recommendation of the analysis is that, in general, long-term gains from diversification are sustainable and persistent, but portfolio managers should be aware that in times of large market movements almost all markets seem to move in the same direction. The U.S. market returns and volatility and the

World Index are more important in explaining security returns and, particularly, volatility in the emerging markets of Asia than in those of Latin America.

To examine the issues of persistency and sustainability of the long-run diversification potential of emerging capital markets, Tsetsekos in Chapter 8 uses co-integration techniques. For thirteen emerging capital markets grouped by geographical regions of the world and the U.S., he finds that the correlation between returns from each market is independent of the investment horizon. For emerging capital markets, he examines the extent to which each one of the emerging markets is weakly efficient and collectively co-integrated. Statistical tests reveal that each one of the thirteen emerging capital markets, when considered in isolation, exhibits weak-form efficiency. Clustering the emerging markets in three groups according to their regional and development status reveals that all of the markets jointly exhibit weak-form efficiency. The lack of co-integration and the independence of markets within these three groups suggest that emerging capital markets are not fully integrated and that there are substantial benefits to be derived from international portfolio diversification.

ASSET AND DERIVATIVES PRICING IN EMERGING CAPITAL MARKETS

Portfolio allocations take into consideration the pricing of financial instruments. Finance models, such as the capital asset pricing model (CAPM) and the arbitrage pricing theory (APT), predict that equity returns are a function of the sensitivity of a financial instrument to global risk factors, which are reflected in the global market portfolio. While this modeling of asset pricing assumes that institutional investors investing in emerging markets reduce country-specific risk through diversification, the recent Mexico crisis shows that developed markets exhibit an asymmetric overreaction to events in other emerging markets, even when those events do not seem to affect the economic fundamentals in developed countries. To explain the strong reaction of developed capital markets to seemingly unrelated events in emerging countries, Buckberg in Chapter 9 empirically tests a proposition that links the pricing of assets in emerging market economies with the portfolio allocation process followed by institutional investors. In a two-factor asset pricing model that includes both the global portfolio and a broad emerging markets portfolio, results from several tests for the period of 1989–95 show that asset pricing is accurate and offers greater precision in pricing than the conventional CAPM.

Recent developments in modeling derivative securities allow for the pricing of several classes of instruments. The original work by Black–Scholes has been expanded to reflect the relaxation of several standard assumptions. For example, the usual Black–Scholes argument requires frictionless markets. There are several instances where derivatives developed for emerging capital markets exhibit high transaction costs and may affect trading in the underlying asset. Hodges et al. discuss stochastic volatility in the pricing and hedging of options and review the most recent research, which has focused on the problems of understanding the nature of the stochastic processes for underlying security and market assets.

DERIVATIVE INSTRUMENTS AND HEDGING IN EMERGING CAPITAL MARKETS

On practical grounds, provided that benefits from diversification exist and there is an interest for portfolio investment flows in emerging country economies, portfolio managers are confronted with three fundamental questions: (a) How are derivatives presently used in some of the representative emerging markets? (b) Are there active markets for derivatives in emerging country economies? and (c) What are the technical details and the appropriate strategy to be followed to hedge portfolio flows in a country with a soft currency?

In Chapter 11, Duke explores alternative hedging objectives for each of the principal types of market participants and presents an analysis of transaction costs, liquidity considerations, risks, and strategic and transactional approaches involving emerging market derivatives. From this analysis, a framework is constructed providing a way to gauge the appropriateness of derivatives uses in managing financial exposures. The article provides a general description of derivatives applications currently in active use in the Asian markets and outlines several future prospects for emerging market derivatives.

When expected future cash flows are denominated in a soft currency, investors or traders are limited to futures and forward contracts, which may not be available in the same soft currency. This implies that investment portfolio flows in emerging capital markets are exposed to considerable currency risk. In Chapter 12, Shen and Wang develop analytical models using Markov switching algorithms, which permit the hedge rations and hedging performances to be different in two states. The application of a cross-hedging two-states approach provides empirical evidence regarding the effectiveness of the cross hedging of New Taiwan dollar exchange rate risk. The results of this analysis show that the second state is an effective hedging state between the two states along with yen futures being an ideal instrument for hedging New Taiwan dollar exchange rate risk.

To hedge relevant exposures, portfolio managers are interested in identifying instruments and contracts traded in emerging markets. Analysis of data reveals that there are several active derivatives markets in emerging country economies. Tsetsekos in Chapter 13 provides a classification of these markets and enumerates the contracts currently traded.

REGULATORY ISSUES AND CENTRAL BANK EXPOSURE

Portfolio management and derivatives hedging are influenced by regulation. In an emerging market there are instances where the derivatives activities influence monetary policy. Papaioannou and Tsetsekos in Chapter 14 examine the preconditions for a well-functioning derivatives market in an emerging economy and analyze the influence of derivatives on its monetary policy. The introduction of derivatives is viewed as an integral part of an economy's financial development. The examination considers the links between derivatives and monetary aggregates and highlights the impact of derivatives on monetary policy and systemic risks. Papaioannou and Tsetsekos suggest that derivatives may (a) distort traditional measures of monetary aggregates; (b) require appreciable changes in macroeconomic parameters for monetary policy to be effective; and (c) increase the credit and risk exposure of underwriters and financial intermediaries, and thus the systemic risks in the financial system. The authors develop the proposition that although beneficial to end-users, derivatives can cause a loss of control by monetary authorities in achieving macroeconomic goals, especially in emerging market economies.

STRUCTURAL FEATURES IN EMERGING MARKETS

2

PATTERNS OF DEVELOPMENT IN EMERGING CAPITAL MARKETS

Michael Papaioannou, *International Monetary Fund*
Lawrence Duke, *Citicorp, Japan*

Over the past two decades, governments of emerging market economies have taken numerous measures to mobilize investment flows from international capital markets to their own new equity markets and to promote efficient capital allocation. Often, these governments have been dedicated to policies that promote macroeconomic stability, allow market forces to work, encourage the private sector as the driving force for economic growth, and enhance the effectiveness and depth of the financial system through scaled-down regulation.

These better known emerging equity markets have become more liquid, less volatile, and more efficient because of greater asset supply, better research, and less extreme economic policy shifts. Moreover, "embryonic" equity markets are emerging with the same characteristics as the emerging markets of the 1970s and 1980s throughout the developing world and in the former centrally planned economies of Eastern Europe and the now-defunct Soviet Union (most notably Indo-China, selected African countries, Russia, and the Baltic states). As financial reforms take root and market institutions appear in the latter countries, their equity market activity is expected to jump in the same manner as in the better known emerging markets. Notable recent incidents of such surges in trading volumes and stock price movements have occurred in Mexico in 1991 and in Korea in late 1992 and early 1993.

The establishment of emerging equity markets is warranted not only because of the domestic capital demand but also because of the willingness of investors to place their funds in such markets. The reform process has allowed these markets to develop as alternative sources of capital for entrepreneurs and government-owned companies attempting to privatize. Nonetheless, the new markets can and have provided investors not only with higher returns than the more established markets of industrial countries, but with more opportunities to diversify their international portfolios.

Emerging equity markets offer potentially attractive rates of return, in part because the combination of low-cost resources and technology transfers often produces large profit margins for firms operating in such environments. Despite their potential benefits, however, the emerging equity markets have as much, if not more, risk than developed markets and have yet to be widely accepted by international investors. In addition to the dangers of macroeconomic and financial and political instability, the following drawbacks to investment in developing countries and transitional economies often are cited: occasional sharp equity price drops, a lack of market liquidity, and inadequate monitoring of insider trading activity. Institutional investors also face bureaucratic restrictions that can limit market access, hinder the settlement of payments, and make repatriating capital difficult. In the last two or three years, a number of countries—especially Mexico and Korea—have initiated serious efforts to eliminate or substantially reduce many of these obstacles.

THE STAGES OF DEVELOPMENT OF AN EMERGING EQUITY MARKET

Although each emerging market has its own idiosyncracies, a broad description of some general phases that a generic—that is, average—emerging equity market goes through can be abstracted from historical experiences and may provide a unifying framework of analysis and a better understanding of the long process of their development. Initially, when a country achieves a degree of economic and political stability and begins implementing growth-oriented policies, equity prices rise. As they do, the market gains the confidence of domestic investors and becomes more widely accepted as an investment alternative to traditional bank deposits and, in many instances, short-term government bonds. Examples of countries that have recently gone through that phase are China, Peru, and Guyana, while examples of countries that are still in that phase are Vietnam, Ghana, and many republics of the former Soviet Union. In the second phase, because the equity market now has some degree of credibility, pressures abroad for greater accessibility and at home for cheaper capital funding lead to a loosening of regulations in the domestic capital market. As deregulation leads to increases in equity market liquidity and to rises in risk-adjusted returns, international investors begin to realize the diversification benefits of investing in such an emerging equity market. Examples of markets in this second phase are the Philippines, India, Pakistan, Colombia, the Czech Republic, and Poland.

In the third, expansion phase because the market now offers the prospect of high returns, new issues of stocks and corporate bonds can be absorbed easily by the investment public, and thus their volume increases rapidly. The number of new issues increases as firms strive to pay down debt and private or newly privatized companies make their initial public offerings. The increased trading activity produces more effective intermediation, while the growing need for a risk transfer mechanism spurs the development of equity and currency-hedging instruments, such as derivatives and index products. Examples of markets that are in the third phase are Malaysia, Indonesia, Thailand, Argentina, Venezuela, Turkey, and Hungary. Finally, as equity risk premia, measured relatively to government Treasury bill rates or an equivalent short-term money market rate, fall to internationally competitive levels, the equity market begins to achieve the stable growth that marks a mature or developed state. Examples of markets in this third phase are Singapore, Korea, Hong Kong, Taiwan, Mexico, Greece, and Portugal.

It should be noted here that the length of these broad phases may vary with the country and the period in which an emerging market's evolution occurs. In general, periods of global economic expansion tend to accelerate the pace of the development of capital markets in general and of emerging equity markets in particular. Furthermore, investors should be aware of the particular phase that an emerging equity market is in so they can assess appropriately the expected returns and risks involved from investing in this specific market. Often, both the returns and the volatility of an equity market tend to be higher during the early phases. Also, governments of emerging equity markets should know the particular phase of development that their markets are in so that they can adopt appropriate policy measures that will speed up the process and aid their smoother evolution.

THE BUBBLE EFFECT

Equity prices tend to fluctuate widely at every phase of an emerging market's evolution. During the early stages, however, prices tend to move more frequently as well as sharply and abruptly as increasing amounts of capital are issued and large inflows of both domestic and foreign funds force stocks to an initial overvaluation. Subsequently, equity prices rise still more, supported by improved domestic economic conditions and increased corporate profits, but the frequency and the intensity of price fluctuations tend to subside.

At this point, domestic market liquidity improves further and foreign portfolio investment picks up. Often, at this stage equity prices begin to rise out of proportion to market fundamentals (that is, to the present discounted value of dividend payments). Equity prices then have reached the peak of a speculative "bubble" phase, setting the stage for a downward correction. As evident from Exhibits 2–1 and 2–2, Korea and Taiwan reached the peak of their bubble phases at the beginning and the end of 1989, respectively. Often, a political or business blunder, misfortune, or perceived or actual mistake in economic policy triggers the downward movement, or "burst of the bubble."

In a downward correction period, investors tend to decrease their equity holdings, creating a surge in their cash balances. Equity issues and interest rates also drop significantly.

E X H I B I T   2–1

Taiwan (WPI)

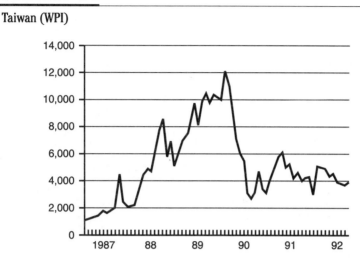

In emerging markets, the fluctuations in price movements common to even the most developed markets are more frequent and exacerbated due to a lack of market liquidity. Only when investors begin to realize that the equity market is being undervalued does the abrupt drop in prices stop. Usually, falling stock prices in relation to current and expected earnings trigger this realization, which subsequently spreads throughout the market and paves the way for renewed market confidence.

As equity prices start to pick up again, domestic investors pour new funds into the equity market, encouraged by the prospect of a repeat of the capital gains realized in the earlier upward surge. International investors often follow suit, and corporations again are encouraged to issue new stock. This is the beginning of another upward movement—and possible overshooting—of equity prices. Close monitoring and preventive measures have helped avert abrupt bursts of a speculative bubble, including the use of "circuit breakers" that prevent an equity index from trading below a prespecified level, based on the previous day's closing price, and adjustments in margin requirements in buying and selling equities and equity derivatives.

Unless sharp downward movements in equity prices are the result of questionable governmental policies, authorities in

EXHIBIT 2-2

Korea Composite Index

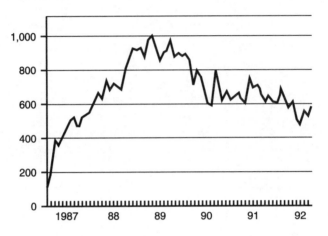

principle should not react by altering their monetary and/or fiscal policies (for example, easing credit conditions or changing withholding tax rates on capital gains). It should be realized that such price fluctuations are part of the natural course of events when undertaking investment risks in an emerging equity market.

PROBLEMS FACING EMERGING EQUITY MARKETS

Frequently, emerging markets have to deal with unique macroeconomic and political risk factors, which are the result of unsettled macroeconomic policy choices and/or volatile political situations, and various other developmental and institutional impediments. The most endemic macroeconomic risks in such countries are monetary instability, along with large budget deficits, inconsistencies in the monetary/fiscal policy mixture, and an overvalued exchange rate. Among the most common developmental and institutional obstacles are small capitalization in relation to the country's gross national product (GNP), limited liquidity of traded instruments, and an outdated and often overregulated financial system. Generally, the implications of such risks and/or impediments are higher returns required by investors, due to the higher uncertainty involved, and higher transaction costs and fees, due to the limited capitalization and market liquidity and the red tape associated with excessive regulation.

Macroeconomic Policy

Some of the most common problems that economies of emerging equity markets face are of a macroeconomic nature. In their attempt to achieve a rather accelerated growth of their investment sector, governments may be tempted to compromise their fiscal and monetary discipline by financing certain public or private sector projects through the government budget or through preferential credit rates. However, it has been proven in the past that such policy deviations will indeed create macroeconomic instability, most often manifested by higher inflation and excessive exchange rate volatility. Depending on the degree to which financing of the public sector occurs through fiscal deficits and the extent to which credit to the government squeezes private investment, such an accelerated growth-oriented policy may endanger the long-term prospects of an economy. Only growth-oriented policies that are formulated within a prudent macroeconomic policy framework can assure a sustained effect on growth and therefore attract international portfolio investment.

Financial Risks

Many investors believe they will face increased market and currency risk exposure in an emerging market due to the reduced market liquidity and the potential for sharp exchange rate depreciations. While emerging markets may be more volatile than established markets, investors may be able to reduce their overall portfolio risk by appropriately diversifying their portfolios through the inclusion of emerging market assets, which usually exhibit different risk and return characteristics than those of developed-market assets.

Furthermore, currency risk is one of the most significant concerns for an international portfolio. However, diversifying currencies can help in reducing such risk if investments are carefully allocated in a global portfolio. Investors also can use cross-hedges, forward contracts, or, in some cases, option-related foreign exchange instruments to insure against currency risk.

Although investors may find ways to reduce uncertainties related to equities and currencies of emerging markets, nonetheless, such uncertainties are considered to be major financial risks by the overwhelming majority of investors and therefore constitute potential obstacles for investments in these markets.

Small Capitalization

Many emerging market economies are faced with the problem of having many small-size firms engaged in domestic production due to the small size of the domestic market or to a less than buoyant local business climate. The small market may be the consequence of insufficient domestic demand due to low incomes and/or small size of population, while an unfavorable business climate may be the result of a stringent institutional, and in particular tax/legal, system and the lack of an appropriate infrastructure, in addition to the previous factors. When the financial structure of firms is such, only a few firms will be eligible to meet the standards of local equity-market listings and therefore the capitalization relative to gross domestic product (GDP) will tend to be small. Small capitalizations often are regarded as a major barrier for international investors because not only do they limit the selection of available investment choices but also they are considered as a prime source for sharp equity price fluctuations (i.e., high volatility).

Liquidity

One major developmental barrier to international investment in emerging stock markets is the lack of liquidity and depth. Many emerging markets are characterized by small trading volumes that effectively shut out large institutional investors, because even what these investors consider to be small trades amount to huge transactions for the markets themselves and could lead to unacceptably high volatility. Lack of liquidity depresses financial transactions in that particular country's emerging equity markets, thus effectively reducing their efficiency. Also, fear of possible price manipulation due to the low volume of instruments may discourage institutional investors from entering undeveloped markets. Liquidity in the latter case is highly dependent on the government's initiative in providing an appropriate legal and accounting system to ensure transparency of financial transactions.

Regulations

Among the most common institutional barriers are regulations that limit foreign investment. International investors face constraints of one kind or another in most of the world's capital markets, but the limitations are most severe in emerging markets. Restrictions and controls on capital flows and exchange transactions, barriers on market entry and exit, inadequate information on securities transactions, a small number of market makers and brokers, and high transaction costs and brokerage fees sharply restrict international investment in many developing countries.

Financial intermediaries, in particular dealers and brokers, need to operate under specific legislation that guarantees compliance with agreements and contracts. Emerging equities markets develop and function well only if participants have confidence in the efficient workings of the financial market system, can trust that the rules of honest trading prevail, and accept specialized government institutions as arbiters in disputes.

Furthermore, differences in accounting rules and standards between developing and developed countries often complicate investment decisions. This limitation is over and above restrictions on foreign investments that many investors may face in their own countries. International investors may be constrained by internal, company-specific or countrywide, provisions on the proportion of foreign assets that they can hold in their portfolios. However, these constraints have been relaxing in countries around the world as the trend toward deregulation accelerates.

Other Risks

Other real-world risks include the possibility that a developing nation's government will institute high withholding taxes, nationalize firms, or restrict the repatriation of dividends and capital. Although such risks can be diversified away to a degree, they cannot be ignored. Finally, management costs in emerging markets tend to be higher than in established markets and can include transaction costs, brokerage fees, custodial fees, management fees, and costs of obtaining market-related information.

Finally, newly emerging market economies are faced with additional problems of a particular nature. Among them are:

1. Economic reform programs, including liberalization, privatization, and restructuring of companies' policies that are incomplete and/or not widely accepted.

2. Formulation and implementation of legal and regulatory codes, as well as other institutional foundations, which are necessary for the orderly functioning of an economic system.

3. Dealing with an underdeveloped financial infrastructure, which includes a lack of technical managers and immense bureaucratic processes.

Especially needed in such countries is the adaptation of a comprehensive regulatory framework that provides rules ranging from equity exchange listings to insider trading, to how companies should prepare their accounts in line with international accounting standards, to protecting property rights, and the issuing of equity shares.

PROMOTING EMERGING EQUITY MARKETS

Many governments of countries with emerging markets have been engaged in various macroeconomic and structural adjustment policies, as well as other institutional changes, in order to promote portfolio investment. Most often, emerging market governments have pursued growth-oriented policies within a framework of relative macroeconomic stability, in an effort to attain long-term, self-sustained growth and ensure a vigorous domestic demand. It is important to note that many emerging market governments have succeeded in instituting such growth policies without seriously impacting their fiscal balances or their monetary discipline. Hence, inflation and exchange rates have been under control, while the crowding out of private investment by public sector financing requirements has been minimal, with a consequent increase in the number of ample-size firms operating in such economies. The growth of domestic demand has encouraged further large scale private investments, which in turn tends to produce larger corporations and therefore higher market capitalization to GDP ratios. As part of their structural adjustment efforts, these governments have cut budget deficits, reduced the economic role of the state (notably through privatization), liberalized internal and external trade, and eased controls on capital flows.

Monetary and Fiscal Policy

As mentioned above, monetary and fiscal policy constitutes a major source of risk in equity markets. This is because monetary instability and fiscal imprudence create financial uncertainty that may seriously impair the functioning and performance of equity markets. For example, unanticipated inflation transfers wealth and income from lenders to borrowers, driving investors out of securities and into the real assets (such as gold and real estate) that traditionally are believed to offer protection against purchasing power risk. Maintaining a stable monetary and budgetary framework is one of the most useful services such governments can provide to financial markets.

The case of Korea is a good example of a country that has pursued growth-oriented policies, coupled with very stable macroeconomic conditions, while instituting a financial reform program in an effort to gain acceptability by international investors. The Korean government followed an open export-oriented program, which succeeded in stimulating private investment and boosting manufactured exports; at the same time, it avoided compromising its macroeconomic discipline. It also should be noted that Korea's subsidized credit system to the export sector from the state-owned banks was fine tuned in such a way that it did not create any serious bottlenecks for the other sectors of the economy. This environment nourished very big and profitable corporations, allowing them to have an early entry to local equity markets and to access funds that helped further their development. Encouraged by the strength of the local corporations and the relatively high capitalization to GDP ratio, international investors have been particularly keen for Korea's equity markets especially following the financial liberalization of recent years.

Financial Liberalization

The implementation of financial liberalization measures has varied widely across emerging market economies, with a small number of them following a fast pace of financial reforms (e.g., Singapore) and the overwhelming majority following a more gradual reform process (e.g., Korea, Mexico, and Turkey). In Korea, the liberalization of interest rates resulted in positive real interest rates, which contributed to significant financial deepening. The ratio of M3 money supply (which includes nonbank financial assets, particularly corporate bonds and commercial paper) to GDP rose sharply in the 1980s, reaching over 100 percent in 1989 and thereafter, and grew faster than the ratio of M2 to GDP. This reflected the more relaxed regulatory environment of the nonbank financial institutions and their ability to offer higher yields on financial instruments than banks. However, although direct credit controls on bank lending were virtually eliminated by the mid-1980s, Korea resorted to informal direct controls toward the end of the 1980s to help offset the monetary impact of the large balance of payments surplus.

Furthermore, Korea undertook measures to reduce obstacles to bank competition and market segmentation by allowing greater freedom of entry, expanding the scope of permissible business activities for different types of financial institutions, and relaxing restrictions on the activities of foreign banks. Simultaneously, it implemented measures to examine bank portfolios, restructure failing financial institutions, and strengthen the supervision of other financial institutions. Korea also undertook measures to encourage the creation and development of money and capital markets, especially equity markets. The development of money markets was fostered by the development of new financial instruments, including central bank and government securities, certificates of deposit, various commercial paper, and repurchase agreements. Since the revision of capital market laws in 1987, the outstanding capital value of stocks and bonds has increased substantially. Although controls on capital flows still remain, capital liberalization measures have taken place since the second half of the 1980s, mainly in the areas of indirect portfolio investment by foreigners and overseas investment by Korean residents. Finally, in March 1990, the managed float system of the won/U.S. dollar rate—wherein account was taken of the movements in a currency basket and developments in Korea's external position—was replaced by a market-average exchange rates system under which the exchange rate floats subject to limits on daily movements. No exchange restrictions on current account transactions exist.

Finally, in today's world of globalization and financial liberalization, governments of emerging market economies are increasingly bounded and to a large degree have followed the general stream of relaxing excessive controls and regulations of their financial systems. In the 1980s, most of the liberalization programs of the domestic financial system were accompanied by the relaxation of restrictions on international capital flows and a shift toward more flexible exchange rate arrangements. Such developments encouraged international investors to actively pursue the placement of their funds in the most liberalized emerging equity markets.

Institutional Reforms

In addition to prudent macroeconomic policies and financial liberalization measures, many emerging market governments have also paid close attention to institutional factors that inhibit portfolio investment. The risks associated with institutional factors involve the tax/accounting and legal systems, the financial infrastructure, and cumbersome bureaucratic procedures. Accounting practices are particularly important: Many emerging markets have instituted accounting systems that are perceived as fair and accurate and have thus gained investors' confidence. In an effort to reduce such uncertainties and ensure fair trading rules, many governments have passed laws ensuring that private contracts are honored and enforced and that appropriate legal provisions exist for the settlement of disputes. They also have instituted special committees with specific mandates to oversee laws and regulations that deal with the transparency issue of financial transactions. Furthermore, governments have attempted to improve the financial infrastructure by allowing the computerization of equity-market dealings, simplifying the procedures for the listing of firms into the equity markets, and relaxing antiquated standards for accepting brokers and brokerage houses in equity transactions, thus significantly reducing transaction costs and management fees in emerging equity markets.

Such initiatives also have succeeded in enhancing the confidence of international investors as the resulting macroeconomic environment has generally improved, the efficiency of private investments has increased, the equity return performance has improved, and the changes in institutions—such as the strengthening of the property rights of borrowers and investors, the elimination of insider dealing, and the increased transparency of financial transactions—have become evident. The Far East Asian countries, most notably Korea, are prime examples of countries that have adapted swift and quick policy measures in the past 5–10 years and in turn succeeded in attracting large sums of foreign capital and encouraging sharp rises in their domestic equity markets. Other countries, such as Mexico, Turkey, Portugal, and Spain, also have instituted policy adjustments and institutional changes at a reasonably fast pace and thus have also experienced an influx of foreign capital flows (see Exhibit 2–3).

The institution of a regulatory framework that ensures market efficiency often improves a market's credibility and helps attract international investment. Credibility can be enhanced, however, only when controls are confined to those needed to correct market failures—such as insider trading and other nonethical or noncompetitive market practices—that may arise in unregulated emerging capital markets.

EXHIBIT 2–3

Portfolio Investment (in millions of (U.S.) dollars)

	1988	1989	1990	1991	1992
Korea	−482	−29	811	3,116	5,742
Mexico	−880	438	−5,359	6,937	6,271*
Turkey	1,178	1,586	547	6,489	2,411
Portugal	1,814	1,050	961	1,895	−2,454**
Spain	2,291	7,989	5,361	17,813	496

Source: International Financial Statistics, June 1993.
Notes: *This figure covers the first two quarters.
**This figure covers the first three quarters

Governments seeking to nurture emerging markets also have followed, in many instances, a relatively slow and gradual adjustment in their policies. Foreign exchange liberalization in particular has drawn special attention, with controls sometimes eased gradually and in line with the improvement in government finances and overall macroeconomic policies, as well as with the development in the legal and institutional framework for financial markets. Such governments have realized that, without sufficient provisions on international capital flows and with liquidity increasing in domestic secondary markets, they could encounter significant capital flight problems and find their foreign exchange reserves endangered if their fiscal or monetary policies or actions were to be questioned by the international financial community.

However, governments have increasingly aborted policies of direct or indirect interventions in capital markets since they have realized that such policies distort efficiency and the information system of the relative price mechanism of investable funds. Financial markets produce and distribute information on returns and risks efficiently through interest rates and securities prices, permitting savers, investors, and borrowers to make rational choices among competing outlets for funds. Government interference may disrupt this process, which is the primary source of information for investors comparing the risk-return characteristics of alternative uses of capital and for entrepreneurs determining where and on what terms they can acquire capital. Efficient capital allocation will take place only if asset prices reflect the investors' undistorted relative evaluation of investment alternatives at any given time.

Especially during their early stages, emerging markets often have relied on some type of government regulation and supervision of financial institutions. Regulation of the securities market, for example, has aimed at providing full disclosure of material information on the securities offered to the public in primary markets and traded in secondary markets. However, some government regulations have not avoided interfering with the capital allocation process among competing uses. In particular, regulatory systems occasionally have administered interest rates on deposits and loans, established government-sponsored financial institutions, provided government guarantees and tax exemptions for loans to certain economic entities, and restricted the market access or activities of certain financial institutions. The implications of such government regulations may be reduced market efficiency and the increased reluctance of investors to place their funds in such emerging markets.

Other Measures

As noted before, emerging equity markets offer potentially attractive rates of return, in part because of the large profit margins for firms that issue equity. Meanwhile, institutional investors, who often make investment decisions based on a long-term view of markets, analyze risk and return characteristics of various emerging equity markets and relate them to that of their entire portfolio. Usually, they select securities across sectors, countries, and asset classes, so that certain portfolio diversification benefits are attained. Due to the small market capitalization of many emerging equity markets, however, even the small size of such institutional investments can boost equity prices out of proportion with fundamentals and create the conditions for the genesis of a bubble-phase. As a precaution against such occurrences, governments of emerging equity markets often have tried to promote market capitalization by encouraging listings of companies in equity exchanges, thus increasing market liquidity. These measures often have worked as deterrents to international investors' concerns over the long-term credibility of an emerging equity market. Note here that most institutional investors tend to place their funds in emerging markets with a long-term view, since (1) entry costs are relatively high in terms of bid-offer spreads, commissions, research, and the like; (2) these funds probably will consist of a relatively small part of the total portfolio; and (3) the realization of upside potential from investing in an emerging market is great, especially, in the long term.

As mentioned above, investors often include their investments in emerging markets as another asset class, even if these investments are small relative to their total portfolio. Emerging markets have tried to encourage portfolio investment by pursuing growth-oriented policies, abolishing credit and exchange restrictions, and offering investors a variety of securities in different sectors and industries. In the process, they have enhanced diversification within and among markets. In addition, optimal investment allocations presume stable inflation and interest rates and a sufficient level of liquidity and trading volume for all asset classes in the portfolio. Offering emerging market securities in more established stock markets can improve liquidity; American Depository Receipts, for example, have been used as vehicles to trade foreign stocks on the New York Stock Exchange.

Derivatives Markets

Although not always essential to the well-being of emerging markets, a derivatives market for instruments such as options and futures has been developed in a selected number of emerging equity market countries as an effective way to promote greater efficiency and provide an outlet for hedging and transferring risk. In principle, these instruments can smooth out and reduce the frequency of market discontinuities and, in addition, provide measures that promote liquidity in emerging markets.

It should be mentioned here, however, that market discontinuities, including the bursting of speculative bubbles, may be the result of excessive volatility stemming from an emerging market's sudden attractiveness to investors who have recognized both the improvement in market fundamentals and the growth potential of the nation's economy. Such discontinuities, although often discounted by investors, have attracted the attention of authorities. However, in markets that are adequately regulated with respect to insider dealing and transactional efficiency, authorities should not be overly concerned about individual investors' trading results per se. Authorities should only be concerned as to whether such movements are a response to inadequate and/or inappropriate macrofinancial policies. Then, authorities need to monitor markets as equity price movements may be an important source of information about the public's sentiment toward certain government actions. Furthermore, authorities should be particularly restrained in exercising their regulatory power and interfering in the markets because, otherwise, they offer free volatility through bubble insurance.

THE FUTURE OF EMERGING EQUITY MARKETS

Many of the better known emerging equity markets have had attractive relative valuations during the past decade; individual issues often have been underpriced, as is evidenced by the relatively faster growth of emerging market economies, on average, in relation to those of more developed countries. If history is any guide for the future, the equity markets of such developing countries will eventually catch up in relative size and valuation with those of developed countries. When this happens, the initial opportunities offered by these markets will gradually evaporate.

Nevertheless, the most exciting opportunities and new challenges for international investors in the 1990s are expected to be presented by the emerging equity markets of the developing countries of Latin America and Asia as well as by the new states of the former USSR and East European bloc, which are likely to grow faster than the world economy as a whole. Like the emerging markets of the 1980s, the newly emerging markets are expected to follow the recent capital market-liberalization trend and thus pose fewer regulatory restrictions to foreign investment. Furthermore, these markets are expected to generate returns that are likely higher and more volatile than those in industrial countries. Nonetheless, emerging markets whose performance does not correlate with that of developed markets will continue to generate diversification benefits for international portfolios and therefore will remain the primary targets of fund managers.

CASE 2-1

KOREA: A CASE STUDY

The emerging market's stages of development are dramatically illustrated by the behavior of the Korean equity market over the past 30 years. Despite the unique geopolitical and cultural characteristics of the Korean economy, the development of its equity market has followed a pattern that echoes the experiences of many other emerging markets, in particular those of other Far East Asian nations.

Korea's equity market transformed itself into an advanced emerging equity market in under three decades. During that time, its total market capitalization (calculated by combining the market capitalizations of all Korean exchanges and adjusting for multiple listings on each) to GDP ratio—an important indicator of how developed a market is—increased rapidly (see Exhibit 2–4). Incidentally, in 1990 the developed markets of the United States, Japan, Australia, and Germany had substantially higher total market capitalization to GDP ratios than the emerging markets of Mexico, Turkey, the Philippines, and India (Exhibit 2–5).

EXHIBIT 2-4

Korea: Total Market Capitalization to GDP Ratio

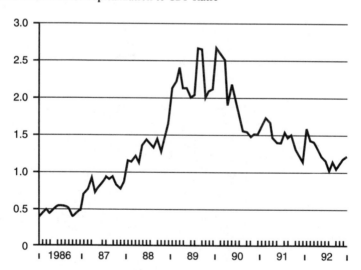

Strong equity performance—the result of growth-oriented policies fueled by domestic investment—marked the early stages of Korea's stock market development after the mid–1960s. Korea's composite index rose sharply as the market progressed rapidly through the developmental stages of its evolution. The depth and breadth of the Korean equity market increased sharply as the trading volume and number of listed issues rose sharply. The process of relaxing exchange and capital controls did not begin until the mid-1980s, but it accelerated in the period 1987–1992. The increase in Korea's equity prices is evidenced in Exhibit 2–2.

E X H I B I T   2–5

Relative Size of Market Capitalization in 1990

Country	Ratio of Market Value of Listed Shares to the Country's Annual GDP
United States	0.56
Japan	0.99
Germany	0.25
Australia	0.82
Mexico	0.14
Turkey	0.14
Philippines	0.13
India	0.13

Sources: IMF International Financial Statistics and International Finance Corporation

Deregulation in 1988–89 prompted huge capital flows into the market. Growing equity returns became increasingly attractive to investors previously restricted to the fixed-income (if relatively high-yield) instruments of the regulated market. The fundamentally sound Korean economy made the more open market even more attractive. The rapid growth of international investment, an enormous expansion of the Korean banking system and over-the-counter (OTC) instruments, and the gradual deregulation of capital markets throughout the world helped support the high stock prices of that period. But the realization that many stock prices had climbed out of proportion to fundamentals caused Korea's composite index to tumble by almost 50 percent since it peaked in the beginning of 1989.

REFERENCES

Auerbach, Robert. *Financial Markets and Institutions.* New York: MacMillan, 1983.

Chuppe, Terry M; and Michael Atkin. "Regulation of Securities Markets: Some Recent Trends and Their Implications for Emerging Markets," WPS 829, The World Bank, January 1992.

Collier, Paul; and Colin Mayer, eds. "The Assessment: Financial Liberalization, Financial Systems and Economic Growth," *Oxford Review of Economic Policy* 5, no. 4 (Winter 1989), pp. 1–12.

Corrigan, E. Gerald. "The Role of Central Banks and the Financial System in Emerging Market Economies," *Federal Reserve Bank of New York Quarterly Review* 15, no. 2 (Summer 1990), pp. 1–7.

Divecha, Arjun; Jaime Drach; and Dan Stefek. "Emerging Markets: A Quantitative Perspective." *Journal of Portfolio Management,* forthcoming.

Dutt, Monish K. *The Development of Emerging Capital Markets: International Experience and Perspectives,* Washington, D.C.: International Finance Corporation, 1991.

Eken, Sena. "Integration of Domestic and International Financial Markets: The Japanese Experience." *Staff Papers* 31. Washington, D.C.: International Monetary Fund, September 1984.

Elton, Edwin J.; and Martin J. Gruber. *Modern Portfolio Theory and Investment Analysis,* 4th edition. New York: John Wiley and Sons, Inc., 1991.

Errunza, Vihang; and Prasad Padmanabhan. "Further Evidence on Benefits of Portfolio Investments in Emerging Markets." *Financial Analysts Journal,* July/August 1988, pp. 76–78.

Flood, Robert P.; and Robert J. Hodrick. "Asset Price Volatility, Bubbles, and Process Switching." *Journal of Finance* 41, no. 4 (September 1986), pp. 831–842.

Garber, Peter M. "Who Put the Mania in Tulipmania?" *The Journal of Portfolio Management,* Fall 1989, pp. 53–60.

Gill, Davis. *Global Investing: The Emerging Markets.* Washington, D.C.: International Finance Corporation, 1987.

Hardouvelis, Gikas A. "Evidence on Stock Market Speculative Bubbles: Japan, United States, and Great Britain." *Federal Reserve Bank of New York Research Paper No. 8810,* April 1988.

International Finance Corporation, Capital Markets Department. *Attractiveness of Emerging Markets for Portfolio Investment.* Washington, D.C.: International Finance Corporation, September 1988.

International Finance Corporation. *Emerging Stock Markets Factbook, 1991.* Washington, D.C.: International Finance Corporation, May 1991.

Juttner, D. Johannes. "Fundamentals, Bubbles, and Trading Strategies: Are They the Causes of Black Monday?" *Kredit und Capital* 22, no. 4 (1989), pp. 470–486.

McKinnon, Ronald I. *The Order of Economic Liberalization: Financial Control in the Transition to a Market Economy.* Baltimore: Johns Hopkins University Press, 1991.

Osugi, K. "Japan's Experience of Financial Deregulation Since 1984 in an International Perspective." *BIS Economic Papers* 26. Basle: Bank for International Settlements, January 1990.

Pardy, Robert. *Institutional Reform in Emerging Securities Markets.* WPS 907, The World Bank, May 1992.

Prywes, Menahem "The Good Work of Financial Crises." *The Columbia Journal of World Business,* Spring 1992, pp. 14–21.

Rudd, Andrew. "International Investing: The Case for the Emerging Markets." In *Global Portfolios: Quantitative Strategies for Maximum Performance,* eds. Robert Z. Aliber and Brian R. Bruce. Homewood, IL: Business One Irwin, 1991, pp. 264–284.

Santoni, G. J. "The Great Bull Markets 1924–29 and 1982–87: Speculative Bubbles or Economic Fundamentals?" *Federal Reserve Bank of St. Louis Review,* November 1987, pp. 16–30.

Shinkai, Yoichi. "The Internationalization of Finance in Japan." *The Political Economy of Japan* 1. Stanford University Press, 1988.

Speidell, Lawrence S. "The Frontier of Emerging Markets: Russia and China." *The Journal of Investing,* Summer 1992, pp. 7–11.

Speidell, Lawrence S.; and Ross Sappenfield. "Global Diversification: In a Shrinking World." *Journal of Portfolio Management,* forthcoming.

Stone, Douglas. "The Emerging Markets and Strategic Asset Allocation." *The Journal of Investing,* Summer 1992, pp. 40–45.

Suzuki, Yoshio. *The Japanese Financial System,* Oxford University Press, 1987.

West, Kenneth D. "Bubbles, Fads, and Stock Price Volatility Tests: A Partial Evaluation." *Journal of Finance* 43, no. 3 (July 1988), pp. 639–656.

3

A SURVEY AND SYNTHESIS OF PROBLEMS AND OPPORTUNITIES IN EMERGING CAPITAL MARKETS

Brian R. Bruce, *President, InterCoast Capital Company*
William Reichenstein, *Pat and Thomas Powers Chair in Investment Management*
Baylor University

PROBLEMS IN EMERGING MARKETS

Emerging stock markets can be found in developing economies around the world. Exhibit 3–1 lists the 25 countries in the International Finance Corporation (IFC) Emerging Markets Index. Moreover, fledgling stock markets in Russia and Eastern Europe hope to continue to develop and achieve the status of emerging stock markets. In this chapter, we will use the term *emerging markets* to mean the more established markets, such as Mexico, and the fledgling markets, such as Russia.

Emerging stock markets pose risks and problems to a U.S. investor beyond those present in investments in U.S. stocks. Duke and Papaioannou (1993) and especially Kautz, Perlow, and Sands (1993) discuss these risks and problems, which include:

E X H I B I T   3–1

Emerging Stock Markets in IFC Indexes

Argentina	Nigeria
Brazil	Pakistan
Chile	Peru
China	Philippines
Colombia	Poland
Greece	Portugal
Hungary	Sri Lanka
India	Taiwan
Indonesia	Thailand
Jordan	Turkey
Korea	Venezuela
Malaysia	Zimbabwe
Mexico	

- Volatility
- Political risks
- Information risks
- Costs
- Liquidity risks
- Currency risks
- Access
- Repatriation of capital
- Diversification
- Fiduciary constraints

Volatility

Emerging stock markets are more volatile than developed stock markets. For example, the Mexican market lost a cumulative 94 percent from year-end 1980 to year-end 1982. From May to November 1992, stock prices on the Shanghai and Shenzhen exchanges in China lost 78 percent and 44 percent, respectively, before rising to new peak levels in February 1993. The Zimbabwe stock market recorded a 174 percent gain between June 1993 and June 1994, its initial year of openness to foreign investors. Moreover, stock-index futures contracts seldom exist on the emerging markets, so investors cannot quickly and cheaply adjust their exposures to an emerging stock market.

Political Risk

"In developed countries, . . . [political] risks are generally evolutionary, not revolutionary. In emerging markets, however, political risks can mean changes that are far from marginal" (Kautz, Perlow, and Sands, p. 44).

In emerging markets, political stability and economic policy often rest in the hands of a government leader. If that leader's future is cast into doubt, markets can respond violently. "An example of this occurred in Brazil, where allegations of campaign finance improprieties against Brazilian President Fernando Collor de Mello led to unusually steep declines in the São Paulo Stock Exchange (Bovespa). When the charges surfaced, the market fell 15.6 percent in a single day, June 29, 1992" (p. 44). Similarly, the death of 90-year-old Deng Xiaoping, the leader of China, is expected to lead to a power struggle. The struggles could bring into question the permanence of his economic reforms.

Political risk also includes the risk of adverse government actions. Although this risk also exists in the U.S. and in other developed markets, the consequences of adverse policies are often more dramatic in emerging markets. For example, the election of President Caldera and the subsequent suspension of constitutional rights caused havoc in the Venezuelan market. Not only did stock prices plunge 41 percent in the second quarter of 1994, but trading liquidity almost disappeared because of foreign investor withdrawal from the Venezuelan market.

Corruption in emerging-markets governments is another form of political risk. India provides one example. In April 1992, news surfaced "that some brokers had diverted huge sums (possibly over $1 billion) from state-owned banks, allegedly with official collusion. On news of the scandal, the Indian market went into a tailspin" (Kautz, Perlow, and Sands, p. 44).

These examples dramatically highlight the potential impact of government action, misaction, and corruption. A later section of this chapter is devoted to a discussion of the government's role in encouraging emerging stock markets.

Information Risk

Information risk encompasses a range of problems. Financial statements in emerging markets seldom follow generally accepted accounting standards. Moreover, disclosure requirements may be lacking. "A lack of stringent accounting practices and generally looser regulatory oversight can pose what some investors term 'management risk,' a polite term for corruption and fraudulent or at least incompetent bookkeeping" (Kautz, Perlow, and Sands, pp. 44–45).

Other forms of information risk include the prevalence of insider trading, which is legal in some emerging markets, and the perception of price manipulations. Moreover, the high inflation rates in some developing countries render financial statements virtually meaningless. Finally, investors must cope with language and culture barriers.

Costs

Costs on emerging market investments exceed costs on domestic investments. Combined daily trading on many emerging exchanges averages less than the daily trading volume on one, mid-sized U.S. stock. Consequently, brokerage fees are larger in emerging markets, as are the bid-ask spreads and the price impacts of trades.

Custodial fees are naturally larger since laws and regulations do not provide the level of safety taken for granted in developed economies. Costs of obtaining information also are higher. Withholding taxes represent a dead-weight loss to pension funds and other tax-deferred investors. Finally, management expenses in emerging markets are very high, since they must reflect the costs of obtaining information and a reward for the specialized knowledge of the emerging markets. For example, the 1993 expense ratio of the emerging market stock funds in

The Individual Investor's Guide to Low-Load Mutual Funds (1994) averaged 1.92 percent.

Liquidity Risk

Trading in emerging markets lacks the depth and breadth of trading in developed markets. Many shares are owned by the government, banks, or families and are not traded. Recall that the Zimbabwe stock market rose 174 percent between June 1993 and June 1994. However, because daily trading volume averaged only $1 million, any attempt to liquidate the stocks would cause the gains to shrink. Thus, from an actual investment standpoint, these results have limited meaning. The trading volume is puny by developed-market standards. The net result is little trading, large bid-ask price spreads, and large price impacts for anyone wishing to buy or sell a reasonable stake in a firm or market.

Currency Risk

Currency risk exists on all foreign-denominated investments, whether in developed or developing markets. A U.S. investor gains when the yen rises, since the yen will then buy more dollars. Thus, currency risk is not unique to emerging markets.

However, three features heighten the currency risk on emerging markets compared to developed markets. First, political risk and currency risk are connected, which means that an investor can get clobbered by falling stock prices and a falling currency. Second, extreme inflation can produce extreme currency risk. "During the four and one-half year period beginning January 1, 1988, and ending June 30, 1992, investors in Argentina and Brazil suffered annualized currency losses of 80 percent to 90 percent" (Kautz, Perlow, and Sands, p. 46). Third, unlike investments in Japan and Germany, a U.S. investor can seldom hedge the currency risk in an emerging market. Forward, futures, swaps, and options contracts provide hedging opportunities for the developed-country currencies. However, these contracts are marks of a developed financial system and they are seldom available on local currencies. Moreover, attempts to hedge a minor currency with contracts on a major currency have generally proved unsuccessful. For example, attempts to hedge the New Taiwan dollar with U.S. dollar currency contracts have generally proven unsuccessful (despite attempts to tie the New Taiwan dollar to the U.S. dollar). Thus, in practice, the currency risk in emerging stock markets usually is larger than the currency risk on Japanese or German stocks, and the currency risk on emerging markets seldom can be hedged.

Access

Emerging markets differ in their willingness to allow foreign funds to enter and leave their markets. Some countries, notably Taiwan, Korea, India, and Venezuela, limit a foreign investor's stake to a small percent of selected stocks, or a government may limit foreign ownership to 20 or 49 percent of a firm's shares. Other markets sell A shares and B shares with foreign ownership limited to B shares. For example, in 1993, B shares in China totaled $700 million or 9 percent of the size of A and B shares combined.

Repatriation of Capital

Access refers to getting capital into a country. Repatriation refers to getting capital out of a country. An exhibit in Kautz, Perlow, and Sands provides a list that discusses the openness of each emerging market. Governments may restrict repatriation of funds either until foreign currency is available, by requiring a lengthy registration process, or until after funds have remained in the country for a minimum number of years. More generally, there always exists the threat that a government will impose future restrictions to the free flow of funds.

Diversification

A handful of firms account for a huge portion of the market value of most emerging market indexes. Moreover, telecommunications and oil firms account for a disproportionate share of these few firms. The net result is that emerging market portfolios lack adequate diversification. However, the company-specific risk of each emerging market and the industry-specific risk of an emerging market portfolio can be eliminated by holding a broad-based, global stock portfolio. An emerging market stock exposure need not imply a larger risk for the portfolio. We will return to this theme later.

Fiduciary Constraint

Some investment committees of plan sponsors prohibit investments in emerging markets. Others allow only a small exposure. Perhaps a more critical factor restricting pension fund investments in emerging markets is a fiduciary bias: If an emerging market strategy proves profitable, the pension manager (or whoever advocated the strategy) receives a pat on the back, but if it turns sour, the pension manager may lose his or her job. This problem is an example of a familiar theme: It is far better for one's reputation to fail conventionally rather than succeed unconventionally.

Another fiduciary constraint on emerging markets is the need to choose a benchmark. Meier (1994) compares six emerging market indexes. Roughly 75 percent of the weight of each index is allocated to Brazil, Korea, Malaysia, Mexico, Taiwan, and Thailand. However, Korea and Taiwan receive substantially different weights across two groups of indexes. Korea and Taiwan combined represent about 5 percent of the weight of the Baring Securities Emerging Markets Index, IFC Investable Index, and Morgan Stanley Capital International (MSCI) Emerging Markets Free Index. The 5 percent reflects foreigners' true access to these markets. Korea and Taiwan combined represent about 25 percent of the weight of the BARRA Emerging Markets Model, MSCI Emerging Markets Global Index, and IFC Global Index. These differences in weights account for dramatic differences in risks and returns. For example, for January 1989 through October 1993, the median annual return of the first group—the investable group—was 27.9 percent, while the median return of the second group was about half as high, at 14.7 percent. Not surprisingly, the investable indexes with their reduced across-country diversification produced more volatile returns.

In this section, we discussed risk factors in emerging markets. "Like any risks, these factors also create opportunities because they represent forms of market inefficiency. Most emerging market specialists are able to add significant value over emerging market indexes, suggesting that risks/inefficiencies can be turned to substantial advantage by skillful managers" (Kautz, Perlow, and Sands, p. 43). In the next section, we will look at the opportunities emerging stock markets present to investors.

EMERGING MARKETS IN THE ASSET MIX

This section reviews the *Journal of Investing (JOI)* articles' opinions about the role of emerging stock markets in a U.S. investor's asset mix. Are emerging stock markets an appropriate asset class and, if so, how much of the portfolio should be devoted to it?

The mean-variance framework is the usual methodology used to assess the role of an asset class in a portfolio. Exhibit 3–2 presents the efficient frontier—that is, the set of mean-variance efficient portfolios. This figure comes from Donayre (1994), but Stone (1992) and Kautz, Perlow, and Sands (1993) also adopt the

EXHIBIT 3–2

Efficient Frontier (January 1, 1985–June 30, 1993)

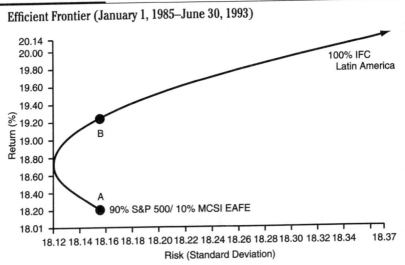

mean-variance framework. The framework requires estimates of the expected return and standard deviation of each asset class and the correlation of returns between each asset class. Point A in Exhibit 3–2 represents the risk and return on a portfolio consisting of 90 percent Standard & Poor's (S&P) 500 and 10 percent EAFE (Europe, Australia, and Far East) Index foreign stocks. Based on returns between January 1985 and June 1993, an investor could have achieved Point B with a higher return and the same risk by placing 4 percent of the portfolio in Latin American equities.

Compared to the developed-country stock returns, emerging-market stock returns have been larger and more volatile, but the developed and emerging market returns have exhibited weak positive correlations. Because of this weak correlation, it has been possible to add some of the more volatile emerging market stocks to a developed-country portfolio without increasing the portfolio's risk. Point B in Exhibit 3–2 has a 4 percent emerging market exposure. Depending upon assumptions, emerging markets can comprise a substantially larger portion of the portfolio without increasing the portfolio risk. For example, Kautz, Perlow, and Sands conclude that "putting as much as two-thirds of an international portfolio in emerging markets will increase return without increasing risk (given our assumptions), relative to an all-EAFE portfolio" (p. 47).

All three papers warn against the blind reliance on historical estimates of returns, standard deviations, and correlations. The strongest case is made by Donayre. He warns that "historical information can be used to support a conclusion, [but] it should never be the underlying basis of that conclusion. It is a pillar, not a foundation" (p. 64). Mean-variance analysis must rely on estimates of the future.

"As is often the case with investments, the future has not mirrored the past. The rush to reap the benefits of international equities has so far been a dismal disappointment. As of the middle of 1993, a plan sponsor who traded in domestic for international equity exposure at the beginning of 1990 when the Japanese market was reaching a crest exchanged the 43 percent cumulative performance of the S&P 500 for the negative 7 percent performance of the EAFE" (p. 64).

Having warned against the blind reliance on historical estimates in the mean-variance framework, Donayre proposes a different approach to assessing the merits of an emerging markets exposure. Exhibit 3–3 summarizes his approach.

First, "a portfolio should be as heavily weighted toward equities as is feasible given the portfolio's liability structure" (p. 65). Investing in emerging markets meets this criterion.

Second, an investor should minimize the portfolio's exposure to any one region, country, or industry by spreading equity risk across the largest feasible universe. Emerging market returns have been weakly correlated with developed-market returns, and this weak relation is expected to continue. Moreover, this type of diversification reduces the risk of having to sell assets at depressed prices. Emerging markets meet this second criterion.

Third, diversification of an equity portfolio should never come at the expense of lower returns. Only invest in emerging markets if they offer expected returns that are at least as large as those available in developed markets.

Finally, "like it or not, sponsors are faced with a timing decision" (p. 66). Prices in emerging markets are so volatile that the choice of entry point can be the critical decision. Donayre rec-

---

E X H I B I T   3–3

Tenets of Portfolio Management

> 1. Maximum allocation to equities
>   - Offers the most favorable mix of risk and return of any established asset class
> 2. Maximum diversification of equity portfolio
>   - Lowers portfolio's vulnerability to any one factor
>   - Increases selling flexibility
> 3. Expected long-term returns of a diversifying equity should be at least equal to those of the existing equity portfolio
>   - Diversification of an equity portfolio should not come at the expense of returns
> **Caveat:** Point of Entry is Crucial
>   - Avoid buying at market peaks
>   - Implement initial allocation over an extended period of time

Source: Donayre (1994).

ommends the use of income averaging. "Plan sponsors should aim to spread their initial allocation over the longest period they can justify, from a minimum period of six months to as much as two or three years" (p. 66).

In short, Donayre advocates the mean-variance framework but warns that the estimates must focus on the future, not the past. Relying on the mean-variance framework and historical returns, "a new asset class looks the most beneficial after it has posted superior returns. For plan sponsors, the best time to present a new asset class to the investment committee is after the asset has performed exceptionally. Unfortunately, because of the investment cycles inherent in all asset classes, extended above-average performance is often a signal that the price of an asset may have peaked.

"And although plan sponsors are well aware of the pitfalls involved in investing near market tops, they have not demonstrated an ability to avoid them—not in the case of the 'nifty-fifty' in the 1970s, real estate in the 1980s, or international equities in the early 1990s. The reason for this failure of wisdom, while analytically complex, may be intuitively simple. It can best be summed up by an adage of the Peruvian Indians, 'A fruit is ripest, and most tempting, just before it spoils.' The Incas knew very little about investments. They knew a lot about human nature" (pp. 66–67).

How Much?

Assuming an investor chooses to invest in emerging markets, the next question is how large should that exposure be. Not surprisingly, opinions vary on this subject.

Kautz, Perlow, and Sands discuss the role of emerging markets in a plan sponsor's portfolio. For those who can tolerate the inherent risks, they advocate that 10 to 25 percent *of the international equity portfolio* be placed in emerging markets. Since they expect international equities to reach 8 percent of the total portfolios of U.S. tax-exempt investors by 1995, they call for an emerging market exposure of 0.8 to 2 percent of a plan sponsor's total portfolio.

If Stone only considered the evidence from the mean-variance framework, he would conclude that emerging markets exposure could reach 15 percent or more of total assets. However, he warns that problems with "[i]nvestability, size, and lack of knowledge about emerging markets actually makes a 15 percent or more portfolio commitment too high" (p. 44). He advocates perhaps a 5 percent exposure for sponsors who can accept the political risks.

Duke and Papaioannou (1993) examine the accessibility of emerging markets to foreign investors and especially institutional investors. They do not rely on the mean-variance framework and do not recommend a specific exposure for emerging markets. However, they conclude that "the new opportunities for investors in the 1990s will come from the emerging equity markets of the previous Soviet Union and Eastern European bloc, as well as from countries in Latin America and Asia that may not have been 'star performers' in the 1980s" (p. 25).

Donayre looks at the specific issue of whether plan sponsors should invest in Latin America. He concludes that Latin American exposure is appropriate if and only if their expected returns are at least equal to those on the existing equities. As of early 1994, he believes that because of "spectacular recent returns [plan sponsors] should proceed with caution. At a minimum, investors should spread their initial allocation over a period of at least two years, and keep in mind that bad implementation can ruin an otherwise good investment decision"(p. 67).

VEHICLES FOR EXPOSURE

There are four major vehicles for getting an emerging market exposure. Kautz, Perlow, and Sands (1993) discuss these vehicles.

Closed-End Mutual Funds

The International Finance Corporation, the private finance arm of the World Bank, helped develop closed-end funds as a vehicle for investing in emerging markets. Closed-end funds have an important advantage compared to open-end funds. An open-end fund stands ready to issue or redeem shares in the investment company (or mutual fund). Thus, net redemptions force a manager to sell fund assets—the common stock in the emerging market. Since emerging markets have little liquidity, a flood of redemptions could cause a liquidity crisis. The closed-end fund eliminates this problem by having the fund's common stock (which represents ownership of the fund's emerging market assets) sold on an organized exchange, usually the NYSE. Investors wanting to exit a closed-end fund must sell the fund's stock on the exchange for whatever it fetches. The price may be at a premium or discount to the fund's net asset value. Regardless, the manager does not need to worry about selling fund assets (i.e., stocks in the emerging markets) to meet redemptions. This arrangement also allows emerging market governments to provide access to their markets while maintaining tight controls.

The closed-end format also provides advantages to investors. They get diversification, professional management, and the liquidity and ease of settlement offered by the U.S. stock markets. However, the authors also note a problem with closed-end funds. "Recent research suggests that closed-end country funds are a poor substitute for direct equity holdings in a foreign market from a diversification standpoint, as fund performance tends to be more closely correlated with U.S. markets than foreign markets. This is particularly true in the case of emerging markets" (p. 49).

According to Bailey and Lim (1992), "One cannot mimic an investment in these popular [emerging] markets merely by purchasing the corresponding country fund." For these reasons, global emerging markets managers may buy country funds to gain exposure to countries that provide limited access to foreigners, such as Taiwan, Korea, and India.

ADRs and GDRs

American Depository Receipts (ADRs) and Global Depository Receipts (GDRs) are a second vehicle to emerging markets exposure. ADRs are negotiable receipts, issued and held by U.S. banks, that represent claims to shares of foreign corporations. The ADR price reflects the price of the common shares in the emerging market adjusted for the exchange rate. GDRs are similar, but they are globally traded receipts held by banks that may or may not be in the U.S.

ADRs and GDRs are typically available on only a few, major foreign firms. For example, ADRs for Telmex, the Mexican telephone company, trade on the New York Stock Exchange (NYSE), but one cannot get an exposure to the smaller Mexican firms through this vehicle. This may remove some of the upside potential (as well as the downside risk) that makes emerging markets exciting. Moreover, investors may find it more efficient to buy Telmex (and other stocks) in Mexico, because ADR liquidity is often low and foreign exchange spreads can be high.

Commingled Funds for Institutions

There are about 30 managers offering emerging markets expertise either on a global or regional (e.g., Latin America) basis. "In general, except for very large funds with significant assets earmarked for emerging markets (more than $25 million to $30 million), a pooled vehicle (a commingled or mutual fund) will be the most cost-effective method of emerging markets investing. Pooling assets lowers costs by spreading the significant trading, custody, and other costs of emerging markets investing over a large number of investors" (Kautz, Perlow, and Sands, p. 49).

Separate Account Management

A plan sponsor can have a separate account managed with an emerging markets mandate. This vehicle is the most flexible but (except for accounts of $25 million or more) it is also the most expensive. Management fees on emerging markets accounts are typically between 1 and 1.25 percent. These are, respectively, about 0.40 and 0.60 percent larger than management fees on EAFE and U.S. stocks.

PORTFOLIO CONSTRUCTION

Even if an investor decides to invest in emerging markets, he still must decide on portfolio weights within the emerging markets segment of the portfolio. Davis (1994) considers several approaches to weighting, including capitalization weights, gross domestic product (GDP) weights, trading weights, and equal weights.

The idea behind capitalization weights is that a country's market cap reflects its risk and return prospects. As we saw earlier, however, country weights vary across emerging market indexes, especially for Korea and Taiwan. Thus, weighting by market capitalization is reasonable, but only if the index contains only accessible stocks.

GDP weighting assumes that the size of the economy reflects country prospects. This weighting scheme places the largest weight on Brazil, followed by Korea, Mexico, India, and Taiwan. As mentioned above, most of Korea and Taiwan are not available to foreign investors.

Trade weighting sounds like an interesting idea. It could minimize liquidity risk. Unfortunately, trade weighting would require investing over 60 percent of the emerging markets portfolio in Taiwan and Korea.

Equal weighting is another possibility. However, it would be difficult to acquire a large enough position in the smaller markets. An alternative weighting scheme would be to give a larger (e.g., 10 percent) allocation to each of the larger countries and a smaller allocation to each of the smaller countries. Perhaps the major flaw in an equal-weighting scheme is the implicit assumption that all markets are equally desirable. In practice, they will neither be equally large, equally accessible, nor equally desirable.

Among the weighting approaches considered, market capitalization with weights based on investable indexes appears most feasible. Of course, an investor could choose a commingled or mutual fund and leave the portfolio construction decision to the manager. To repeat, "most emerging markets specialists are able to add significant value over emerging market indexes" (Kautz, Perlow, and Sands, p. 43).

EMERGING MARKET LIFE CYCLE

Is there an emerging market life cycle? Duke and Papaioannou (1993) think so. They list the following stages in the healthy development of an emerging market:

1. Strong equity performance as a result of economic and political stability and growth-oriented policies;
2. Increased confidence, and thus acceptance, of the equity market as an investment alternative to bank deposits and the bond market for domestic investors;
3. Deregulation of domestic capital markets as a result of internal pressures for cheaper capital funding of firms and international challenges for accessibility;
4. Realization of the diversification benefits for domestic and international investors as a result of the higher domestic liquidity and increased risk-adjusted returns;

5. Rapid increase of new issues of stocks and bonds as a result of better economic prospects and profit opportunities;

6. Greater volumes of issuance by firms striving to optimize their capital structures, by privately held companies eager to make initial public offerings, and by governments determined to privatize publicly owned companies;

7. More efficient intermediation as a result of increased trading activity;

8. Development of equity and currency derivatives, as well as index products, as a result of the increased necessity for a risk transfer mechanism; and

9. Stable (plateau) growth of equity market activity as equity risk premiums fall to internationally competitive levels. At this latest phase, the emerging market is close to, if not at, a mature or developed stage of its life (pp. 22–23).

They illustrate the life cycle with the Japanese stock market. Exhibit 3–4 presents the Nikkei 225 index over the past 40 years. The early stages of Japan's post-war stock "market development are marked by strong equity performance as a result of growth-oriented policies fueled by domestic investment" (p. 24). The relaxation of exchange and capital controls and the expansion of derivative markets in the 1980s prompted huge domestic capital flows into the Japanese equity market. Duke and Papaioannou interpret the stock market crash that began in 1990 as a "pernicious

EXHIBIT 3–4

Japan: Total Market Capitalization to GDP Ratio

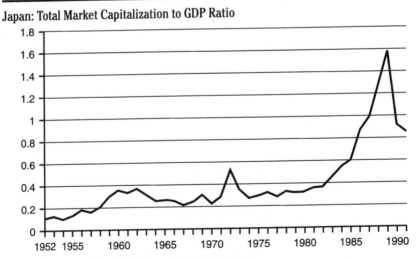

Source: IMF International Financial Statistics and Tokyo Stock Exchange

bubble" caused by unchecked investor euphoria and a lack of attention to the relation between stock prices and economic fundamentals. It is important to note that the crash occurred in a developed stock market and is not a typical feature of the final stages of an emerging market.

ROLE OF GOVERNMENT

This final section discusses several of the papers devoted to the role of government in encouraging an emerging market. The article by Duke and Papaioannou (1993) applies across countries, while articles by Speidell (1992, 1993) and Wong and Bauman (1993) provide examples specific to China.

The role of the government is to promote policies that allow market forces to work. It should provide the legal structure to protect property rights and allow individuals to pursue their self interest through the freedom to enter private contracts. The government should interfere with the people's right to freely enter contracts only when clear and substantial externalities exist. Duke and Papaioannou echo this free-market position:

- To be genuinely successful, governments must promote policies that allow market forces to work and encourage the private sector to be the driving force for economic growth.
- Financial markets are built on implicit or specified contracts and property rights. Development of emerging markets depends critically on a government's initiative to provide an appropriate legal and accounting framework that assures savers and borrowers of their property rights and secures the enforcement of financial contracts.
- Governments should encourage the development of a comprehensive legal and institutional framework for equity markets.
- For equity markets to allocate resources most productively, regulations should merely correct market failures that would arise in totally unregulated markets.

Many articles emphasize the critical role of the economic system in development. Stone (1992) calls the political organization and the administrative competence of the government the most important variables in a country's long-term economic growth. Differences in economic growth rates have not been linked statistically to factor endowments. China offers an excellent example. "By 1978, it became clear to the national leadership that an economy that relied almost exclusively on centralized planning and bureaucratic control had resulted in stagnant productivity, extensive inefficiency, and low morale among the population. Other countries that chose to follow a market-oriented economic strategy (especially the newly industrialized economies of Hong Kong, Singapore, South Korea, and Taiwan) had achieved economic miracles despite the fact that in the early 1950s they were not appreciably better off than China" (Wong and Bauman, p. 12).

Everywhere it has been tried, socialist planning has proven to be an abysmal failure. Against this background of failure, economic reforms in China were launched in 1978. Deng Xiaoping, the reform leader, implemented systematic reform by replacing central planning with more local control. He created seven Special Economic Zones, within which prices are relatively free and many other governmental restraints to free trade have been removed. The growth and prosperity of these zones stand in stark contrast to the rest of the country. "The best example is Shenzhen, north of Hong Kong, where the population has soared to 1.7 million from 50,000 in 1980, and industrial output is up to U.S. $3.8 billion (40 percent exported), compared with only $11 million ten years ago. Expansion continues at a double-digit pace, and the city boasts a growing skyline of office towers and luxury hotels. In February 1992, Deng Xiaoping made a special visit to Shenzhen to endorse the economic reforms that have led to its 40 percent annual growth rate. Throughout China, 'Shenzhen Speed' has come to symbolize success" (Speidell 1992, p. 10). The market system works.

A cornerstone of the market system is private ownership of the means of production. China must establish the necessary legal and ethical reforms to insure these rights. As of 1993, there were no basic legal laws to protect the rights of shareholders. However, these rights were being established, including the rights of shareholders to participate in earnings and dividends, to vote on management, and to receive fair treatment in the event of bankruptcy.

China needs to develop other features of the foundation of a market economy, as well. "Accounting standards, corporate disclosure, and shareholder information are areas where China needs to show rapid progress in order to attract a large number of long-term fundamental investors" (Maisonneuve, 1994). "The current account and reporting system is not well-defined and offers no provision for bad debts or depreciation. Neither does it consolidate the accounts of subsidiaries . . . . The purpose of auditing is for tax assessment, not for providing a true and fair view of a company's financial statements to its shareholders" (Wong and Bauman, p. 17).

"Meetings on both the Shenzhen and Shanghai stock exchanges have focused on how to improve the stock market, and participants show impressive understanding and commitment on both the corporate and regulatory levels. Pending are standards on insider dealing, timing of corporate disclosure, communication with investors, and improvement of the Chinese regulatory body" (Maisonneuve, 1994, p. 98). In China, as in the U.S. and other developed countries, many of these safeguards can be provided by industry self regulation instead of government regulation.

Despite the progress to date, risks remain that China will diverge from its path of economic reform. Although Deng Xiaoping has installed reform-minded personnel in key positions, a political struggle is expected to follow his death. The 1997 unification of Hong Kong with China represents another potential trouble spot. Hong Kong supported the demonstrators in Tiananmen Square, which "severely strained relations" with China (Speidell 1993, p. 8). "China now faces increased pressure for democracy in Hong Kong from British Governor Christopher Patten. . . . China has responded harshly to Patten's proposals and has indicated that it considers its right to govern more important than Hong Kong's economic prosperity" (Speidell 1993, p. 8). A violent reaction by the people of Hong Kong to unification would endanger China's cherished and critical most-favored-nation status. To give one example of its importance, the loss of most-favored-nation status would cause import duties on toys to rise from 7 percent to 70 percent (Speidell 1993, p. 8).

Several articles refer to the greater freedoms in recent years of the Chinese people. For example, Speidell (1993) quotes several friends in Shanghai who feel that "China has more freedom of speech today than at any time in its history" (p. 9). He also says that oppression is not a feature of daily life for most Chinese. However, "more freedom of speech" implies that restrictions remain. And most people being free of daily oppression means that some are not. How would the people of Hong Kong react to the loss of freedom of speech? And to repeat, "China . . . considers its right to govern more important than Hong Kong's economic prosperity" (Speidell 1993, p. 8). Political risks in China, as in other emerging markets, remain a reality.

SUMMARY

The *Journal of Investing* (*JOI*) has become a major outlet for literature in emerging stock markets. In this chapter, we synthesized our material from 1992–94 articles in the *JOI* around six themes. First, we discussed the problems and unique risks of investing in emerging markets. These include huge volatility, political risks, information risks, high costs, liquidity risks, currency risks, limited access, problems in repatriating capital, lack of diversification, and plan sponsor fiduciary constraints. Despite these risks, many scholars believe that emerging markets provide plan sponsors with the chance to raise portfolio returns without raising portfolio risk.

Second, we examined the role of emerging markets in an investor's asset mix. Historical returns on emerging markets often exceed returns on developed markets, and the low correlations of returns between emerging and developed markets imply that the extra volatility on emerging markets need not raise the portfolio's risks. Mean-variance analysis typically suggests that a small emerging markets exposure can improve the portfolio's risk-return trade-off.

Next, we examined, respectively, the methods available to acquire an emerging market's exposure and the available methods of portfolio construction. Except for very large plans, the most cost-effective methods of acquiring an emerging markets exposure are commingled funds and mutual funds.

Following a brief review of one author team's view of an emerging market life cycle, we turned to the role of government in encouraging its emerging stock market. First and foremost, the government should promote policies that allow market forces to work. It must provide a legal structure that protects private property, including the protection of shareholder rights. Many emerging stock markets are found in countries trying to break the failed central planning dictates of their socialist history. China serves as an excellent example of both the dramatic growth and the increased productivity that accompany a change to a market economy, as well as the difficulty of making that political change.

REFERENCES

American Association of Individual Investors. *The Institutional Investor's Guide to Low-Load Mutual Funds*, 13th ed. Chicago, IL: American Association of Individual Investors, 1994.

Bailey, W.; and J. Lim. "Evaluating the Diversification Benefits of the New Country Funds." *Journal of Portfolio Management*, Spring 1992, pp. 74–80.

Davis, L. H. "Portfolio Composition for Emerging Market Equities." *Journal of Investing*, Winter 1994, forthcoming.

Donayre, F.X. "Investing in Latin America: Good Idea, Bad Time?" *Journal of Investing*, Summer 1994, pp. 63–67.

Duke, L. K.; and M. G. Papaioannou. "Accessing Emerging Stock Markets: Prerequisites for International Investors." *Journal of Investing*, Summer 1993, pp. 18–25.

Kautz, L. B.; H. D. Perlow; and G. Sands. "Emerging Markets: A Framework for Institutional Investments." *Journal of Investing*, Spring 1993, pp. 41–50.

Maisonneuve, V. "China: The New International Equities Market." *Journal of Investing*, Fall 1994, pp. 95–98.

Meier, J. "A Comparison of Emerging Markets Benchmarks." *Journal of Investing*, Summer 1994, pp. 58–62.

Speidell, L. S. "Checklist for China." *Journal of Investing*, Summer 1993, pp. 6–11.

Speidell, L. S. "The Frontier of Emerging Markets: Russia and China." *Journal of Investing*, Summer 1992, pp. 7–11.

Stone, D. "The Emerging Markets and Strategic Asset Allocation." *Journal of Investing*, Summer 1992, pp. 40–45.

Wong, K.A.; and W. S. Bauman. "China: Is Now the Time to Invest?" *Journal of Investing*, Summer 1993, pp. 12–17.

III

PORTFOLIO ALLOCATION ISSUES IN EMERGING MARKETS

4

OPTIMAL PORTFOLIO ALLOCATION IN EMERGING CAPITAL MARKETS

Lawrence S. Speidell, *Batterymarch Financial Management*
Ross Sappenfield, *Capital Research and Management Company*

This chapter reviews the arguments for global investing, discusses the risk of rising correlations, and concludes that emerging equity markets have an important role to play in effective diversification.

THE CASE FOR GLOBAL INVESTING

There is much interest in increasing the international exposure of portfolios. Much of this increase is due to perceived higher returns for non-U.S. equities, but part of the appeal of non-U.S. markets comes from diversification. Exhibit 4–1 illustrates three points about diversification:

1. Global markets have wide differences in historic returns and risk (measured by the standard deviation of annual returns).

2. Emerging markets shown in gray (defined by the International Finance Corporation) have had higher risk and return than the developed markets.

3. The EAFE, (Europe, Australia, and Far East) Index has had lower risk than most of the individual countries that compose it.

EXHIBIT 4-1

10-Year Compound Returns and Standard Deviation of Returns

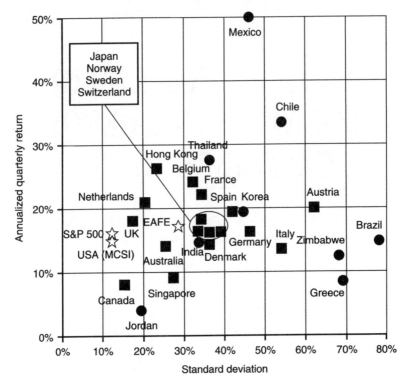

One of the benefits of diversification is that markets tend to move independently, so their returns balance one another. The effect of this low correlation can be seen by comparing the effect of different mixes of two assets, such as the Standard & Poor's (S&P) 500 and the EAFE Index. The historic five year correlation of EAFE with the S&P has been 0.61. This "*r*" statistic converts to an *r*-squared of 0.36, indicating that 36 percent of the return of one index can be explained by the other. Because 64 percent of the return of each index is independent, there are significant benefits from combining them. If we begin with a 100 percent S&P portfolio and move to a mix of 90 percent S&P with 10 percent EAFE, we not only increase the return from 15.8 percent to 16.1 percent, but we lower the risk from a

EXHIBIT 4-2

10-Year Average Returns and Standard Deviation of Returns through 1990

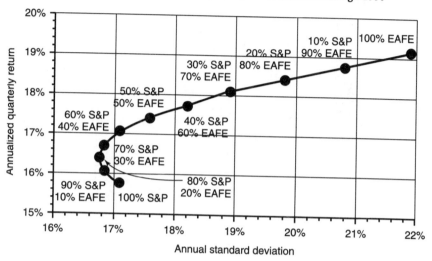

17.1 percent standard deviation to 16.8 percent, as shown in Exhibit 4–2.

The benefits do not end there, because the lowest risk portfolio has 20 percent EAFE, a standard deviation of 16.7 percent, and a return of 16.4 percent. If we are content with the original S&P risk level, we can go to 40 percent EAFE and have a 17.1 percent return, 130 basis points higher than the S&P alone. For most investors, the ideal asset mix would be a point on the curve where the slope of the line flattens to equal their risk preference (i.e., where the amount of incremental return is too little to warrant accepting additional standard deviation).

Because returns vary, even over 10 year periods, it is worthwhile to repeat our analysis with historical data using differing beginning and ending points, as shown in Exhibit 4–3. Again we see patterns with a "boomerang" shape, suggesting optimal EAFE weights between 30 percent and 50 percent, depending on the period chosen. This is true even in periods when the EAFE return was below that of the S&P, such as in 1982 and 1984. The diversifying benefit of EAFE during these periods was still great enough to lower overall risk significantly, with only a slight decline in returns.

10-Year Average Returns and Standard Deviation of Returns

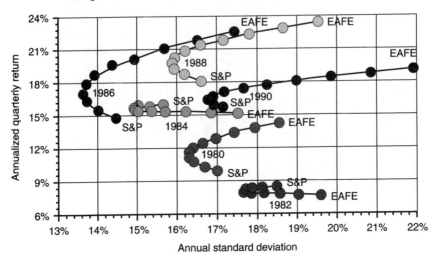

THE CHALLENGE OF ESTIMATES BASED ON AN UNCERTAIN PAST

While it is easy to see what would have worked in the past, there is a high degree of instability in historical data, which makes the asset allocation decision particularly difficult. As shown in Exhibit 4–4, returns vary widely when measured over trailing five-year periods (our return figures are annualized averages based on quarterly data).

In addition to EAFE and the S&P, Exhibit 4–4 shows the International Finance Corporation (IFC) Index of emerging markets. Although its history is short, it has had a higher return than the other indexes. While the EAFE Index had similar high returns in the late 1980s, these were mostly due to Japan, whereas the IFC's high returns have been much more broadly based. In projecting future returns, we are inclined to be conservative. While EAFE returns were higher than the S&P by 10 percent or more in the late 1980s, the higher trading costs and maturing of non-U.S. developed markets lead us to estimate a 1–2 percent return advantage in the future over the S&P. Similarly, for the IFC, while future returns could continue to remain high, we estimate a realizable return premium, after trading costs, of 3–5 percent.

EXHIBIT 4-4

5-Year Trailing Average Total Returns

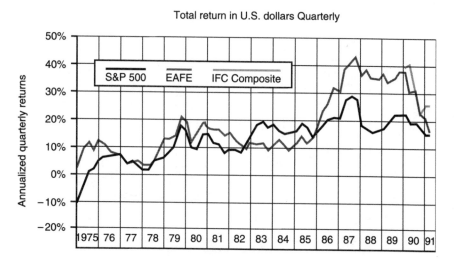

Total return in U.S. dollars Quarterly

Although risk levels are somewhat more stable, they also vary, as shown in Exhibit 4–5. For the future, it may be appropriate to estimate standard deviations of 18 percent for the S&P, 20 percent for the EAFE, and 35 percent for the IFC Index.

CORRELATION RISK

Most discussions of risk begin and end with standard deviation of returns, which can be divided into systematic market risk (or beta) and specific stock risk. Another form of risk is correlation risk. This is the risk that a seemingly diversified portfolio will prove to be undiversified in the future because its assets will begin to move uniformly rather than independently.

There are several trends that may cause correlations among assets to increase:

1. Institutional portfolios represent a larger portion of trading.

In the U.S., for example, institutions account for 70 percent of total trading volume today, compared with 40 percent in 1960. This trend means that fewer decision makers control larger amounts of trading, and those decisionmakers tend to be more alike and driven by similar inputs.

2. Indexing tends to bind stocks together.

EXHIBIT 4-5

Standard Deviation of Returns

5 year trailing standard deviation of total returns in U.S. dollars

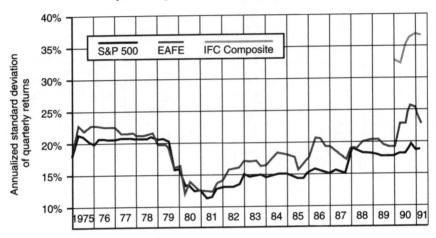

Today, indexed equity portfolios in the U.S. exceed $220 billion and represent over 50 percent of assets for some institutions. Similar index funds also are growing abroad. The likelihood that trading signals will affect all these portfolios simultaneously is high. Large buy and sell decisions by index funds drive every stock in the index regardless of the merits of each individual member.

3. The common market is linking the economic fortunes of European countries.

Over time, increasing integration of the fiscal and monetary policies of member nations is likely. Eventual centralized security trading also is probable. These factors will bind all European equities closer together. Meanwhile, similar unifying trade zones may develop in Asia and the Americas.

4. "Global events" are likely to occur more frequently.

The growth of world trade makes companies in all countries mutually dependent. Meanwhile, the advance of instantaneous communication means that markets respond simultaneously to global news. Cable News Network (CNN) broadcasts now are received even in Moscow.

The impact of global events is shown clearly in Exhibit 4–6, which plots the quarterly returns of the U.S. and German stock

EXHIBIT 4-6

Five Years of Quarterly Returns

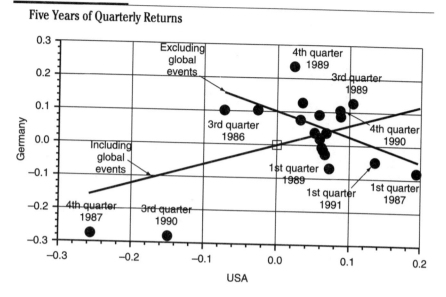

markets over the past five years. The outlying data points represent the fourth quarter of 1987 (The Great Crash) and the third quarter of 1990 (the Iraqi invasion of Kuwait). Two regression lines are shown; the one with a negative slope, indicating a negative correlation, excludes the fourth quarter of 1987 and the third quarter of 1990, while the other includes them and shows a positive slope. Although history will not repeat itself, global events are likely to occur again, and in our view, their frequency will increase.

Exhibit 4–7 shows how the correlation between the U.S. and other developed countries has changed over time. With all periods included, the correlations are at or near their highs, but without the "global events" they are lower. Japan is the only exception, possibly due to the heavy influence of government controls on the market in 1987. It is our expectation that all of these charts will show irregular uptrends during the 1990s as their economies become more interlocked. One result will be a straightening of the boomerang curves of Exhibit 4–2 and 4–3. Ultimately, asset allocation could simply be a choice of maximum tolerable risk along a straight line between the S&P and the EAFE Index.

EXHIBIT 4–7

Correlation of Developed Country Markets with the United States (5 Year Trailing)

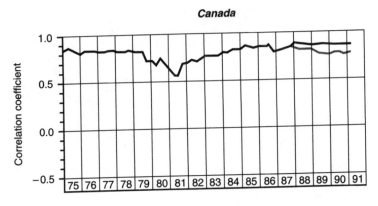

Canada

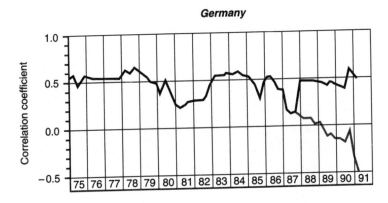

Germany

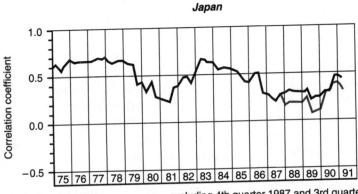

Japan

including all quarters   excluding 4th quarter 1987 and 3rd quarter 1990

EXHIBIT 4–7   *Continued*

Correlation of Developed Country Markets with the United States (5 Year Trailing)

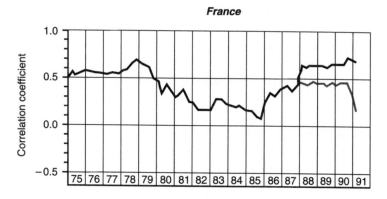

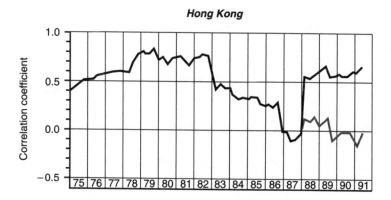

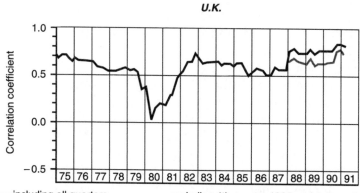

———— including all quarters   ———— excluding 4th quarter 1987 and 3rd quarter 1990

THE EMERGING MARKET SOLUTION

There is a solution to the risk of rising asset correlations. As institutional trading and global events increase the correlation of developed markets, the relative diversification advantage of emerging markets becomes greater. The correlations of several emerging markets with the U.S. are shown in Exhibit 4–8. Not only are they often significantly below the correlation levels of the developed markets, but several of the curves are trending down.

Exhibit 4–9 summarizes the correlation coefficients of 17 developed equity markets and 18 emerging equity markets versus the U.S. over the past five years. The correlations in column A include all quarters while those in column B exclude the global events of the fourth quarter of 1987 and the third quarter of 1990. These events posed much greater risk to portfolios that included only developed countries than to portfolios that included emerging markets. The average correlation of developed markets with the U.S. is 0.62 including the global events and 0.17 without them, an increase of 0.45. This compares with an average emerging market correlation over all periods of 0.22, which is still low and only 0.15 higher than the correlation without global events.

With this review of correlations, we can analyze the optimal weighting in emerging markets depending on their expected correlaton with the rest of a global portfolio. For the first step, our analysis assumes no excess return for emerging markets or for EAFE versus the S&P. It includes these markets on the basis of their diversification benefit due to low correlation. In order to study the effect of emerging markets specifically, we assume a fixed EAFE/S&P correlation of 0.61, which is the historic result over the past five years.

The result is shown in Exhibits 4–10 and 4–11. If the emerging market correlation with the S&P is 0.25, for example, the optimal emerging market weight ranges from 12.9 percent to 40.7 percent when the emerging market/EAFE correlation varies from plus 1 to minus 1. (At the same time, the percent invested in the S&P drops to zero because of the better fit of emerging markets with EAFE.)

The next step is to expand this analysis to include the impact of the positive estimated excess returns for EAFE and the emerging

E X H I B I T   4–8

Correlation of Emerging Country Markets with the United States (5 Year Trailing)

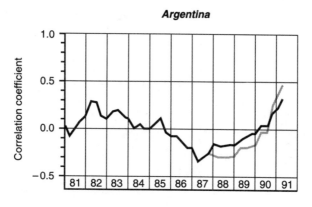

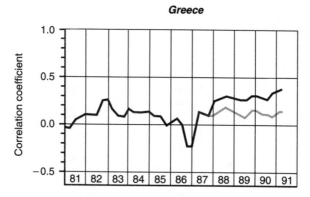

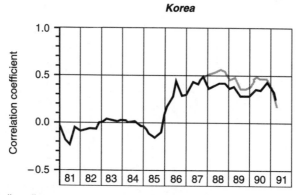

E X H I B I T 4–8 *Continued*

Correlation of Emerging Country Markets with the United States (5 Year Trailing)

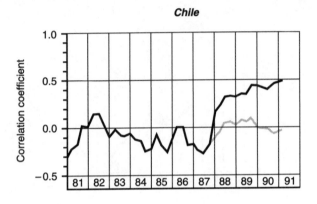

Chile

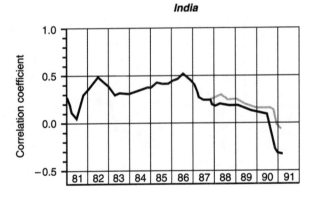

India

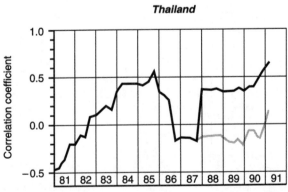

Thailand

—————— including all quarters   —————— excluding 4th quarter 1987 and 3rd quarter 1990

EXHIBIT 4-9

Correlation Coefficients of Quarterly Returns with S&P 500 (Total Returns in U.S.$, five years ended 1Q 1991)

	Correlation Coefficient Including All Quarters	Correlation Coefficient Excluding 4Q 1987 & 3Q 1990	Effect on Correlation Coefficient of Global Events	1987 4Q Return	1990 3Q Return
	(A)	(B)	(A − B)		
Developed Markets[1]					
United States	1.00	1.00	0.00	−22.7%	−13.8%
Australia	0.75	0.52	0.23	−36.9%	−2.7%
Austria	0.21	−0.31	0.52	−1.9%	−29.0%
Belgium	0.63	0.13	0.50	−17.5%	−13.6%
Canada	0.87	0.78	0.09	−18.4%	−7.5%
Denmark	0.28	0.01	0.27	−0.3%	−8.6%
France	0.68	0.17	0.51	−20.0%	−21.3%
Germany	0.47	−0.52	0.99	−24.1%	−24.8%
Hong Kong	0.66	0.01	0.65	−40.3%	−16.8%
Italy	0.44	−0.30	0.74	−14.1%	−24.0%
Japan	0.43	0.31	0.12	−2.6%	−25.5%
Netherlands	0.75	0.26	0.49	−17.7%	−7.6%
Norway	0.61	0.05	0.56	−39.1%	−4.4%
Singapore/Malaysia	0.86	0.42	0.44	−37.0%	−23.9%
Spain	0.55	0.23	0.32	−10.1%	−25.3%
Sweden	0.77	0.37	0.40	−22.7%	−28.8%
Switzerland	0.72	0.12	0.60	−20.7%	−20.1%
United Kingdom	0.81	0.73	0.08	−15.9%	−10.0%
Mean of Developed Markets:	0.62	0.17	0.45	−20.0%	−17.3%

1. Source: MSCI Indexes & S&P 500.

Continued on page 76

markets. To simplify this, we have assumed that the optimal solution for a hypothetical investor would be the highest return with a risk level equal to the S&P alone (i.e., that point on the "boomerang" curve of Exhibit 4–3 that lies directly above the S&P). Second, we have assumed that the EAFE excess return is fixed at 1 percent while varying the estimated emerging market return. Finally, we have used the historic five year standard deviations of EAFE, the S&P, and the IFC Index.

EXHIBIT 4-9   *Continued*

	Correlation Coefficient Including All Quarters	Correlation Coefficient Excluding 4Q 1987 & 3Q 1990	Effect on Correlation Coefficient of Global Events	1987 4Q Return	1990 3Q Return
	(A)	(B)	(A − B)		
Emerging Markets[2]					
Argentina	0.34	0.48	−0.14	−5.7%	5.1%
Brazil	0.23	0.18	0.05	−27.6%	−3.9%
Chile	0.49	−0.03	0.52	−22.1%	−6.1%
Columbia	−0.02	−0.28	0.26	11.5%	−10.7%
Greece	0.37	0.15	0.22	−20.3%	−22.4%
India	−0.32	−0.06	−0.26	2.9%	53.7%
Jordan	0.10	−0.04	0.14	5.6%	−14.5%
Korea	0.24	0.16	0.08	7.1%	−15.5%
Malaysia	0.86	0.48	0.38	−33.0%	−19.0%
Mexico	0.76	0.26	0.50	−77.7%	−11.1%
Nigeria	0.03	0.14	−0.11	−1.7%	6.3%
Pakistan	−0.29	−0.37	0.08	4.0%	4.6%
Philippines	0.31	−0.04	0.35	2.5%	−41.9%
Portugal	0.55	0.17	0.38	−52.8%	−18.4%
Taiwan	0.54	0.16	0.38	−45.9%	−45.2%
Thailand	0.66	0.15	0.51	−30.6%	−27.8%
Venezuela	−0.22	0.15	−0.37	18.2%	122.9%
Zimbabwe	−0.64	−0.43	−0.21	31.4%	21.8%
Mean of Emerging Markets:	0.22	0.07	0.15	−13.0%	−1.2%

2. Source: IFC Indexes.

The results are shown in Exhibits 4–12 and 4–13. If we assume a high 0.6 correlation of emerging markets with *both* EAFE and the S&P, then assuming a 4 percent excess return (the midpoint of our range earlier), the emerging market weighting would be 3.1 percent of the total portfolio. Using lower correlation estimates, however, increases the emerging market weightings dramatically. Interestingly, once the expected excess return is higher than 2 percent, changes in return do not influence the portfolio weight nearly as much as changes in correlation. Our best estimate of the expected correlation of emerging markets versus EAFE and the S&P is 0.4. At this level, assuming 4 percent excess return in emerging markets, the optimal

EXHIBIT   4-10

Allocation of Optimal Portfolio

Emerging Markets versus S&P 500		Emerging Markets versus EAFE								
		−1	−0.75	−0.5	−0.25	0	0.25	0.5	0.75	1
−1	% S&P 500	34.1	55.9	66.4	66.4	66.4	66.4	66.4	66.4	66.4
	% EAFE	30.4	10.6	0	0	0	0	0	0	0
	% Emerging	35.4	33.4	33.6	33.6	33.6	33.6	33.6	33.6	33.6
−0.75	% S&P 500	15.1	43.1	62.5	68.5	68.5	68.5	68.5	68.5	68.5
	% EAFE	47.1	24.3	6.2	0	0	0	0	0	0
	% Emerging	37.7	32.6	31.3	31.5	31.5	31.5	31.5	31.5	31.5
−0.5	% S&P 500	0	27.7	51.7	68.7	71.1	71.1	71.1	71.1	71.1
	% EAFE	59.3	38.6	18.9	2.6	0	0	0	0	0
	% Emerging	40.7	33.7	29.4	28.9		28.9	28.9	28.9	28.9
−0.25	% S&P 500	0	3.1	40.3	60.2	74.7	74.7	74.7	74.7	74.7
	% EAFE	59.3	58.3	30.8	14.5	0	0	0	0	0
	% Emerging	40.7	38.7	28.9	25.3	25.3	25.3	25.3	25.3	25.3
0	% S&P 500	0	0	23.9	53.3	68.6	79.7	79.7	79.7	79.7
	% EAFE	53.3	60.5	45	23.9	11.4	0	0	0	0
	% Emerging	40.7	39.5	31.1	22.0	20	20.3	20.3	20.3	20.3
0.25	% S&P 500	0	0	0	47.2	67.4	77.3	84	87.1	87.1
	% EAFE	59.3	60.5	62.2	31.9	18.2	10.8	4.2	0	0
	% Emerging	40.7	39.5	37.8	21	14.4	11.9	11.8	12.9	12.9
0.5	% S&P 500	0	0	0	38.4	76.6	84.5	85.7	85.7	85.7
	% EAFE	59.3	60.5	62.2	40.6	18	14.4	14.3	14.3	14.3
	% Emerging	40.7	39.5	37.8	21	5.4	1.1	0	0	0
0.75	% S&P 500	0	85.7	85.7	85.7	85.7	85.7	85.7	85.7	85.7
	% EAFE	59.3	14.3	14.3	14.3	14.3	14.3	14.3	14.3	14.3
	% Emerging	40.7	0	0	0	0	0	0	0	0
1	% S&P 500	85.7	85.7	85.7	85.7	85.7	85.7	85.7	85.7	85.7
	% EAFE	14.3	14.3	14.3 ·	14.3	14.3	14.3	14.3	14.3	14.3
	% Emerging	0	0	0	0	0	0	0	0	0

Note: Assumes correlation of EAFE with S&P 500 of .61, zero alpha for all asset classes, and historical standard deviations of returns.

weight is 13.8 percent. Raising the estimated excess return to 10 percent causes only a 0.7 percent increase in weighting; lowering the expected correlation to 0.3 increases the optimal weight by over 7 percent, to 21.4 percent. At a 0.3 correlation, we still would want 14.4 percent in emerging markets even if the excess return were only 1 percent, the same as our estimate for the EAFE excess return.

EXHIBIT 4-11

Optimal Zero Alpha Allocation to Emerging Markets
Assuming 0.61 EAFE/S&P 500 Correlation

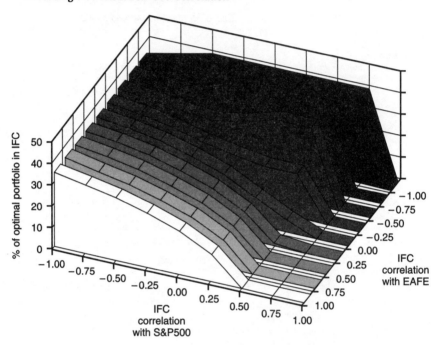

EXHIBIT 4-12

Emerging Markets Portfolio Optimization

Assumptions:

	Return	Standard Deviation	
S&P 500	0.0%	18.6%	
EAFE	1.0%	25.3%	EAFE/S&P Correlation = 0.6
Emerging Markets		36.8%	

Continued

Optimal Allocation to Emerging Markets (% of Portfolio for Portfolio Variation equal to S&P 500)

Emerging Markets Excess Returns versus S&P	Correlation with S&P and EAFE								
	− 0.2	− 0.1	0.0	0.1	0.2	0.3	0.4	0.5	0.6
0.0%	24.0	21.3	18.3	15.0	11.4	7.2	2.0	0.0	0.0
1.0%	34.7	31.6	28.2	24.3	19.8	14.4	8.1	1.1	0.0
2.0%	41.4	38.1	34.3	29.9	24.8	18.7	11.8	4.9	0.4
3.0%	44.8	41.3	37.3	32.7	28.0	20.5	13.1	6.5	2.1
4.0%	46.6	42.9	38.7	33.9	28.2	21.4	13.8	9.4	3.1
10.0%	49.1	45.2	42.3	35.6	29.5	22.4	14.5	7.7	4.0

Optimal Allocation to Emerging Markets (% of Portfolio, Portfolio Variation = S&P 500)

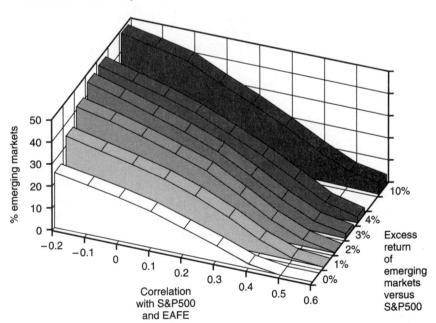

A final analysis shows the effects of changing risk tolerance on the solution. Here we assume the emerging markets excess return is 4 percent and the correlation is 0.4. As shown in Exhibit 4–14, at the lowest level of risk, emerging markets represent 4.4 percent of the portfolio. As risk tolerance rises, however, the emerging market commitment grows substantially.

E X H I B I T   4–14

Optimal Portfolio Allocation

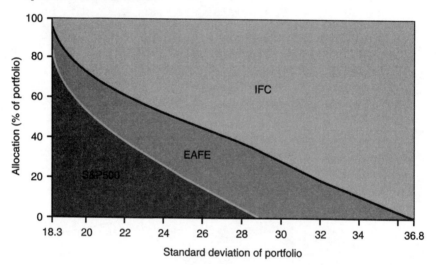

CONCLUSION

Risk and return have received considerable attention in studies of asset allocation. Typically, the most uncertainty has focused on estimates of return while standard deviation and correlation have been assumed to be relatively stable. Correlations among markets have been changing, however, as demonstrated by the October 1987 crash and the July 1990 invasion of Kuwait. Similar global events are likely to occur with increasing frequency due to improved communications, rising trade, the growing interdepedence of countries, and the increasing number of global investors. In the 1990s, more equity assets will move together because of simultaneous decisions by investors, reducing the diversification of global portfolios.

As the diversification of developed markets is reduced, emerging equity markets become increasingly important in asset allocation. Conservative assumptions suggest optimal emerging market weightings of 10–15 percent, compared with current levels of 0–1 percent for typical institutional portfolios. Although limited liquidity will prevent most large portfolios from achieving this target, the greatest rewards will accrue to those investors who establish sizable positions in emerging markets before they become more widely used.

REFERENCES

Hunter, John B.; and T. Daniel Coggin. "An Analysis of the Diversification Benefit from International Equity Investment." *Journal of Portfolio Management,* Fall 1990.

Wainscott, Craig B. "The Stock-Bond Correlation and its Implications for Asset Allocation." *Financial Analysts Journal,* July–August 1990.

CHAPTER

5

PORTFOLIO ALLOCATION AND COMMODITY RISK MANAGEMENT IN EMERGING COUNTRY ECONOMIES

Stijn Claessens and Panos Varangis, *International Economics Department
The World Bank*

INTRODUCTION

It is clear that better management of international commodity price risk could have a valuable role in the great majority of developing countries since they continue to bear large commodity price exposures on both exports and imports.[1] Exports often are concentrated in a few primary commodities with positively correlated price movements. For 36 developing countries, the share of primary commodities to total exports exceeded 50 percent for the year 1990 or 1991 (see Exhibit 5–1). In several developing countries, a single commodity accounts for more than 90 percent of total export earnings (for example, coffee in Burundi, Burkina Faso, and Uganda, and oil in Nigeria). Overall, primary commodities accounted for 68 percent of exports of low-income developing countries and 44 percent of high-income developing countries.

---

1. For earlier empirical work on this area see Gemmill (1985), Rolfo (1980), and McKinnon (1967), among others.

E X H I B I T   5–1

Export Concentration for Developing Countries

Country	Commodities	Share
Hungary	Nonferrous metals;	100.0
Algeria	Crude petroleum; natural gas; petroleum refined	99.0
Kiribati	Seeds other fixed oils; fresh fish; crude veg materials	98.8
Seychelles	Prepared fish; fresh fish; salted fish	95.9
Fr. Guiana	Shell fish; rice; fresh fish	94.7
Venezuela	Crude petroleum; nonferrous metals; nonferrous metal scrap	94.7
Nepal	Crude veg materials; seeds other fixed oils; jute	94.2
Faeroe Islds	Fresh fish; salted fish; shell fish	93.0
Reunion	Sugar and honey; shell fish; alcoholic beverages	92.5
Trinidad And	Petroleum refined; crude petroleum; sugar and honey	91.8
Guadeloupe	Fruit & nuts; sugar and honey; alcoholic beverages	87.0
Jordan	Crude fertilizers; fresh veg; fruit & nuts	84.1
Ecuador	Crude petroleum; fruit & nuts; shell fish	81.8
Paraguay	Cotton; seeds soft fixed oil; meat fresh	81.0
Togo	Crude fertilizers; cotton; coffee	80.6
Barbados	Sugar and honey; alcoholic beverages; edible products	78.2
Ethiopia	Coffee; hides & skins; exc furs; fresh veg	78.2
Bangladesh	Shell fish; jute; hides & skins, exc furs	77.3
El Salvador	Coffee; sugar and honey; shell fish	76.9
Sri Lanka	Tea; natural rubber; fruit & nuts	75.0
Mexico	Crude petroleum; fresh veg; nonferrous metals	72.4
Singapore	Petroleum refined; nonferrous metals; natural rubber	72.2
Pakistan	Cotton; rice; shell fish	68.9
Peru	Nonferrous metals; base metal ores; animal feed	67.8
Panama Ex.Cz	Fruit & nuts; shell fish; sugar and honey	66.8
Tunisia	Crude petroleum; soft fixed veg oils; shell fish	66.8
Kenya	Coffe; tea; petroleum refined	65.3
Colombia	Coffee; crude petroluem; coal	65.2
Bolivia	Natural gas; base metal ores; nonferrous metals	64.9
Egypt	Crude petroleum; petroleum refined; nonferrous metals	64.7
Indonesia	Crude petroleum; natural gas; petroleum refined	63.4
Chile	Nonferrour metals; base metal ores; fruit & nuts	62.9
Guatemala	Coffee; sugar and honey; fruit & nuts	61.1
Uruguay	Wool; meat fresh; rice	58.0
Oman	Nonferrous metals; tobacco manufactured; fresh fish	57.3
Malaysia	Crude petroleum; nonsoft fixed veg oil; wood rough	52.4

Continued

E X H I B I T   5–1   *Continued*

Country	Commodities	Share
Senegal	Soft fixed veg oils; petroleum refined; prepared fish	52.3
Poland	Coal; nonferrous metals; sulphur	46.9
Yugoslavia	Nonferrous metals; base metal ores; wood shaped	46.0
Turkey	Fruit & nuts; fresh veg; tobacco unmanufactured	45.9
Macau	Wood; shell fish; nonalcohol beverages	44.0
Morocco	Crude fertilizers; shell fish; fruit & nuts	41.0
Taiwan	Meat fresh; nonferrous metals; fresh fish	40.8
Argentina	Animal feed; soft fixed veg oils; seeds soft fixed oil	40.7
Brazil	Iron ore; nonferrous metals; animal feed	40.5
Thailand	Shell fish; rice; prepared fish	39.7
India	Tea; iron ore; petroleum refined	33.2
China	Crude petroleum; fresh veg; maize unmilled	27.5

Source: The World Bank, International Economics Department.

Although the dependency of developing countries on exports of primary commodities has declined during the last 20–30 years, it is still quite high. Imports also are influenced by commodity prices, particularly those of fuels and food. Oil and food grains account for a large share of the import bill for a large number of developing countries, particularly the low-income group.

The most widely used approaches in the developing countries' management of external exposures to commodity price risk have not, by and large, proved successful. These include domestic and international commodity price stabilization schemes, contingent finance, reserves management, and export diversification. With recent innovations in financial markets, it appears that market-based financial risk management techniques may assist developing countries in hedging commodity price risks to a significant extent. Furthermore, developing countries could link their exposure in commodities to the form of finance used to obtain loans or finance projects at more favorable terms. For example, developing countries and companies in such countries could sell call options in products they produce to reduce the nominal interest costs.

Some developing countries have been hedging themselves through use of traditional short-dated market-based instruments. But very few developing countries have been able to access the long-dated (up to 10-years maturity) derivative instruments, such as commodity swaps, long-dated options, and commodity-linked bonds, which would permit much more comprehensive price risk management. On the whole, little of developing countries' exports or imports are hedged routinely. The creation of domestic futures exchanges usually is not the most effective approach, as they do not necessarily diversify the risk externally. Furthermore, developing countries do not have the necessary human and institutional capital to warrant the creation of future markets. They will likely find that removal of impediments to the use of existing international futures markets will provide a large degree of risk reduction.

So why do so few countries attempt to manage their commodity price risk in this way? We can identify a number of barriers that prevent them from doing so. Most importantly, the capacity to hedge has been hindered by domestic restrictions on access to international financial markets, the incompleteness of domestic (financial) markets (e.g., the inability to enter and enforce fixed-price contracts), and distortions introduced by (government) policy. Underlying causes typically have been legal, regulatory, and institutional constraints that have adversely affected the private sector's capacity to hedge. Other important constraints have included lack of familiarity with the market instruments and their strategic use, misconceptions that confuse speculation with hedging, and low credit standing in global financial markets.

The limited use of commodity risk management instruments by developing countries motivated the World Bank in 1990 to set up a program of technical assistance (TA), supported by research, to help various entities in developing countries improve their management of commodity price risk. The program, which has given assistance in Algeria, Chile, Colombia, Costa Rica, Hungary, Indonesia, Nigeria, Papua New Guinea, Poland, Trinidad, Tobago, Tunisia, Uganda, and Venezuela, has focused on raising awareness of external exposures (in commodity prices, currencies, and interest rates); convincing policy makers and the entities exposed of the benefits of using market instruments; and assisting in the implementation of risk management strategies.

This chapter discusses the experience of the World Bank TA program with encouraging use of market-based hedging instruments in developing countries. The structure of the chapter is as follows. First we discuss the trend toward the trading of commodities as assets and show the benefits of looking at commodities as assets for both developing and industrial countries. Next, we outline the different mechanisms available for risk management and the benefits to developing countries of using market-based commodity risk management instruments. We then go on to describe some of the experiences of developing countries with futures and options exchanges and some of the experiences with over-the-counter markets in developed as well as developing countries. Next we discuss the barriers to increased commodity risk management in developing countries and then turn to the implications of developing domestic futures markets as well as other domestic forms of risk management. Finally, we provide concluding remarks.

COMMODITIES AS TRADED ASSETS

It is commonly observed that commodities are increasingly being traded as assets. This is particularly true for the permanently storable ones (i.e., metals), but it is also true for other commodities. The fact that commodities have become tradable as assets changes their price behavior significantly—their prices are more forward-looking (and thus [real] interest rate sensitive) and less driven by contemporaneous demand and supply factors.

Empirical evidence bears this out. Palaskas and Varangis (1989) found that real interest rates have a significant impact on commodity prices. A 1 percent increase in the real interest rate will cause a 2.2 percent reduction in the price of metals and minerals. The same increase in the real interest rate will cause a 1.2 percent reduction in the prices of agricultural food and a 1.7 percent reduction in agricultural raw material prices. Note the greater impact of interest rate increases on metals and minerals prices (more storable) than on agricultural food prices (less storable). This result also conforms to the view that metals and minerals are more tradable as assets than are the other commodities.

The increased tradability of commodities also implies that one needs to define properly the rate of return on commodities. If a commodity trades as a financial asset, it foregoes the opportunity cost of money (the interest rate) if it is kept untraded (i.e., in the ground or in stock). Cash commodity prices (i.e., acquiring the commodity left in the ground) reflect this opportunity cost and thus the rate of return on cash prices will consequently underestimate the total rate of return available on commodities. The total rate of return on a commodity thus should be defined as the sum of two parts: the cash commodity price return as well as the opportunity cost of money. Using this definition of total return, it is likely that commodities have performed quite well as an asset compared to many other assets.

One example of the use of this total return concept is the Goldman Sachs Commodity Index (GSCI). This index includes cash commodity prices as well as the opportunity cost of money (short-term T-bills). In addition, the GSCI includes the so-called roll yield—defined as the difference between the spot price (or the nearby futures contract) and the next-to-nearby futures price in the previous period. As many commodities were in backwardation during the period 1970–92, the roll yield was a positive 4 percent. Putting these three components together the total rate of return on the GSCI over the period was 15 percent. This was higher than the Standard & Poor's (S&P) 500 and substantially above the World Bank commodity price index of 33 commodities (WB33), which saw only an average annual increase of about 2.5 percent. The difference between the performances of the GSCI and the World Bank index (apart from the differences in the weights) is largely due to the fact that the GSCI includes the opportunity cost of money (the T-bill rate) while the WB33 only includes the spot return. Commodities have thus not performed as poorly as often stated.

This analysis has two important implications for developing countries. One, to increase the rate of return that developing countries receive on their commodities, they could have the commodities "earn" the opportunity cost of capital (i.e., sell them forward in some form and in that way earn the opportunity rate of return). This forward selling can be done through borrowing funds in the traditional way while at the same time selling futures, either through commodity-linked loans or through a combination of commodity derivatives and loans (further discussed below).

There are, of course, some serious constraints to selling commodities forward on a large scale. Some of these constraints are legal (e.g., the negative pledge clauses commonly found in commercial bank agreements), while others are economic (e.g., the risk that countries will overcollateralize and in that way lower their international credit standing). Nevertheless, this way of operating is becoming more common. The best example is current practice in financing gold mines; the majority of new mining activity is financed with gold loans, or with traditional loans with future gold revenues immediately swapped into fixed payment revenues. Similarly, many farmers in developed countries finance their crops using futures hedges, and in this way reap the opportunity costs of borrowing from their commodities.

The second important implication is that commodities as traded assets can be attractive investment opportunities from an industrial country investors point of view. Not only have commodities a high rate of return (when properly measured), but they also offer large diversification potential as they have negative correlations with most other assets and, in general, are effective inflation hedges. They can thus move the efficient frontier of risk-return trade offs upwards (i.e., achieving a higher return for a given standard deviation or a lower standard deviation for a given return), even if it is assumed that the rate of return on commodities will not continue to be above that of other assets. The effect of moving upwards along the efficient frontier is shown in Exhibit 5–2 where investing in the S&P500 alone (the commodity share is zero) is dominated by including up to 50 percent commodities in the portfolio as the rate of return is higher for equal or lower variance. (The graph is based on the 1970–92 rates of returns on the GSCI and S&P500.)

This is arguably a favorable case as the rate of return on the GSCI exceeded that on the S&P500, while the correlation between them was -0.32. If one were to assume that the rate of return on the GSCI will be much less in the future (e.g., 7 percent), then the frontier will slope downward from the S&P-point, thus still achieving lower variance but also lower returns. This is done in Exhibit 5–3.

Building on these concepts, one can show that commodities offer some diversification potential even when other assets are

Frontier including Commodities
(share of GSCI)

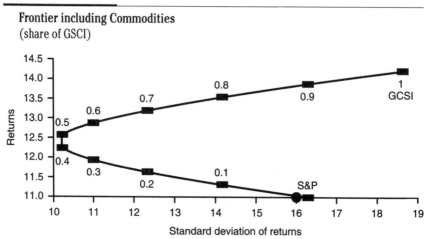

included in the portfolios—both from the developing countries' side (e.g., their stocks markets as represented in the Emerging Market Data Base of the IFC) as well as from the industrial countries' side (e.g., stocks as well as bonds and real estate from different countries). The net result remains that investors in industrial countries would benefit from including some amount of commodity price-linked assets.[2]

MARKET-BASED VERSUS OTHER COMMODITY RISK MANAGEMENT INSTRUMENTS

There are three general types of risk management instruments that can be used to cope with terms of trade shocks arising from (primary) commodity price changes: (a) self-insurance, including reserve management policies, macroeconomic policies, domestic price stabilization schemes (such as buffer funds), and

---

2. Recently, managed funds (funds put together by individuals or institutions to undertake future market operations) have been active in commodity markets, as means to diversity investors' portfolios. A 1988/89 survey by CFTC showed that funds accounted for an average 1 to 6 percent of open interest and volume on medium-sized and large commodity futures markets in the United States. Since then, that share has probably grown given the growth of managed funds. Analysts consider managed funds an important potential source of growth for commodity exchanges.

E X H I B I T   5-3

Frontier including Commodities
(share of GSCI, assuming ror.GSCI = 7%)

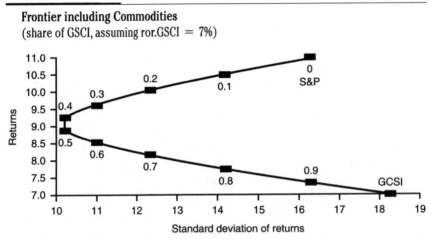

activity diversification; (*b*) third party insurance (i.e., transfer-ring part or all of the price risk to parties outside the country through the use of international financial markets); and (*c*) other schemes such as international commodity price stabilization agreements and compensatory financing schemes. These instruments are not exact substitutes and they also may serve different functions, but they all can play a role in managing the risks from price instability.

A negative factor in the use of self-insurance schemes is the high cost they impose on the economy in terms of the funds required; moreover, often they prove to be not very effective when most needed. They also can have negative spillovers into other sectors of the economy. In particular, the developing countries' experience with commodity stabilization funds (CSFs) has not been satisfactory, with the vast majority of the funds experiencing severe liquidity problems as well as being used for social objectives unrelated to price stabilization. Even if they had been used only for their stated objective of price stabilization, a CSF still would not last very long given how commodity prices typically behave.[3]

---

3. For an illustration of the mechanics of commodity stabilization funds with an application to copper and oil, see Arrau and Claessens (1992).

Recent empirical work on commodity prices by Deaton (1992) shows that most commodity prices eventually revert to their mean—a requirement for a stabilization fund to be viable—but only very slowly, with an average reversal time measured in years, not months. Because of this, a CSF has to be very large to be effective or the country needs to have ample access to foreign borrowing opportunities.[4] For domestic, political reasons, large CSF is not feasible—it is too much subject to spending pressures from domestic constituencies—and sovereign risk prohibits the necessary access to foreign borrowing. As a small CSF is not effective, Deaton argues that there is little scope for countries to stabilize their domestic consumption levels through a CSF or through borrowing in the international capital markets. Furthermore, CSFs tie up scarce funds which could be better used in other sectors of the economy. A general problem with self-insurance schemes, which do not involve the use of external assets, is that they only redistribute the risks within the country; they do not diversify the risks outside the country to entities better able to bear such risks.

Countries previously relying on CSF-type schemes for their exports (such as Côte d'Ivoire, Cameroon, Burundi, Rwanda, and Ghana) have begun to abandon them. Nigeria dropped its cocoa price stabilization scheme in 1986 while Madagascar abandoned its coffee price support scheme in 1989. The only funds so far that have worked with some success are the coffee fund in Colombia, the Copper Stabilization Fund in Chile, and the Mineral Resource Stabilization Fund in Papua New Guinea.

International commodity price stabilization agreements have been tried for several commodities but in most instances they have had a short life span—often breaking down when their stabilizing influence could have been most useful. Compensatory financing schemes can perform a useful role by providing funds after a price decline. However, by their very nature, they are ex-post instruments and therefore can mitigate only part of the adverse effect of a price decline.

---

4. Larson and Coleman (1991) have argued that using options to complement a CSF will make it more likely that the CSF will survive in the short term. However, they argue that whether or not a stabilization fund is hedged, it will inevitably generate large amounts of debt.

These poor experiences with various price stabilization schemes have led the private sector in many industrial countries to the use of short-dated futures and options to hedge and manage short-dated commodity exposures. As we will see in the next section, the use of these market-based risk management instruments in developing countries is limited.

THE USE OF EXISTING COMMODITY EXCHANGES BY DEVELOPING COUNTRIES

To What Extent Do Developing Countries Use U.S. Commodity Exchanges?

Very little has been recorded regarding the participation of developing countries in commodity futures markets (an early reference is Powers and Tosini, 1977). This is partly due to the fact that developing countries have only recently shown a significant interest in using these instruments, but it also reflects the unavailability of data. Due to the confidential nature of most such transactions, information has been quite difficult to access. A recent paper by Umali (1992), using data from the U.S. Commodity Futures Trading Commission (CFTC) for the period January to December 1991, provides for the first time an indication of developing countries' participation in U.S. futures exchanges. Exhibit 5–4 shows the open interest held by foreign traders from different geographic regions in the various commodities. Exhibit 5–5 shows the percentage of open interest in U.S. futures contracts attributed to foreigners during 1991. It can be seen that the share of developing countries in total open interest is quite small. In most cases, its value was less than 1 percent. Further, most of the activity from developing countries has been concentrated in grains, soybeans, and foodstuffs (mainly coffee and cocoa).

Exhibit 5–6 shows regional participation as a percentage of total foreign participation. Europe and Canada account for most of the foreign participation in U.S. exchanges. Among developing countries, the most active in U.S. exchanges have been the Central and South American countries. Sub-Saharan Africa has been almost absent from the U.S. exchanges, except for minor activity in foodstuffs. Developing countries in Asia also have hardly used the U.S. exchanges.

E X H I B I T 5–4 Reportable Open Positions in U.S. Futures Exchanges for Selected Commodities Held by Foreign Traders, 1991

| Commodity Group | Type of Position | Asia | | | Middle East and Africa | | | Central & S. America | Europe & Canada | Centralized Economies | Open Positions | |
		Developed	Developing	Total	ME+ N. Afric	S.-Saharan	Total				Total Foreign	Total Position
Grains & Soybean complex	Long	102988	2927	105915	2452	300	2752	56694	418094	6570	590025	
	Short	124990	10716	135706	6105	0	6105	30327	414356	3497	589991	7181635
Grains	Long	37755	0	37755	1133	300	1433	13866	179497	4173	236724	
	Short	114603	10320	124923	3993	0	3993	2163	129195	3099	263373	4147026
Soybean complex	Long	65233	2927	68160	1319	0	1319	42828	238597	2397	353301	
	Short	10387	396	10783	2112	0	2112	28164	285161	398	326618	3034609
Livestock products	Long	374	0	374	123	0	123	2184	12775	0	15456	
	Short	50	0	50	71	0	71	3409	15865	0	19395	1440801
Foodstuffs	Long	114771	7344	122115	3468	0	3468	34072	661309	0	820964	
	Short	137241	430	137671	1215	17625	18840	20328	857647	0	1034486	2591979
Industrial materials	Long	90739	0	90739	5399	78	5477	41945	427767	0	565928	
	Short	93865	180	94045	4093	1681	5774	58668	460625	0	619112	6366129
Metals	Long	53579	1783	55362	10686	0	10686	24004	219928	0	309980	
	Short	23962	330	24292	17565	0	17565	13481	270726	0	326064	3138254
Financial instruments	Long	676615	20	676635	3393	0	3393	187697	1204685	0	2072410	
	Short	746785	1190	747975	35040	0	35040	203194	1717341	0	2703550	19202471
Currencies	Long	25081	0	25081	3878	0	3878	59304	179887	0	268150	
	Short	2065	0	2065	3527	0	3527	25654	319716	0	350962	2680597

Notes: The data were compiled from CFTC "01" report forms, which are filed daily by futures commission merchants, clearing members, and foreign brokers. It lists all reportable-sized futures positions carried. These annual figures (January–December) are the sum of month-end values.

The countries included in the regional groupings are as follows: Developed Asia—Australia, Hong Kong, Japan, New Zealand, Republic of Korea, Singapore, and Taiwan; Developing Asia—India, Indonesia, Malaysia, Philippines, and Thailand; Middle East and North Africa—Bahrain, Egypt, Israel, Jordan, Kuwait, Lebanon, Moroco, Muscat, Oman, Saudi Arabia, Tunisia, Turkey, and the United Arab

Continued

EXHIBIT 5-4 Continued

Emirates: Sub-Saharan Africa—Liberia, South Africa, Swaziland; Central and South America—Argentina, Bahamas, Bermuda, Brazil, Chile, Cayman Islands, Colombia, Costa Rica, Dominican Republic, Ecuador, El Salvador, Guatemala, Honduras, Mexico, Netherlands Antilles, Peru, Paraguay, Panama, St. Vincent, Trinidad, Tobago, Turks and Calcos Islands, Uruguay, Venezuela, British Virgin Islands, and West Indies; Europe and Canada—Austria, Belgium, Canada, Cyprus, Denmark, Ireland, England, Finland, France, Federal Republic of Germany, Gibraltar, Greece, Holland, Ireland, Italy, Liechtenstein, Luxembourg, Monaco, Netherlands, Norway, Portugal, Spain, Sweden, and Switzerland; Centralized Economies (including formerly centralized economies)—Bulgaria, China, Czechoslovakia, Hungary, Romania, and the Commonwealth of Independent States.

The commodities included in the commodity groupings are: Grains—corn, wheat, oats, rice; Soybean complex—soybean, soybean meal, and oil; Livestock products—live cattle, feeder cattle, hogs, and pork bellies; Foodstuff—cocoa, coffee, orange juice, potatoes, corn syrup, and sugar; Financial instruments—certificates of deposit, CPI-W index, Commodity Research Bureau futures price index, corporate bond indexes, GNMA mortgages, municipal bonds, stock indexes, Treasury bills, Treasury bonds, Treasury notes, and U.S. dollar index; Metals—gold, platinum, and silver; Currencies—Eurodollars, European currency unit, and foreign currencies; and Industrial goods—aluminum, copper, cotton, crude oil, gasoline, lumber, heating oil, palladium, and propane gas.

Source: Division of Economic Analysis, CFTC, 1992.

EXHIBIT 5-5

Percentage of Reportable Regional Open Interests over Total Open Interests in U.S. Futures Exchanges for Selected Commodities, 1991

Commodity Group	Type of Position	Asia Developed	Asia Developing	Asia Total	Middle East and Africa M.E.+ N. Afric	Middle East and Africa Sub-Sahar	Middle East and Africa Total	Central & S. America	Europe & Canada	Centralized Economies	Foreign Total Positions
Grains & Soybean complex	Long	1.43	0.04	1.47	0.03	*	0.04	0.79	5.82	0.09	8.22
	Short	1.74	0.15	1.89	0.09	0.00	0.09	0.42	5.77	0.05	8.22
Grains	Long	0.91	0.00	0.91	0.03	0.01	0.03	0.33	4.33	0.10	5.71
	Short	2.76	0.25	3.01	0.10	0.00	0.10	0.05	3.12	0.07	6.35
Soybean complex	Long	2.15	0.10	2.25	0.04	0.00	0.04	1.41	7.86	0.08	11.64
	Short	0.34	0.01	0.36	0.07	0.00	0.07	0.93	9.40	0.01	10.76
Livestock products	Long	0.03	0.00	0.03	0.01	0.00	0.01	0.15	0.89	0.00	1.07
	Short	*	0.00	*	*	0.00	*	0.24	1.10	0.00	1.35
Foodstuffs	Long	4.43	0.28	4.71	0.13	0.00	0.13	1.31	25.51	0.00	31.67
	Short	5.29	0.02	5.31	0.05	0.68	0.73	0.78	33.09	0.00	39.91
Industrial materials	Long	1.43	0.00	1.43	0.08	0.00	0.09	0.66	6.72	0.00	8.89
	Short	1.47	*	1.48	0.06	0.03	0.09	0.92	7.24	0.00	9.73
Metals	Long	1.71	0.06	1.76	0.34	0.00	0.34	0.76	7.01	0.00	9.88
	Short	0.76	0.01	0.77	0.56	0.00	0.56	0.43	8.63	0.00	10.39
Financial instruments	Long	3.52	*	3.52	0.02	0.00	0.02	0.98	6.27	0.00	10.79
	Short	3.89	0.01	3.90	0.18	0.00	0.18	1.06	8.94	0.00	14.08
Currencies	Long	0.94	0.00	0.94	0.14	0.00	0.14	2.21	6.71	0.00	10.00
	Short	0.08	0.00	0.08	0.13	0.00	0.13	0.96	11.93	0.00	13.09

Note: *—Value less than 0.05 percent.

Source: Division of Economic Analysis, CFTC, 1992.

Percentage of Reportable Regional Over Total Foreign Open Interests in U.S. Futures Exchanges for Selected Commodities, 1991

Commodity Group	Type of Position	Asia			Middle East and Africa			Central & S. America	Europe & Canada	Centralized Economies
		Developed	Developing	Total	M.E.+ Afric	Sub-Sahar	Total			
Grains & Soybean complex	Long	17.45	0.50	17.95	0.42	0.05	0.47	9.61	70.86	1.11
	Short	21.19	1.82	23.00	1.03	0.00	1.03	5.14	70.23	0.59
Grains	Long	15.95	0.00	15.95	0.48	0.13	0.61	5.86	75.83	1.76
	Short	43.51	3.92	47.43	1.52	0.00	1.52	0.82	49.05	1.18
Soybean complex	Long	18.46	0.83	19.29	0.37	0.00	0.37	12.12	67.53	0.68
	Short	3.18	0.12	3.30	0.65	0.00	0.65	8.62	87.31	0.12
Livestock products	Long	2.42	0.00	2.42	0.80	0.00	0.80	14.13	82.65	0.00
	Short	0.26	0.00	0.26	0.37	0.00	0.37	17.58	81.80	0.00
Foodstuffs	Long	13.98	0.89	14.87	0.42	0.00	0.42	4.15	80.55	0.00
	Short	13.27	0.04	13.31	0.12	1.70	1.82	1.97	82.91	0.00
Industrial materials	Long	16.03	0.00	16.03	0.95	0.01	0.97	7.41	75.59	0.00
	short	15.16	0.03	15.19	0.66	0.27	0.93	9.48	74.40	0.00
Metals	Long	17.28	0.58	17.86	3.45	0.00	3.45	7.74	70.95	0.00
	Short	7.35	0.10	7.45	5.39	0.00	5.39	4.13	83.03	0.00
Financial instruments	Long	32.65	*	32.65	0.16	0.00	0.16	9.06	58.13	0.00
	Short	27.62	0.04	27.67	1.30	0.00	1.30	7.52	63.52	0.00
Currencies	Long	9.35	0.00	9.35	1.45	0.00	1.45	22.12	67.08	0.00
	Short	0.59	0.00	0.59	1.00	0.00	1.00	7.31	91.10	0.00

Note: *—Value less than 0.05 percent.

Source: Division of Economic Analysis, CFTC, 1992.

While the participation of developing countries in U.S. futures exchanges appears low, as recorded in these data, some trades may not be recorded as originating from developing countries as they go through third-parties. Further, these data relate to U.S. futures exchanges only, which probably explains why Central and South American participation is much greater than that of other developing country regions. European and Asian futures exchanges data may tell a different story about Asia's and Sub-Saharan Africa's participation in foreign exchanges.

These data do not include the over-the-counter markets, which have expanded rapidly in recent years. For the longer end of the hedging spectrum, we think largely of commodity swaps.[5] Since commodity swap contracts are only a very recent development, the swap markets are not yet as active as the currency and interest rate swap markets. However, the commodity swap markets have been growing and, according to estimates from the Bank for International Settlements, the total amount of the commodity-indexed swap and option markets is between $40 and $50 billion. The depth of the over-the-counter markets for oil-linked instruments has increased considerably in recent years. The market for energy swaps is estimated to be at least $25 billion per annum. Aluminum, copper, nickel, zinc, and jet fuel also can be swapped, but the markets are thinner (i.e., there is an inability to enter into swaps in large volumes at prices close to the current quoted prices). As mentioned, swaps and other longer-dated instruments have been mostly used in the mineral and energy sectors in industrial countries (investments in gold mining often are financed with gold loans).

One point that is worth emphasizing here is that the commodity swap and, in general, the over-the-counter markets do not necessarily reduce the need for or compete with the futures/option markets. For example, the spread of oil-linked instruments both has relied on and been a factor in the development of long-dated futures contracts in the oil market. Banks and

---

5. Commodity swaps are basically the same as currency and interest rate swaps. But a commodity swap is not exactly a series of commodity forward contracts; unlike a currency or an interest rate swap, it does not involve deliveries of physical commodities. However, it should be noted that the economic consequences are approximately equal to those of a series of forward contracts.

other intermediaries that offer over-the-counter instruments often hedge portions of the risk they have assumed on established futures/options markets. We could go even further and argue that if developing countries became more active in commodity swaps for the soft commodities, this would give support to the development of longer-dated futures contracts in soft contracts where there is little liquidity or where contracts do not exist at present.

Some more encouraging signs of the participation by developing countries in international hedging markets exist on an anecdotal basis. We know that in a few developing countries the private sector as well as state enterprises already use these instruments in a routine fashion. For instance, Ghana, Cameroon, and Côte d'Ivoire consistently have sold forward a significant fraction of their next year's cocoa exports at a fixed price.[6] Sugar exporters in the Philippines, Costa Rica, Guatamala, and Thailand have used fixed-price agreements to lock in profit margins for sugar exports. China and Mexico have used futures and options frequently to hedge sugar imports (Laughlin and Falloon, 1990). China also has used futures/options markets to hedge grain imports. In Indonesia, no formal restrictions exist on the use of external risk management tools and some coffee, cocoa, and rubber exporters routinely hedge. Similarly, in Malaysia and Brazil, coffee and cocoa exporters routinely use the New York and London futures/options markets to hedge their risk. In Costa Rica and Colombia, some private coffee exporters have been hedging for quite some time (even though the legal framework did not permit it until recently in Colombia). In general, for domestic commodity markets that are not distorted by government intervention and where the commodity traded has low basis risk with that traded in an existing commodity exchange, the private sector tends to use futures contracts.

In addition, we know that some state enterprises that are involved in commodity exporting or importing and other intermediaries taking on exposure to international prices also have

---

6. By doing that, these Sub-Saharan cocoa producers benefit from the forward premium, that is, "the opportunity rate of return" associated with forward sales (see the previous section).

used these instruments.[7] For example, Mexico's finance minister recently reported significant participation in the oil futures and options markets.[8] The state-owned copper company of Chile, Codelco, has used copper hedging instruments to manage part of its risk exposure. During the Gulf War, Brazil, Chile, and El Salvador hedged imports of oil through their central banks and state oil companies.[9] Other oil companies also have used oil derivatives (short-dated) to hedge their transaction exposures.

Commodity Futures Exchanges in Developing Countries

Commodity futures exchanges are not only found in developed countries. A number of developing countries have developed their own commodity futures exchanges. Interest in establishing new commodity futures exchanges in developing countries has increased in recent years. Existing commodity futures/options exchanges in developing countries are the following:

> *Bolsa de Mercadorias & Futuros (BM&F), Brazil:* This exchange trades U.S. dollar-denominated futures contracts in live cattle, arabica coffee, robusta coffee, cotton, and calves. U.S. dollar-denominated options are traded on arabica coffee and gold options on actuals. As of January 1993, the futures contracts on robusta coffee, cotton and calves were inactive (no open interest). Little open interest was registered in futures contracts on arabica coffee and live cattle and in options on arabica coffee, while there was liquidity (significant open interest) in gold options on actuals.
>
> *Budapest Commodity Exchange (BCE), Hungary:* The BCE was founded in late 1989. The three main futures contracts that

---

7. Use of financial instruments can in many cases be supplemented and complemented by contingent financing arrangements or an increase of foreign reserves in times of high commodity export prices (as, for example, in the case of Mexico, Venezuela, Nigeria, and Ecuador in the recent period when oil prices were high). However, internal political pressures may reduce the effectiveness of these self-insurance instruments.

8. One of the motivations mentioned by the Mexican authorities for participation in the futures market was to reassure investors that the economic program and budget would, to a significant extent, be insulated from oil price movements. This shows that hedging can be an effective way of underwriting structural adjustment programs (which often entails increased external exposures) and enhancing investor confidence.

9. See *The Wall Street Journal*, March 11, 1991.

they trade are wheat, corn, and hogs. Of these, the wheat and corn contracts are liquid while the hog contracts are not liquid. For all three contracts, however, liquidity has been increasing rapidly. In 1990, there were 2,136 contracts traded, while in 1992, there were 50,000 contracts traded (mostly wheat and corn). The value of trades increased from under U.S. $10 million in 1990 to U.S. $115 million in 1992. BCE now plans to include energy and interest rate contracts. The Chicago Mercantile Exchange (CME) and the Chicago Board of Trade (CBOT) are making recommen-dations for necessary improvements to increase the possibility of BCE succeeding as an exchange.

Kuala Lumpur Commodity Exchange (KLCE), Malaysia: KLCE lists five futures contracts: crude palm oil, tin, RDB olein, crude palm kernel oil, and cocoa. Of these, tin and RBD palm olein were inactive as of January 1993, while the open interest in crude palm kernel oil and cocoa was very low, making them effectively inactive. The open interest (last trading day in January 1993) in crude palm oil (7,500 contracts) represented roughly 187,500 tons or 2.8 percent of Malaysia's annual palm oil production. Thus, there seems to be some liquidity, although not much, in that contract.

Mercado de Futuros y Opciones (MERFOX), Argentina: MERFOX lists two livestock futures contracts: one in local currency and another in U.S. currency. Also, MERFOX lists one U.S. dollar-denominated livestock options contract. There is not sufficient liquidity in any of these contracts. In fact, liquidity in January 1993 in each of these contracts was about a third of what it was during January 1992.

Singapore International Monetary Exchange (SIMEX), Singapore: The three commodity futures contracts traded at SIMEX are gold, gasoline, and high sulfur fuel oil. The gasoline and gold contracts are almost inactive, while there is some liquidity in the high sulfur fuel oil. The open interest in the latter was equivalent to about 7 million barrels in January 1993 with daily trading volumes equivalent to around 1 million–2.5 million barrels. However, most of the liquidity is concentrated in the first two nearby contracts.

Rubber Association of Singapore: The Rubber Association of Singapore (RAS) used to be a forward market for rubber but moved to futures trading in 1992. There is an active arbitrage between the Kobe (Japan) and RAS. Kobe operates a rubber contract with contract prices used as a reference for domes-tic physical trade.

Thus, of the 23 futures/options contracts listed in the five commodity exchanges in developing countries reviewed, five are inactive (zero open interest in January 1993) and only for eight is there some liquidity.[10] Also, with the exception of MERFOX in Argentina, open interest has been growing in all of the commodity exchanges during the last 2–3 years. The best functioning exchange in terms of contracts traded has by far been the BCE. It should be mentioned that, almost exclusively, the users of these futures/options exchanges have been local individuals and corporations; there has been little, if any, foreign participation.[11]

Overall, the experience so far of commodity futures exchanges in developing countries has not been encouraging. Despite this, a number of developing countries have plans, some very preliminary, some more concrete, to establish commodity futures exchanges. Among them are: Mexico (agricultural commodities), Turkey (cotton), Indonesia (robusta coffee and possibly some other commodities), Morocco (orange juice, cereals), some of the former Soviet Union Republics (mainly agricultural commodities), and Chile. Certainly, this list is not exhaustive.

The factors determining the success of a commodity futures/ options contract are further discussed later in this chapter. We now turn to the barriers to using externally traded commodity risk management tools.

BARRIERS TO USING FINANCIAL RISK MANAGEMENT TOOLS

On the whole, the data and anecdotal evidence show that little of developing countries' exports and imports are hedged routinely. Why do so few countries attempt to manage their commodity

---

10. The contracts that posted zero open interest in January 1993 also posted zero open interest in January 1992. So it seems that they have been inactive for some time.
11. Futures exchanges in developing countries such as BM&F (Brazil) and SIMEX (Singapore) are not pure commodity exchanges but also operate quite successful, liquid financial futures/options contracts. The BM&F and SIMEX are two exchanges that have had relative success in financial contracts but not in commodity contracts. The rest of the exchanges mentioned operate strictly in commodities. However, there are plans for the BCE to launch an interest rate contract.

price risk using international hedging markets? There are a number of barriers that prevent these countries from doing so. We will discuss each of these in turn.

Domestic Barriers

Legal and Regulatory Barriers

Many developing countries have exchange controls that prevent the purchase of collateral required for the use of futures. Other developing countries have laws prohibiting access to international futures markets completely. In Colombia, for example, until recently laws were in place prohibiting the use of external risk management instruments. Only after the Colombian government changed the legal framework was the private sector allowed to hedge interest rate, commodity price, and currency risks.

Institutional Barriers

Often, various parties in a developing country are exposed to external price risks in a complex and non-transparent manner due to institutional arrangements, market failures, or (policy-induced) distortions or regulations. Consequently, incentives for any party to engage in risk management may be poor or force the party least able to to carry the risks. Typically, as a result of market failures or policy-induced distortions (or simply due to limited bargaining power), the majority of risks will fall either upon the small producers and consumers—who do not possess the means to manage them effectively, lacking the expertise to access international financial markets and hedge themselves externally or to hedge or allocate risk internally—or be absorbed by the government budget.[12]

Some examples can help to illustrate. In Costa Rica, coffee price risk is incurred in a complex manner by exporters, intermediaries, and final producers. The party least able to engage in risk management—the producer—is, however, incurring most of the coffee price risk and the parties most able to engage in risk management—the exporters and millers—have the least incentive to do so. In Colombia, one of the major reasons private

---

12. In many developing countries, state enterprises face a "soft" budget constraint. As a consequence, there is little incentive to manage commodity price, exchange rate, or interest rate risks.

exporters have no incentive to hedge for longer periods is that export contracts are not "opened" by the institution supervising coffee exports for longer than three months. As a consequence, domestic costs and fees (which are regulated) to be paid for exports three months ahead remain uncertain and, in effect, represent a larger risk to the private exporter than international coffee price risks. Even though an international hedging market exists with a horizon longer than three months and with little basis risk, exporters do not use it and, in the end, the producers have to absorb the price risk.

Government Intervention
In some developing countries, intervention by the government may greatly diminish the price risk incurred by the private sector and thus reduce the incentive for the sector to manage risk. This may happen, for example, through explicit or implicit guarantee schemes such as price stabilization schemes, deposit insurance of banks, and guaranteed exchange rate coverage. In some circumstances, the tax system may present a deterrent against hedging as net profits may be less exposed to external price risks than gross profits. As a private company only will be interested in hedging net profits, its incentive to hedge will accordingly be less (implying that tax revenues, the difference between gross and net profits, are exposed to price risk).[13]

Following are some specific examples of the negative effects of government intervention. In Brazil, movements in many domestic commodity prices differ from international prices, leading to difficulties in using international financial instruments. Domestic prices differ from international prices not for the traditional reasons, for example, due to the existence of basis risk (differences in grades of the commodity), but because of government intervention in the spot (cash) market and other policy-induced distortions. In response, trading company subsidiaries of commercial banks now issue short-term certificates of deposit linked to domestic commodity prices. As a result, a domestic hedging (futures) contract has been created and, at face value, some risk reduction has been achieved. In principle, however,

---

13. For industrial countries it is generally argued that the tax system provides an incentive to hedge as the tax schedule in convex (in the underlying commodity price).

the use of international financial markets would have been preferable.

A similar situation existed very recently in Argentina, where the grain sector was burdened by high levels of direct and indirect taxation, an expensive marketing system, and other government regulation. As a result, domestic prices were not related in a very systematic fashion to world prices. The recent liberalization of the Argentine grain sector, including the abolishment of the National Grain Board (which acted as regulator as well as trader), should do much to bring domestic prices closer in line with international prices and, in that way, allow greater use of international hedging instruments.

These examples make it clear that the measurement of exposures and the need for hedging should not only be looked at from the viewpoint of the country as a whole but should take into account the perspectives of entities within that country, such as marketing boards, farmers, co-operatives and private exporting or importing companies—corresponding to the distinction of who bears what risk. The distribution of risks and the interdependencies between risk bearers depends upon the institutional structure in commodity production, processing, marketing, and distribution. Hence, the design of a coherent hedging strategy can be a complex undertaking that needs to balance the concerns of all participants, in both the public and private sectors.

Know-How

It should be realized that risk management activities require considerable knowledge of financial instruments and an appropriate institutional framework within which to carry out hedging operations. Expertise is required in understanding the risk structure of the company or economy, in identifying appropriate risk management instruments, and in making and supervising hedging transactions. Unfortunately, many developing countries lack the necessary expertise for these operations. Furthermore, an institutional framework may be necessary to introduce adequate reporting, recording, monitoring, and evaluating mechanisms and to establish internal control procedures that can protect against speculative transactions.[14]

---

14. This is absolutely necessary for publicly owned entities, but private entities require this, too.

Awareness

Another important barrier to the use of these instruments is a general lack of familiarity at the policy level with these market instruments and their strategic uses and misconceptions that confuse speculation with hedging. An inadequate understanding of the techniques and instruments also is often a constraint in many developing countries. Many policymakers expect, for example, that risk management will lead to consistently higher profits, lower debt service payments, higher export prices, or, conversely, lower import prices. However, risk management effects a tradeoff between the assurance of predictable costs against *future* uncertain external price movements that could produce either large windfall gains or losses. Whether risk management avoids losses or gains to the economy depends on the (ex-post) trend in prices, which cannot be anticipated.

The fact that policymakers are not aware that using risk management tools may entail "costs"—in terms of foregone higher revenues or lower expenses—can lead to successful hedging programs being perceived as failures or prevent potentially attractive hedging programs from getting started. In this respect, options, in spite of their often-mentioned connotation as having a "speculative" payoff profile, can have advantages over the use of futures. With options, at most the premium is lost; thus, their use may suffer less from any political backlash arising from having locked in a fixed price.

Barriers Related to Technology

Critical preconditions needed for the effective use of risk management instruments may not always be in place in developing countries. Technical factors, such as transportation, storage, time differences, data processing and, especially, communications bottlenecks, can represent barriers.

Fundamental Barriers

Basis Risk and Liquidity

Arguably, the lack of hedging by developing countries in part arises because the international markets for commodity risk management are incomplete from the point of view of many exporters or importers. There is often no well-matched hedging tool available for a particular commodity (e.g., tropical fruits)[15] or there is a considerable mismatch between the characteristics of the commodity to be hedged and those specified in the hedging tool. This does not necessarily imply that the other, more traditional risk management tools are preferable—or that a country should establish a domestic futures exchange. Before drawing such conclusions, an analysis of the causes, nature, and magnitude of the mismatch is required.

The mismatch may be with respect to maturity or with respect to type. Maturities are generally limited to one to two years in the futures and options markets; long-dated, over-the-counter or capital market instruments often are not available for the risk in question. While the short-dated hedge might in principle be "rolled over" (i.e., renewed at maturity), so as to duplicate a long-dated hedge,[16] in practice the protection offered by a rollover will be considerably less than that of a long-dated instrument because of the basis risk arising from changes in the relationship between spot and futures prices. While using these instruments may significantly reduce the near-term exposure of many countries to price risk, hedging for longer periods will be far from perfect.

Basis risk also arises from the differences in type or in the characteristics of the commodity to be hedged and those specified in the hedging instrument. This is the risk that over a given period of time the price of the commodity to be hedged will not move in lockstep with the price of the market hedging instrument. The reason for this is the existence of many grades of a commodity (e.g., different grades of crude oil) and only a limited number of liquidly traded hedging tools.

We have found that for many commodities both sources of basis risk are small, however. For example, in simulations of hedging of oil exports or imports, we found that by using short-dated futures (less than six months' maturity), 75 percent to

---

15. There always will be hedging tools available for other assets (either substitutes or complements) that can serve as hedging tools, even though with large basis risks.

16. Whether (in the absence of basis risk) there is exact equivalence between a rollover and a long-dated instrument will depend upon the price process applicable: full equivalence would hold if, for example, the price behaved like a so-called random walk over time. But few prices appear to conform to this pattern exactly.

85 percent of the near-term price risk could be eliminated over the period 1985–90 for most crude oils, implying basis risk of 15 percent to 25 percent (Claessens and Varangis, 1991). This level of basis risk is not high, considering the large variety of crude oils we used (the American Petroleum Institute (API) varied from 25° to 40°). Using longer dated futures for hedging oil prices, the other form of basis risk became more important, but not to a great extent: About 70 percent of price risk in excess of six-month horizons could be eliminated for most crude oils.

We also have simulated hedging strategies for coffee exports (Claessens and Varangis, 1993). The strategy involved selling short-dated futures for a coffee exporter in Costa Rica over the period 1980–90, to set up hedges over the coming crop period. The contracts were renewed at maturity. The hedging strategy resulted in a reduction in risk, as measured by the standard deviation of prices, of 75 percent (i.e., three-quarters of the intraperiod variability in the realized price compared to the spot price prevailing at the time of initiating the hedge was eliminated through hedging.[17] For shorter periods, we found the basis risk for a Costa Rican exporter to be around 6 percent. Running the same simulation for a Colombian exporter, we found that basis risk for short periods (one to two months ahead) was around 13 percent.

Analysis conducted on cotton prices indicates that for those cotton producers where there is little government intervention, cash prices move closely together; however, for cotton sectors in which the government heavily intervenes (e.g., Egypt), prices deviate considerably from their closest substitute (Varangis et al., 1992). Similarly, in the case of crude oil, the prices of Mexico, Colombia, and Ecuador tend to move closely together and also with the West Texas Intermediary (WTI)—the crude oil underlying NYMEX's sweet light crude contract. In contrast, Venezuelan crude prices do not follow the above prices very closely, even though

---

17. It is important to appreciate that this reduction in risk applies only to risk within short-term periods. The average transaction costs were about 0.5 percent of contract value, largely accounted for by the cost of funding collateral for margin requirements. The average price received was actually higher than without hedging by about 2 percent, due to an unexpected downward trend in coffee prices over the chosen period.

Venezuelan crudes are close in quality to the other Latin American crudes. The basis risk appears to be due mainly to the pricing policies adopted by Venezuela. For similar reasons, grain prices in Argentina and Brazil do not closely follow world price movements; there is government intervention in the form of direct and indirect taxes, tariffs and subsidies, and cumbersome regulations.

Basis risk as well as liquidity will remain an important issue for all types of financial commodity risk management instruments. While for the commodities analyzed (and many others), basis risk need not be a serious constraint to using existing futures markets, we cannot expect that the markets for commodity risk management instruments will develop sufficiently well for all commodities. At the short end of the hedging spectrum, the introduction of new instruments will likely continue to be constrained by inadequate liquidity.

Constraints will be even more severe at the longer end. The development of markets in swaps and other long-term risk management instruments for perishable crops such as coffee, cocoa, and cotton is inherently more problematic, in part because of the seasonality of production and the high cost of storage. The development of markets for long-dated instruments for these commodities can thus be expected to take some time.

Premiums

The up-front costs of some risk management instruments can be an issue for countries that already have problems in raising foreign funds. Purchases of options, caps, and floors (that is, a series of options) require a significant premium up front, usually accounting for a significant portion of the amount of the underlying asset to be hedged. However, futures and collars for an importer (buying a call and selling a put) or exporter (selling a call and buying a put) can be implemented at very low cost.

Creditworthiness

Developing countries' credit standing often has prevented commercial banks and bond market investors from dealing with them—whether governments or private entities.[18] Because short-dated,

---

18. Political risk can be a considerable part of the creditworthiness constraint.

exchange-traded futures and options are subject to margin requirements, the credit risk is effectively overcome. Also, options
bought—regardless of their maturity and whether they have been
bought through an exchange or over-the-counter—have no credit
risk on the side of the developing country.

However, forward, swap, and options (if sold) contracts involve a consideration of the counterparty's creditworthiness. The
longer the performance period (the length of the contract), and
the greater the volatility of the underlying price, the greater the
credit risk. Since many developing countries lack sufficient credit
standing, their access to long-dated risk management instruments
will be limited. Most market participants are, for example, reluc-
tant to offer entities in even the more creditworthy developing
countries swap contracts that extend beyond one year.

However, encouraging signs exist as private borrowers in
several developing countries now are afforded better access to
foreign finance. In some cases, borrowers are required to turn to
collateral or other forms of security (such as pledges of future re-
ceivables). Private entities in some developing countries also are
using short-dated swaps for hedging purposes. For instance, in
Papua New Guinea, Mexico, and Chile, export financing is report-
edly combined regularly with commodity swaps. The commodity
swaps form part of a hedging package by providing price assurance for future exports.[19]

Another example of how credit risks can be overcome comes
from Chile. In Chile, an intermediary in the copper industry,
ENAMI, offers its customers (producers) the possibility of guaran-
teeing a minimum price for their copper exports in exchange for
which the producers agree to share in any upward price movements. ENAMI covers this guarantee through a series of options
and futures transactions in the international markets. Risk management is important for these producers since their marginal
costs of production are quite high. Performance (credit) risk on
the part of the private producers is minimal for ENAMI as it has a
natural monopsony on purchases from the producers, while as a
semistate entity, ENAMI has a good credit standing abroad.

---

19. In addition, the proceeds from the future exports might be deposited in an offshore
    escrow account.

ESTABLISHING OWN VERSUS USING EXISTING COMMODITY FUTURES/OPTIONS MARKETS[20]

Why Establish a Futures Market?

The desire of some developing countries to set up their own commodity futures/options exchanges (CFOE) is related to three factors: (1) their desire to improve the price discovery process in their country and to obtain more meaningful forward prices; (2) the notion that, if a particular commodity accounts for a large portion of a country's economic activity, it should also be priced in that country's marketplace; and (3) the benefit of lower basis risk (as we observed above, for some comodities no futures contracts exist).[21] In addition, many developing countries consider a CFOE the logical next step after the development of stock and financial markets. Below we analyze in more detail, some of the reasons for establishing a CFOE.

The two main benefits that could arise from establishing a domestic futures market are improved price discovery and reduced basis risk. Domestic futures markets may have less basis risk because the futures contract represents the local cash commodity more closely than any other hedge instrument. Delivery at a nearby location also will reduce basis risk. Other important benefits include: more publicly available information; improved transmission of price and other commodity-related information; improved credit systems; more responsive capital markets; uniformity in repayment rules and market surveillance; reduced transaction costs; and more accurate forward prices (Peck, 1985).

The two most important functions performed by futures markets are facilitating the management of risk and establishing forward prices. Forward prices provide information to decision makers, which can lead to a more efficient allocation of

---

20. This section benefited greatly from the presentations and discussions in the Workshop "Risk Management in Liberalizing Economies: Issues of Access to Futures and Options Markets," organized by the World Bank, Paris, France, June 3–5, 1992. Particular mention should be made of the presentations by R. Leuthold (University of Illinois) and P. Catania (Chicago Board of Trade).
21. General spillover effects of a domestic futures market on capital markets, public information, and the credit system are also often mentioned as motivations.

resources. Forward prices can be established by forward markets or futures exchanges. Forward cash contracts, or forward contracts, often proceed the development of futures contracts. Forward and futures markets develop from well-functioning, cash (spot) markets and add the time dimension. Forward and futures markets often exist side-by-side, complementing each other.

However, futures and forward contracts perform different roles. Forward contracts usually are not fungible (i.e., liquid) because they are tailored to the particular market circumstances and the transfer of the contract requires an evaluation of the credit risk of the counterparty. Futures contracts are standardized and trade on organized exchanges; and, as no credit risk is involved, contracts of the same maturity provide perfect substitutes. Hedgers and speculators are attracted to futures markets because futures contracts provide them with liquid, standardized financial instruments to assist them in the management of their risks. Portfolio managers can use the relationships between individual futures prices and returns on other financial instruments to hedge their overall exposures.

Conditions for Establishing a Domestic Futures Market

The most basic precondition for the establishment of a domestic futures market is a competitive, well-functioning spot (cash) market with transparent prices. This implies that the spot market should not be monopolized by either private firms or public entities. Additional conditions include a well-functioning infrastructure in place for product grading, distribution, transportation, and storage. Also required is a legal structure and system of property rights and enforceable contracts. Traders must be knowledgeable about the concept of ownership and be aware of the associated risk. In these basic preconditions must be included a stable and credible currency, reliable credit markets, the existence of a range of well-functioning financial institutions, and a system that can enforce repayment rules and provisions for liquidation in cases of bankruptcy.

Following these basic preconditions is a set of conditions related to the futures trading itself. There must be a sufficient number of traders, speculators, and financial institutions interested in such a futures exchange. A country cannot depend only on producers and consumers to achieve a viable futures market. The involvement of foreign firms also is necessary to achieve external diversification of the risk. Rules for trading and procedures for solving disputes and conflicts and for preventing manipulation of prices need to be established. Very critical is the establishment of a clearinghouse that has sufficient financial resources to become an intermediary to all trades and serve as a counterparty to all transactions. A well-functioning clearing house establishes the financial integrity of the futures market; without it, traders will not have the necessary confidence to use it.

While the above conditions provide the basis for establishing a *futures exchange*, they cannot indicate whether a particular *futures contract* will be successful or not. The main conditions for a successful futures contract can be summarized as follows. First, commodity prices and futures prices must be closely correlated. Second, the underlying commodity must be standardized in terms of size, grade or quality, place of delivery and month of maturity (i.e., a representative price exists, so that contracts become fungible and homogeneous).[22] These conditions are broad in nature and by no means guarantee the success of a futures contract. It is sobering that a large percentage, about two-thirds, of futures contracts introduced in existing and viable exchanges in industrial countries have not been successful, making it doubtful that futures contracts introduced in developing countries will succeed where the necessary preconditions are not all in place.[23]

---

22. For agricultural commodities, a grading system will be necessary to allow a wide variety of commodities to be included in the contract. This is typically done by applying necessary discounts and premia to the representative price. In addition, for a contract to be effective as a hedging instrument, the cash price for each of the varieties needs to be closely correlated with the futures price. The detailed specifications of the futures contract must be parallel to the activities and traditions of the spot market (Leuthold, 1992).

23. Black's (1986) empirical findings suggest that the success of a futures contract depends on the price variability, the size of the cash market, the presence or absence of an efficient cross hedge for the underlying commodity, and the contract design features.

Benefits and Costs of Establishing Domestic Futures Markets

The benefits and costs of a domestic exchange should be compared with the benefits and costs of using existing (foreign) futures exchanges. The existing (foreign) futures exchanges have an advantage in being well established in terms of rules and regulations and very liquid. Higher levels of liquidity may mean reduced transaction costs that can outweigh the basis and exchange rate risks. The major risks when using existing (foreign) futures exchanges are basis risk (discussed above) and exchange rate risk. When a country's currency is relatively stable, trading in an existing (foreign) futures exchange may be sensible given the higher liquidity and lower transactions cost. A thinly traded domestic futures market can potentially have higher execution costs and higher basis risk than the basis and currency risks combined of using an existing futures exchange.

Practical experience bears out that foreign exchanges often are preferred. Brazilian and Malaysian cocoa exporters prefer to use the New York Coffee, Sugar, and Cocoa Exchange (CSCE) rather than the Kuala Lumpur or BM&F (Brazil) exchanges.

Major Barriers to Establishing Domestic Futures/Options Markets

While the establishment of a domestic commodity futures market has a number of advantages, existing conditions in developing countries make it hard for commodity futures exchanges to be effective. The experience to date in developing countries (presented earlier in this chapter) has not been encouraging. The most important barriers to establishing future exchanges in developing countries are:

1. Lack of infrastructure in areas such as communications, transportation, and information processing.
2. Underdeveloped commercial and financial sectors.
3. Government controls over commodities most likely to be traded on a futures market.
4. Government regulations restricting the use of futures/options markets and/or the free flow of funds necessary to trade in such markets.

5. Lack of legal and regulatory frameworks necessary in establishing futures/options markets.

6. Insufficient capital among potential market participants to forestall counterparty risk (i.e., insufficient capital to form a viable clearing entity).

While this list is not exhaustive, it is relatively comprehensive and represents the experiences of developing countries in trying to establish these markets as well as the experiences of various analysts who have dealt with this issue.

Commodity Forward Cash Markets

The creation of forward cash markets often has preceded the creation of a futures/options market. Also, forward and futures markets often coexist and complement each other. Forward markets may provide an instrument for risk management (hedging) in cases where there is no futures contract for that commodity (or there is very high basis risk) or when it is not feasible to establish a full-fledged futures exchange domestically as not all preconditions are in place.

However, the creation of forward commodity markets is not justified only on risk sharing or hedging grounds. Forward commodity markets may serve to provide short-term storage finance to domestic agents in a commodity's marketing system. Forward commodity markets have been in existence in several developing countries. However, they tend to be of a bilateral (over-the-counter) nature, with no regulations and without the necessary legal status. Bilateral forward arrangements, while they provide cash contracts with the needed intertemporal dimension, do not reduce transaction costs or increase the flow of information in the market. The reason for this is that bilateral forward arrangements tend to be very specific, designed to the needs of the two parties involved and thus not liquid. In addition, the lack of regulations and monitoring may increase the incidence of defaults (performance risk) and, if defaults occur, adequate legal institutions do not exist to resolve the situation.

The above arguments indicate that the government can play a role in creating the conditions for a formal, forward commodity market. This does not necessarily imply that the government should be involved directly. Forward commodity markets can be developed by the private sector exclusively. Thus, the question that arises is, Why do we have so few of them in developing countries? There are three preconditions related to the creation of a forward commodity market.[24] These are: (*a*) the establishment of an appropriate legal framework; (*b*) the development of the appropriate institutional infrastructures; and (*c*) governmental policies.

Our discussion below of these preconditions focuses on the case in which warehouse receipts are traded. This is because the development of contractual arrangements in which warehouse receipts for various commodities can be explicitly borrowed and lent intertemporally can serve as a first step in the development of a forward market for the commodity. Trading in warehouse receipts also reduces the costs of exporters and processors of managing the risks in scarcity in a particular commodity market (Glaessner, et al., 1990).

Legal

There are three areas where a legal framework needs to be developed. First, legal regulations must ensure the validity of warehouse receipts by law and allow them to be negotiable and transferable. Banks can then issue securities backed by these receipts. Banks also can then pull together these warehouse receipts and use them as collateral to back securities. This securitization can match assets with liabilities and thus provide benefits to banks, local processors, and exporters. In addition, the legal concept of "novation" needs to be established, as it does not exist in many developing countries. According to this concept, the clearing corporation (house) is a legal entity between the transacting parties. Thus, while the rights associated with the trade in commodities are with the transacting parties, the clearinghouse takes the credit risk. The legal system further needs to provide bankruptcy codes, provisions for collateral liquidation, and uniformity in the warehouse documents.

Institutional Infrastructure

There is a need to standardize cash contracts and make information about prices accessible. Back-office functions also need to be developed. In some countries, the double-entry system that elim-

---

24. For an extensive discussion on this topic, see Glaessner, et al. (1990).

inates the physical transfer of securities does not exist. A clearing system also needs to be developed. This system assures that trades can be reconciled, that is, it determines the accountability for the exchange of money and securities between the counterparties to a securities trade.

Government Policies

The stability of the macroeconomic environment is important in the development of forward commodity markets. The government should avoid intervention in the physical market for the commodities in terms of subsidized credit programs, price support programs, or trade interventions. Such interventions will tend to reduce the need for risk sharing and reduce the demand for forward contracts. Finally, the government needs to examine its tax codes to make sure they do not provide disincentives for parties to get involved in forward transactions.

CONCLUDING REMARKS

Many developing countries could benefit from improved commodity price risk management. The performance of the traditional risk management instruments—commodity stabilization funds, buffer stocks, and international commodity agreements—has not been satisfactory. Market-based risk management instruments, such as futures, options and swaps, provide for more efficient risk management and also externalize the commodity price risks. Few developing countries have been using hedging instruments, however, and the experience of commodity exchanges in developing countries has not been encouraging.

Experience and theoretical work (see Priovolos and Duncan, 1991) have shown that market-based financial instruments can offer large benefits if used coherently. A coherent risk management strategy involves: (1) diagnosing domestic market failures and policy-induced distortions; (2) designing solutions to creditworthiness constraints; (3) taking account of the domestic institutional structure governing the commodity in question; and (4) possibly, integrating the management of all external exposures. In addition to a lack of awareness of and misconceptions about the role of hedging instruments, domestic legal, regulatory, and institutional structures are the most important barriers to the use of the full range of internationally available commodity-linked market instruments, including the recent innovations of commodity-linked swaps, loans, bonds, and long-dated options.

There does not appear to be strong justification for the establishment of domestic futures markets in developing countries. Establishment of commodity futures exchanges in developing countries requires several preconditions that are not met by most of these countries. If the existing commodity exchanges do not offer the necessary hedging instruments and if establishing a domestic exchange is not advisable, the development of formal and regulated forward markets for commodities may be a good option for providing risk sharing and price discovery.

REFERENCES

Arrau, P.; and S. Claessens. "Commodity Stabilization Funds." *PR Working Paper No. 854.* The World Bank, 1992.

Black, D. G. "Success and Failure of Futures Contracts: Theory and Empirical Evidence." *Monograph Series in Finance and Economics, Monograph 1986-1.* Salomon Brothers Center for the Study of Financial Institutions, Graduate School of Business Administration, New York University, 1986.

Claessens, S.; and P. Varangis. "Hedging Crude Oil Imports in Developing Countries." *PR Working Paper No. 755.* The World Bank, 1991.

Claessens, S.; and P. Varangis. "Risk Management Strategies in the Costa Rican Coffee Sector". In *Commodity Risk Management and Finance*, Vol. II, ed. S. Claessens and R. Duncan. Oxford University Press (forthcoming), 1993.

Deaton, A. "Commodity Prices, Stabilization, and Growth in Africa." Mimeograph, Princeton University, 1992.

Futures Industry Association. *International Open Interest Report*, various issues.

Gemmill, G. "Optimal Hedging on Futures Markets for Commodity-Exporting Nations." *European Economic Review* 27 (1985) pp. 2245–61.

Glaessner, T.; J. Reid; and W. Todd. "A Framework for Reform in Developing Private Markets for Agricultural Stock Financing." Technical Paper, Latin America Technical Department, Trade, Finance and Industry Division, The World Bank, 1990.

Larson, D. F.; and J. Coleman. "The Effects of Options-Hedging on the Costs of Domestic Price Stabilization Schemes." *PR Working Paper No. 653.* The World Bank, 1991.

Laughlin, T. J.; and W. D. Falloon. "Catch-22 Solutions for Less Developed Countries." *Corporate Risk Management*, September 1990, pp. 26–29.

Leuthold, R. M. "Access to Futures and Options Markets: Own Versus Existing Markets." Paper presented at the workshop "Risk Management in Liberalizing Economies: Issues of Access to Futures and Options Markets," June 3–5, 1992, Paris, France.

McKinnon, R. "Futures Markets, Buffer Stocks, and Income Instability for Primary Products." *Journal of Political Economy* 75, no. 6 (1967), pp. 844–61.

Palaskas, T.; and P. Varangis. "Primary Commodity Prices and Macroeconomic Variables, A Long-Run Relationship." *PR Working Paper No. 314.* The World Bank, 1989.

Peck, A. E. "The Economic Role of Traditional Commodity Futures Markets." In *Futures Markets: Their Economic Role*, ed. A. E. Peck. Washington D.C.: American Enterprise Institute for Public Policy Research, 1985.

Powers, M. J.; and P. Tosini. "Commodity Futures Exchanges and the North-South Dialogue." *American Journal of Agricultural Economics.* 59, no. 5 (December 1977).

Priovolos, T.; and R. Duncan, eds. *Commodity Risk Management and Finance.* Oxford University Press, 1991.

Rolfo, J. "Optimal Hedging Under Price and Quantity Uncertainty: The Case of a Cocoa Producer." *Journal of Political Economy* 88, no. 1 (1980), pp. 100–116.

Umali, D. "Agricultural Futures Markets: The Developing Country Experience." Paper presented at the workshop "Risk Management in Liberalizing Economies: Issues of Access to Futures and Options Markets", June 3–5, 1992, Paris, France.

Varangis, P.; E. Thigpen; and T. Akiyama. "Risk Management Prospects for Egyptian Cotton." *PR Working Paper No. 1077.* The World Bank, 1993.

The Wall Street Journal. "Mexico's Move to Lock in Oil Prices in Gulf Crisis Means It Can Stay Calm Now as the Market Softens." *The Wall Street Journal,* Monday, March 11, 1991.

IV

ISSUES OF VOLATILITY AND CO-INTEGRATION IN EMERGING CAPITAL MARKETS

6

INTERNATIONAL CORRELATIONS IN LATIN AMERICAN EMERGING EQUITY MARKETS

Mitchell Ratner, *Rider University*

INTRODUCTION

As the world's major industrial markets experience the slow growth of the global recession of the 1990s, investors are turning their attention to the emerging stock markets. Due to its close proximity, U.S. investors have taken a renewed investment interest in Latin America.

The potential gain to investors through international portfolio diversification has gained much attention in recent years. Extending modern portfolio theory to the international arena suggests that diversification among markets having imperfectly correlated returns is an effective way to reduce portfolio risk without impairing the portfolio's expected return. Applying the market model framework to international investment implies that portfolio risk is determined by the degree of variability among international stock indexes.

The stock indexes of the Group of Seven (G–7) industrialized countries (and others) have been exhaustively studied from numerous perspectives. However, little is known about the volatile emerging markets of Latin America. Emerging stock markets contain features that differentiate them from the markets of industrialized countries. In addition, the Latin American countries presently are undergoing major infrastructural changes due to the deregulation and privatization of major industries.

This chapter examines the correlation structure of the emerging markets of Latin America utilizing a recent sample from 1982–1990. Its primary focus is the extent to which security prices in Latin American stock markets are influenced by both the United States and other Latin stock markets. Pair-wise tests devised by Granger (1969), Sims (1972), and Geweke, Meese, and Dent (1982) are used to examine the integration between the market returns of these countries.

PREVIOUS RESEARCH

Grubel (1968), Bertoneche (1979), Lessard (1976), and Roll (1988) have all conducted empirical research on international stock market investment. These studies typically focus on the nature of the correlation coefficients between stock market indexes. A stock index providing a low correlation coefficient relative to the domestic country is viewed as a defensive investment, which demonstrates risk-reducing properties in portfolio diversification. Hamao, Masulis, and Ng (1990) examine the time-varying volatility of international stock prices. A vector autoregression approach investigating the transmission of innovations across markets is demonstrated by Eun and Shim (1989). Cumby (1990) shows that increased international equity market integration is consistent with consumption-based asset pricing models.

Prior investigation of the behavioral relationship between stock market indexes has produced conflicting results. Panton, Lessig, and Joy (1976) find a strong stable intercountry correlation structure for short- and intermediate-term investment. Watson (1980) finds evidence to support a stable structure during medium- and long-term investment; Philippatos, Christofi, and Christofi (1983) support only intermediate-term stability; and Maldonado and Saunders (1981) find stability only for very short periods of time. Given the dynamic nature of the international capital markets, much of this research is outdated.

There is considerable evidence on the lead-lag relationship between national stock indexes in the literature. Agmon (1972) notes the integration in the movements among the equity markets of the United States, Germany, Japan, and the United Kingdom. Hilliard (1979) uses spectral analysis to examine market movements among 10 countries during the mid–1970s; his results do not indicate significant lead-lag relationships. More recent studies have focused on bidirectional causality between equity markets. Schollhammer and Sand (1987) and Khoury, Dodin, and Takada (1987) find interdependencies among 13 and 4 countries, respectively. Other recent studies examining bidirectional causality include Swanson (1988), Mathur and Subrahmanyam (1991), and Cochran and Mansur (1991).

LATIN AMERICAN MARKET CHARACTERISTICS

Selected characteristics of Latin American stock markets are presented in Exhibit 6–1. These markets are small and undeveloped as compared to those of the industrial world vis-a-vis market capitalization. Hours of operation are limited, market access is somewhat restricted, and there is a high degree of market concentration among the 10 largest stocks on each exchange. Investment returns

E X H I B I T   6–1

Selected Latin American Stock Market Characteristics[1]

	Country			
	Argentina	Brazil	Chile	Mexico
Hours of operation (per day)	4.0	3.5	1.5	8.0
Market concentration (% market capitalization of 10 largest stocks)	67.7%	22. 5%	47.2%	36. 3%
Number of firms per exchange	174	574	217	200
Inflation (mid-1991)	l44%	367%	23%	22%

Source: Information obtained from the *Emerging Market Fact Book*, Washington D.C.: International Finance Corporation, 1991.

1. The Chilean stock market conducts four 1.5-hour trading sessions.

in Latin America are among the highest in the world; each of these markets has experienced gains topping 100 percent in a given year.

The United States maintains a strong trade and monetary relationship with each of these countries, accounting for up to 30 percent of their imports and exports each year. On a monetary level, stock quotes in each of these countries often are reported in U.S. dollar terms. Argentina's Economy Minister Domingo Cavallo fixed the parity of the Argentine currency directly to the U.S. dollar in 1991.

The most important trade issue affecting the future of business in Mexico is clearly the North American Free Trade Agreement (NAFTA) between the United States, Canada, and Mexico. The Southern Cone Common Market (MERCOSUL) is scheduled to take effect in 1995. This agreement, between Argentina, Brazil, Uruguay, and Paraguay, is intended to harmonize fiscal and monetary policies among these countries. The MERCOSUL is actually an extension of a 1986 trade agreement between Argentina and Brazil.

DATA AND CAUSALITY TEST METHODOLOGY

This chapter examines the four largest equity markets of Latin America: Argentina, Brazil, Chile, and Mexico. Weekly stock returns are derived from daily closing prices from January 1982 through December 1990. The Argentine Buenos Aires Stock Exchange General Index, the Brazilian Ibovespa Index, the Chilean Index General de Precios de Acciones (IPGA) index, and the Mexican Bolsa Mexicana de Valores (MBV) index are obtained from official stock exchange information in each country. Due to the high level of inflation in Latin America, all of the stock returns are converted into U.S. dollars. The Standard & Poor's 500 series for the United States is obtained through *Barrons*. Although daily data is available, a weekly sampling is used to avoid some of the problems associated with daily data. As noted by Lo and MacKinlay (1988), daily data may contain biases due to non-trading, asynchronous pricing, and day-of-the-week effects. The tests are conducted on an annual basis from 1982–1990, and full sample and subsample tests are conducted from 1982–1990, 1982–1985, and 1985–1990.

Granger (1969) proposed that an independent variable, X, is said to *Granger-cause* Y if Y can be better forecasted using past values of both Y and X rather than past Y values alone. The Granger test regresses Y on lagged values of Y and lagged values of X and tests the lags of X. Sims (1972) developed a two-sided distributed lag model of causality theoretically equivalent to the Granger test, but different in application. The Sims test regresses X on past, present, and future values of Y and tests the leads of Y. Geweke, Meese, and Dent (1982) discovered that the Sims test sometimes failed to correct for serially correlated residuals. The authors suggest a modified test of Sims causality that includes lagged values of the dependent variable but still tests the leads of the independent variable.

Causality tests are performed to investigate the effects of unidirectional causality between the U.S. stock returns and the returns of the four largest markets of Latin America. The pairwise causality tests for Granger, Sims, and Geweke, Meese, and Dent (GMD) are tested empirically as follows:

$$R_{LA,t} = \alpha + \sum_{i=1}^{4} \beta_i R_{LA,t-i} + \sum_{i=1}^{4} \gamma_1 R_{US,t-i} + E_t \qquad (6.1)$$

$$R_{US,t} = \alpha + \sum_{i=4}^{4} \beta_i R_{LA,t-i} + E_t \qquad (6.2)$$

$$R_{US,t} = \alpha + \sum_{i=4}^{4} \beta_i R_{LA,t-i} + \sum_{i=1}^{4} \gamma_1 R_{US,t-i} + E_t \qquad (6.3)$$

where R_{US} represents the U.S. stock market returns, R_{LA} represents the Latin American stock market returns, and ε is the random error term. In Equation (6.1), the U.S. is said to Granger-cause changes in a Latin American country if the lagged coefficients of R_{US}, as a group, are significantly different from zero. From Equation (6.2), the U.S. Sims test causes changes in Latin America if the lead coefficients of the R_{LA} variable, as a group, are significantly different from zero. Lastly, the U.S. GMD test causes changes in Latin America if the lead coefficients of the R_{LA} variable, as a group, are significantly different from zero in Equation (6.3). The choice of four weeks is arbitrarily selected as the lag length. Geweke, Meese, and Dent (1982) show that test results in cases such as these are insensitive to lag length selection.

Ordinary least squares (OLS) regression is the estimation procedure used to test the relationships in Equations (6.1) through (6.3). In order to examine the significance of the causal direction precisely, F statistics are constructed as follows:

$$F = \frac{\dfrac{(SSE_r - SSE_u)}{(df_r - df_u)}}{\dfrac{SSE_u}{df_u}}$$

where SSE_r and SSE_u denote the sums of squared errors from the estimations of the restricted and unrestricted equations, and df_r and df_u are the degrees of freedom.

CAUSALITY TEST RESULTS

Empirical results from tests for unidirectional causality between the U.S. and Latin American equity markets are presented in Exhibit 6-2. The findings for the three tests, Granger, Sims, and GMD, are generally consistent across all countries and test periods. With minor exceptions, significant evidence of causality is not observed throughout the test period. On an annual basis during the 1982–1985 period, there does not appear to be significant causality between the U.S. and any Latin American market.

During the annual tests from 1986–1990, the U.S. → Argentina market relationship demonstrates the greatest significance in all three tests at the 1 percent level in 1986. The U.S.→ Chile relationship provides little support for causality, with 10 percent significance in the Granger test in 1987, 5 percent significance with the Sims test in 1988, and 10 percent significance in the GMD test in 1988. No significant causality is demonstrated between U.S.→ Brazil in any time period. The U.S.→ Mexico market relationship is the most consistent with significant findings of causality in 1986, 1987, and 1988.

The long-term findings for 1982–1990, 1982–1985, and 1986–1990 find weak support for U.S.→ Mexico causality at the 10 percent level of significance. No other long-term evidence is indicated between the U.S. and any other Latin American market. These findings are essentially consistent with the annual data. Due to Mexico's close proximity and relatively high level of trade with the U.S., it is no surprise that the U.S.→ Mexico relationship is the strongest of the markets.

EXHIBIT 6-2

Causality Tests Between U.S. and Latin American Market Returns[1,2]

			F-Statistics Reported			
Country	1982	1983	1984	1985	1986	1987
U.S.→AR:						
Granger	0.32	0.96	0.48	0.58	5.55*	0.53
Sims	0.69	0.83	1.40	0.49	4.90*	1.86
GMD	0.66	0.42	1.28	0.70	5.00*	1.64
U.S. →CH:						
Granger	0.15	0.65	0.16	1.28	0.99	2.29***
Sims	1.32	0.41	0.24	0.56	1.44	1.73
GMD	1.15	0.60	0.43	0.64	1.42	1.52
U.S. →BR:						
Granger	1.26	1.09	1.35	1.19	1.40	1.03
Sims	0.72	0.63	1.01	1.24	1.88	1.14
GMD	0.60	0.94	0.89	1.04	1.72	1.29
U.S. →ME						
Granger	1.47	1.01	0.77	0.10	2.16***	2.85**
Sims	1.22	0.68	0.56	0.25	1.54	4.02*
GMD	1.58	1.02	0.44	0.36	2.59***	4.57*
Country	1988	1989	1990	1982–90	1982–85	1985–90
U.S.→AR:						
Granger	1.99	1.38	0.47	0.62	0.12	0.90
Sims	1.97	1.13	0.51	0.62	0.24	0.76
GMD	1.97	1.66	0.32	0.64	0.24	0.83
U.S.→CH:						
Granger	1.48	0.36	0.59	0.87	0.52	0.98
Sims	3.28**	0.25	0.52	1.23	1.22	1.44
GMD	2.56***	0.34	0.52	1.29	1.19	1.42
U.S.→BR:						
Granger	1.17	0.35	0.25	0.77	0.12	1.39
Sims	1.62	0.66	0.28	1.02	0.21	1.88
GMD	1.73	0.35	0.42	1.05	0.22	1.73
U.S.→ME:						
Granger	2.64**	0.66	0.09	2.20***	2.07***	2.16***
Sims	2.56***	0.77	0.25	1.55	1.92	1.53
GMD	2.75***	0.86	0.25	2.15***	2.22***	2.59***

Note: *, **, and *** indicate significance at the I percent, 5 percent, and I0 percent levels, respectively.

1. GMD stands for Geweke, Meese, and Dent test.

2. The arrows indicate the direction of causality.

Causality Between Latin Markets

Given the level of business transactions and economic policy co-ordination that exists among Latin American countries, this section examines causality between each of the Latin American markets. Exhibit 6–3 contains the results for both unidirectional and bidirectional causality tests between Argentina, Brazil, Chile, and Mexico for the same test periods as in Exhibit 6–2. Considering the high correlation between the Granger, Sims, and GMD procedures, only the Granger causality test results are reported. The Granger methodology is as follows:

$$R_{LA1,\,t} = \alpha + \sum_{i=1}^{4} \beta_i R_{LA1,\,t-i} + \sum_{i=1}^{4} \gamma_i R_{LA2,\,t-i} + \varepsilon_t \quad (6.4)$$

$$R_{LA2,\,t} = \alpha + \sum_{i=1}^{4} \beta_i R_{LA2,\,t-i} + \sum_{i=1}^{4} \gamma_i R_{LA1,\,t-i} + \varepsilon_t \quad (6.5)$$

In pair-wise tests, unidirectional causality is observed if the lagged coefficients of the $LA2$ variable in Equation (6.4) are significantly different from zero, while the lagged coefficients on the $LA1$ variable from Equation (6.5) are insignificantly different from zero. Bidirectional causality is indicated if the $LA2$ coefficients in Equation (6.4) and the $LA1$ coefficients from Equation (6.5) are both significant at the same time.

On an annual basis, bidirectional causality is not observed between any of the four Latin American countries. Unidirectional causality is observed, but the evidence is weak. The tests between Argentina–Brazil and Argentina–Chile offer the strongest evidence of causality, with significant coefficients at either the 10 percent or 5 percent level for three years each. The strongest evidence of causality among all of the countries occurs in 1982 and 1983 with significance at the 1 percent level for three pairs of countries. Weak evidence is indicated among some of the countries at the 10 percent level during the 1985–1986 period. Negligible evidence of causality is indicated after 1986.

For the entire sample period, 1982–1990, bidirectional causality is observed between Argentina–Mexico. During the 1982–1985 period, unidirectional causality from Argentina to Chile exhibits the greatest significance at 1 percent, while other

EXHIBIT 6–3

Granger Causality Tests Between Latin American Markets

	F-Statistics Reported					
Country	1982	1983	1984	1985	1986	1987
CH→AR	1.94	0.44	1.19	1.10	0.51	0.57
AR→CH	1.97	2.28***	0.25	2.72**	0.37	0.63
BR→AR	0.12	0.65	0.45	1.36	2.11***	2.40***
AR→BR	0.19	1.63	0.35	0.52	1.41	0.85
ME→AR	0.47	2.48***	0.65	0.15	3.04**	0.52
AR→ME	0.86	1.40	1.30	2.28***	0.68	0.96
CH→ME	4.32*	1.56	0.38	0.25	1.35	0.88
ME→CH	0.88	0.97	0.48	0.55	1.22	1.38
CH→BR	0.69	4.69*	1.94	0.36	0.59	1.05
BR→CH	0.41	0.60	3.28**	0.33	1.18	0.08
ME→BR	4.57*	1.60	1.94	0.59	1.35	1.94
BR→ME	0.14	0.25	0.56	0.06	1.44	0.75
Country	1988	1989	1990	1982–90	1982–85	1985–90
CH→AR	0.86	2.27***	0.07	0.39	1.77	0.20
AR→CH	1.15	0.53	1.16	0.94	3.79*	0.15
BR→AR	1.64	1.36	1.55	1.33	2.10***	1.33
AR→BR	2.06	1.92	2.40***	1.44	0.87	1.02
ME→AR	1.73	0.38	0.88	2.43**	0.07	4.25*
AR→ME	0.53	0.74	0.62	2.15***	1.99	0.80
CH→ME	1.59	1.40	0.99	0.83	0.69	0.82
ME→CH	0.58	1.06	1.59	0.42	0.51	0.06
CH→BR	0.41	0.42	0.52	0.13	1.63	0.49
BR→CH	0.99	1.13	0.20	0.94	2.55**	0.23
ME→BR	1.05	0.79	0.55	1.07	2.08***	1.25
BR→ME	0.63	1.30	0.27	0.19	0.67	0.17

Note: *, **, and *** indicate significance at the l percent, 5 percent, and l0 percent levels, respectively.

countries experience causality with less significance. During the 1985–1990 period, causality from Mexico to Argentina is significant at the l percent level. No other significant causality is observed.

Contemporaneous Causality

Granger (1969) suggests a further test to examine the level of integration between equity markets. The Granger equation, Equation (6.1), can be modified to include a contemporaneous variable:

$$R_{LA,t} = \alpha + \sum_{i=1}^{4} \beta_i R_{LA,t-i} + \sum_{i=1}^{4} \gamma_i R_{US,t-i} + \delta R_{US,t} + \varepsilon_t \quad (6.6)$$

Equation (6.6) tests for contemporaneous adjustments between the United States and Latin American countries. Contemporaneous adjustment between Latin American countries is tested by replacing the U.S. variable with another Latin American country.

The results for the contemporaneous adjustments are found in Exhibit 6–4. The findings indicate only sporadic significance among all countries and time periods. On an annual basis, contemporaneous adjustments are significant at the 5 percent level between U.S.–Chile in 1988 and U.S.–Mexico in 1990. Weaker evidence at the 10 percent level also is apparent. In the long-term, contemporaneous adjustment is significant for U.S.–Chile during 1985–1990 and U.S.–Mexico during 1982–1990. No significant integration is indicated between the U.S. and Argentina or Brazil above the 10 percent level.

There is also very little evidence of market integration between Latin American countries during this time period. On an annual basis, the strongest evidence of market integration is between Brazil–Chile in 1982 and Argentina–Mexico in 1984, at the 1 percent level. Infrequent contemporaneous adjustment is indicated among other pairs of Latin American countries at the 5 percent and 10 percent levels. In the long-term tests, Brazil–Chile, in 1982–1990 and 1985–1990, demonstrates the greatest contemporaneous adjustment at the 5 percent level.

CONCLUSIONS

This chapter applies causality tests to examine the relationship between stock market returns in the United States and the four largest equity markets of Latin America. Granger, Sims, and Geweke, Meese, and Dent tests are performed to test unidirectional causality from the United States to Argentina, Brazil, Chile,

EXHIBIT 6-4

Contemporaneous Adjustments in Granger Causality Tests

	F-Statistics Reported					
Country	1982	1983	1984	1985	1986	1987
U.S.–AR	1.80	0.11	3.68***	0.08	0.02	0.19
U.S.–BR	0.09	0.05	0.02	1.19	0.79	1.63
U.S.–CH	0.01	0.01	1.58	0.12	1.38	2.52
U.S.–ME	0.79	1.08	2.28	1.84	3.61***	0.03
AR–BR	1.30	0.11	1.45	0.75	0.71	0.56
AR–CH	0.67	0.30	2.21	5.49**	0.10	1.43
AR–ME	0.85	0.17	11.38*	3.01***	0.52	0.99
BR–CH	14.55*	0.26	0.47	0.01	0.05	2.66
BR–ME	1.04	3.11***	0.93	0.26	0.63	2.55
CH–ME	2.17	3.21***	0.01	0.05	0.07	3.79***
Country	1988	1989	1990	1982–90	1982–85	1985–90
U.S.–AR	0.48	3.24***	0.28	0.04	0.01	0.12
U.S.–BR	2.00	0.03	0.11	0.24	0.09	0.05
U.S.–CH	5.64**	0.09	0.62	3.43***	0.10	6.37**
U.S.–ME	1.32	1.38	6.30**	4.81**	1.15	2.49
AR–BR	0.09	0.56	0.01	0.49	0.20	0.43
AR–CH	0.85	6.37**	1.33	1.48	3.32***	0.05
AR–ME	0.07	3.74***	0.14	0.49	0.29	0.09
BR–CH	0.32	4.33**	0.01	5.75**	0.29	6.18**
BR–ME	2.35	0.36	1.24	1.76	0.55	1.39
CH–ME	0.01	0.92	0.05	3.48***	1.00	2.95***

Note: *,**, and *** indicate significance at the 1 percent, 5 percent, and l0 percent levels, respectively.

and Mexico, individually. Bidirectional Granger tests are applied between the Latin American countries, and contemporaneous Granger tests are applied among all countries. The empirical results reveal that the market returns among all countries in this study are largely independent of one another.

On both an annual and subperiod basis, all three causality tests confirm that the United States market generally has weak or no influence on any of the four Latin American countries. As expected, the U.S.–Mexico relationship appears to be the most significant. Unidirectional and bidirectional tests between the Latin American countries also demonstrate both weak and inconsistent influences among all of the Latin American markets. Granger tests for contemporaneous adjustments are consistent with the causality results that indicate weak and inconsistent adjustments among all of the markets. Surprisingly, the Argentina–Brazil relationship is no more significant than the other linkages, even though these two countries maintain long-term trade arrangements.

Regardless of the level of significance, all of these results provide valuable information to the international investor. The fact that one market cannot consistently forecast changes in another market supports the notion of market efficiency in these markets. The absence of significant contemporaneous adjustments indicates that these markets are essentially nonintegrated. Insight into the factors that influence market returns helps investors formulate ex ante optimal investment portfolios. The empirical findings presented here suggest that investment in the emerging markets of Latin America can result in a reduction of risk in a diversified international portfolio.

REFERENCES

Agmon, T. "The Relations Among Equity Markets: A Study of Share Price Co-Movements in the United States, United Kingdom, Germany and Japan." *Journal of Finance*, September 1972, pp. 839–856.

Bertoneche, M. "An Empirical Analysis of the Interrelationships Among Equity Markets Under Changing Exchange Rate Systems." *Journal of Banking and Finance* 4 (1979), pp. 397–405.

Cochran, S. J.; and I. Mansur. "The Interrelationships Between U.S. and Foreign Equity Market Yields: Tests of Granger Causality." *Journal of International Business Studies*, 1991, pp. 723–736.

Cumby, R. E. "Consumption Risk and International Equity Returns: Some Empirical Evidence." *Journal of International Money & Finance* 9 (1990), pp. 182–192.

Eun, C. S.; and S. Shim. "International Transmission of Stock Market Movements." *Journal of Financial and Quantitative Analysis* 24 (June 1989), pp. 241–256.

Geweke, J.; R. Meese; and W. Dent. "Comparing Alternative Tests of Causality in Temporal Systems." *Journal of Econometrics*, 1982, pp. 161–194.

Granger, C. W. "Investigating Causal Relationships by Econometric Models and Cross-Spectral Methods." *Econometrica* 37 (1969), pp. 424–38.

Grubel, H. J. "Internationally Diversified Portfolios: Welfare Gains and Capital Flows." *American Economic Review*, December 1968, pp. 1229–1314.

Hamao, Y.; R. Masulis; and V. Ng. "Correlations in Price Changes and Volatility Across International Stock Markets." *Review of Financial Studies* 3 (1990), pp. 281–307.

Hilliard, J. "The Relationship Between Equity Indices on World Exchanges." *Journal of Finance* 34 (March 1979), pp. 103–114.

Lessard, D. R. "World, Country, and Industry Relationships in Equity Returns." *Financial Analysts Journal*, January–February 1976, pp. 32–38.

Khoury, S. J.; B. Dodin; and H. Takada. "Multiple Time-Series Analysis of National Stock Markets and Their Structure: Some Implications." In *Recent Developments in International Banking* 1, eds. S. J. Khoury and A. Ghosh. Lexington, MA: Lexington Books (1987), pp. 169–186.

Lo, A. W.; and A. C. Mackinlay. "Stock Market Prices Do Not Follow Random Walks: Evidence from a Simple Specification Test." *Review of Financial Studies* 1 (1988), pp. 41–66.

Maldonado, R.; and A. Saunders. "International Portfolio Diversification and the Inter-Temporal Stability of International Stock Market Relationships, 1957–78." *Financial Management*, Autumn 1981, pp. 54–63.

Mathur, I.; and V. Subrahmanyam. "An Analysis of the Scandinavian Stock Indices." *Journal of International Financial Markets, Institutions & Money*, 1991, pp. 91–114.

Panton D. B.; V. P. Lessig; and O. M. Joy. "Comovement of International Equity Markets: A Taxonomic Approach." *Journal of Financial and Quantitative Analysis*, September 1976, pp. 415–432.

Philippatos, G. C.; A. Christofi; and P. Christofi. "The Inter-Temporal Stability of International Stock Market Relationships: Another View." *Financial Management*, Winter 1983, pp. 63–69.

Roll, R. "The International Crash of October 1987." *Financial Analysts Journal*, September–October 1988, pp. 19–35.

Schollhammer, H.; and O. Sand. "Lead-Lag Relationships Among National Equity Markets: An Empirical Investigation." In *Recent Developments in International Banking* 1, eds. S. J. Khoury and A. Ghosh. Lexington, MA: Lexington Books (1987), pp. 149–168.

Sims, C. A. "Money, Income, and Causality." *American Economic Review*, 1972, pp. 540–552.

Swanson, P. E. "Interrelationships Among Deposit and Eurocurrency Deposit Yields: A Focus on the U.S. Dollar." *Financial Review*, February 1988, pp. 91–94.

Watson, J. "The Stationarity of Inter-Country Correlation Coefficients: A Note." *Journal of Business Finance and Accounting*, Summer 1980, pp. 297–303.

7

LINKAGES AND VOLATILITY IN EMERGING CAPITAL MARKETS

Reena Aggarwal, *Georgetown University*
Ricardo Leal, *University of Nevada*

INTRODUCTION

This chapter builds on the recent literature of stock market linkages. Almost all of the studies conducted so far have been limited to developed countries, particularly the U.S., the U.K, and Japan. This chapter examines 10 of the most important markets of Asia and Latin America: Argentina, Brazil, Chile, Mexico, India, Malaysia, the Philippines, Korea, Taiwan, and Thailand, besides the U.S. and Japan. Also included in the analysis are the Morgan Stanley World Index, the Far East Index, the Latin American Index, and the Emerging Markets Index. This allows an analysis of two of the fastest-growing economic regions of the world. It also allows a study of the level of intraregional and interregional stock market integration. The grouping of data by region lets us examine factors common for each region. The regions have faced different economic and political problems, while the markets also differ in terms of regulations, trading systems, and transaction costs.

This chapter examines whether the globalization of world markets has actually brought these stock markets closer together within their regions and outside their regions. The financial press maintains that there has been rapid globalization of financial markets. However, despite the casual evidence supporting global linkages, a number of academic studies have found low correlations, implying a high degree of independence among the world's stock exchanges.

We find the correlations are relatively low not only among the countries outside the geographic region but also within the same region. Day-to-day linkages are relatively weak between markets but, as the time period is increased from daily to monthly returns, the correlations increase. The linkages are particularly strong between the emerging markets and the U.S./World Index during periods of large market movements, both negative and positive. U.S. returns and the World Index returns are important in explaining returns and volatility in emerging markets. Similarly, volatility in the emerging markets can be explained to some extent by volatility of the U.S. and World Index returns.

Previous studies have made a strong case for international portfolio diversification in a mean-variance portfolio framework. The comovement of world exchange indexes and stocks indicates that movements in most Asian and Latin American markets show little similarity with the markets of North America or Europe. Therefore, a strong case has been made for diversifying into these markets. It also has been documented that if there exists close economic ties between countries, then the relationships between their stock markets also will be strong. Further, the globalization of markets and economies in the last decade should, in general, have resulted in stronger linkages between the markets of the world.

Some recent studies examine the interdependence among the major world stock markets. They focus on analyzing how news from one international market influences another market's volatility process. In general, they find that there is not much comovement among these markets when they are represented by stock market indexes. Studies also have investigated the transmission mechanism of stock price movements (innovations) and volatility across international stock markets. Eun and Shim (1989) find that stock market innovations in the U.S. are rapidly transmitted to the rest of the world, whereas stock market innovations in other national markets have little impact on the U.S. Hamao, Masulis, and Ng (1990) document significant price volatility spillovers from the U.S. market to Japan and the U.K. A stronger relationship across international industries is found by Roll (1992).

Research addressing the linkages among emerging markets is very limited. Errunza, Losq, and Padmanabhan (1992) investigate the integration between emerging markets and the United States. They conclude that, while markets cannot be considered integrated, they are not completely segmented. Aggarwal and Rivoli (1989) find some evidence of linkages between the Asian markets and the U.S. An earlier study by Lessard (1973) examines the period between 1958–68 and reports that the stock markets of Latin America are independent of each other and that returns within each country are due to country-specific factors.

DATA AND METHODOLOGY

The data consist of daily closing values for the following indexes: the Standard and Poor's (U.S.); the Nikkei Average (Japan); the Bolsa Indice General (Argentina); the BOVESPA São Paulo Stock Exchange Index (Brazil); the IGPA Index (Chile); the Seoul Composite Index (Korea); the Kuala Lumpur Composite Index (Malaysia); the BMV General (Mexico); the Manila Composite Index (Philippines); the Taipei Weighted Price Index (Taiwan); and the Bangkok SET Index (Thailand). Except for the Nikkei, which is price-weighted, all of the other indexes are value-weighted and do not include dividends.

Asian index data are collected from the *Asian Wall Street Journal* for all the Asian markets except Korea and Taiwan, for which data are provided by the respective stock exchanges. The Brazilian index is collected from the São Paulo Stock Exchange monthly bulletin. The Argentine index is obtained from the daily *La Nación* and from the Buenos Aires Stock Exchange. The Chilean and Mexican data are provided by the Santiago and Mexican Stock Exchanges, respectively. The Morgan Stanley World Index, the Far East Index, the Emerging Markets Index, and the Latin American Index also are used in the analysis. The latter two indexes became available only from 1988 onward.

The analysis in this chapter covers the period from January 1982 to December 1993. Exchange rates are obtained from *The Wall Street Journal* daily. On the days the exchange rates were not reported (due to U.S. holidays), the exchange rate is fitted as the average of the two adjacent days so that there are no missing values in the foreign exchange rate series. All country returns are calculated in local currencies and also adjusted for U.S. dollar returns:

$$R_{i,t} = Ln \left(\frac{I_{i,t}/I_{i,t-1}}{X_{i,t}/X_{i,t-1}} \right) \tag{7.1}$$

First, correlations are estimated based on daily and monthly returns for the full sample period. Next, five of the largest market movements upward (downward) in U.S. returns are identified. Daily correlations are then estimated for a five-day window surrounding each of these events in order to examine linkages during periods of large movements in the U.S. markets.[1] All returns are aligned to adjust for time differences.

Two sets of regression models are estimated using monthly returns. In the first case the dependent and independent variables are in terms of returns, while in the second case they are in terms of volatility. Volatility is measured by standard deviation during the month. The independent variables are the U.S., Japan, World, Emerging Markets, Latin American, and Far East indexes. Therefore,

$$R_{i,t} = a_i + b_i R_{j,t} \tag{7.2}$$

where, R_{it} are monthly returns on one of the emerging market indexes and R_{jt} are monthly returns on a major index.

Similarly,

$$\sigma_{i,t} = a_i + b_i \sigma_{j,t} \tag{7.3}$$

where $\sigma_{i,t}$ is the variance based on daily returns for the month for an emerging market index and $\sigma_{j,t}$ is the corresponding variance for the major market.

---

1. The five largest upward movements took place on October 21, 20, and 29 of 1987 and August 17 and November 3 1982. The five largest downward movements took place on October 19 and 26 of 1987, January 8 of 1988, October 13 of 1989, and October 16 of 1987.

EMPIRICAL RESULTS

Descriptive Statistics

The mean daily dollar-adjusted returns vary from a high of 0.15 percent for the Latin American Index to a low of 0.02 percent for India as reported in Exhibit 7–1. The Latin American and the Emerging Market indexes were introduced in 1988 by Morgan Stanley. Since 1988, many emerging markets have experienced bull markets as reflected in the high mean returns for these indexes. It is clear that the emerging markets of Asia and Latin America are much more volatile than the developed markets. The lowest standard deviation is for the World Index, at 0.78 percent. The World Index is mainly made up of the developed markets and also benefits from the most diversification. Argentina has the highest standard deviation at 4.57 percent, followed by Brazil at 4.09 percent. The Asian markets are far less volatile than the Latin American markets.

E X H I B I T   7–1

Descriptive Statistics
Daily Returns (1982–1993) in percent

Country	Mean	Std.Dev.	Skew.	Kurt.	Autocorr.	Obs.
Asia						
India	0.02	1.88	4.57*	12.95*	19.14*	1774
Malaysia	0.06*	1.05	−1.24*	16.94*	122.35*	2767
Philippines	0.08*	1.77	−0.67	15.10*	58.11*	2806
South Korea	0.07*	1.35	4.17*	3.88*	8.58	2809
Taiwan	0.08*	2.14	−1.59*	3.40*	57.38*	2758
Thailand	0.09*	1.64	−4.79*	48.07*	56.52*	2750
Latin America						
Argentina	0.14	4.57	−1.73*	30.11*	34.81*	2845
Brazil	0.06	4.09	−0.43	3.32*	29.39*	2810
Chile	0.07*	1.73	−1.19*	27.54*	17.62*	2879
Mexico	0.11*	2.79	−1.49*	23.44*	103.01*	2865
Major Markets						
Japan	0.04	1.45	−0.43	13.36*	6.98*	2796
U.S.	0.05*	1.03	−3.98*	90.10*	24.26*	2939

The unconditional distribution for most markets is non-normal. Most markets have negative skewness which is statistically significant for the U.S., World, and many emerging market indexes. India and Korea are the only countries that have significant positive skewness. All of the 16 return series examined here, including the U.S., have fat tails, as indicated by the kurtosis. All markets, except South Korea, also have significant autocorrelation in daily returns.

Correlation Analysis

Exhibit 7–2 reports correlation coefficients between countries using both daily and monthly returns for the full sample period, 1982–1993. Because of the time difference between the U.S. and Asia, the U.S. and World returns are lagged by one day while obtaining correlations for Asia.

Correlations between the Emerging Market Index/Latin America Index and the U.S./World Index during the time period 1988–1993 are higher than they are for the individual countries for the full sample period, 1982–1993. This suggests correlations have increased over time as also shown by Aggarwal and Leal (1994). The correlations between the broader market indexes also suggest that as the frequency of time is increased from daily to monthly returns, the correlations tend to be higher in magnitude. An examination of individual country correlations indicates evidence of regional integration.

Exhibit 7–3 presents the correlations around the five periods when the U.S. market moves up the most and down the most during the years 1982 to 1993. During periods of very large market movements, the correlations are extremely high. All Asian markets, except South Korea and Taiwan, show significant correlations with the U.S., ranging from 0.82 for Japan to 0.56 for Thailand. A similar scenario is true for the five largest down markets, with the correlations ranging from 0.77 to 0.62. However, in the case of Latin America, only Chile has significant correlations with the U.S. in both up and down markets. It is possible that an examination of the last few years will show other countries, such as Mexico, also showing significant linkages.

Univariate regression results of each emerging country return as the dependent variable and a developed market (U.S. or Japan) or broad market index as the independent variable are reported in Exhibit 7–4. The coefficients of the World and U.S.

EXHIBIT 7-2

Correlations Between Returns 1982–93
Daily/Monthly

Asia	India	Malaysia	Philippines	S. Korea	Taiwan	Thailand	USA	World
Japan	−.01/−.13	.27*/.16	.08*/.19*	.04/.32*	.12*/.22*	.15*/.15	.12*/.30*	.66*/.78*
India		.05/−.13	.00/−.09	−.06*/−.07	−.02/−.13	−.04/.01	−.03/−.04	.00/−.10
Malaysia			.13*/.09	.08*/−.05	.12*/.05	.22*/.16*	.12*/.25*	.32*/.24*
Philippines				.02/.10	.08*/.18*	.16*/.32*	−.03/.16	.07*/.27*
S. Korea					.08*/.13	.10*/.05	.01/.15	.05*/.27*
Taiwan						.15*/.40*	.01/.23*	.10*/.28*
Thailand							.03/.36*	.13*/.36*

Latin America	Brazil	Chile	Mexico	USA	World
Argentina	.08*/−.03	.06*/.05	.05*/.17*	.03/.01	.06*/−.04
Brazil		.08*/.04	.04/−.02	.04*/.11	.08*/.17*
Chile			.05*/.18*	.07*/.11	.05*/.07
Mexico				.12*/.24*	.16*/.18*

Morgan Stanley Index	USA	World
World	.68*/.76*	
Emerging	.11*/.26*	.27*/.34*
Latin America	.16*/.28*	.22*/.29*
Far East	.12*/.28*	.78*/.79*

Note: *Significant at the five percent level.

143

EXHIBIT 7-3

Five Largest Up Markets/Five Largest Down Markets
Correlations Between Returns, 1982–93

Asia

	India	Malaysia	Philippines	S. Korea	Taiwan	Thailand	USA	World
Japan	-.27*/-.22	.64*/.66*	.66*/.61*	.51*/.61*	.15/.15	.26/.30	.82*/.77*	.36/.32
India		.24/.24	.24/.43	.26/.43	-.19/.11	.25/.51	.64*/.43	.64*/.67*
Malaysia			.39/.69*	.20/.54*	.12/.37	.56*/.87*	.78*/.73*	.71*/.65*
Philippines				.71*/.59*	.58*/.59*	.52*/.67*	.68*/.71*	.68*/.64*
S. Korea					.11/.40	.33/.49	.42/.63*	.31/.51*
Taiwan						.39/.43	.07/.16	.23/.16
Thailand							.56*/.62*	.82*/.75*

Latin America

	Brazil	Chile	Mexico	USA	World
Argentina	-.01/.06	.40/.47	.03/-.01	.31/.24	.27/.23
Brazil		.03/.24	.26/.56*	.21/.17	.67*/.69*
Chile			.25/.53*	.89*/.78*	.62*/.60*
Mexico				.32/.43	.46/.67*

Note: *Significant at the 5 percent level.

indexes are significant for each of the Asian markets, except India. The Far East Index is a significant explanatory variable for all six of the Asian countries. Japanese returns are significant for all the Asian countries except India.

In the case of Latin America, the World Index, Emerging Markets Index, and Latin American Index returns are significant only in the case of Brazil and Mexico, while the U.S. returns are significant only for Mexico. Brazil is an important part of the Emerging Market Index and the Latin American Index. The results suggest that the Asian countries are more integrated intraregion and interregion than the Latin American countries.

When the above regressions are repeated to examine the relationship between the volatility of the markets by using the standard deviation of returns as the variable, the results are even stronger, as seen in Exhibit 7–5. Almost all of the Asian markets, except India, have significant relationships with the developed markets of the U.S. and Japan. The broader indexes also are significant explanatory variables for most of these markets. The Indian market behaves quite differently than other Asian markets, possibly because the Indian economy has been quite a closed one in the past. However, the economic reforms of the last 2–3 years may result in India also becoming integrated with the rest of the world. The Latin American countries show a little more integration in terms of volatility (Exhibit 7–5) as compared to returns (Exhibit 7–4).

SUMMARY AND CONCLUSIONS

This chapter examines intraregion and interregion linkages in the emerging markets of Asia and Latin America. Most of these market returns exhibit negative skewness, fat tails, and autocorrelation. Emerging markets in general and Latin American markets of Brazil and Argentina in particular, are very volatile. Based on the correlations and regression estimates, the evidence suggests that emerging markets are not only linked with other regional markets but also are linked with the rest of the world. The results are stronger for Asia than for Latin America.

Even though market linkages are increasing over time, the correlations are low enough to result in significant benefits from

EXHIBIT 7-4

Univariate Regression Models with Monthly Returns

$$R_{i,t} = a_i + b_i R_{j,t}$$

	World			U.S.			Emerging			Latin/Far East			Japan		
	Const	Coeff	R²	Const	Coeff	R²	Const	Coeff	R²	Const	Coeff	R²	Const	Coeff	R²
Asia															
India	1.11	-.18	.01	1.00	-.07	.00	1.71	-.06	.00	1.25**	.17**	.03	1.08	-.14	.02
Malaysia	-.81	.90*	.06	-.75	.89*	.06	.18	-.17	.00	-.33	.36**	.03	-.28	.35*	.03
Philippines	.97	.62*	.07	1.24	.37**	.03	.52	.60*	.16	1.25	.32*	.05	1.31	.25*	.04
South Korea	.81	.44*	.07	1.02**	.24**	.02	-.17	.46*	.14	.87	.32*	.10	.93	.31*	.10
Taiwan	1.05	.89*	.08	1.28	.69*	.05	-2.26*	1.96*	.73	1.46	.42*	.05	1.51	.40*	.05
Thailand	1.17**	.69*	.13	1.22**	.67*	.13	1.30	.61*	.20	1.63*	.20*	.03	1.67*	.17**	.02
Latin America															
Argentina	1.78	-.21	.00	1.55	.03	.00	2.93	.21	.00	2.65	.01	.01			
Brazil	.59	.92*	.03	.95	.59	.01	-.12	1.48*	.12	-5.19*	2.48*	.66			
Chile	.40	.18	.01	.31	.28	.01	1.60	-.05	.00	1.46	.01	.00			
Mexico	1.46	.75*	.03	1.32	.94*	.05	2.58*	.74*	.26	2.34*	.51*	.23			

Note: *Significant at the 5 percent level.
**Significant at the 10 percent level.

EXHIBIT 7-5

Univariate Regression Models with Volatility

$$\sigma_{i,t} = a_i + b_i \sigma_{j,t}$$

	World			U.S.			Emerging			Latin/Far East			Japan		
	Const	Coeff	R²	Const	Coeff	R²	Const	Coeff	R²	Const	Coeff	R²	Const	Coeff	R²
Asia															
India	1.56*	.10	.00	1.79**	−.17	.01	2.54	−.53	.04	1.28*	.40	.06	1.08*	.45*	.10
Malaysia	.36*	.78*	.30	.46*	.50*	.29	.55*	.32*	.12	.37*	.41*	.29	.54*	.28*	.14
Philippines	1.11*	.56*	.05	1.22*	.32*	.04	.88*	.68*	.14	1.05*	.42*	.09	1.13*	.29*	.05
South Korea	.93*	.41*	.06	1.16*	.06	.00	1.08*	.38*	.08	.72*	.45*	.22	.66*	.44*	.27
Taiwan	1.14*	.97*	.11	1.40*	.47*	.06	.63*	1.83*	.62	1.06*	.70*	.16	.98*	.65*	.18
Thailand	.49*	1.06*	.11	.65*	.65*	.10	.57*	.98*	.19	.59*	.61*	.10	.44*	.61*	.14
Latin America															
Argentina	3.05*	1.23*	.03	3.38*	.59	.02	1.34**	2.85*	.16	.18	3.02*	.20			
Brazil	3.29*	.64	.02	3.77*	−.04	.00	3.65*	1.00*	.07	2.56*	1.59*	.19			
Chile	.97*	.73*	.05	1.16*	.27**	.02	.96*	.64*	.07	1.55*	.00	.00			
Mexico	.75*	2.08*	.16	.75*	1.64*	.23	1.66*	−0.01	.00	1.15*	.40	.02			

Note: *Significant at the 5 percent level.
**Significant at the 10 percent level.

diversification. However, it is important for portfolio managers to keep in mind that Latin American markets have very different risk-return characteristics than the Asian markets. Therefore, it is important to diversify outside of one emerging market region. It also is important to realize that during periods of very large market movements in the U.S., the correlations between country returns become very high as all markets tend to follow in the same direction. Therefore, during periods of disaster, there is no safe place to hide.

REFERENCES

Aggarwal, Reena; and Ricardo Leal. "Integration and Anomalies in the Emerging Markets of Asia and Latin America." Forthcoming in *Advances in International Stock Market Relationships and Interactions,* eds. J. Doukas and L. Lang. Greenwood Publishing, 1994.

Aggarwal, Reena; and Pietra Rivoli. "Seasonal and Day-of-the-Week Effects in Four Emerging Stock Markets." *The Financial Review* 24, no. 4, (1989), pp. 541–550.

Campbell, J.Y.; and Y. Hamao. "Predictable Stock Returns in the United States and Japan: A Study of Long-Term Capital Market Integration." *Journal of Finance* 47, no. 1 (1992), pp. 43–69.

Errunza, V.; E. Losq.; and P. Padmanabhan. "Test of Integration, Mild-Segmentation, and Segmentation Hypothesis." *Journal of Banking and Finance* 16, no. 5 (1992), pp. 949–972.

Eun, Cheol S.; and Sangdal Shim. "International Transmission of Stock Market Movements." *Journal of Financial and Quantitative Analysis* 24, no. 2 (1989), pp. 241–256.

Hamao, Y.R.; R. W. Masulis; and V. Ng. "Correlation in Price Changes Across International Stock Markets." *Review of Financial Studies* 3, no. 1, (1990), pp. 281–307.

King, Mervyn; and Sushil Wadhwani. "Transmission of Volatility Between Stock Markets." *Review of Financial Studies* 3, no. 1 (1990), pp. 5–33.

Lessard, Donald R. "International Portfolio Diversification: A Multivariate Analysis for a Group of Latin American Countries." *Journal of Finance* 28 (1973), pp. 619–633.

Roll, Richard. "Industrial Structure and the Comparative Behavior of International Stock Market Indices." *Journal of Finance* 47, no. 1 (1992), pp. 3–42.

8

CO-INTEGRATION AND THE INVESTMENT HORIZON IN EMERGING CAPITAL MARKETS

George Tsetsekos, *Drexel University*

INTRODUCTION

Several Asian and Latin American stock markets and a handful of others are referred to as "emerging" by the International Finance Corporation. Academic research has addressed in considerable depth the benefits of diversifying into emerging capital markets (Errunza, 1983, 1988 and Bailey and Stulz, 1990). Favorable diversification benefits typically are found because of low correlations among equity returns. In most studies, correlations are estimated from equity returns based on short return intervals spanning from one month to one quarter.

To assess the diversification benefits in emerging capital markets, however, the use of correlations corresponding to short-term horizons is inappropriate for at least two reasons. *First,* transaction expenses or other market imperfections that are especially present in emerging capital markets may cause investors to maintain long-run investment horizons; therefore, diversification benefits ought to be assessed on return correlations measured in the long run rather than over short intervals. *Second,* correlations of returns based on short-term horizons may not capture potential long-term trends found in emerging capital markets. Given systematic events affecting all countries, international capital markets may share a common trend. Correlations based on short horizon returns may be misspecified because they do not capture the presumed long-run trend present in emerging markets. The presence of a trend makes the benefits diversification for emerging capital markets limited in the long run (Kasa, 1992).

While the above reasons draw into question the usefulness of correlations based on short-term investment horizons in assessing diversification in emerging capital markets, it is still possible under certain circumstances that the correlation between the returns in these markets may be independent of the investment horizon. This is possible only when there are independent stochastic trends driving the markets, as opposed to a common stochastic trend.

THE CONCEPT OF CO-INTEGRATED MARKET RETURNS

A relatively new statistical technique called co-integration allows for useful insight into the nature of long- versus short-run correlations. The technique identifies stochastic trends present in time series. Academic research has shown that if two time series are co-integrated, a single stochastic trend tends to drive the pair (Stock and Watson, 1988). In the long run, the behavior of the common trend dominates the behavior of the two series. In essence, the common stochastic trend ties the variables together and unique shocks die out as each variable reverts toward the common trend. Over long horizons, the common stochastic trend results in a correlation of 1.0 between the two co-integrated series.

The application of this methodology for two emerging markets reveals important insight for portfolio management, especially regarding diversification benefits. If two emerging stock markets are co-integrated, a common stochastic term will tie the markets together and diversification will be obviously limited. When more than two markets are involved, the interpretation becomes less clear. In a recent paper (DeFusco, Geppert and Tsetsekos, 1994), we show that with N emerging markets, if the number of stochastic trends is less than N, then the correlation between any pair of country returns depends on the investor's investment horizon. Only when the number of trends equals the number of markets, N, are the correlations independent of the investor's investment horizon. If, instead, there is just one trend present in all markets, the correlation between all pairs of country returns will approach 1.0 in the long run.

When emerging capital markets are cointegrated, the correlation between the returns is a function of the length of an investor's investment horizon. Because correlations are dependent on the length of the investor's horizon, previous studies that have used weekly or monthly return data to estimate the correlations among capital market returns may have overestimated the long-run diversification potential of international investing. Given that each investment horizon yields different correlations, monthly return data will yield only the correlation for a monthly investment horizon. For any other investment horizon, the monthly estimates will be inappropriate. Co-integrated markets yield correlations that are much higher than previously estimated.

To examine the long-run diversification potential of 13 emerging markets, we use the Johansen (1988) and Johansen and Juselius (1990) co-integration tests. We arrange the emerging capital markets in three geographical regions of the world. We find that none of the three regions combined with the U.S. are co-integrated. These findings indicate that independent stochastic trends generate the returns in these markets—not just one common trend. Therefore, the correlation between the returns in these markets is independent of the investment horizon. Using weekly data, we find the correlation between these markets to be low. Because none of the markets are co-integrated, long-run correlations can be assessed with weekly data.

METHODOLOGY AND DATA
Testing for Co-integration

Many economic time series seem to be characterized by statistical processes that are nonstationary. A nonstationary series has the tendency to become arbitrarily large or small over time. For instance, the Standard & Poor's (S&P) 500 and the *Financial Times*–Actuaries (FT–A) indexes may best be characterized as series that become arbitrarily large over time. Even though the level of each individual index is nonstationary, it is possible that the two series do not wander too far from each other. In statistical terms, if some linear combination of the levels of the two share price indexes is stationary, the two series are referred to as cointegrated.

Tests of co-integration are conducted in two phases. In the first phase, each of the series must be found to be integrated of the same order (i.e., the number of times that we must difference each series before it is stationary). These tests are referred to as *unit root* tests. In this chapter, we use four regression models to test for the presence of a unit root. A summary of the models is presented below.

Model 1: $\Delta y_t = \alpha_0 + \rho y_{t-1} + u_t$ $H_0 : \rho = 0$

Model 2: $y_t = \alpha_0 + \rho y_{t-1} + u_t$ $H_0 : \rho = 1$

Model 3: $\Delta y_t = \alpha_0 + \alpha_1 t + \rho y_{t-1} + u_t$ $H_0 : \rho = 0$

Model 4: $y_t = \alpha_0 + \alpha_1 (t - T/2) + \rho y_{t-1} + u_t$ $H_0 : \rho = 1$

In models 1 and 3, the disturbance terms are assumed to be serially uncorrelated. Models 2 and 4 allow for serial correlation in the disturbance term. Dickey and Fuller (1979) show that the common test statistic, the usual "*t*-ratio" for the null hypothesis $\rho = 0$, does not have a *t* distribution even in the limit as the sample size becomes infinite. The distribution of the *t*-ratio, denoted as t_μ for model 1 or t_τ for model 3 to distinguish it from the conventional *t* statistic, has selected percentiles, as given in Fuller (1976, p. 373). The Phillips and Perron tests (1988) with and without trends are presented as models 2 and 4 above, with associated test statistics denoted as $Z(t_\alpha^*)$ and $Z(t_{2\hat{\alpha}})$. In the Phillips and Perron models, the null hypothesis is $\rho = 1$ with the stationary alternative $\rho < 1$. Asymptotic critical values for $Z(t_\alpha^*)$ and $Z(t_{2\hat{\alpha}})$ are found in the subtables of Table 8.5.2 of Fuller (1976, p. 373).

Once the series have been found to be integrated of the same order, the second phase of the co-integration procedure can begin; this phase involves the application of statistical tests to detect significance in the results. Several different tests of co-integration have been developed.[1] The approach used in this chapter is based on Johansen (1988) and Johansen and Juselius (1990).

Data

We collected 228 weekly price index levels published by the International Finance Corporation (IFC) for 13 emerging capital markets from January 1989 to May 1993. We selected the following countries for examination: Brazil, Chile, Colombia, Greece, Mexico, Venezuela, Korea, Philippines, Taiwan, Malaysia, Thailand, Portugal, and Turkey.

For each emerging capital market, IFC reports index levels in U.S. dollars using the Friday closing stock prices. If Friday is a holiday, the last transaction price is used in the calculation of the price index. Stocks selected for inclusion in the country indexes are based on market capitalization, liquidity, and industry classification. The indexes include actively traded stocks that are broadly diversified by industry and whose combined market values are approximately 60 percent of total market capitalization at the end of each year. Stocks are not selected on the basis of their availability to foreign investors. In a few instances, the IFC may include more than one class of stock for the same company in the index. All IFC price indexes are weighted by market capitalization. Weekly data on the Standard & Poor's (S&P) 500 index is collected from the daily indexes file maintained by the University of Chicago's Center for Research in Security Prices for the time period January 1989 to December 1992. S&P 500 data from January 1993 to May 1993 are collected from *The Wall Street Journal*. Due to limitations on dividend data, all tests are performed on price levels only.

---

1. Several researchers have developed tests for co-integration and methods for estimating co-integrating vectors. All of these tests involve locating the "most stationary" linear combinations (among all the possible ones) of the time series in question. Estimation methods of co-integration have been proposed with ordinary least squares, nonlinear least squares, and principal components. Johansen and Johansen and Juselius use maximum likelihood estimation in a fully specified error correction model.

RESULTS

Descriptive Statistics and Unit Root Tests

In Exhibit 8–1 we report summary statistics for the 13 emerging capital markets and the United States. During the period from January 1989 to May 1993, Brazil has the largest weekly return of 4.95 percent, while Korea experiences the biggest loss at −0.17 percent. We find that only the mean weekly returns of the United States, Chile, Colombia, and Mexico are significantly different from zero. Of the 13 markets, Brazil has the largest level of volatility as reported by its variance of 0.00864 and its interquartile range of 11.20 percent. For comparison purposes, the United States has the lowest variance of 0.00032.

As discussed earlier, for two series to be co-integrated, the series must be integrated of the same order. Tests of the order of

EXHIBIT 8–1

Summary Statistics of Weekly Returns for 13 Emerging Capital Markets and the United States

Country	Mean	Variance	Skewness	Kurtosis	Interquartile Range
Brazil	0.0495	0.00864	−0.683	4.058	0.112
Chile	0.0060**	0.00101	0.455	0.319	0.043
Colombia	0.0059**	0.00164	1.484	7.445	0.029
Mexico	0.0067**	0.00087	−0.364	0.530	0.036
Venezuela	0.0047	0.00136	0.402	1.638	0.062
Korea	−0.0017	0.00136	0.812	1.352	0.047
Philippines	0.0018	0.00179	−1.160	6.147	0.042
Taiwan	−0.0002	0.00389	−0.199	2.777	0.067
Malaysia	0.0028	0.00080	−0.818	4.730	0.028
Thailand	0.0037	0.00189	−0.889	9.654	0.043
Greece	0.0025	0.00276	0.589	2.017	0.060
Portugal	−0.0012	0.00085	0.514	2.695	0.030
Turkey	0.0035	0.00571	0.278	0.312	0.090
United States	0.0020*	0.00032	−0.322	1.035	0.022

Notes: Data on the 13 emerging markets covers the time period January 1989 to May 1993.
** Statistically different from zero at the 5 percent level of significance.
* Statistically different from zero at the 10 percent level of significance.

integration are conducted for individual countries with unit root tests. We compute adjusted Dickey–Fuller (ADF) $(t_\mu$ no trend; t_τ with trend) and Phillips–Peron $[Z(t_\alpha^*)$ no trend; $Z(t_{\hat\alpha})$ with trend] test statistics. Unit root tests are corrected for possible serial correlation and autoregressive heteroskedasticity. For all countries, we cannot reject the (null) hypothesis of the presence of a unit root. Further testing on the first differences of each stock price index series does not indicate the presence of a second unit root. Because all country stock index levels are integrated of order 1, all are potential candidates for co-integrated markets.

Co-integration Tests

The Johansen and Juselius co-integration test is applied to three mutually exclusive groupings of national stock markets based on their geographical region. Each of the groupings below also includes the U.S. The groups are as follows:

Latin America: U.S. and Brazil, Chile, Colombia, Mexico, and Venezuela,

Pacific Basin: U.S. and Korea, Philippines, Taiwan, Malaysia, and Thailand,

Mediterranean: U.S. and Greece, Portugal, and Turkey.

Within each of the above groupings, we are unable to identify co-integrating relationships among the emerging countries. In the long run, country stock return indexes do not exhibit any tendency to move together. In addition, the lack of co-integration implies that the correlation between pairs of markets does not depend on the investment horizon. Consequently, it is appropriate to infer longer investment horizon return correlations based on data for weekly returns. Using these data, we can detect to what extent correlations between national indexes are low and thus ascertain possible gains from diversification.

In Exhibit 8–3 we present the correlation coefficients of the weekly returns. The correlation levels reported in the exhibit are similar to those reported in several other academic studies (for example, Errunza, 1983, 1988 and Bailey and Stulz, 1990). Correlations on average are quite low and, for many combinations, even negative. The average correlation is 0.11; the maximum is 0.52

EXHIBIT 8–2

Trace and Maximum Eigenvalue Test Statistics for Co-integration

Number of Co-integrating Vectors	Group I		Group II		Group III	
	Trace Test	Maximium Eigenvalue	Trace Test	Maximum Eigenvalue	Trace Test	Maximum Eigenvalue
0	57.11	27.51	66.93	27.82	23.98	13.56
1	29.61	12.99	39.12	16.40	10.32	5.85
2	16.61	10.83	22.71	14.68	4.46	4.46
3	5.77	5.01	8.03	5.78	na	na
4	0.76	0.76	2.24	2.24	na	na

Group I	Latin America: Brazil, Chile, Colombia, Mexico, and Venezuela.
Group II	Pacific Basin: Korea, Philippines, Taiwan, Malaysia, and Thailand.
Group III	Mediterranean: Greece, Portugal, and Turkey.

Notes: The trace test examines the suitability of at most the number of co-integrating vectors indicated below. The maximium eigenvalue test examines the suitability of the number of co-integrating vectors indicated below versus that number plus one.

na = Test not applicable for three countries.

None of the above statistics are significant at the 5 percent level.

(Malaysia and Thailand); and the minimum is −0.16 (Taiwan and Venezuela). The distances that separate these countries do not appear to influence the degree of correlation. Even countries that are located within the same region of the world have low and/or negative correlations. It appears that substantial gains from diversification exist among the 13 emerging markets. Correlations between the 13 emerging markets and the S&P 500 index range from a maximum of 0.37 (with Mexico) to a minimum of −0.13 (with Venezuela). Taken together, these results present evidence for substantial gains from diversification in emerging capital markets.

EXHIBIT 8-3

Correlation Coefficients of Weekly Returns for 13 Emerging Capital Markets and the United States for the Period January 1989 to May 1993

	Bra	Chi	Col	Mex	Ven	Kor	Phil	Tai	Mal	Thai	Gre	Por	Tur	U.S.
Bra	1.00	0.12	0.10	0.09	-0.1	0.04	0.03	0.13	0.16	0.10	0.10	0.14	0.13	0.10
Chi		1.00	-0.03	0.04	-0.10	0.09	0.06	0.04	0.04	0.002	0.06	0.06	-0.04	0.03
Col			1.00	-0.01	0.004	-0.13	0.06	0.06	-0.02	0.03	0.03	0.03	0.16	0.02
Mex				1.00	-0.02	0.09	0.20	0.21	0.38	0.23	0.12	0.18	0.02	0.37
Ven					1.00	-0.01	-0.04	-0.16	-0.03	-0.07	-0.09	-0.06	-0.03	-0.13
Kor						1.00	-0.06	0.06	0.18	0.17	-0.05	0.09	0.02	0.16
Phil							1.00	0.24	0.31	0.23	0.14	0.23	0.14	0.17
Tai								1.00	0.28	0.23	0.09	0.16	0.26	0.18
Mal									1.00	0.52	0.23	0.30	0.26	0.25
Thai										1.00	0.23	0.31	0.23	0.24
Gre											1.00	0.40	0.30	0.05
Por												1.00	0.28	0.24
Tur													1.00	0.05
U.S.														1.00

Countries are as follows: Brazil, Chile, Colombia, Mexico, Venezuela, Korea, Philippines, Taiwan, Malaysia, Thailand, Greece, Portugal, Turkey, and the United States

CONCLUSIONS

In this chapter we use co-integration tests to examine the long-run diversification potential of 13 emerging capital markets. Co-integration tests are conducted based on geographical regions of the world using the Johansen (1988) and Johansen and Juselius (1990) procedure. None of the three regions examined possess co-integrated markets. Returns in emerging capital markets are generated from independent stochastic trends and correlations are independent of the investment horizon. We find that the correlations between countries are low, with an average correlation of 0.11. The independence of markets within the emerging markets regions suggests that diversification across emerging capital markets is effective.

REFERENCES

Bailey, W.; and R. M. Stulz. "Benefits of International Diversification: The Case of Pacific Basin Stock Markets." *Journal of Portfolio Management* 16 (1990), pp. 57–61.

Dickey, D. A.; and W. A. Fuller. "Distributions of the Estimates for Autoregressive Time Series with a Unit Root." *Journal of the American Statistical Association* 74 (1979), pp. 427–432.

DeFusco, R. A.; J. M. Geppert; and G. P. Tsetsekos. "Long-Run Diversification Potential in Emerging Capital Markets." Working Paper 33–14. Drexel University, 1994.

Errunza, V. R. "Emerging Markets: A New Opportunity for Improving Global Portfolio Performance." *Financial Analysts Journal*, September–October 1983, pp. 51–58.

—————. "Further Evidence on the Benefits of Portfolio Investments in Emerging Markets." *Financial Analysts Journal*, July–August 1988, pp. 76–78.

Fuller, W. A. *Introduction to Statistical Time Series*. New York: Wiley & Sons, 1976.

Johansen, S. "Statistical Analysis of Cointegrating Vectors." *Journal of Economic Dynamics and Control* 12 (1988), pp. 231–254.

Johansen, S.; and K. Juselius. "Maximum Likelihood Estimation and Inference on Cointegration—with Applications to the Demand for Money." *Oxford Bulletin of Economics and Statistics* 52, no. 2 (1990), pp. 169–210.

Kasa, K. "Common Stochastic Trends in the International Stock Market." *Journal of Monetary Economics* 29 (1992), pp. 95–124.

Perron, P. "Trends and Random Walks in Macroeconomic Time Series: Further Evidence from a New Approach." *Journal of Economic Dynamics and Control* 12 (1988), pp. 297–332.

Phillips, P. C. B. "Time Series Regression with a Unit Root." *Econometrica* 55 (1987), pp. 277–301.

Phillips, P. C. B.; and P. Perron. "Testing for a Unit Root in Time Series Regression." *Biometrika* 75 (1988), pp. 335–346.

Stock, J. H.; and M. W. Watson. "Testing for Common Trends." *Journal of the American Statistical Association* 83 (1988), pp. 1097–1107.

V

ASSET AND DERIVATIVE PRICING IN EMERGING CAPITAL MARKETS

9

INSTITUTIONAL INVESTORS AND ASSET PRICING IN EMERGING MARKETS

Elaine Buckberg, *International Monetary Fund*

No conventional model of equity markets can explain the dramatic declines in developing country stock markets, referred to as the Tequila effect, that occurred in the wake of the Mexican financial crisis beginning in late 1994. Standard finance models, such as the capital asset pricing model (CAPM) and arbitrage pricing theory (APT), predict that all equity returns should be a function of the stock or portfolio's sensitivity to global risk factors, such as commodity prices or returns on the world portfolio. To the extent that the crash of the Mexican market only reflected news about Mexican fundamentals, it would have been expected to have only a very small impact on the world portfolio, since Mexico represents less than 2 percent of global stock market capitalization. With only a small impact on the world portfolio, the impact of the Mexican crash on other developing country stock markets would have been expected to be insignificant.

A new model of asset pricing is needed to explain why other developing country equity markets responded so strongly to the Mexican devaluation, while the world's major stock markets were unmoved. The contagion effect among developing country stock markets, and particularly within Latin America, suggests that investors do not analyze these markets solely in the context of global risk factors. This is consistent with the behavior of institutional investors, who appear to treat developing country equity markets as a separate asset class, first deciding what share of their portfolio to allocate to industrial and developing country equity markets, respectively, and then allocating the funds within each asset class. Moreover, the across-the-board (albeit short-lived) liquidation of developing country equity holding in the wake of the Mexican devaluation suggests that portfolio managers (1) had not substantially differentiated among developing country equity markets based on their individual risks, and (2) had interpreted the peso devaluation to signal that underlying risks in other economies might be higher than they had recognized.

ASSET PRICING WITH DEVELOPING COUNTRY EQUITIES AS A SEPARATE ASSET CLASS

According to the capital asset pricing model (CAPM), investors should allocate their funds among risky assets according to the assets' expected rates of return relative to the expected return on the market portfolio.[1] Investors divide their wealth between a riskless asset and risky assets or portfolios; the representative investor would hold a portfolio of risky assets identical to the market portfolio.[2] An investor would deviate from holding the market portfolio only if by doing so he could improve the efficiency of his overall portfolio, increasing his expected return without accepting additional risk. As such, the only factor that should affect investors' demand for an asset is that asset's return covariance with the market portfolio. If we assume that investors invest globally, then the market portfolio is the world stock portfolio and the rate of return on each country's stock market should be a function of that market's return covariance with the world stock portfolio:

---

1. All returns are measured in excess of the riskless rate of return.
2. Assuming zero transactions or informational costs and assuming that assets are infinitely divisible, a representative investor would hold each equity in proportion to its share in the world portfolio, such that his or her portfolio would be identical to the world portfolio in composition.

$$r_{jt} = \alpha + \beta_w r_{wt} + u_t \qquad (9.1)$$

where r_{jt} is the expected return on market j and r_{wt} is the expected return on the world portfolio.[3] Therefore, if developing country equity markets are part of the global market, the return in any given market j should be proportional to that market's covariance with a capitalization-weighted world portfolio. Higher expected returns in any market should be exploited by investors who shift their portfolios into that market until the excess returns are eliminated and the CAPM equation again holds.

The composition of institutional investor portfolios, however, suggests that investors do not determine their holdings based solely on each developing country equity's relationship to the world portfolio, without regard to other factors. In particular, investors have not allocated as much of their portfolios to developing country equities as the CAPM would have suggested based on historical return patterns. Over the period from December 1988 to December 1992, investors could have substantially improved the efficiency of their portfolios, increasing returns without accepting additional risk, by increasing their holdings of developing country equities.[4]

The low proportion of developing country equities in investor portfolios suggests that investors intentionally limit their developing country holdings to a lower share than potentially optional. Because many developing country markets are very illiquid, only a few investors could achieve an apparently optimal portfolio allocation between developing and industrial country equities. If all portfolio managers tried to shift simultaneously into developing country equities, stock prices would be quickly driven up and expected returns driven down, reducing the optimal portfolio share of developing country equities. As such, the portfolio share invested in developing country equities may be

---

3. All returns are calculated in excess of the holding yield on a constant one–month maturity U.S. Treasury bill intended to represent the riskless rate of return.
4. By shifting from a portfolio composed entirely of the *Financial Times*–Actuaries (FT–A) World Index to a portfolio composed of 50 percent of the IFC Emerging Markets Data Base (EMDB) Investable Composite Index and 50 percent the FT–A World Index, investors would have increased the return on their portfolios from roughly 7 to 17 percent, while slightly decreasing portfolio variance from about 17 to 16 percent.

optimal once liquidity problems are considered. Alternatively, the underallocation of assets to developing country stocks might simply indicate that the realized returns on these securities have been much better than expected.[5]

WHY INSTITUTIONAL INVESTORS MAY TREAT DEVELOPING COUNTRY EQUITIES AS A DISTINCT ASSET CLASS

Investors may believe that developing country equities are subject to larger shifts in investor sentiment (than equities in mature markets) and other classwide risks and, as such, they may consider them to be riskier as a class than the variance of their individual returns might suggest. Aitken (1995) explains that if institutional investors together influence a significant share of developing country equities and jointly experience a shift in sentiment away from developing country markets, they may push asset prices out of line with the assets' underlying economic fundamentals. Arbitrage traders (who trade on the basis of economic fundamentals) would normally be expected to buy the assets that become undervalued and offset the trend. However, the magnitude of their potential loss, should asset prices fall further and thus force them to liquidate before prices recover, may limit arbitrage traders' willingness to purchase the undervalued assets. Institutional investors could then create self-fulfilling shifts in investor sentiment toward developing country equities as a class, where investors sell their developing country securities because they expect prices to decline, and prices decline because investors sell.

Using a variance ratio test on asset return data to evaluate developing country market stability in 1989–91 and 1992–95, Aitken finds that the variance ratios increase profoundly in the

---

5. Bekaert and Urias's (1995) analysis of the diversification benefits from emerging market closed-end funds versus the IFC EMDB indexes suggests that the high returns on the indexes may overstate the effective return once transaction costs and other barriers to investment are considered. Bekaert and Urias assume that returns on closed-end funds approximate achievable returns inclusive of all transactions and other costs. They find statistically significant diversification benefits from U. K. emerging market funds, but not from comparable U.S. funds.

later period, when institutional investors play a larger role in developing country stock markets.[6] He interprets these results as indicating that institutional investor participation has had a destabilizing, rather than stabilizing, impact on these markets. Notably, the increases in variance ratios are greatest for the EMDB composite indexes, indicating that developing country equities as a class are more subject to destabilizing noise trading than are the individual markets.

Restrictions on institutional investors' behavior may contribute to their treating developing country equities as a separate asset class. Dedicated developing country mutual funds are forced to keep the vast majority of their assets in developing country securities at all times, whereas many broadly based mutual funds are limited in the proportion of assets that can be invested in developing country securities by the portfolio allocation guidelines outlined in their prospectuses.

Portfolio allocation by risk-based asset class also is consistent with the allocation of pension fund assets between stocks and bonds, where the share of assets invested in stocks typically is substantially lower than the proportion that would maximize the portfolio's expected return.[7] Benartzi and Thaler (1995) present myopic loss aversion as a plausible explanation of such low-risk portfolio allocations, and this explanation also seems relevant to the apparent underallocation of assets to

---

6. The variance ratio test begins with the proposition that if a stock price reflects all available information about asset fundamentals, then under certain conditions, an asset's price can then be expected to follow a random walk as the current price would be the best forecast of future prices. Under a random walk, actual future prices would on average remain in a range that would widen linearly over time, such that the return variance would increase proportionately with the period over which the asset is held and the variance ratio would equal one:

$$VR = \frac{\left[\dfrac{\sigma_T}{T}\right]}{\sigma_1} = 1$$

where σ_T is the return variance over a T-week period and σ_1 is the return variance over one week. If, however, the ratio exceeds one, price increases today would signal future price increases and indicate that deviations from asset fundamentals may be exploding rather than mean-reverting.

7. Benartzi and Thaler cite 60 percent stocks and 40 percent bonds and Treasury bills as typical asset-allocation proportions. Leibowitz and Langetieg indicate that for a twenty-year horizon, the stock to bond ratio should exceed 100 percent most of the time.

high-variance developing country equities. If investors are loss-averse, their utility loss from a marginal loss in asset value exceeds their utility gain from an equally sized gain in asset value.[8] Kahneman and Tversky (1979) formalize loss aversion as a utility function defined over changes in wealth, rather than levels of wealth, that is concave for gains, but convex for losses and steeper for losses than gains.[9] Essentially, loss-averse investors attempt to maximize expected returns subject to a downside risk constraint, which may induce them to hold fewer high-variance assets than would be suggested in models that assume investors' utility is symmetric with respect to changes in wealth.

Based on their downside risk constraint, loss-averse investors may determine how much of their equity portfolio to allocate to high-variance developing country equities versus lower variance industrial country equities—a share that will be lower than if investors were maximizing the expected return of their portfolio—and then allocate their assets within each class. Kramer and Smith (1995) have observed that the price behavior of mutual funds specialized in Mexican equities is consistent with loss-aversion. They interpret the shift in fund prices from trading at a premium (relative to the underlying portfolio value) as indicating that investors did not want to realize paper losses on their closed-end fund shares.[10]

---

8. Benartzi and Thaler also present myopic loss aversion as an explanation for the equity premium puzzle—the return premium, typically estimated at 6.5 percent, which investors demand on stocks relative to bonds. Benartzi and Thaler attribute the premium to the fact that stocks have both upside and downside risk, whereas a bond often is treated as having no downside risk if held to maturity. However, even if held to maturity, bonds have downside risk in the form of default risk.

9. Loss-averse investors will demand a return premium for accepting additional variance risk, regardless of the asset's covariance with the market portfolio and, due to the utility function's convexity over losses, the magnitude of the premium will increase more than one-for-one with increases in an asset's variance. Hence, loss aversion is in contradiction to the capital asset pricing model.

10. The size of the return premium that loss-averse investors will demand is greater if the investor evaluates his portfolio over short-time horizons, as do institutional investors. Benartzi and Thaler observe that institutional investors typically operate with relatively short horizons tied to the length of time they expect to remain in their job; in addition, investment managers' portfolio performance is evaluated annually, and their bonuses are set accordingly. Similarly, De Bondt and Thaler (1994) observe that institutional investors have higher turnover ratios than individual investors.

A TWO-CLASS ASSET PRICING MODEL

Portfolio allocation by asset class suggests that a two-factor asset pricing model may be more appropriate to describe returns in developing country equity markets. If investors first determine what percentage of their portfolio to allocate to developing versus industrial country markets and then distribute those funds across developing country stock markets, the return in developing country equity market j would depend both on the world market return (where the world portfolio is composed of assets in mature stock markets) and on the return on a broad portfolio of developing country stocks (the developing country market portfolio):

$$r_{jt} = \alpha + \beta_w r_{wt} + \beta_{em} r_{emt} + u_t \qquad (9.2)$$

where $r_{j,t}$ is the expected return on market j; $r_{w,t}$ is the expected return on the world portfolio (the FT–A World Index); and $r_{em,t}$ is the expected return on the IFC EMDB Global Composite Index. The coefficient $\beta_{em,t}$ represents the covariance between the expected return in market j and the expected return on a capitalization-based developing country equity portfolio, where the return an investor would require to hold the portfolio of market j—as opposed to holding the developing country market portfolio—would be an increasing function of that covariance.[11] If investors select each asset based only on its relation to the world portfolio, as the CAPM predicts, β_{em} should not be significantly different from zero. Any significant β_{em} would be consistent with investors treating developing country equities as a separate class, allocating within that class according to market j's relationship with returns on the developing country portfolio, and would signify a rejection of the CAPM.[12]

---

11. The IFC EMDB Global Composite portfolio is used to proxy a true capitalization-weighted portfolio of developing country equities.

12. This is the case even if expected returns are correlated with one another within the asset class—any two developing country assets that are correlated with one another should affect expected returns only through their impact on the world portfolio. When using actual returns as a proxy for expected returns, however, a nonzero coefficient on the developing country portfolio can reflect two possibilities: (1) the traditional one-factor CAPM is insufficient to explain investor behavior; or (2) unanticipated shocks to asset returns are shared across developing countries. If an unanticipated shock to one country spreads to others because investors, who treat developing country assets as a class, shift their sentiment regarding other markets, a nonzero coefficient would imply that the strict one-factor CAPM did not hold.

DATA DESCRIPTION

The data for stock exchanges in developing countries come from the Emerging Markets Data Base (EMDB) compiled by the International Finance Corporation (IFC). The EMDB has both global and investable indexes for each market, as well as the overall Composite, Latin Americans and Asian indexes used in this chapter. This chapter treats the general indexes, constructed as based on all the stocks in the market, as representative portfolios of local stocks to examine the behavior of the overall stock market.[13] The IFC's consistent methodology across countries makes its indexes preferable to local indexes for statistical analysis, although the local indexes may be watched more closely by market participants.[14] EMDB indexes typically include 10 to 20 percent of listed stocks, selected on the basis of high trading volume or large capitalization or to give the index an industry composition representative of the market overall; indexes are capitalization-weighted. Like many industrial market indexes, the IFC indexes are biased toward local blue chip stocks. The analysis below uses end-week data on total returns (prices plus accrued dividends) evaluated in U.S. dollars from January 1989 to April 1995; all returns are calculated in excess of the holding yield on a U.S. Treasury bill one month from maturity, which serves as the riskless rate. The markets studied are in Argentina, Brazil, Chile, Colombia, India, Jordan, Korea, Mexico, Malaysia, the Philippines, Taiwan Province of China, Thailand, and Venezuela.

The world market portfolio is represented by the Financial Times-Actuaries (FT-A) World Index. The FT–A World Index has an advantage over other standard global indexes (such as the Morgan Stanley Capital International [MSCI] world index) in that it includes developing country stocks as well as industrial country stocks. As such, the FT–A World Index will reflect, as the CAPM market portfolio should, changes in prices in the developing country markets under study, a factor that has become increasingly important over time; emerging markets accounted for 12 percent of world market capitalization at the end of 1994.

---

13. The investable indexes include only those stocks accessible to foreign investors.
14. The IFC indexes are available only weekly, whereas local indexes are available on every trading day and, in some cases, continuously throughout the day.

Again, data is end-week total returns, evaluated in U.S. dollars and in excess of the holding yield on a U.S. Treasury bill one month to maturity, for January 1989 to April 1995.

Data statistics for raw returns (*not* excess returns) are presented in Exhibit 9–1, and excess return correlations between the individual markets and the multicountry indexes are presented in Exhibit 9–2.

ESTIMATES OF THE ASSET PRICING MODEL

Ordinary least squares (OLS) estimates of the two-factor model of Equation (9.2) indicate that the addition of the developing country market portfolio substantially improves the explanation of returns in individual developing country equity markets relative to the standard CAPM of equation (9.1). In weekly data covering the

EXHIBIT 9-1

Data Statistics for Emerging Markets, the World, and IFC Portfolios[1]

Market	Mean	Standard Deviation
Argentina	5.88	28.55
Brazil	3.87	20.50
Chile	3.39	8.87
Colombia	3.60	12.01
India	1.35	10.19
Jordan	0.93	5.60
Korea	0.31	8.89
Mexico	2.29	10.41
Malaysia	1.63	6.60
Philippines	1.86	10.38
Taiwan Province of China	1.22	13.54
Thailand	2.45	9.21
Venezuela	2.04	14.48
FT–A World	0.66	3.99
IFC-G Composite	1.04	6.19
IFC-G Latin America	2.51	9.91
IFC-G Asia	0.81	6.82

1. The emerging markets composite index and the indexes for each emerging market are from the IFC Emerging Markets Data Base global indexes. The world market is represented by the *Financial Times*–Actuaries (FT–A) World Index. All series are monthly from December 1988 to April 1995.

E X H I B I T   9–2

Correlations Between Excess Returns in Emerging Markets and the World and IFC Portfolios[1]

$$r_{j,t} - \alpha + \beta_w r_{w,t} + \beta_{em} r_{em,t} + \beta_{Asia} r_{Asia,t} + \beta_{Lat\,Am,t} + u_t$$

Market	FT–A World	IFC-G Composite	IFC-G Latin America	IFC-G Asia
Argentina	—	0.05	0.23	−0.04
Brazil	0.20	0.40	0.82	0.14
Chile	0.05	0.22	0.39	0.09
Colombia	0.01	0.05	0.06	0.01
India	−0.04	0.07	−0.01	0.10
Jordan	0.12	0.12	−0.05	0.14
Korea	0.20	0.34	0.10	0.38
Mexico	0.27	0.39	0.59	0.17
Malaysia	0.47	0.47	0.17	0.49
Philippines	0.03	0.08	0.05	0.08
Taiwan Province of China	0.24	0.79	0.12	0.86
Thailand	0.28	0.44	0.16	0.44
Venezuela	−0.09	−0.04	0.05	−0.08
FT–A World	—	0.39	0.27	0.33
IFC-G Composite	—	—	0.49	0.17
IFC-G Latin America	—	—	—	0.17

1. Returns are calculated in excess of the holding yield on a U.S. Treasury bill with one month to maturity. The emerging markets composite index and the indexes for each emerging market are from the IFC Emerging Markets Data Base global indexes. The world market is represented by the *Financial Times*–Actuaries (FT–A) World Index. All series are weekly from the period December 31, 1988, to April 28, 1995.

period of January 1989 to April 1995, the one-factor CAPM specification can be rejected in favor of the two-factor specification for 8 of 13 markets, including the largest and most liquid of the developing country equity markets (Taiwan Province of China, Malaysia, Mexico, and Brazil) (See Exhibit 9–3).[15] The estimated two-factor equations explain up to 63 percent of returns in individual markets, with explanatory power highest in some of the largest and most liquid markets (Malaysia, Mexico, Taiwan Province of China, and Thailand). Explanatory power is very low, however, and the model

---

15. Using an *F* test, the CAPM can be rejected with 95 percent confidence in seven markets (Brazil, Chile, Korea, Mexico, Malaysia, Taiwan Province of China, and Thailand) and with 90 percent confidence for India.

is rejected in markets that are either legally or practically closed to foreign investors (Colombia, India, and Venezuela). Argentina is an interesting exception where the equation has little explanatory power despite the presence of substantial foreign investment.[16] The coefficient on the developing country portfolio is statistically significant in eight markets.[17] The coefficient on the world portfolio is significant in 5 of the 13 markets.

Monthly data, which may be less affected by noise and better able to demonstrate longer term relationships, produce similar results. Two developing country equity markets are most sensitive to the world portfolio in monthly data (Korea and the Philippines) (See Exhibit 9–3). In monthly data, the CAPM can be rejected in favor of the two-factor model in eight markets. The CAPM is no longer rejected for India; however, the CAPM is rejected for the Philippines in monthly, but not weekly, data.

A perfect test of Equation (9.2) is impossible in that expected returns cannot be observed. The OLS results above use ex post realized returns as an estimate of ex ante expected returns on the assumption that ex post returns are equal to expected returns plus some forecast error:

$$r_{j,t} = E_{t-1}[r_{jt}] + \epsilon_t \qquad (9.3)$$

where ϵ_t is assumed to be independent and identically distributed (i.i.d.). An alternative approach is conditional or expectational estimation, as used in Harvey (1989, 1991) and Buckberg (1995), among others, which attempts to more closely capture ex ante expected returns by using an information set Z_{t-1} to calculate expected returns and then use these returns to estimate the expected moments of Equations (9.1) and (9.2). Generalized method of moment (GMM) conditional estimates (not shown here) were found to be weak with large standard errors and few significant coefficients. The weak coefficients may indicate that the model specification is inappropriate for the data or, more likely given the far stronger OLS results, that the instruments provide a poor estimate of expected returns.

---

16. Tests on a split sample (presented below) indicate that the rejection may be due to substantial structural change in the Argentine market's behavior. The CAPM model is rejected in favor of the two-factor model for 1992–95, but not for 1989–91.

17. The estimates of β_{em} may be biased upward somewhat because the return on market j, $r_{j,t}$, may have a significant weight in determining $r_{em,t}$.

EXHIBIT 9-3

Two-Factor Model for 13 Emerging Markets, Weekly and Monthly Data, 1989–95[1]

$$r_{j,t} = \alpha + \beta_w r_{w,t} + \beta_{em} r_{em,t} + u_t$$

Market	Weekly Data				Monthly Data			
	β_w (t-statistic)	β_{em} (t-statistic)	Adj. R²	$F_{1,305}$ (p-value)	β_w (t-statistic)	β_{em} (t-statistic)	Adj. R²	$F_{1,57}$ (p-value)
Argentina	-0.12 (0.29)	0.25 (0.80)	-0.003	0.84 (0.36)	-0.32 (0.38)	0.12 (0.18)	-0.028	0.03 (0.85)
Brazil	0.26 (0.86)	1.33 (5.49)	0.161	44.04 (—)	0.25 (0.43)	1.71 (3.95)	0.236	18.45 (—)
Chile	-0.08 (0.68)	0.30 (4.04)	0.043	14.97 (—)	-0.13 (0.50)	0.52 (3.59)	0.085	8.03 (0.01)
Colombia	-0.03 (0.30)	0.09 (0.87)	0.002	0.71 (0.40)	-0.22 (0.52)	0.05 (0.22)	-0.025	0.03 (0.86)
India	-0.19 (1.12)	0.18 (1.68)	0.004	2.70 (0.10)	-0.35 (1.17)	0.10 (0.48)	-0.012	0.22 (0.64)
Jordan	0.13 (1.84)	0.09 (0.95)	0.014	1.77 (0.18)	0.30 (1.41)	0.01 (0.11)	0.021	0.01 (0.92)
Korea	0.16 (1.25)	0.43 (5.43)	0.119	28.79 (—)	0.70 (3.07)	0.29 (2.63)	0.233	4.06 (0.05)

Continued

EXHIBIT 9-3 Continued

	Weekly Data				Monthly Data			
Market	β_w (t-statistic)	β_{em} (t-statistic)	Adj. R^2	$F_{1,305}$ (p-value)	β_w (t-statistic)	β_{em} (t-statistic)	Adj. R^2	$F_{1,67}$ (p-value)
Mexico	0.32 (2.44)	0.53 (4.48)	0.159	33.81 (—)	0.04 (0.18)	0.74 (3.96)	0.177	14.10 (—)
Malaysia	0.58 (6.41)	0.41 (5.10)	0.313	43.59 (—)	0.47 (2.98)	0.39 (4.17)	0.301	11.77 (—)
Philippines	0.02 (0.09)	0.63 (2.39)	—	1.65 (0.20)	0.73 (2.13)	0.49 (2.35)	0.224	6.77 (0.01)
Taiwan Province of China	−0.25 (2.25)	1.84 (17.19)	0.627	468.25 (—)	−0.19 (−0.85)	1.68 (8.87)	0.550	78.18 (—)
Thailand	0.31 (1.93)	0.65 (4.56)	0.204	49.40 (—)	0.38 (1.22)	0.38 (1.94)	0.095	4.05 (0.55)
Venezuela	−0.27 (1.11)	−0.01 (0.07)	0.007	0.01 (0.93)	−0.26 (0.58)	−0.44 (−1.31)	0.018	1.92 (0.17)

1. Linear regressions with heteroskedasticity-consistent errors. Estimates of constant terms are not shown. Returns are calculated in excess of the holding yield on a U.S. Treasury bill with one month to maturity. The emerging markets composite index and the indexes for each emerging market are from the IFC Emerging Markets Data Base (EMDB) global indexes. The world market is represented by the *Financial Times*–Actuaries (FT–A) World Index. Weekly data cover the period from December 31, 1988, to April 28, 1995; monthly data cover the period of January 1989 to April 1995.

Given the significant structural changes in developing country equity markets in recent years, including the significant increase in foreign and institutional investor participation, the one- and two-factor equations also are estimated over two subsamples of weekly data: January 1989 to December 1991, and January 1992 to April 1995. During the 1989–91 period, many developing countries imposed substantial restrictions on foreign investment in their stock markets, with 1991 being a significant turning point in a number of countries' regulations. The 1992–95 period reflected both liberalized foreign investment regimes and a significant increase in institutional investor participation in developing country stock markets. The increase in institutional investor involvement relates not only to improved market access but also to increased interest in the high yields offered by developing country equities due to the decline in interest rates and equity returns in the U.S. and other industrial countries.

The results indicate that the two-factor model is a more appropriate description of developing country asset pricing in the 1992–95 period, when foreign and institutional investors played a large role in these markets, than in the 1989–91 period or for the full sample. For 1992–95, the two factor model dominates the CAPM in 11 of 13 markets, where the exceptions are Colombia and Jordon, versus only 7 of 13 markets in the 1989–91 sample and 8 of 13 in the full sample (see Exhibit 9–4). In 12 markets, asset prices are more sensitive to other emerging markets than to the world portfolio in the 1992–95 period (versus nine for the full sample and seven in the 1989–91 sample.)[18] For Argentina, the Philippines, and Venezuela, the CAPM is rejected in favor of the two-factor model for 1992–95, although the CAPM is preferred over the full sample; in all three cases, β_{em} is higher in the 1992–95 tests and, for Argentina and the Philippines, β_w is also higher. These results suggest a significant structural change in developing country equity pricing following the large-scale entry of institutional investors, particularly an increased sensitivity of developing country markets to each other, consistent with portfolio allocation by asset class.

---

18. The exception is Jordan.

EXHIBIT 9-4

Two-Factor Model for 13 Emerging Markets. Weekly Data, 1989–91 and 1992–95[1]

$$r_{j,t} = \alpha + \beta_w r_{w,t} + \beta_{em} r_{em,t} + u_t$$

Market	January 1989–December 1991				January 1992–April 1995			
	β_w (t-statistic)	β_{em} (t-statistic)	Adj. R^2	$F_{1,150}$ (p-value)	β_w (t-statistic)	β_{em} (t-statistic)	Adj. R^2	$F_{1,152}$ (p-value)
Argentina	-0.36 (0.60)	-0.06 (0.13)	-0.010	-0.02 (0.89)	0.60 (1.80)	1.22 (5.08)	0.216	28.81 (0.00)
Brazil	0.48 (1.20)	0.91 (3.18)	0.111	12.09 (0.00)	-0.17 (0.44)	2.54 (8.93)	0.296	61.83 (0.00)
Chile	-0.03 (0.17)	0.17 (1.97)	0.009	2.97 (0.09)	-0.16 (0.78)	0.69 (5.02)	0.137	25.82 (0.00)
Colombia	-0.01 (0.08)	0.05 (0.47)	-0.012	0.17 (0.68)	-0.06 (0.24)	0.19 (0.68)	-0.008	0.81 (0.37)
India	0.04 (0.23)	-0.06 (0.51)	-0.011	0.32 (0.57)	-0.67 (1.71)	0.84 (3.79)	0.067	11.88 (0.00)
Jordan	0.22 (2.34)	0.11 (0.93)	0.035	1.59 (0.21)	-0.07 (0.65)	-0.01 (0.13)	0.011	0.01 (0.92)
Korea	0.26 (1.67)	0.31 (3.40)	0.132	10.36 (0.00)	-0.05 (0.20)	0.78 (5.13)	0.146	26.31 (0.00)

Continued

EXHIBIT 9–4 *Continued*

Market	January 1989–December 1991				January 1992–April 1995			
	β_w (t-statistic)	β_{em} (t-statistic)	Adj. R^2	$F_{1,150}$ (p-value)	β_w (t-statistic)	β_{em} (t-statistic)	Adj. R^2	$F_{1,152}$ (p-value)
Mexico	0.50 (4.70)	0.19 (2.16)	0.219	6.29 (0.01)	−0.01 (0.24)	1.52 (5.24)	0.292	59.00 (0.00)
Malaysia	0.61 (5.20)	0.34 (3.47)	0.380	22.36 (0.00)	0.50 (3.76)	0.61 (4.60)	0.239	25.13 (0.00)
Philippines	0.10 (0.28)	0.66 (1.88)	−0.001	0.66 (0.42)	−0.10 (0.53)	0.49 (2.94)	0.050	9.80 (0.00)
Taiwan Province of China	−0.37 (3.00)	2.15 (20.92)	0.820	627.43 (0.00)	−0.04 (0.17)	0.92 (5.53)	0.166	29.86 (0.00)
Thailand	0.61 (2.84)	0.53 (2.99)	0.253	19.33 (0.00)	−0.38 (1.97)	0.92 (5.24)	0.187	37.42 (0.00)
Venezuela	−0.43 (1.37)	0.22 (1.01)	0.037	1.64 (0.20)	0.22 (0.71)	0.65 (2.41)	0.043	6.47 (0.01)

1. Linear regressions with heteroskedasticity-consistent errors. The t-statistics appear in parentheses. Estimates of constant terms are not shown. Returns are calculated in excess of the holding yield on a U.S. Treasury bill with one month to maturity. The emerging markets composite index and the indexes for each emerging market are from the IFC Emerging Markets Data Base (EMDB) global indexes. The world market is represented by the *Financial Times*–Actuaries (FT–A) World Index. Weekly data cover the period of December 31, 1988, to April 28, 1995; monthly data cover the period of January 1989 to April 1995.

ASSET PRICING WITH REGIONAL PORTFOLIO ALLOCATION

The existence of region-specific developing country mutual funds also suggests that investors may be managing portfolios on a regional basis. The sharper and more sustained drop in Latin American stock markets after the Mexican devaluation, as compared to Asian markets, lends support to this observation. Similarly, Latin markets were substantially correlated in the months following the Mexican devaluation but were far less correlated with Asian markets. Perceived common macroeconomics characteristics across Asian and Latin American economies, respectively, support investors' tendencies to classify markets by region.

If investors made their portfolio allocation decisions by region and considered the relative returns among individual markets only as a second step, then returns in Latin American markets would be a function only of other Latin American markets and not of non-Latin markets; the same could be expected to hold among developing country equity markets in Asia. More specifically, returns in Argentina would be a function of their covariance with returns on a portfolio of Latin American equities, but they would not depend on their covariance with returns on a portfolio of developing Asian market equities. For Argentina β_{LatAm} would be statistically significant and β_{Asia} would be zero in the equation

$$r_{j,t} = \alpha + \beta_w r_{w,t} + \beta_{em} r_{em,t} + \beta_{Asia} r_{Asia,t} + \beta_{LatAm} r_{LatAm,t} + \epsilon \quad (9.4)$$

where $r_{\text{LatAm,t}}$ is the return on a Latin American portfolio (proxied by the IFC Global Latin American returns index) and $r_{\text{Asia,t}}$ is the return on an Asian portfolio (proxied by the IFC Global Asia returns index). β_{em} will reflect covariance with the emerging markets in Africa, Europe, and the Middle East that are included in the IFC Composite Index. In OLS estimates of Equation (9.4) for 13 markets over the period January 1989 to April 1995, the results are varied (See Exhibit 9–5).[19] The regional portfolio only has explanatory power for returns in Brazil, Chile. Malaysia, and the Taiwan Province of China. However, for Mexico and Korea, the IFC

---

19. The estimates of β_{em} and the regional betas may be biased upward somewhat because the return on market j, $r_{j,t}$, may have a significant weight in determining $r_{em,t}$ or the regional return.

EXHIBIT   9–5

Four-Factor Model for 13 Emerging Markets[1]

$$r_{j,t} = \alpha + \beta_w r_{w,t} + \beta_{em} r_{em,t} + \beta_{Asia} r_{Asia,t} + \beta_{LatAm} r_{LatAm,t} + u_t$$

Market	β_w (t-statistic)	β_{em} (t-statistic)	β_{Asia} (t-statistic)	β_{LatAm} (t-statistic)	Adj. R^2 (t-statistic)
			Weekly Data		
Argentina	−0.28 (−0.68)	1.12 (0.64)	−1.11 (0.92)	0.47 (0.81)	0.052
Brazil	−0.11 (−0.60)	−0.55 (0.61)	0.42 (0.61)	2.05 (10.22)	0.672
Chile	−0.14 (−1.26)	0.03 (0.09)	0.03 (0.10)	0.34 (3.05)	0.151
Colombia	−0.05 (−0.44)	1.26 (2.39)	−0.95 (2.30)	−0.22 (1.90)	0.007
India	−0.18 (1.01)	−0.51 (0.83)	0.57 (1.21)	0.10 (0.67)	−0.004
Jordan	0.15 (2.06)	0.48 (1.31)	−0.25 (0.99)	−0.18 (1.86)	−0.026
Korea	0.18 (1.49)	−0.87 (1.96)	1.07 (3.04)	0.21 (1.77)	0.149
Mexico	0.20 (1.70)	2.11 (3.12)	−1.53 (−2.97)	0.12 (0.79)	0.403
Malaysia	0.60 (6.39)	−0.61 (1.46)	0.85 (2.70)	0.15 (1.46)	0.341
Philippines	0.02 (0.05)	−1.03 (−0.76)	1.26 (1.11)	0.44 (0.83)	0.005
Taiwan Province of China	−0.14 (1.66)	0.38 (0.96)	1.42 (4.59)	−0.12 (1.32)	0.741
Thailand	0.33 (2.03)	0.28 (0.52)	0.34 (0.81)	— (0.02)	0.206
Venezuela	−0.31 (1.25)	1.38 (1.95)	−1.16 (1.18)	−0.19 (1.08)	0.012

1. Linear regressions with heteroskedasticity-consistent errors. Estimates of constant terms are not shown. Returns are calculated in excess of the holding yield on a U.S. Treasury bill with one month to maturity. The emerging markets composite index and the indexes for each emerging market are from the IFC–EMDB global indexes. The world market is represented by the FT–A World Index. All series are weekly from December 31, 1988, to April 28, 1995.

composite portfolio has explanatory power beyond the regional term; the Latin American portfolio return is not statistically significant in explaining Mexican returns, which would be consistent with the view that investors treat Mexican securities as a benchmark for other Latin American country securities.

Another reason that the CAPM might fail to describe asset pricing in developing country equity markets could relate to the fact that much of the foreign funds entering these markets are channeled through U.S.-based mutual funds and investment banks, and that the U.S. is a common destination for flight capital from many developing countries. It therefore seems plausible that returns in developing country equity markets could respond more to covariance with the U.S. portfolio than the world portfolio. However, tests of an expanded version of Equation (9.2) adding the returns on a U.S. and Canadian market portfolio, did not improve the explanation of return behavior in any of the 13 developing country stock markets tested.

CONCLUSION

This chapter proposes that portfolio allocation by asset class on the part of institutional investors can explain the very strong response of developing country stock markets to events in another developing country market, even when the events in the other country do not seem to affect economic fundamentals outside its own borders. A good example of such behavior, of course, was the widespread selling of developing country securities across the board in the immediate wake of the Mexican devaluation in December 1994. This chapter argues that this can be explained if institutional investors allocate their portfolios according to a two-step process—first determining what share of their portfolios to invest in developing country versus industrial country stock markets and then allocating their funds among developing country markets. To determine whether developing country stocks are priced as a function of other developing country stocks, rather than solely as a function of the world market portfolio, as assumed by the CAPM, this chapter presents a test of a two-factor pricing model. In the two-factor model, returns on the developing country market are evaluated as a function of returns on a broad emerging market portfolio and returns on the world portfolio.

The tests indicate that the two-factor model dominates the CAPM in most of the developing country markets studied. Over the full sample period of 1989–95, the CAPM is rejected in favor of the two-factor model for 8 of 13 markets. However, for the period 1992–95, when institutional investor involvement in developing country markets was greatest, the two-factor model dominates the CAPM far more strongly. Over 1992–95, the CAPM is rejected in favor of the two-factor model in 11 of the 13 markets studied, with Jordan and Colombia as the exceptions. The two-factor estimates also indicate that returns in developing country markets are more sensitive to changes in returns on the composite developing country stock portfolio than to the world portfolio in 12 of the 13 markets. The significant structural change suggests that the increased role of institutional investors in these markets has increased their sensitivity to each other—which is logical only if investors make investment decisions in developing country markets primarily by comparing the markets to each other, and not by comparing each market to the world portfolio.

REFERENCES

Aitken, Brian. "Impact of Institutional Investors' Trading on Developing Country Stock Prices." *IMF*, unpublished manuscript, 1995.

Aziz, Jahangir. "Market Participation and Asset Price Volatility." Paper presented at the North American Economics and Finance Association Annual Meetings, Washington, D.C., January 6–8, 1995.

Bekaert, Geert. "Market Integration and Investment Barriers in Emerging Equity Markets." *World Bank Economic Review*, January 1995, pp. 75–108.

Bekaert, Geert; and Campbell R. Harvey. "Emerging Equity Market Volatility." Standard University mimeo, April 9, 1995.

Bekaert, Geert; and Campbell R. Harvey. "Time-Varying World Market Integration." National Bureau of Economic Research Working Paper No. 4843, August 1994.

Bekaert, Geert; and Michael S. Urias. "Diversification, Integration and Emerging Market Closed-End Funds." National Bureau of Economic Research Working Paper No. 4990, January 1995.

Benartzi, Sholmo; and Richard Thaler. "Myopic Loss Aversion and the Equity Premium Puzzle." *Quarterly Journal of Economics*, February 1995, pp. 73–92.

Buckberg, Elaine. "Emerging Stock Markets and International Asset Pricing." *World Bank Economic Review*, January 1995, pp. 51–74.

De Bondt, Werner F. M.; and Richard H. Thaler. "Financial Decision-Making in Markets; and Firms: A Behavioral Perspective." National Bureau of Economic Research Working Paper No. 4777, June 1994.

The Economist. "Too Little, Not Too Much." *Economist*, June 24, pp. 72–73.

Hansen, Lars Peter; John Heaton; and Masao Ogaki. GMM programs for GAUSS. Funded by the National Science Foundation, 1992.

Harvey, Campbell R. "The World Price of Covariance Risk." *Journal of Finance*, March 1991, pp. 111–157.

Kahneman, Daniel; and Amos Tversky. "Prospect Theory: An Analysis of Decision Under Risk." *Econometrica*, March 1979, pp. 263–291.

Kramer, Charles; and R. Todd Smith. "Recent Turmoil in Emerging Markets and the Behavior of Country-Fund Discounts: Renewing the Puzzle of the Pricing of Closed-End Mutual Funds." IMF Working Paper WP/95/68, July 1995.

Lee, Charles M.; Andrei Schleifer; and Richard H. Thaler. "Investor Sentiment and the Closed-End Fund Puzzle." *Journal of Finance*, 1991, pp. 75–109.

Leibowitz, M. L.; and T. C. Langetieg. "Shortfall Risks and the Asset Allocation Decision: A Simulation Analysis of Stock and Bond Risk Profiles." Salomon Brothers Research Department, January 1989.

10

RECENT DEVELOPMENTS IN PRICING DERIVATIVE ASSETS

Stewart Hodges, Michael Selby, Les Clewlow, Chris Strickland, and Xinzhong G. Xu, *Financial Options Research Centre*

INTRODUCTION

It is now twenty years since Black and Scholes (1972) presented an empirical test of their option pricing formula within the context of determining the efficiency of the pre-Chicago Board of Exchange (CBOE) options market. In that paper they state "we hope to establish the empirical validity of our model as a forerunner to more complicated models of other option forms." As every reader will know, the degree of their success was almost unprecedented in the field of finance. There is no need for us to recount the speed and variety of much subsequent work: the explosion of theoretical work including the binomial model, leading to general notions of risk neutral valuation alongside the innovation of new financial products (financial engineering) featuring derivatives on interest rates and foreign exchange (FX) as well as on equities.[1] In this chapter we survey what we regard as the most striking developments in this area over the last 12 months or so.[2]

Significantly, most of the topics we see as of current research importance were flagged within the early Black–Scholes paper. The relaxation of the important assumptions of a constant term-structure of interest rates and constant instantaneous volatility of returns has led to important areas not explicitly addressed during the 1970s and not really considered until the last five years. These developments have been motivated both by the implications of empirical studies and by the growing variety of risk-management instruments, initiated in part by the swaps market. This relaxation of the original Black–Scholes assumptions has been continued with regard to transactions costs—an area that has brought financial economists in closer contact with stochastic optimal control theorists, whose tools of stochastic and semi-martingale calculus had been used by financial economists since the original contributions of Black and Scholes (1973) and Merton (1973), among others. Finally, from a period in which valuation formulas were developed from strong assumptions of the (exogenously defined) stochastic processes for the underlying asset prices, we now are seeing much more emphasis on the idea of 'consistency with equilibrium' as an additional constraint to the usual 'no-arbitrage' one.

---

1. The definition of a derivative security does not seem to be generally agreed upon. Merton (1990), on pages 10 and 429, defines derivative securities to be "securities with contractual payoff structures that are contingent on the prices of one or more traded securities." In this chapter, we shall be less specific and interchangeably use contingent claim contracts with derivative securities. One reason for this is that most, if not all, of the technology that we use for pricing a security is actually independent of whether the underlying source of value is a traded asset. Of course, when the underlying asset is a traded asset, we are able to obtain the (desired) required prices without making explicit assumptions about tastes and preferences. However, a very large part of today's options markets, for example interest related securities, do not meet the requirement that the underlying asset be tradable. Practitioners, however, refer to interest-rate based options as interest-rate derivatives. It seems preferable to use a language that will be understood explicitly by both academics and practitioners.

2. This is now an extremely large field, which continues to grow rapidly. Our selection is necessarily a subjective one that in part reflects our own research priorities.

The focus of our chapter is on the areas we have just described: We believe these to have been the most exciting so far and believe they will continue to be so for the foreseeable future.

The chapter is organized as follows: In the next section we review developments in models for interest rate derivatives, including the role of volatility in the term structure. The second section reviews other recent work on stochastic volatility in option pricing. The third section describes work on option valuation when there are transactions costs involved in trading the underlying asset. The fourth section describes equilibrium issues related to option pricing. Finally, we comment briefly on other important topics which lack of space prevents us from covering in more detail.

INTEREST RATE DERIVATIVES

In this section we survey alternative models for pricing interest rate derivative securities and also look at the relationship between the volatility of interest rates and the shape of the term structure.

Early Models

During the late 1970s and the early 1980s models for interest rate derivatives were based on models developed to explain the term structure of interest rates.

The earliest models (e.g., Vasicek [1977]) started from an assumed process for the short-term interest rate and an assumed form for the price of interest rate risk. They also used the now conventional no-arbitrage condition to solve for the form and process of the entire term structure. Cox, Ingersoll, and Ross (CIR) (1985) pointed out the inherent dangers in closing such models by assuming a specific functional form for the risk premium and developed their term structure model from an intertemporal general equilibrium asset pricing model. Both models can be characterized by their assumptions about the short-term interest rate, which is assumed to be the single source of uncertainty:

$$dr(t) = \kappa(\theta - r(t))dt + \sigma(r)dz \qquad (10.1)$$

where $r(t)$ is the short rate, at time t, and dz is a Wiener process. The instantaneous drift represents the process as mean-reverting.

In the Vasicek paper, the short rate is assumed to follow the Ornstein–Uhlenbeck diffusion process with the volatility of the process $\sigma(r)$ set equal to a constant σ. In the CIR paper, the volatility of the short rate increases with the square root of the rate itself.

Although this approach to pricing interest rate derivatives has the important advantage that all derivatives are valued on a common basis (i.e., it is a whole term structure approach), it has the severe disadvantage that the term structures provide a limited family that does not correctly price many traded bonds.

By valuing interest rate derivatives with reference to a theoretical yield curve rather than the actually observed curve, equilibrium models produce contingent claims prices that disregard key market information affecting the valuation of any interest rate derivative security. The most obvious market data that could be used to price interest rate derivatives are the term structure of interest rates and the term structure of interest rate volatilities. Many models currently appearing in the literature are what we term "whole term structure models," and an underlying motivation for the models has been to provide a unifying framework; unifying in both the sense of using as much market data as possible from which to build the models and in trying to price and hedge the whole range of interest rate dependent securities.

Models That Fit an Initial Term Structure

Ho and Lee (HL) (1986) were the first authors to build a model that set out to model the dynamics of the entire term structure in a way that was automatically consistent with the initial (observed) term structure of interest rates. In much the same way that the Black–Scholes model, for pricing options on stocks, can be inverted to obtain the implied volatility of stock prices consistent with the option price, Ho and Lee reasoned that the same principle could be applied to the pricing of bonds. The Ho and Lee model is developed in the form of a binomial tree relating future movements of the yield curve explicitly to its initial state. The authors estimate the parameters of the discrete time binomial process including the risk neutral probability. Unfortunately, for large step sizes, the parameters are not independent, making estimation problematic (see Heath, Jarrow, and Morton [1990b]). Although the authors do not discuss the issue of convergence, a number of other authors (e.g., Dybvig [1988c] and Jamshidian [1988]) show that the continuous time limit can be characterized by the short rate process:

$$dr(t) = \theta(t)dt + \sigma dz \qquad (10.2)$$

where $\theta(t)$, the drift during the short time interval dt, is a function of time in order to make the model consistent with the initial term structure of interest rates. This model attracted a great deal of attention: practitioners in particular liked being able to fit any term structure exactly as well as the binomial form of the model. Another advantage was that the valuations are preference independent. However, there were some severe drawbacks, too. As can be seen from Equation (10.2), the model describes the whole volatility structure by a single parameter σ, implying that spot rates and forward rates that differ in their maturity are all equally variable, all future spot rates are normally distributed, and all possible yield curves at a future time are parallel to each other. A further difficulty of the model is that it incorporates no mean reversion and, as a result, there is a high probability that future interest rates will become negative. Subsequent work in this area has therefore aimed to keep the advantages of the Ho and Lee approach while eliminating these kinds of problems.[3]

Black, Derman, and Toy (1990) have developed a model to match the observed term structure of spot interest rate volatilities as well as the term structure of interest rates that is currently popular. As with Ho and Lee, the model developed describes the evolution of the entire term structure in a discrete-time binomial lattice framework. The continuous time limit of the model is given by the stochastic differential equation:

$$d \log r(t) = \left[\theta(t) - \frac{\sigma'(t)}{\sigma(t)} \log r(t) \right] dt + \sigma(t) dz \qquad (10.3)$$

---

3. Regretfully, for the purposes of this chapter, we have no space to comment on the analyses of Black and Karasinski (1991), Jamshidian (1989, 1991a, 1991b), and Turnbull and Melino (1991).

This model incorporates two functions of time; the first, $\theta(t)$, is chosen so that the model fits the term structure of spot interest rates, and the second, $\theta(t)$, is chosen so that it fits the term structure of spot rate volatilities. In this model, changes in the short rate are lognormally distributed, with the advantage being that interest rates cannot become negative. Once $\theta(t)$ and $\sigma(t)$ are chosen, the future short rate volatility is entirely determined, and an unfortunate consequence of the model is that, for certain specifications of the volatility function $\sigma(t)$, the short rate can be mean-fleeing rather than mean-reverting. Unfortunately, analytic solutions are not available for the prices of bonds or the prices of bond options.

Heath, Jarrow, and Morton (HJM) (1990a, 1990b, and 1992) sought to construct a family of continuous time stochastic processes for the term structure, consistent with the observed initial term structure data. In order to model the dynamics of the term structure, we can choose between equivalent formulations in terms of bond prices, short-term interest rates, or forward rates. HJM chose to model forward instantaneous interest rates, due to volatility considerations concerned with the maturity of zero coupon bonds, and so they take as given the initial forward rate curve.

The forward rate curve's dynamics are exogenously given by the equation:

$$f(t,T) = f(0,T) + \int_0^t \alpha\,(v,\,T,\,\omega)dv + \sum_{i=1}^n \int_0^t \sigma_i(v,\,T,\,\omega)dW_i(v)$$

(10.4)

where $f(0,T)$ is a fixed initial forward rate curve; $\alpha\,(v,T,\omega)$ is the instantaneous forward rate's drift, with ω signifying an arbitrary path of the evolution of interest rates; σ_i are the volatilities of the forward rates; and W_i denotes the ith Weiner process (for $i = 1$, . . . , n).

Equation (10.4) is expressed in its most general form, with n independent Brownian motions determining the stochastic fluctuation of the forward rate curve. HJM (1992) show that prices of pure discount bonds satisfy a stochastic differential equation that states that the instantaneous return on the T-th maturity bond has a drift rate equal to the spot rate plus a term premium that is a function of the forward rate's drift and volatility and volatilities that are also a function of the forward rate volatilities. It can be shown that the HJM model is consistent with bond prices converging to par at maturity and the behavior of the instantaneous rate. By applying the insights of Harrison and Kreps (1979), the process is shown to be arbitrage-free, and contingent claim values are obtained via an application of Harrison and Pliska (1981).

The HJM paper highlights two examples which aid the reader's understanding of the model's practical applications. The first is the single factor, continuous time limit of HL, which leads to a modified Black–Scholes formula for the value of a European bond option, with the second example involving two sources of randomness also leading to a closed-form solution.

Motivated by practical considerations and the desire to value all interest rate contingent claims on a consistent basis, while retaining the ability for the model to provide a perfect fit to observed market data, Hull and White (HW) (1990) derived two one-state variable models for the short rate. HW sought to reconcile the tractability of the Vasicek and CIR models with the consistency of a model that fits the initial yield curve. Their proposed models can be seen, and are presented as, extensions of the Vasicek and Cox–Ingersoll–Ross models due to the similarity of the nature of the short-rate processes to those presented in the original papers:

$$dr = [\theta(t) - \phi(t)r]dt + \sigma(t)dz \qquad (10.5)$$

$$dr = [\theta(t) - \phi(t)r]dt + \sigma(t)\sqrt{r}dz \qquad (10.6)$$

Hull and White propose that the three functions of time, $\theta(t)$, $\phi(t)$ and $\sigma(t)$, are chosen so that the models, determined by Equations (10.5) and (10.6), fit the initial term structure of interest rates, the term structure of spot rate volatilities, and the anticipated variability across time of the instantaneous spot rate. The first model leads to normally distributed interest rates and lognormally distributed bond prices, with the resulting disadvantage that interest rates can become negative. The model leads to analytical solutions for European option prices. The second model eliminates the possibility of negative interest rates but is not as analytically tractable as the first, Jamshidian (1990) independently analyzed the general Gaussian model, highlighting the important role played by the variance structure of the model.

The Variance of Rates and the Term Structure

Attractive though the class of models just described may be, they are not without their dangers. At any date we must estimate functions for the term structure of interest rates, the term structure of volatility, and the time path of volatility. However, just as with implied volatility in a conventional options model, when we look at market prices at a later date, there is no guarantee that they will be consistent with the previously estimated functions. In particular, choosing volatility functions to some extent independently of fitting to the term structure of interest rates poses the danger that we may ignore the information that the shape of the term structure contains about the anticipated volatility of interest rates. Convexity considerations or other more formal analysis lead very easily to relationships between the concavity of spot rates with respect to maturity and the prospective volatility of interest rates.

The relationship between the shape of the yield curve and interest rate volatility has been studied empirically by Brown and Dybvig (BD) (1986), Litterman, Scheinkman, and Weiss (LSW) (1991), and, theoretically, by Brown and Schaefer (BS) (1991).

BD's principal motivation was to test the single factor CIR model of the term structure. They discovered that an implied volatility of the short-term rate could be identified from the fitted term structure at any date, and they demonstrated that this seemed to have some predictive power, even though the single factor model is misspecified. LSW find that a measure of volatility obtained from the yield curve, as a linear function of pure discount bond yields, explains nearly 70 percent of the variation in the volatility implied from the prices of options on Treasury bond futures. Prompted by this seemingly robust feature of the relationship between the shape of the term structure and the level of interest rate volatility, BS develop a relatively simple relation between the forward interest rate curve, the level of interest rate volatility, and the level of bond price volatility, or duration, for a general class of equilibrium type models which they refer to as the "affine yield class." This class includes both the Vasicek and CIR models.

Longstaff and Schwartz (1991) develop a remarkable two-factor model of the term structure of interest rates drawing upon the same general equilibrium framework as CIR (1985). The choice of the model's two factors, the short rate and the volatility of the short rate—both of which are observable and intuitively appealing—allow contingent claim prices to reflect both the current level of interest rates and the current level of interest rate volatility. The authors obtain closed-form solutions for the prices of pure discount bonds and options on pure discount bonds in this two-factor setting (a strong attraction of the model), but for other more complex applications, numerical solutions are required. The two factors allow a richer variety of possible yield curves than the one-factor equilibrium models discussed earlier, but generally will be inconsistent with an observed initial curve. Although a model based on the two factors of the short-term interest rate and its instantaneous volatility is a most exciting step forward, their joint processes were necessarily chosen for their analytical tractability rather than their empirical realism. A more natural formulation is provided by Fong and Vasicek (1991, 1992), which gives rise to solutions involving special functions. We look forward to further work in this area.

STOCHASTIC VOLATILITY

Motivation

Ever since the early empirical work of Black and Scholes (1972), it has been evident that volatility is a central problem in option pricing. That early study found that historical measures of volatility give rise to an errors-in-variables problem. By now there is massive evidence that, for most asset processes, we have distributions with fat tails, due in part at least to the volatility changing through time. Option prices, too, exhibit related effects of implied volatilities that vary through time and non-linear exercise price ('smile') effects of higher implied volatilities for in- or out-of-the-money options. (See, for example, Shastri and Wethyavivorn [1987].)

This has provided a clear motivation for the development of option pricing models for asset processes where the volatility itself is stochastic. Since options effectively enable the volatility to be traded, it is also unsurprising that we have simultaneously seen considerable new work on modeling and forecasting asset volatility. Autoregressive Conditional Heteroskedasticity (ARCH) models, especially their generalizations to Generalized ARCH (GARCH) and Exponential GARCH (EGARCH) have become standard tools of analysis in this field. We refer the reader to the special journal issues edited by Campbell and Melino (1990) and by Engle and Rothschild (1992).

The natural way to develop option pricing models under stochastic volatility is to write down diffusion equations for the joint process of the underlying asset and its volatility and use some kind of numerical technique to integrate (or simulate) the required solutions. The early papers by Hull and White (1987), Johnson and Shanno (1987), Scott (1987), and Wiggins (1987) all make use of this, along with the idea that option prices could be computed if the risk premium for the volatility could be identified. The difficulty is to find functional forms for the processes that combine a degree of realism with reasonably simple calculations for option values. There is also a tension between this approach and ARCH models for which there is no clear correspondence to diffusion equations (see Nelson [1990]).

Recent Models

This is an awkward literature to survey. There are now quite a few different approaches, none of which seems as yet to dominate the others or to provide quite the ideal solution. Exhibit 10–1 provides a summary of recent models of which we are aware. All of these models enable volatility to command a risk premium. The models differ in whether changes in volatility can be correlated with asset returns, in the computational approach, and on the plausibility of the process for the volatility.

Duan (1991) provides a model for a GARCH process. He assumes Hyperbolic Absolute Risk Aversion (HARA) utility in order to obtain a risk neutral valuation relationship and uses simulation to compute numerical values from the model. Hull and White (1988) extend their earlier work to allow the volatility to be instantaneously

EXHIBIT 10-1

Summary of Stochastic Volatility Models

Authors	Correlation	Solution Technique
Duan (1991)	n/a	Monte Carlo simulation
Hull and White (1988)	Nonzero	Series solution
Madan and Seneta (1990)	Zero	Approximate formula or Single integration
Scott (1992)	Nonzero	Single integration
Stein and Stein (1991)	Zero	Double integration

correlated with the security price. They assume a square root process for the variance. Madan and Seneta (1990) propose a model of a continuous-time pure jump process that provides the variance with a gamma distribution, and the resulting compound distribution enables high levels of kurtosis to be generated.

Stein and Stein (1991) assume a mean-reverting arithmetic process for the volatility. They are able to derive a quasi-closed form formula for the probability distribution of the security by using Fourier inversion of the characteristic function. Option values are computed by integrating the stock price distribution numerically. This model specification suffers two drawbacks. First, it is possible for negative volatility to occur, and second, it assumes that the correlation between stock returns and volatility is zero.

Scott (1992) also uses a square root process for the variance in a model that also includes stochastic interest rates. There are no restrictions on the correlation between the stock return and volatility and between the interest rates and volatility. A quasi-closed form solution for prices of index options has been derived also by using the Fourier inversion formula for probability distribution functions. To value options, only univariate numerical integration is needed.

Empirical Work

Recent empirical studies have tended to work with equity index options (e.g., Heynen, Kemna, and Vorst [1991], Hull and White [1987, 1988], and Scott [1992]) or currency options (Chesney and Scott [1989] and Melino and Turnbull [1990]). The general conclusions from these studies are that equity returns and volatility are negatively correlated, and that stochastic volatility models price options more accurately than the alternative simpler models. The risk premium on volatility risk is generally hard to estimate, though Melino and Turnbull have found that it has a significant effect on the option prices. It does not seem to be known whether these models enable more accurate hedging to be undertaken.

A New Approach

An entirely new approach to volatility hedging and pricing has recently been described by Dupire (1992). The aim is to develop continuous-time no-arbitrage pricing with stochastic volatility, without the need to specify any volatility risk premium. It does this by working with conditions for the evolution of option prices to preclude arbitrage, in a way that is entirely parallel to the Ho and Lee approach to term structure modeling. A key assumption is that a continuum of options in exercise price and time to maturity are traded and are priced consistent with no arbitrage within the continuum. All that we require in reality is that those options that are traded are priced consistent with the continuum. Since the variance can be traded, it will not command a risk premium and we can assume the drift is the risk-neutral drift (which Dupire shows how to compute). Option prices can then be computed as the discounted risk-neutral expectation of the payoff.

TRANSACTION COSTS
Early Work

The construction of hedging strategies that best replicate the outcomes from options (and other contingent claims) in the presence of transactions costs is an important problem that has seen significant recent advances. Delta hedging is central to the theory of option pricing. Arbitrage valuation models, such as that of Black and Scholes (1973), depend on the idea that an option can be perfectly hedged using the underlying asset, thus making it possible to create a portfolio that replicates the option exactly. Hedging also is widely used to reduce risk, and the kind of delta hedging strategies implicit in Black and Scholes are commonly applied, at least approximately, by participants in options markets. Optimal hedging strategies are therefore of direct practical interest. Much of the theory of options assumes that markets are frictionless. The analysis of delta-hedging strategies under transactions costs also provides more general insight into the valuation issues that arise where the nature of the market dictates that trading is discontinuous, or where the asset processes are such that the market is incomplete and contingent claims are not spanned by existing securities.

The first paper to consider the problem of replicating options' payoffs using delta hedging under transactions costs was Leland (1985). The issue is particularly interesting because the usual Black–Scholes strategy, implemented as rebalancings at discrete intervals, tends to an infinite quantity of expected transactions as the frequency of rebalancings is increased.[4] Leland's analysis is set in a continuous-time framework and assumes proportional transactions costs. It describes how, by making an adjustment to the variance (depending on the exogeneously specified revision frequency), the Black–Scholes formula can be used to hedge with a zero-expected replication error and with a standard deviation that tends to zero with the length of the rebalancing interval. Neuhaus (1989) contributes some further insight to this approach. However, this method is in no sense an optimal one. It is worth explaining briefly the intuition behind the variance adjustment. The seller of an option (either a call or a put), hedging risk by delta-hedging, is forced to buy stock whenever the stock price has increased and, conversely, sell it whenever it has fallen. The spread on trading the stock makes it as if the stock movement was greater than its actual movement, leading to a need to increase the volatility used for valuation and hedging. On the other hand, someone delta-hedging a long option position has the opposite experience and must make a downward adjustment to the volatility.

---

4. It is well known that with discrete rabalancings at equal time intervals, the expected transactions turnover is proportional to the square root of the number of rebalancings.

Discrete-time Formulations

Recent contributions to the transactions costs literature may be conveniently classified according to whether the analysis is set in a discrete or continuous-time framework and whether or not it involves a utility function. Merton (1990) provides a single period working of exact replication of an option under proportional transactions costs in a binomial tree. Boyle and Vorst (1992) have extended this in an elegant way to many periods in what amounts to a reworking of Leland's analysis in a discrete binomial tree. Interestingly, they obtain a variance adjustment that differs from Leland's by a factor of $\sqrt{\frac{2}{\pi}}$: This is essentially because, although the binomial tree provides the same variance of return as the continuous process which it approximates, it distorts the expected absolute change over any small time interval.

Edirisinghe, Naik, and Uppal (1991) develop replication approaches based on both linear programming and dynamic programming. In their analysis, they minimize the initial cost of obtaining a terminal payoff at least as large as that from the option being hedged. They show that allowing a cash surplus in some states of the world can significantly reduce the replication cost compared to the "exact replication" of Boyle and Vorst, particularly when transactions costs are high. Another advantage of this approach is that the model is also applicable to contingent claims whose payoff is nonconvex.

Portfolio Selection with Transaction Costs

The continuous-time literature on replication under transactions costs represents the outcome of extensions to Merton's (1971) work on portfolios that maximize expected utility over an infinite horizon. Constantinides (1986) and Magill and Constantinides (1976) were the first papers to consider this problem under transactions costs, albeit in a heuristic manner. Important control theory formulations and solutions were subsequently derived in the papers by Davis (1988), Davis and Norman (1990), Eastham and Hastings (1988), Taksar, Klass and Assaf (1988), and Dumas and Luciano (1991). The papers by Davis show rigorously that, whereas in Merton's world without frictions the ratio of risky to safe assets is managed to remain constant, under proportional transactions costs it should be managed to remain between a pair of constants (which bracket the constant for the zero-cost case). The pair of constants define a *no-transaction* region: Transactions are undertaken only to return to the region when the portfolio strays outside it. While these papers are concerned with optimal policies, they are not directly concerned with the problems of replicating (or similarly hedging) contingent claims by means of the underlying asset.

Continuous-Time Option Valuation Under Costs

A continuous-time formulation for option valuation under transactions costs was first developed by Hodges and Neuberger (1989). The mathematical analysis has been treated in a more rigorous fashion by Davis and Panas (1991) and by Davis, Panas, and Zariphopoulou (1992), and further work also has been presented in Hodges and Clewlow (1992). The approach is a preference-dependent one, using optimal control theory techniques to maximize the expected utility of the delta-hedged option payoff.

For numerical tractability, an exponential utility function is used, as this reduces the number of state variables to two. For a highly risk-averse parameter value, this gives very tight replication similar to the dominance criteria of Edirisinghe, Naik, and Uppal, with correspondingly widely set reservation prices for buying or selling the option. For low risk aversion, the replication is much looser, with reservation prices that are closer together and tend to the Black–Scholes value for the limiting risk-neutral case. The solutions exhibit properties of both Leland's variance adjustment and also the *no-transaction* region of the continuous-time portfolio selection papers. Only with a fixed-cost component as well as (or instead of) a variable one would it be appropriate to jump into the interior of the control region for delta (which is now a function of both the asset price and time). Both the width and shape of the control region for delta depend on whether a short or long options position is being hedged. As in Leland's analysis, short options imply a flattening of delta as a function of the underlying and long options positions imply the converse. The technique can handle portfolios of options without any requirement for monotonicity in the payoff profile.

GENERAL EQUILIBRIUM AND CONTINGENT CLAIMS

A major strength of the option theory initiated by Black and Scholes, and by Merton, is that, because it is a relative pricing theory, when dynamic spanning can be implemented, the value of a derivative security can be obtained on the basis of "no-arbitrage" and, therefore, a full equilibrium analysis is unnecessary.

The full power and elegance of this approach was developed by Cox and Ross (1976), Harrison and Kreps (1979), and Harrison and Pliska (1981). A key feature of these papers is that the securities markets are what we now term 'dynamically complete' (see, for example, Duffie and Huang [1985]). Further, they all assume that prices are consistent with equilibrium. Indeed, Harrison and Kreps introduce the term "viable" to refer to this consistency and undertake a considerable analysis focusing on the properties of viability. It should, therefore, not be surprising that there is a significant and important linkage between derivative securities pricing and general equilibrium analysis. However, until the last few years, the explicit consistency and role of equilibrium has been relegated in importance because of the power of the "no-arbitrage" approach to pricing.

The "no-arbitrage" approach to securities pricing relies heavily upon the "consistency with equilibrium" assumption. The pitfalls in this area were explicitly discussed by Cox, Ingersoll, and Ross (1985), as we already have mentioned. However, until quite recently very little explicit work had been undertaken to address the question "Can a general equilibrium model be constructed in which a given stochastic behavior of prices will result from more primitive assumptions on agents' preferences, endowments, information structures, and beliefs?" (Bick [1987], p. 259).

The importance of understanding the exact nature of equilibrium depends critically on the context. The pricing of an option via the Harrison and Pliska paradigm will give the correct value and hedging information for that derivative security. It is not usually necessary to understand the nature of equilibrium risk premia in order to price and hedge options or minimize risks. On the other hand, information about equilibrium expected returns is essential for efficient investment decisions. The use of derivative securities for implementing dynamic asset allocation schemes of a variety of types is becoming a day-to-day activity for many fund managers in the United States and elsewhere.

Investment decisions clearly depend simultaneously both on preferences and on risks and expected rates of return. Recent work has highlighted the simplifications that occur when markets are dynamically complete. Dybvig (1988a) has shown how the opportunity to synthesize Arrow-Debreu pure securities (using options or dynamic replication) enables multiperiod problems to be reduced to single period ones, and that, with the assumption of state-independent utility maximization (or something slightly weaker), a pricing model for probability distributions can be obtained. Under such assumptions there are also strong implications for portfolio management. Dybvig (1988b) shows that a necessary condition for efficient portfolio management is that wealth at future dates should be monotonic decreasing in the state-price density function, and he provides a quantification of the losses from path dependent strategies [5] that violate this condition.

The characterization of a market equilibrium is a topic of continuing fundamental importance in financial economics. Papers by Bick (1987, 1990), He and Leland (1991), Hodges and Carverhill (1992), and Stapleton and Subrahmanyam (1990) advance our knowledge of the nature of general equilibria that are consistent with Black–Scholes option valuation.

The issue is motivated by three aspects. First, in option pricing, the dynamics for the underlying asset are generally taken as a "primitive assumption," rather than being derived endogenously within the model. Second, because so much of option pricing has essentially concerned itself with relative valuation (with information concerning tastes and preferences embedded within the price of the underlying assets), it was not possible to identify assumptions that would give rise to a general diffusion process. Third, the dynamics of the market portfolio and the behavior of its risk premium are of particular interest.

Bick (1987) and Stapleton and Subrahmanyam (1990) derive necessary conditions for the process of a market index asset to describe a Geometric Brownian Motion and show (perhaps unsurprisingly) that this involves a representative agent with constant proportional risk aversion (CPRA) utility. Bick (1990)

---

5. Cox and Leland (1982) seem to have been the first to comment on the relationship between path independence and portfolio efficiency.

considers the relationship between more general diffusion processes and the possible utility functions of the representative agent. He provides both necessary and sufficient conditions for viability and demonstrates that, not only is the set of viable diffusions very restricted, but quite common stochastic processes, such as the Ornstein-Uhlenbeck (that is used in the Vasicek term-structure of interest rates model), are not consistent with equilibrium if applied to the market portfolio. This line of inquiry has been extended in the work of Hodges and Carverhill (1992) and He and Leland (1991), which derives necessary conditions for the market risk premium in general equilibrium economies that support Black–Scholes option pricing.

This work begins to shed new light on the growing literature that suggests that equity market returns are to some extent predictable (see, for example, Poterba and Summers [1988] and Fama and French [1988]). Apparent observed mean reversion could be explained by consistently time-varying equilibrium risk premia, and in order to test whether this applies to the markets that we observe, we must first be able to characterize what kinds of variation in risk premia are consistent with a general equilibrium model.

OTHER AREAS OF RESEARCH

Before concluding, we shall briefly comment on some of the many topics that we have been unable to discuss in detail. There are various reasons for the omissions.

First, some topics, such as the valuation of American style and exotic options (such as average-rate or look-backs) are, in our opinion, a continuation of the original Black–Scholes/Merton work. Also, for these in particular, there are already excellent up-to-date surveys by Myneni (1992) and Rubinstein (1991). Further, much of the work represents the presentation of standard approaches in various areas in applied mathematics, such as variational inequalities, in order to give alternative characterizations of the finance problems. Although this often gives a numerical analytical approach new to the finance literature, there do not appear to be any significant financial economic insights. Frequently, the "discussions" are very mathematical. Indeed, many of the articles are being written by mathematicians/probabilists and are being published in mathematics/probability journals. In fact, we express some concern over this direction, as frequently this work increases the divide between academia and the practitioners.

Second, the focus of this chapter has been on traded instruments. We, therefore, feel that this is not the appropriate place to discuss the growing interest in the value of real options. This is an area that has received an impetus over the last two or three years due to the interest of mainstream economists such as Pindyck (1991) and Dixit (1992) and includes a recent interesting (and important) paper by Ingersoll and Ross (1992) on project valuation with interest rate uncertainty within a Cox, Ingersoll, and Ross framework. One key aspect of much of the work in this area is to recognize the value of the embedded options, particularly with respect to the option to invest now or delay.

There still seems to be a dearth of good and innovative empirical work in the area. Econometric analysis in the field of derivative securities is particularly difficult because of the joint hypotheses relating to the validity of the derivative pricing model and the derivative and underlying asset price processes. The other vital point, which also has led to some strange results, is the need for simultaneous observation of the underlying and derivative prices. Harvey and Whaley (1991, 1992) point out that this can easily lead to inconsistent results. However, it also is encouraging to see papers such as those by Longstaff (1990) and Bates (1991), which develop theoretical models designed to explain securities prices and then test them in a traditional way. We cannot leave empirical work without commenting on the many papers based on the use of ARCH and its generalizations for examining prices and volatility. Although there are tensions between tractability for option modeling and for econometric estimation, it is important that mainstream econometricians now are bringing their knowledge and experience to bear, and this augurs well for the future.

Although Black and Scholes motived their formula by corporate liability valuation, until recently there were relatively few signs of interest in this area. However, possibly motivated by developments in the swaps markets, there is renewed interest in the valuation of "risky" corporate securities and financial products where the option to default now is being explicitly recognized. Cooper and Mello (1991) is a good example. The original Black and Scholes (1973) paper held out high hopes in this sort of area: "Since almost all corporate liabilities can be viewed as combinations of options, the formula and the analysis that led to it are also applicable to corporate liabilities such as common stock, corporate bonds, and warrants." The hopes of pricing credit risk in an options framework have not really been fulfilled. The option theoretic approach generally predicts significantly smaller credit premia than actually observed. Authors such as Ramaswamy and Sundaresan (1986), Babbs (1991), and Jarrow and Turnbull (1990) have to assume some premium expected return on risky debt securities emanating from an unstated imperfection in markets (which seems to admit arbitrage). While a number of plausible reasons for such imperfections can be stated, they should be encompassed within a more complete theory.

Finally, we have commented neither on contract design nor market microstructure. Although they are key areas for practitioners and have received some academic attention, we feel that the problems are so difficult that the insights from existing analyses are very limited. For example, we know very little about what makes some contracts more liquid than others, or the affect of different market structures (e.g., different forms of screen-based trading or open-outcry). We think that, over the next five years, both of these areas will develop and the embedded options for market makers will have to be analyzed.

CONCLUSIONS

This chapter has reviewed recent developments in modeling derivative securities. In particular, we have focused on developments in:

- "Whole term structure models" for valuing interest rate derivatives.
- Models of stochastic volatility in pricing and hedging other kinds of options.
- Valuing options when transactions costs affect trading in the underlying asset.
- The role of general equilibrium analysis in the field of contingent claims.

Brief mention is made of some other topics in the options literature. It is noteworthy that work on options has directed major new resources at the problems of understanding the nature of the stochastic processes for underlying security market assets, both through the key focus on volatility and asset distributions and through the new insights contingent claims theory provides into market equilibrium. In this sense, we believe that the derivative securities area has, within the last year or two, come full circle in feeding back into those parts of the finance literature from which it came.

REFERENCES

Babbs, S. "Interest Rate Swaps and Default-Free Bonds: A Joint Term Structure Model." FORC Preprint 91/27, December 1991.

Bates, D. S. "The Crash of '87: Was it Expected? The Evidence from Options Markets." *Journal of Finance* 46, no. 3 (1991), pp. 1009–1045.

Bick, A. "On the Consistency of the Black–Scholes Model with a General Equilibrium Framework." *Journal of Financial and Quantitative Analysis* 22, no. 3 (1987), pp. 259–275.

Bick, A. "On Viable Diffusion Price Processes of the Market Portfolio." *Journal of Finance* 45, no. 2 (1990), pp. 673–689.

Black, F.; E. Derman; and W. Toy. "A One-Factor Model of Interest Rates and Its Application to Treasury Bond Options." *Financial Analysts Journal*, January–February, 1990, pp. 33–39.

Black, F.; and P. Karasinski. "Bond and Option Pricing when Short Rates Are Lognormal." *Financial Analysts Journal*, July-August 1991, pp. 52–59.

Black, F.; and M. Scholes. "The Valuation of Option Contracts and a Test of Market Efficiency." *Journal of Finance* 27, no. 2 (1972), pp. 399–418.

Black, F.; and M. Scholes. "The Pricing of Options and Corporate Liabilities." *Journal of Political Economy* 81 (1973), pp. 637–659.

Boyle, P.; and T. Vorst. "Option Replication in Discrete Time with Transaction Costs." *Journal of Finance* 47, no. 1 (March 1992), pp. 271–293.

Brown, R. H.; and S. M. Schaefer. "Interest Rate Volatility and the Term Structure." Paper presented at the Second International *Conference of the Centre for Research in Finance*, IMI Group, Rome, September 1991.

Brown, S. J.; and P. H. Dybvig. "The Empirical Implications of the Cox, Ingersoll, Ross Theory of the Term Structure of Interest Rates." *Journal of Finance* 51 (1986), pp. 617–630.

Campbell, J. Y.; and A. Melino (Eds). "Econometric Methods and Financial Time Series." *Journal of Econometrics* 45 (1990), pp. 1–2.

Chesney, M., and L. Scott. "Pricing European Currency Options: A Comparison of the Modified Black–Scholes Model and a Random Variance Model." *Journal of Financial and Quantitative Analysis* 24, no. 3 (1989), pp. 267–284.

Constantinides, G. M. "Capital Market Equilibrium with Transaction Costs." *Journal of Political Economy* 94 (1986), pp. 842–862.

Cooper, I. A.; and A. S. Mello. "The Default Risk of Swaps." *Journal of Finance* 46, no. 2 (1991), pp. 597–620.

Cox. J. C.; J. E. Ingersoll; and S. A. Ross. "A Theory of the Term Structure of Interest Rates." *Econometrica* 53 (March 1985), pp. 385–408.

Cox, J. C.; and H. E. Leland. "On Dynamic Investment Strategies." Proceedings of the Seminar on the Analysis of Security Prices, Centre for Research in Security Prices, University of Chicago, 1982.

Cox, J. C.; and S. A. Ross. "The Valuation of Options for Alternative Stochastic Processes." *Journal of Financial Economics* 3 (January–March 1976), pp. 145–66.

Davis, M. H. A. "Local Time on the Stock Exchange." *Stochastic Calculus in Application*, ed. J. R., Norris. Pitman Research Notes in Mathematics, 1988.

Davis, M. H. A.; and Norman A. R. "Portfolio Selection with Transactions Costs." *Mathematics of Operations Research*, 15 (November 1990), pp. 676–713.

Davis, M. H. A.; V. G. Panas; and T. Zariphopoulou. "European Option Pricing with Transaction Costs." Working Paper, Imperial College, London, 1992.

Davis, M. H. A.; and V. G. Panas. "European Option Pricing with Transactions Costs." *Proceedings 30th IEEE Conference on Decision and Control,* December (1991), pp. 1299–1304.

Dixit, A. "Investment and Hysteresis." *Journal of Economic Perspectives* 6, no. 1 (Winter 1992), pp. 107–132.

Duan, J.C. "The GARCH Option Pricing Model." WP, Faculty of Management, McGill University, Montreal, February 1991.

Duffie, D.; and C. Huang. "Implementing Arrow-Debreu Equilibrium by Continuous Trading of Few Long-Lived Securities." *Econommertrica* 53 (November 1985), pp. 1337–56.

Dumas, B.; and E. Luciano. "An Exact Solution to a Dynamic Portfolio Choice. Problem under Transactions Costs." *Journal of Finance* 46 (June, 1991), pp. 577–595.

Dupire, B. "Arbitrage Pricing with Stochastic Volatility." WP, Société Générale Division Options, Paris, May, 1992. Presented at the French Finance Association Annual Meeting, June 1992.

Dybvig, P. H. "Distributional Analysis of Portfolio Choice." *Journal of Business* 61 (1988a), pp. 369–393.

Dybvig, P. H. "Inefficient Dynamic Portfolio Strategies, or How to Throw Away a Million Dollars." *Review of Financial Studies* 1, no. 1 (1988b), pp. 67–88.

Dybvig, P. H. "Bond and Bond Option Pricing Based on the Current Term Structure." Working Paper, Olin School of Business, University of Washington, 1988c.

Eastham, J. F.; and K. J. Hastings. "Optimal Impulse Control of Portfolios." *Mathematics of Operations Research* 13 (November 1988), pp. 588–605

Edirisinghe, C.; V. Naik; and R. Uppal. "Optimal Replication of Options with Transactions Costs." Working Paper, July 1991, Faculty of Commerce, University of British Columbia.

Engle, R. F.; and M. Rothschild (Eds). "ARCH Models in Finance." *Journal of Econometrics* 53 (1992), pp. 1–2.

Fama, E. F.; and K. R. French. "Dividend Yields and Expected Stock Returns." *Journal of Financial Economics* 22 (1988), pp. 3–25.

Fong, H. G.; and O. A. Vasicek. "Fixed-Income Volatility Management." *Journal of Portfolio Management* (1992) pp. 41–46.

Fong, H. G.; and O. A. Vasicek. "Omission Impossible." *Risk Magazine* 5 (1992), pp. 63–65

Harrison, J. M.; and D. Kreps. "Martingales and Arbitrage in Multiperiod Securities Markets." *Journal of Economic Theory* 20 (July 1979), pp. 381–408.

Harrison, J. M.; and S. Pliska. "Martingales and Stochastic Integrals in the Theory of Continuous Trading." *Stochastic Processes and Their Applications* 11 (1981), pp. 215–260.

Harvey, C. R.; and R. E. Whaley. "S&P 100 Index Option Volatility." *Journal of Finance* 46, no. 4 (1991), pp. 1551–1561.

Harvey, C. R.; and R. E. Whaley. "Market Volatility Prediction and the Efficiency of the S&P 100 Index Option Market." *Journal of Financial Economics* 31, no. 1 (1992), pp. 43–73.

He, H.; and H. Leland. "Equilibrium Asset Price Processes." Finance Working Paper #221, Haas School of Business, University of California at Berkeley, December 1991.

Heath, D.; R. Jarrow; and A. Morton. "Contingent Claim Valuation with a Random Evolution of Interest Rates." *The Review of Futures Markets* 9, no. 1 (1990a), pp. 54–76.

Heath, D.; R. Jarrow; and A. Morton. "Bond Pricing and the Term Structure of Interest Rates: A Discrete Time Approximation." *Journal of Financial and Quantitative Analysis* 25, no. 4 (December 1990a), pp. 419–440.

Heath. D.; R. Jarrow; and A. Morton. "Bond Pricing and the Term Structure of Interest Rates: A New Methodology for Contingent Claims Valuation." *Econometrica* 60, no. 1 (1992), pp. 77–105.

Heynen, R.; A. G. Z. Kemna; and A. C. F. Vorst. "Analysis of the Term Structure of Implied Volatilities." Working Paper 9220A Econometric Institute, Erasmus University, Rotterdam, 1991.

Ho, T. S. Y.; and S-B Lee. "Term Structure Movements and Pricing Interest Rate Contingent Claims." *Journal of Finance* 41, no. 5 (December 1986), pp. 1011–1029.

Hodges, S. D.; and A. P. Carverhill. "The Characterization of Economic Equilibria which Support Black–Scholes Option Pricing." *The Economic Journal* (forthcoming), 1992.

Hodges, S. D.; and L. J. Clewlow. "Optimal Delta-Hedging Under Transactions Costs." Paper Presented at the Financial Options Research Centre's 5th Annual Conference, University of Warwick, June 1992.

Hodges, S. D., and A. Neuberger. "Optimal Replication of Contingent Claims Under Transactions Costs." *The Review of Futures Markets* 8 (1989), pp. 222–239.

Hull, J.; and A. White. "The Pricing of Options on Assets with Stochastic Volatilities." *Journal of Finance* 42, no. 2 (1987), pp. 281–300.

Hull, J.; and A. White. "An Analysis of the Bias in Option Pricing Caused by A Stochastic Volatility." *Advances in Futures and Options Research* 3 (1988), pp. 29–61.

Hull, J.; and A. White. "Pricing Interest Rate Derivative Securities." *The Review of Financial Studies* 3, no. 4 (1990).

Ingersoll, J. E.; and S. A. Ross. "Waiting to Invest: Investment and Uncertainty." *Journal of Business* 65, no. 1 (1992), pp. 21–29.

Jamshidian, F. "The One-Factor Gaussian Interest Rate Model: Theory and Implementation," Working Paper, Financial Strategies Group, Merrill Lynch Capital Markets, New York, 1988.

Jamshidian, F. "An Exact Bond Option Formula." *Journal of Finance* 44 (1989), pp. 205–209.

Jamshidian, F. "The Preference-Free Determination of Bond and Option Prices from the Spot Interest Rate." *Advances in Futures and Options Research* 4 (1990), pp. 51–67.

Jamshidian, F. "Bond and Option Evaluation in the Gaussian Interest Rate Model." *Research in Finance* 9 (1991a), pp. 131–170.

Jamshidian, F. "Forward Induction and Construction of Yield Curve Diffusion Models." Working Paper, Financial Strategies Group, Merrill Lynch Capital Markets, New York, March 1991b.

Jarrow, R. H.; and S. M. Turnbull. "Pricing Options on Financial Securities Subject to Credit Risk." Working Paper, Johnson Graduate School of Management, Cornell University, 1990.

Johnson, H.; and D. Shanno. "Option Pricing when the Variance Is Changing." *Journal of Financial and Quantitative Analysis* 22, no. 2 (1987), pp. 143–151.

Leland, H. E. "Option Pricing and Replication with Transaction Costs." *Journal of Finance* 40 (1985), pp. 1283–1301.

Litterman, R.; J. Scheinkman; and L. Weiss. "Volatility and the Yield Curve." *Journal of Fixed Income* 1, no. 1 (June 1991), pp. 49–53.

Longstaff, F. "The Valuation of Options on Yields." *Journal of Financial Economics* 26, no. 1 (1990), pp. 97–121.

Longstaff, F.; and E. Schwartz. "Interest Rate Volatility and the Term Structure: A Two-Factor General Equilibrium Model." Paper Presented at the European Finance Association Meetings, 1991.

Madan, D. B.; and F. Milne, "Option Pricing with V. G. Martingale Components." *Mathematical Finance* 1, no. 4 (1991), pp. 39–55.

Madan, D. B.; and E. Seneta. "The Variance Gamma (V. G.) Model for Share Market Returns." *Journal of Business* 63, no. 4 (1990), pp. 511–524.

Magill, M. J. P.; and G. M. Constantinides. "Portfolio Selection with Transaction Costs." *Journal of Economic Theory* 13 (1976), pp. 245–263.

Melino, A.; and S. M. Turnbull. "Pricing Foreign Currency Options with Stochastic Volatility." *Journal of Econometrics* 45 (1990), pp. 239–265.

Merton, R. C. "Optimum Consumption and Portfolio Rules in a Continuous Time Model." *Journal of Economic Theory* 3 (1971), pp. 373–413.

Merton, R. C. "Theory of Rational Option Pricing." *Bell Journal* 4 (1973), pp. 141–183.

Merton, R. C. *Continuous-Time Finance*. Cambridge, MA: Basil Blackwell, 1990.

Myneni, R. "The Pricing of the American Option." *Annals of Applied Probability* 2, no. 1 (1992), pp. 1–23.

Nelson, D. B. "ARCH Models as Diffusion Approximations." *Journal of Econometrics* 45 (1990), pp. 7–38.

Neuberger, A. "Option Replication with Transaction Costs—An Exact Solution for the Pure Jump Process." Working Paper, London Business School, June 1992.

Neuhaus, H. "Discrete Time Option Hedging." Doctoral Dissertation, London Business School, 1989.

Pindyck, R. S. "Irreversibility, Uncertainty and Investment." *Journal of Economic Literature* 29, no. 3 (1991), pp. 1110–1148.

Poterba, J. M., and L. H. Summers. "Mean Reversion in Stock Prices: Evidence and Implications." *Journal of Financial Economics* 22 (1988), pp. 27–59.

Ramaswamy, K.; and S. M. Sundaresan. "The Valuation of Floating Rate Instruments." *Journal of Financial Economics* 17 (1986), pp. 251–272.

Rubinstein, M. "Exotic Options." Finance Working Paper #220, Haas School of Business, University of California at Berkeley, December 1991.

Scott, L. "Option Pricing When the Variance Changes Randomly: Theory, Estimation and an Application." *Journal of Financial and Quantitative Analysis* 22, no. 4 (1987), pp. 419–438.

Scott, L. "Stock Market Volatility and the Pricing of Index Options: An Analysis of Implied Volatilities and the Volatility Risk Premium in a Model with Stochastic Interest Rates and Volatility." WP, Department of Finance, University of Georgia, 1992.

Shastri, K.; and K. Wethyavivorn. "The Valuation of Currency Options for Alternate Stochastic Processes." *Journal of Financial Research* 10, no. 2 (1987), pp. 283–293.

Shreve, S. "A Control Theorist's View of Asset Pricing." Working Paper, Carnegie Mellon University, April 1989. Presented at Workshop on Applied Stochastic Analysis, Imperial College, London, April 7, 1989.

Stapleton, R. C.; and M. G. Subrahmanyam. "Risk Aversion and the Intertemporal Behaviour of Asset Prices." *The Review of Financial Studies* 3, no. 4 (1990), pp. 677–693.

Stein, E. M.; and J. C. Stein. "Stock Price Distributions with Stochastic Volatility: An Analytical Approach." *Review of Financial Studies* 4, no. 4 (1991), pp. 727–752.

Taksar, M.; M. J. Klass; and D. Assaf. "A Diffusion Model for Optimal Portfolio Selection in the Presence of Brokerage Fees." *Mathematics of Operations Research* 13 (1988), pp. 277–294.

Turnbull, S. M.; and F. Milne. "A Simple Approach to Interest Rate Option Pricing." *Review of Financial Studies* 4, no. 1 (1991), pp. 87–120.

Vasicek, O. "An Equilibrium Characterization of the Term Structure." *Journal of Financial Economics* 5 (1977), pp. 177–188.

Wiggins, J. B. "Option Values under Stochastic Volatility: Theory and Empirical Estimates." *Journal of Financial Economics* 19 (1987), pp. 351–372.

VI

DERIVATIVE INSTRUMENTS AND HEDGING IN EMERGING CAPITAL MARKETS

11

DERIVATIVES IN EMERGING MARKETS

Lawrence K. Duke, *Citibank Tokyo*

OVERVIEW

The derivatives business has witnessed enormous change over the past few years, with the seemingly constant introduction of new products and derivatives strategies. In contemplating the use of derivatives in risk management, it is important to first step back and outline the objectives and constraints that a financial participant confronts in managing the risk exposures of the business and the investment and trading portfolios. It immediately becomes obvious that different financial participants will have different objectives and constraints in managing business and portfolio risk. For instance, in describing the financial needs of corporate treasurers and fund managers, the objectives will be different for each. Investor objectives (which cover the needs of fund managers) include the expectations of exceeding a given benchmark return while maintaining or reducing risk. The benchmarks (e.g., the EAFE Index, and the Salomon Brothers Global Bond Index) will be different for most fund managers as their skills in bond selection, stock selection, quantitative analysis, and so on will be different. Relatedly, fund managers have a tendency to view markets as a series of country indexes or baskets as opposed to only a collection of individual securities. As such, there will, from time to time, be requirements for fund managers to change their asset allocations and country exposures. Analogously, corporate treasurers generally will look to reduce risk with the lowest cost hedges. They also will look for ways to reduce their funding costs. Conversely, traders will be seeking high total returns while operating on a daily marked-to-market basis. They also may look for longer term position-taking with respect to views on price, volatility, or spreads between financial instruments. These differing objectives will impact the strategic decisions involved in exposure management and the potential use of derivatives therein.

CONSTRAINTS, TRANSACTION COSTS, LIQUIDITY CONSIDERATIONS, AND RISKS

It is also important to consider the various costs and constraints that financial participants face in managing exposures. One of the most important is transaction costs. It is an important academic observation that the process of reducing transaction costs in financial dealings has been an important way for financial managers to add value to a business or portfolio. In addition, if potential deals or structures involve higher transaction costs, there should be other attributes of the deal that will enhance value to the investor and originator in such a way to make up for such costs. Exhibits 11–1 and 11–2 provide a comparison between the transaction costs in the largest equity stock and futures markets and the costs associated with equity swaps in selected Asian markets. In this comparison, a disparity exists between the low transaction costs associated with the largest equity futures markets and the costs incurred in transacting equity swaps in selected Asian markets, as shown in the exhibits. In addition, Exhibit 11–1 also illustrates the significant transaction costs savings associated with futures relative to stocks themselves. With respect to Asian equity swaps, implicit stock commissions and taxes have a dramatic impact on the

EXHIBIT 11-1

Estimated Round-Trip Transaction Costs as Percentages of Amounts Invested

Cost	United States	Japan	United Kingdom	France	Germany
Stocks					
Commissions	0.14%	0.20%	0.20%	0.10%	0.10%
Market Impact (a)	0.55	0.70	0.90	0.55	0.50
Taxes	0.00	0.30	0.50.	0.00	0.00
Total	0.69%	1.20%	1.60%	0.85%	0.60%
Average Stock Price in U.S. dollars (b)	$39.10	$27.30	7.73	$158.60	$385.65
Futures					
Commissions	0.01%	0.08%	0.02%	0.04%	0.03%
Market Impact (a)	0.05	0.05	0.10	0.10	0.05
Taxes	0.00	0.00	0.00	0.00	0.00
Total	0.06%	0.11%	0.12%	0.14%	0.08%

Source: Association of Investment Management and Research Conference, Apr 13–14 1993.

Note: Statistics are representative of $25 million, capitalization-weighted, indexed portfolio executed as agent, does not include settlement and custody fees.

(a) Trader estimate.

(b) Local indexes: S&P 500, Nikkei 225, FTSE 100, CAC–40. and DAX. respectively.

(c) All contracts are quarterly except for the CAC40.

high level of transaction costs (see Exhibit 11–2). Liquidity considerations also are quite important in assessing different approaches to exposure management. Liquidity is the ability to execute a transaction within an expected time frame. The demand for liquidity surges when a major market trend emerges. It is this factor that provides the information value associated with very liquid markets, where transactions will be done cheaper, earlier, and quicker. Conversely, the lack of liquidity in Asian stock markets, when looked at on an index or basket basis, negatively impacts the attractiveness of doing business in these markets.

Other potential obstacles to financial management involve the various risks that may be involved with the use of one of the variety of financial instruments, including derivatives. Price or market risk is an obvious risk associated with virtually

EXHIBIT 11-2

Estimated Transaction Costs as Percentages of Amounts Invested for Select Asian Stock Markets

Index	Dvd Yield	Dvd With Tax	Eff. Dvd Yield	Common (round trip)	Stamp (round trip)	Transaction Tax	Misc. Cost	Dead Weight Cost	Capital gain tax
Hang Seng	3.00%	0.00%	3.00%	0.70%	0.30%	0.00%	0.00%	1.00%	
Taiwan	1.23%	20.00%	0.98%	0.70%	0.00%	0.30%	0.00%	1.00%	0.60%
Singapore	1.57%	27.00%	1.15%	2.00%	0.20%	0.00%	0.02%	2.22%	
Thailand	2.33%	10.00%	2.10%	2.00%	0.00%	0.00%	0.02%	2.02%	15.00%
Indonesia	1.98%	0.00%	1.98%	2.00%	0.20%	0.00%	0.00%	2.20%	
Malaysia	1.49%	32.00%	1.01%	2.00%	0.30%	0.00%	0.02%	2.32%	
Philippines	0.53%	35.00%		2.00%	0.25%	0.25%	0.02%		

Source: Citibank Hong Kong.

all instruments. The purpose of hedging is to reduce such risk, while active management is the ability to assume such risks. Other risks include credit risk (which is lesser for futures by virtue of the margining system), regulatory risk (due to changes in regulations or tax laws), basis risk (the difference in price/volatility between the derivative and the underlying position), rolling risk (the price fluctuations associated with rolling over derivative contracts or other financial instruments), and internal risk (due to an organizational lack of comfort with derivatives). Users of financial products should thoroughly understand the nature of these risks both in order to evaluate the risk-reward tradeoffs and to control the risks as much as possible. Credit risk and basis risk control are especially notable with respect to derivatives. It is important to incorporate these risk factors in exposure management decisions. A final constraint on these decisions may include restrictions pertaining to investments (time horizon, concentration), risk, use of capital, and liquidity limits. Notwithstanding the above, the dynamics of financial deal-making can be driven by a process that mitigates one or more of these types of risks; this is why derivatives play an integral role in finance.

STRATEGIC AND TRANSACTIONAL APPROACHES USING DERIVATIVES

Strategic approaches using derivatives fall into three main categories. The first one involves the identification of arbitrages between two markets on the basis of perceived valuations. The main participants in this type of strategy usually are market-makers who have significant flows of business in one of the two markets. This type of activity will have a strong tendency to increase the efficiency of the markets by enhancing liquidity and lowering transaction costs. An example of this type of approach is the program trading performed in several of the markets included in Exhibit 11–1. Program trading involves transactions in the respective equity and equity futures/options market that capture the arbitrage spread by taking advantage of high volumes and low securitized borrowing costs. The second category, asymmetrical asset allocation and portfolio insurance, describes strategies that involve deviations from payoffs associated with traditional equity or other market exposures (which have symmetrical return patterns). For instance, institutional investors (principally fund managers) have been able to use derivatives such as a synthetic put, which provides downside protection while preserving substantial upside potential (asymmetrical distribution). The synthetic put involves no up-front payment of option premium (some funds still are restricted or discouraged from paying option premiums) and is constructed through the sale and purchase of futures or physical stock at prices determined by traditional or specially tailored option pricing models. The third category, dynamic asset allocation, involves the use of derivatives to change the asset allocation of a given fund without the purchase or disposal of securities, potentially reducing transaction costs and maintaining incentive for the individual fund managers.

Transactional approaches involve very specific applications. A good way to describe these approaches is "where there is friction, there is opportunity." Many of the applications involve derivative structures that reduce one or more of the variety of risks and constraints described earlier. One approach involves tax arbitrage. Many deals in derivatives are directly or indirectly motivated by adding value through tax reductions. Withholding and other taxes can be reduced or eliminated by using derivatives. Regulatory arbitrage is another transactional approach that can bear fruitful results for financial managers by the use of structured instruments (e.g., equity-linked notes) that have the risk/reward profile investors require but are ordinarily subject to regulatory restrictions. This approach may improve performance through more efficient asset allocation, as well. Yield enhancement is a third approach that may add value through structures that likely have imbedded options. However, it is important to realize what is being given up (e.g., reduced upside participation, less risk reduction, less creditworthy counterparty) for the enhanced yield. A fourth example of a transactional approach using derivatives is benchmark arbitrage, which is a special case of yield enhancement whereby the structure is designed in such a way that the reward profile provides an enhanced return exceeding a given benchmark.

Given the above overview, a framework can be constructed to gauge the appropriateness of the use of derivatives in managing exposures.

RATIONALE BEHIND THE USE OF EMERGING MARKET DERIVATIVES

The quantitatively derived structures and complex allure of derivative products may make them appear magical. However, the recent publicized events concerning several large companies incurring sizable losses in derivatives trading has broken the spell. It is therefore important to motivate the use of derivatives both in terms of the objectives discussed earlier in this chapter and in conjunction with comparisons with traditional financial instruments as per the framework. The best way to demonstrate this is through using the Asian equity markets as an example. The challenge for dealing in these markets is overcoming the high costs and their occasional illiquid conditions. When market conditions are bullish, as they were in 1993, participants are not very concerned about these shortcomings. However, when conditions change, these concerns become very important indeed. Exhibits 11–1 and 11–2 portray on a relative and an absolute basis, the high transaction costs associated with equity swap deals in selected Asian markets. It would appear that equity swaps (which will be covered in detail later) and other over-the-counter (OTC) equity options incur significantly higher transaction costs than do some exchange-traded futures and options, where transaction costs are as low as 75–100 bp. However, there are hidden costs in dealing with the Asian derivative exchange markets. One major cost is attributed to inefficiencies that are due to the difficulty of shorting equities (borrowing equities), this results in additional hedging costs in sales of futures. Another significant cost is that incurred by rolling risk (the process by which the nearest contract position is squared out before maturity and the next nearest contract is purchased). A final cost involves the lack of liquidity in the contracts that have farther out future dates than the nearest contracts. The net result is that the existing futures and options exchanges (principally Hong Kong) are very valuable in encouraging investment in the respective Asian markets, but there are still onerous costs in financially managing many of the financial participants' exposures without the use of OTC derivatives. Moreover, it is even more problematic to trade in those countries without futures and options exchanges. It is important to describe the transactional environment in many of the emerging markets. The characteristics include complicated tax laws, regulatory constraints, a high level of commission in dealing securities, high bid-offer spreads, extreme difficulty or impossibility (in a couple of markets) for nonresidents to invest directly, and burdensome policies regarding the repatriation of funds. These dealing conditions result in high costs and reduced liquidity. Perceptions of manipulation in a few of the region's currency and capital markets also impact liquidity conditions. Additionally, for longer term deals, the lack of liquidity in local long-term interest rate markets also is an obstacle, frequently resulting in the absorption of currency risk in such deals. Thus, the general state of Asian financial deal-making can be described as systematic institutional rigidity, where the liquidity conditions and "bubble nature" of these markets must be considered in executing financial strategies. Derivative strategies that overcome these large transactional impediments, despite relatively high transaction costs, will add value for financial participants, as long as these strategies are consistent with the objectives of the specific investor, trader, or corporation.

EMERGING MARKET DERIVATIVES PRODUCTS AND APPLICATIONS

Some brief examples of how derivative strategies may be applied in effective ways are as follows:

1. To capture tax advantages between local and offshore jurisdictions.
2. To diversify risk between different markets without cash movements (asset allocation).
3. To initiate investments in markets that are restricted for or closed to overseas investors.
4. To segment exposure to specific areas by using derivatives to close out undesired exposures (e.g., to assume risk in Taiwan equities but not the New Taiwan dollar).

E X H I B I T   11–3

Countries with Stock Index Futures

Country	World Index
Australia (a)	1.3%
Canada (a)	1.8
Denmark	0.3
France (a)	3.3
Germany	3.3
Hong Kong	1.4
Japan (a)	25.4
Netherlands	1.5
New Zealand	0.1
Spain	0.9
Sweden	0.7
Switzerland	2.0
United Kingdom (a)	10.5
United States (a)	42.8
Total as of December 31, 1992	95.3%

Sources: Commodity Futures Trading Commission and FT-Actuaries World Markets Monthly.
(a) Approved for use by U.S. Investors.

5. To capture the regulatory advantages of a domestic investor from offshore.

6. To reduce the cost of funding for a corporate issuer.

As an illustration, the following discussion provides an introduction to equity derivative products and applications currently in use in Asian markets. Exhibit 11–3 provides a list of the availability of equity index futures by country. The list would seem to reflect the growing awareness among national authorities of the importance of futures markets in attracting equity investment. However, the potential for index futures for the individual Asian countries remains unexplored (with the exception of Hong Kong). Exhibits 11–4A and 11–4B provide information on the price movements of selected Asian equity markets over a period of 18 months. As can be seen from the exhibits, there has been significant volatility in most of the markets, with

EXHIBIT   11-4A

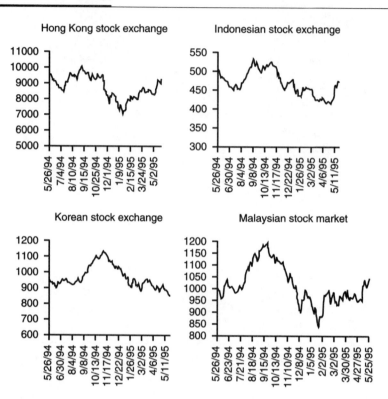

"bubbles" breaking at times. As futures markets develop, their liquidity often can exceed the underlying securities markets themselves, resulting in more efficiency and lower transaction costs, as exemplified by the Standard & Poor's (S&P) 500 index futures in the United States. Examples of futures-related derivatives applications include the use of enhanced index strategies, which combine index futures (or swaps) with cash management or fixed-income products to earn an incremental return over the index. With futures trading on global stock indexes (and potentially more in Asia), an exposure can be easily created that participates in the upside or downside moves in the underlying index. The funds in excess of the initial margin can be invested in cash-enhanced strategies that can add an incremental return to the underlying index return. Some of the incremental return can be considered compensation for taking on credit risk. Any cheap-

E X H I B I T   11–4B

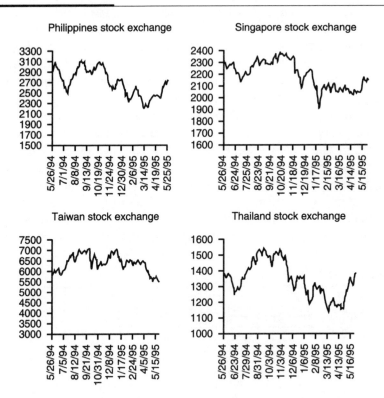

ness in the futures would be an added benefit to long exposure strategies.

Another increasingly popular derivative application involves equity swaps. Equity swaps are variants of traditional fixed-floating interest rate swaps. Equity-linked swaps differ from traditional interest rate swaps primarily in that the returns from an equity index may vary over a wider range of returns on most fixed- or floating-rate notes (see Exhibit 11–5). Options can be imbedded within the swap structure, as in the case of interest rate swaps. The primary attraction for using equity swaps, as has been explained earlier, is their capability to overcome transactional impediments, such as taxes and regulations, which make ownership of equities expensive or impossible in many markets. Many of these impediments occur in cross-border investing, and the cross-border market is the dominant market for such swaps.

Variations of these swaps include equity-equity, equity-commodity, and structured swaps. The first two variations are self-explanatory. The third variation, structured swaps, represents a combination of one of the two basic swaps with another financial product. In general, the other financial product will be an interest rate, equity, or currency product. Examples of structured swaps include leveraged swaps (a basic swap with an embedded equity option), upside swaps (an equity call option with an amortized premium), cross-currency equity swaps (an equity swap with a currency swap and the swap spread swap (see Exhibit 11–6). The swap spread generally is quoted as a spread over or under the interest rate side. As with other types of financial transactions, credit risk and cost considerations are important. The periodic settlement of swaps can mitigate the credit risk by reducing the term or level of exposure. Margin agreements and settlement pools also can

EXHIBIT 11–5

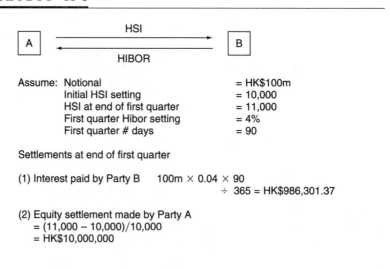

Assume: Notional   = HK$100m
         Initial HSI setting   = 10,000
         HSI at end of first quarter   = 11,000
         First quarter Hibor setting   = 4%
         First quarter # days   = 90

Settlements at end of first quarter

(1) Interest paid by Party B   100m × 0.04 × 90
                                  ÷ 365 = HK$986,301.37

(2) Equity settlement made by Party A
    = (11,000 − 10,000)/10,000
    = HK$10,000,000

EXHIBIT 11–6

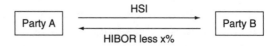

Party A pays the performance on the Hang Seng Index and receives Hibor less x. The swap spread is x.

serve to reduce counterparty exposure. As an aside, a small group of major financial institutions has the capability to significantly reduce the high hidden costs ordinarily associated with traditional equity investment in the Asian region through equity swaps. This cost reduction may result from having a physical presence in a local market, leveraging a global network, or through customer deal flows. From an investment manager's viewpoint, equity swaps and derivatives also can improve a portfolio's diversification by the process that fewer investment managers will be required to cover all desired asset classes. In addition, equity swaps can be used in structured paper for those financial participants that have restrictions in dealing with derivatives directly. A comparative illustration of common hedging strategies is presented in Exhibits 11–7 and 11–8. In each of these exhibits note the payoff patterns, the reflection of view on future price action and volatility, and the range of returns for each hedging strategy.

Structured (exotic) options are basic options with additional structures. As an example, exotic options can be imbedded in equity swaps. Current examples of exotic options include barrier options (in which option terms include a barrier level where options knock in or out), complex (quanto) options (in which the payoff is defined in terms of more than one variable, for example,

EXHIBIT 11–7

Summary Comparison of Option Hedging Strategies

Strategy	Return (Cost)	Return (Cost Range)	Upside Limit	Downside Limit
Selling futures	0		4.0%	4.0%
Selling calls (5% OTM)	3.75%	<11.25%	11.25	None
Buying put (5% OTM)	(4.00)	>(5.85)	None	(5.85)
Zero-premium collar		(2.10)		
(5% OTM)	(0.25)	to 7.90	7.90	(2.10)
Collar with put spread		(1.70)		(1.70)
(5% OTM put)				
5–15% OTM	0.15	to 11.15	11.15	to (11.70)

Source: Association of Investment Management and Research Conference, April 13–14, 1993.

E X H I B I T   11-8

Most Common Hedging Strategies

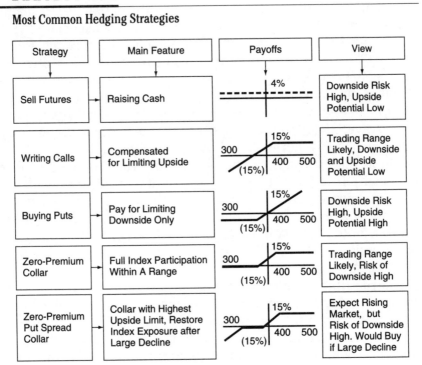

Source: Association of Investment Management and Research Conference, April 10–14, 1993.

the Hong Kong dollar value of the S&P 500), and chooser options (in which the holder can choose at some specified point in time whether the option is a call or a put). The use of specific derivative strategies needs to incorporate objectives, costs, and constraints as well as a comparison with alternative financial strategies before the financial decision is made. It may be a more appropriate strategy to use the underlying securities instead of fancy derivatives structures. Alternatively, the direct use of exchange-traded derivatives might be more attractive to the market participant. Financial managers need to consider both their capabilities in managing derivatives, especially in managing rolling risk, and the expertise of the back office in monitoring derivatives-related risks. In the case of Asian equity markets, derivatives will play an important role in reducing the costs of investing in the region, especially in the restrictive regulatory and tax environment that currently exists.

FUTURE PROSPECTS FOR DERIVATIVES

Common sense would seem to dictate a strong need for equity futures exchanges for each country in general. This would encourage foreign investment in local markets through lower transaction costs and more price transparency. Additional benefits to be derived include a lowered cost of capital for local corporations which, in turn, would foster higher economic growth for the country. For the investor and financial community, it would lower hedging costs and increase the efficiency of local markets through enhanced liquidity. Derivatives are not just an add-on but are an integral part of the financial manager's and investor's tool kit. Derivative transactions can be win-win deals for both the principal and the intermediary, but the transaction must make sense in terms of the framework described above. As such, financial institutions that deal in derivatives need to communicate the descriptions and rationale of specific derivatives strategies in a user-friendly manner. As emerging market derivatives become more widely understood and accepted, they will play a progressively more valuable role in opening up these markets to foreign investment and much-needed liquidity.

12

CROSS-HEDGING CURRENCY INVESTMENT FLOWS IN AN EMERGING MARKET

Chung-Hua Shen, *National Central University, Taiwan*
Lee-Rong Wang, *Chung-Hua Institution for Economic Research, Taiwan*

INTRODUCTION

How does a trader or investor cover foreign exchange risk when the expected future cash flow is denominated in a minor currency? Forward and futures markets are generally not yet available for these currencies. In this situation, the foreign exchange risk can be offset only through cross hedging (i.e., the commodity being hedged is different from the commodity underlying the futures contract). Identifying effective cross-hedging strategies typically involves employing the risk-minimizing methodology by regressing the change in the spot price against the change in the futures price through the ordinary least squares (OLS) method, where the estimated slope coefficient and R^2 of this regression are viewed as the measure of the optimal hedge ratio and the degree of hedging effectiveness, respectively.[1]

The primary purpose of this chapter is to identify the ideal hedging instrument for a minor currency, such as the New Taiwan (NT) dollar, in hedging exchange rate risk. The unavailability of an NT dollar futures market and a limited forward market in Taiwan have encouraged the practice of cross-hedging among Taiwan's exporters and importers.[2] If a high R^2 and a significant hedge ratio are found, the cross-hedging of NT dollar exchange rate risk through the major foreign currency futures is thus possible. However, employment of the OLS method to estimate the hedge ratio and R^2 may yield a misleading result. Previous studies involving hedging performance of the futures market have been subject to the criticism of having a stable hedge ratio. For example, Grammatikos and Saunders (1983) find that the hedge ratios for five major foreign currency futures are actually unstable over time. Malliaris and Urrutia (1991) demonstrated that the hedge ratios and the measures of hedging effectiveness follow a random walk. Such a stability assumption seems particularly questionable in view of the considerable volatility and turbulence that have occurred since the recent deregulation of Taiwan's foreign exchange market. The risk of the exchange rate of the NT dollar against the U.S. dollar may be greatly reduced if effective cross-hedging strategies can be identified under the scenario of changing hedge ratios and hedging performance.

Identifying the changing hedge ratios and hedging performances involves the application of a two-state, first-order Markov switching model (Hamilton 1988, 1989, 1990). The hedge ratios and hedging performances of cross-hedging on the NT dollar are assumed here as being different in two regimes, and they switch back

---

1. The estimated coefficient and R^2 have been extensively examined. Hedge ratios and measures of hedging effectiveness are estimated for GNMA futures by Ederington (1979), Hill, Liro, and Schneeweis (1983); for foreign currency futures by Hill and Schneeweis (1982), Grammatikos and Saunders (1983), Grammatikos (1986), and Benet (1990, 1992); for T-bond futures by Hill and Schneeweis (1984); for CD futures by Overdahl and Starleaf (1986); for T-bill futures by Ederington (1979), Franckle (1980), and Howard and D'Antonio (1984); and for stock market index futures by Figlewski (1984, 1985) and Junkus and Lee (1985).

2. This limitation is due to active intervention by the monetary authority in Taiwan. Also, small-and medium-sized companies, which comprise a large part of Taiwan's export and import enterprises, may not be capable of accessing the forward market.

and forth according to the Markov chain. The Markov model argues that the outliers or some superficially irregular observations, which are typically ignored in the traditional estimation, may possibly form another systematic pattern. Restated, the observed futures data may be generated by the weighted average of two distributions along with each distribution having its own hedge ratio and R^2. The weights, which are permitted to evolve over time, reveal the probabilities of effective/ineffective hedging states in the next period. Therefore, findings of low hedge ratios and R^2s by traditional tests (e.g., Gon and Chen [1992] in a study of cross-hedging on the NT dollar) do not necessarily imply that the cross-hedging is irrelevant. The ignored irregular observations may possibly constitute a high R^2, implying an opposite result.

Exhibit 12–1 plots the relative frequency (histogram) of futures price changes of the British pound (BP), Canadian dollar (CD), Japanese yen (JY) and German mark (DM). The plots for the BP and CD futures show that the change in futures prices may have two modes. The plots for the JY and DM futures exhibit the typical high peaks and fat tails that also are consistent with the argument of mixture of two normal distributions. These primary findings, together with recently observed financial data, have been demonstrated by many studies as possibly having resulted from a finite mixture distribution;[3] as a result, the application of a Markov switching model may be justified. The traditional estimation technique, which assumes a single distribution, may bias the estimation results if the population is actually a finite mixture of two normal distributions.

The organization of this chapter is as follows. The cross-hedging model is introduced in the next section. A two-state Markov switching model is then discussed, followed by the data and estimation results.

---

3. For example, the joint distribution of price and quantity is contended by Harris (1986) and Tauchen and Pitts (1983) as being a mixture distribution. The observed long tail and mass peak of the stock return are hypothesized by Turner et al. (1990) as possibly have arisen from two normal distributions. Growth of the U.S. GNP was discovered by Hamilton (1989) as following a Markov process. The observed long swing in the exchange rate is demonstrated by Engle and Hamilton (1990) as being a consequence of the mixture of normal distributions. Shen (1994) cannot reject that the relationship between the NT–U.S. dollar spot and forward exchange rates shifts according to a Markov law.

EXHIBIT 12–1

Relative Frequency of Futures Price Changes

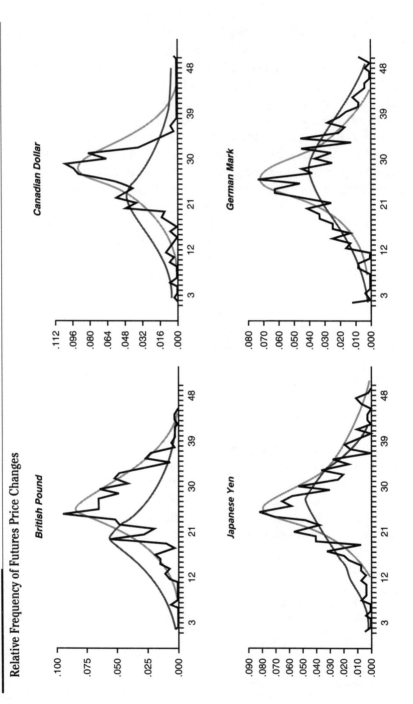

THE CROSS-HEDGING MODEL

Cross-hedging entails the use of a futures contract in a currency to reduce the risk related to a spot position in another currency that differs materially in location, type, grade, or maturity date. Nevertheless, the choice of an appropriate hedging instrument is not obvious for minor currencies (e.g., the NT dollar). The success of any hedging instrument must be related to the strength (and stability) of the correlation between movements in the spot price and the futures (hedge) price.

The basis for the empirical tests is a model in which a risk averse agent is assumed to minimize the variance of his end-of-period wealth, W[4]

$$Min_\beta L = VAR(W_\tau) \tag{12.1}$$
$$W_\tau = S_\tau - S_t - \beta(F_\tau - F_t)$$

where β is the number of futures contracts sold($+$) or purchase($-$) per spot position (i.e., hedge ratio); W_τ is the end-of-period wealth distribution at time τ; S_τ and S_t ($\tau - t$ represents the hedging period) are the spot prices at which it can be sold at times τ and t, respectively; and F_τ and F_t are the prices of the futures contract at times τ and t, respectively. The value of β that minimizes the variance of W_τ is the ratio of the covariance of $(S_\tau - S_t)$ and $(F_\tau - F_t)$ to the variance of $(F_\tau - F_t)$,[5] which is correspondent to the OLS regression of

$$y_t = \alpha + \beta f_t + \epsilon_t \tag{12.2}$$

where $y_t = S_\tau - S_t$ and $f_t = F_\tau - F_t$.

Moreover, since N different futures contracts may possibly exist and be available, Anderson and Danthine (1981) develop a single futures hedging methodology to include the possibility of portfolio futures hedges. The simple regression, Equation (12.2), is thus extended toward the multiple regression to estimate the portfolio futures hedge ratios

$$y_t = \alpha + \beta(1)f_t^1 + \beta(2)f_t^2 + \cdots + \beta(N)f_t^N + \epsilon_t \tag{12.3}$$

---

4. A more general model maximizes expected utility, rather than minimizing risk. However, the majority of papers in previous literature employ Equation (12.2) since the latter provides a more concise expression for estimation.

5. See Johnson (1960), Stein (1961), and Ederington (1979) for the derivation.

where $\beta(i)$ $(i = 1, 2, \ldots, N)$ is the hedge ratio for contract i and f_t^i is the change in the futures price for contract i during the hedging period $(\tau - t)$. The generalization to multiple futures contracts suggests that, in the case of multiple cross-hedgings, the partial (given remaining futures prices) correlation coefficient between the change in the spot price and the change in the price of a futures contract is a better indicator of the usefulness of that contract for hedging purposes than is the simple correlation coefficient. Thus, the optimal hedge against a long spot position may conceivably involve a long futures position (i.e., in which the hedge ratio has a negative sign) in a contract—even when the (simple) correlation between the spot and that futures price is positive.

THE MARKOV SWITCHING MODEL

The Model

The Markov switching model assumes that the data are simultaneously sampled from two normal distributions (two states). The states are not directly observable but can be estimated via a maximum likelihood method. Estimates of each state, as well as the above-mentioned weights, can be obtained given initial values of all parameters (see below for details) by employing nonlinear updating rules. What the two states are remains unknown before the estimation. The weights inform which state has the dominant power at each period.

This unobserved state, denoted s_t, characterizes the state or regime. Equation (12.2) can therefore be rewritten as

$$y_t = \alpha_{s_t} + \beta_{s_t} f_t + \epsilon_t \qquad (12.4)$$

where

$$\alpha_{s_t} = \begin{cases} \alpha_1 & \text{if } s_t = 1 \\ \alpha_2 & \text{if } s_t = 2 \end{cases}$$

$$\beta_{s_t} = \begin{cases} \beta_1 & \text{if } s_t = 1 \\ \beta_2 & \text{if } s_t = 2 \end{cases}$$

The evolution of the unobservable state variable is assumed to follow a two-state Markov chain

$$Pr(s_t = 1 \mid s_{t-1} = 1) = p_{11}$$
$$Pr(s_t = 2 \mid s_{t-1} = 1) = p_{12}$$
$$Pr(s_t = 1 \mid s_{t-1} = 2) = p_{21}$$
$$Pr(s_t = 2 \mid s_{t-1} = 2) = p_{22}$$

with $p_{11} + p_{12} = p_{21} + p_{22} = 1$. The respective notations $Pr(\cdot)$ and $P(\cdot)$ refer to a discrete probability set and a probability density function. The model expressed in Equation (12.4) is similar to Hamilton (1988) except the expected value μ_3 in his model is replaced by $\alpha_{st} + \beta_{st} f_t$.

This Markov chain is presumed to be independent of the lagged y once one places conditions on s_{t-1}. The observation also can be thought of as drawing from a mixture of two normal distributions. The state in each period determines which of the two normal densities is applied toward generating the model. The market is assumed to switch between two states according to transition probabilities.

Maximum Likelihood Estimation of Parameters

For simplicity, let $x_t = (1, f_t)$ represent the set of independent variables at period t and $\phi'_{s_t} = (\alpha_{s_t}, \beta_{s_t})$. Equation (12.4) can therefore be written in a more compact form as

$$y_t = x_t \phi_{s_t} + \epsilon_t \qquad (12.5)$$

The capital letters X_t and Y_t represent all of the information available up to period t:

$$X_t = (x_1, x_2, \ldots, x_t)'$$

$$Y_t = (y_1, y_2, \ldots, y_t)'$$

Following convention, θ is used to refer to the entire unknown parameters set:

$$\theta = (\alpha_1, \alpha_2, \beta_1, \beta_2, \sigma^2, p_{11}, p_{22})$$

Assuming the state is known, the sample likelihood function conditional on the given state is

$$P(y_t \mid s_t; x_t, \theta) = \frac{1}{\sqrt{2\pi}\sigma} \exp\left[\frac{(y_t - x_t \phi_{s_t})^2}{-2\sigma^2}\right] \qquad (12.6)$$

Searching for an θ that maximizes Equation (12.6) is desired here. The estimation consists of three parts. First, the filter probabilities

$Pr(s_t \mid Y_t; X_t, \theta)$, which use the information up to time t, are estimated. Second, the smoothed probabilities $Pr(s_t \mid Y_T; X_T, \theta)$ are derived by using the filter probabilities. Different from the filter inference, the full sample of ex post available information can be utilized in deriving the smoothed probability.[6]

Third, the smoothed probabilities finally are used for weighting data and implementing the OLS regression. The weighted observations are calculated as

$$y_t^{(j,=)} = y_t \cdot \sqrt{Pr(s_t = j \mid Y_T; X_T, \theta)}$$
$$x_t^{(j,=)} = x_t \cdot \sqrt{Pr(s_t = j \mid Y_T; X_T, \theta)}$$

The left-hand side denotes the weighted observations and uses the notation to distinguish between the original observations. The superscript j denotes the present state. Once weighted data are obtained, the hedge ratio at state j is

$$\phi_j = [X_T^{(j,=)'} X_t^{(j,=)}]^{-1} [X_T^{(j,=)'} Y_t^{(j,=)}] \tag{12.7}$$

The hedging performance at state j, R_j^2, is obtained by summing over all observations

$$R_j^2 = 1 - \frac{\sum_{t=1}^{T} [y_t^{(j,=)} - x_t^{(j,=)} \phi_{s=j}]^2}{\sum_{t=1}^{T} [y_t^{(j,=)} - \sum_{t=1}^{T} y_t^{(j,=)} / T]}$$

and other statistics

$$\sigma^2 = \frac{\sum_{j=1}^{2} \sum_{t=1}^{T} [y_t^{(j,=)} - x_t^{(j,=)} \phi_{s=j}]^2}{T}$$

$$p_{ij} = \frac{\sum_{t=1}^{T} Pr(s_t = j, s_{t-1} = i \mid Y_T; X_T, \theta)}{\sum_{t=1}^{T} Pr(s_{t-1} = i \mid Y_T; X_T, \theta)}$$

$$\rho = Pr(s_t = j \mid Y_T; X_T, \theta)$$

These three steps are repeated until the convergence criterion is satisfied. The convergence criterion chosen is the absolute difference of new and old sets of all parameters less than 10^{-8}. The estimations are tried with difference initial values until a global solution is reached. The estimation of the multiple cross-hedgings, Equation (12.3), is similar to that of single cross-hedging, and thus is not derived here.

---

6. Detailed derivations for the filter and smoothed probabilities are provided in Hamilton (1990).

Testing the Null of Markov Switching Model

Whether the parameters of the two states are the same or not is tested next. The three tests concerned here are

$$H_0^{(1)}: \alpha_1 = \alpha_2$$

$$H_0^{(2)}: \beta_1 = \beta_2$$

and

$$H_0^{(3)}: p_{11} = 1 - p_{22}, \quad a_1 \neq \alpha_2 \quad \beta_1 \neq \beta_2$$

The first two hypotheses examine the equality of the parameters of the two states. The third hypothesis examines whether or not the probability of the current state is affected by that of the previous state, that is, $p_{11} = p_{21}$. The Markov model under $H_0^{(3)}$ therefore comprises an i.i.d. sequence with individual densities given by the following mixture of two normals:

$$P(y_t | X_t, \theta) = \frac{p_{11}}{\sqrt{2\pi}\sigma} \exp\left[\frac{(y_t - x_t\phi_1)^2}{-2\sigma^2}\right] + \frac{(1 - p_{11})}{\sqrt{2\pi}\sigma} \exp\left[\frac{(y_t - x_t\phi_2)^2}{-2\sigma^2}\right]$$

$$(12.8)$$

See Engle and Hamilton (1990) for the rationale for this test.

The Wald tests for $H_0^{(1)}$, $H_0^{(2)}$, and $H_0^{(3)}$, respectively, are

$$\frac{(\hat{\alpha}_1 - \hat{\alpha}_2)^2}{\widehat{Var}(\hat{\alpha}_1) + \widehat{Var}(\hat{\alpha}_2) - 2\widehat{Cov}(\hat{\alpha}_1, \hat{\alpha}_2)} \approx \chi^2(1)$$

$$\frac{(\hat{\beta}_1 - \hat{\beta}_2)^2}{\widehat{Var}(\hat{\beta}_1) + \widehat{Var}(\hat{\beta}_2) - 2\widehat{Cov}(\hat{\beta}_1, \hat{\beta}_2)} \approx \chi^2(1)$$

$$\frac{[\hat{p}_{11} - (1 - \hat{p}_{22})]^2}{\widehat{Var}(\hat{p}_{11}) + \widehat{Var}(\hat{p}_{22}) + 2\widehat{Cov}(\hat{p}_{11}, \hat{p}_{22})} \approx \chi^2(1)$$

THE DATA

To enable comparison over similar time periods, futures price data for the contracts calling for delivery of BP, CD, DM, and JY during the period July 1987 to March 1992 are collected using the weekly Wednesday settlement prices of nearby contracts traded in the International Monetary Market (IMM) of the Chicago Mercantile Exchange (CME). These currencies are chosen for this study because Japan, Germany, Canada, and Great Britain are important trading partners of Taiwan and also because the futures contracts for these currencies are actively traded. The weekly Wednesday prices are used with the intention of eliminating the weekly effect: If no trading occurs on one particular date, the data of the latest trading date is used instead. Spot exchange rates come from the *Financial Statistics Monthly* of the Republic of China, where the interbank closing rates of the NT dollar against the U.S. dollar on each corresponding Wednesday are used.

Furthermore, to avoid irregular futures price movements that are sometimes observed in the expiration month, the old contract is replaced when the futures contract moves into its expiration month and a new contract is used in the next expiration month. Also, the hedging period of each contract, $\tau - t$, is assumed to be four weeks.[7]

THE RESULTS

As a standard of comparison, Equations (12.3) and (12.4) are first estimated by the OLS method. Exhibit 12–2 reports the estimation results in which panel A contains the results of single cross-hedgings and panels B, C, and D contain those of multiple cross-hedgings. In the case of single cross-hedgings, the hedge ratios of BP and JY are significantly different from zero and, for both currencies, the effectiveness of hedging performance is 2.3 percent. However, the hedge ratios of DM and CD in single cross-hedgings are not significantly different from zero and the effectiveness of their hedging performance is only 1 and 0.8 percent, respectively. The results of panel A do not support the use of foreign currency futures to effectively reduce the NT exchange risk.

When two futures contracts are considered (panel B of Exhibit 12–2), the hedge ratio of BP remains significant even when the second foreign futures DM or CD is considered. However, the hedge ratio of BP becomes insignificant when the second

---

7. According to Grammatikos and Saunders (1983), the two-week hedging period is the most commonly found assumption in the empirical literature on financial futures hedging. However, some experimentation was attempted with shorter (one-week) and longer (four-week) periods without substantially altering the results reported.

Single Distribution Model—OLS Method

A. Single Cross-Hedging

	β	R^2
BP	0.0219*	0.023
	(2.35)	
JY	0.0586*	0.023
	(2.36)	
DM	0.043	0.010
	(1.56)	
CD	0.085	0.008
	(1.41)	

B. Multiple Cross-Hedging——Two Futures

	$\beta(1)$	$\beta(2)$	R^2
BP JY	0.013	0.034	0.027
	(0.97)	(0.97)	
BP DM	0.025**	− 0.014	0.023
	(1.78)	(0.32)	
BP CD	0.020*	0.067	0.027
	(2.18)	(1.11)	
JY DM	0.055**	0.006	0.022
	(1.76)	(0.17)	
JY CD	0.057*	0.080	0.030
	(2.31)	(1.33)	
DM CD	0.042	0.081	0.017
	(1.51)	(1.34)	

C. Multiple Cross-Hedging—Three Futures

	$\beta(1)$	$\beta(2)$	$\beta(3)$	R^2
BP JY DM	0.017	0.037	− 0.021	0.028
	(1.06)	(1.04)	(0.48)	
BP JY CD	0.010	0.038	0.072	0.033
	(0.77)	(1.07)	(1.19)	
BP DM CD	0.023	− 0.009	0.065	0.028
	(1.58)	(0.22)	(1.08)	
JY DM CD	0.055**	0.005	0.079	0.030
	(1.74)	(0.13)	(1.32)	

D. Multiple Cross-Hedging—Four Futures

	$\beta(1)$	$\beta(2)$	$\beta(3)$	$\beta(4)$	R^2
BP JY DM CD	0.014	0.040	− 0.017	0.070	0.033
	(0.86)	(1.12)	(0.39)	(1.16)	

Notes: absolute t-value in parenthesis *: significance at the 5 percent level. **: significance at the 10 percent level.
Constant term is not reported. U.S./JY is multiplied by 100; U.S./NT is multiplied by 20.

futures JY is included. Similar results can be found in the case of JY, for which the hedge ratio remains significant when the second foreign futures DM or CD is employed. The hedge ratios of both DM and CD remain insignificant in a two-contract cross-hedging model. The R^2s in panel B are noted to slightly increase, thus leading to the conclusion that adding one more futures contract in a regression will not help investors in hedging risk.

The multiple-hedgings with three or four futures contracts make almost all coefficients insignificant (panels C and D of Exhibit 12–2). The R^2s, ranging from 0.028 to 0.033, indicate that the potential for risk reduction still remains low. Consequently, the OLS estimation results in Exhibit 12–2 illustrate that the use of cross-hedgings to avoid NT dollar exchange rate risk is ineffective. This pessimistic conclusion is consistent with that of Gon and Cheu (1992).

Whether cross hedging is actually ineffective or not is the concern of this chapter. Exhibit 12–3 reports the Markov Switching (MS) estimation results of each single cross-hedging. The estimated parameters of the two states are strikingly different from another. As shown in the exhibit, the insignificant hedge ratios and low R^2s of each futures contract in state 1 yield similar results as those in the OLS estimation. State 1 can thus be referred to as an ineffective hedging state. In contrast, the hedge ratios of employing different foreign futures in state 2 are all significantly different from zero; in addition, the hedging effectiveness of the different futures of this state are all high, ranging from 0.746 (BP) to 0.958 (JY). Thus, at least 74.6 percent and at most 95.8 percent of the exchange rate risk of the NT dollar can be reduced in state 2. State 2 can thus be referred to as an effective hedging state. The completely different behavior of these two states signifies that the single distribution model does not fully utilize all available information. Moreover, in contrast to OLS estimation, where only BP and JY are significant, many hedge ratios here become significant—regardless of the states—implying that the MS method improves the efficiency of estimations.

Once the parameters of each state have been obtained, then whether the samples are indeed generated by two normal

E X H I B I T   12–3

Mixture Distribution Model: Markov Switching Method
Single Cross-Hedging
$y_t = \alpha_s + \beta_s f_t + \epsilon_t$

		β	p_{ii}	R^2
BP	State 1	0.020	0.965	0.043
		(0.253)		
	State 2	−0.052*	0.822	0.746
		(2.17)		
	χ^2-test	[9.24*]	[8.45*]	
JY	State 1	0.040**	0.984	0.014
		(1.87)		
	State 2	−0.339*	0.371	0.958
		(3.06)		
	χ^2-test	[11.39*]	[10.62*]	
DM	State 1	0.032	0.967	0.014
		(1.30)		
	State 2	−0.163*	0.833	0.760
		(2.15)		
	χ^2-test	[4.01*]	[148.9*]	
CD	State 1	0.160*	0.970	0.059
		(3.22)		
	State 2	0.453*	0.836	0.780
		(3.18)		
	χ^2-test	[7.00*]	[112.0*]	

Notes: Absolute t-values in parentheses.
*: Significance at the 5 percent level.
**: Significance at the 10 percent level.
$p_{ii} = Pr(s_t = i \mid s_{t-1} = i)$.
χ^2-test: Chi-squared statistics of $H_0^{(2)}$ and $H_0^{(3)}$.
U.S./JY is multiplied by 100; U.S./NT is multiplied by 20.

distributions or not can be examined. Three null hypothesis, $H_0^{(1)}$, $H_0^{(2)}$, and $H_0^{(3)}$ are tested; however, only the latter two are reported, as the constants are typically not of interest. As shown by the χ^2 test in Exhibit 12–3, all of the null hypotheses are rejected. That is, all single cross-hedgings reject the null hypothesis that the data are sampled from a univariate distribution and favor the assumption of a finite mixture of two normal distributions. The MS model appears appropriate for the cross-hedging of the exchange rate risk here.

Exhibit 12–4 (a) to (d) plot the smoothed probabilities of state 2 for each single cross-hedging. Although state 2 is an effective hedging state, the probability of its occurrence during the studied periods is mostly close to zero. Restated, state 1 has a dominant influence over the two states most of the time. This inference may possibly account for why OLS estimators reject the usefulness of cross-hedging at the 95 percent confidence interval, as OLS estimation reflects the properties of the majority of the data.

However, avoiding exchange rate risk is still possible, as revealed by the previous MS estimation results. The smoothed probabilities of state 2, although not occurring quite often, are sometimes close to 1. During the following two periods, the high probabilities of state 2 signify that the effective hedging state dominates. Any investors desiring to hedge the exchange rate risk during these periods are likely to succeed. The first period ranges from August 1, 1989 (the 85th observation), to June 14, 1989 (the 100th observation), at the time when the Central Bank of China (Taiwan) abolished the former central-rate system on April 3, 1989, and allowed the bid-ask principle to be applied toward both interbank and retail tradings in foreign exchange markets.[8] The second period ranges from October of 1991 (the 220th observation) to February of 1992 (the 240th observation). At that time, the Central Bank of China reopened the forward foreign exchange market, in an effort to facilitate the hedging of exchange rate risk by export and import traders.[9] Forward foreign exchange markets may provide useful information and, consequently, enhance the effectiveness of cross-hedging management. More detailed research on this issue, however, is required.

Results of multiple cross-hedgings are reported in Exhibits 12–5–12–7. Similar results are observed as those in Exhibit 12–3.

---

8. The former system had employed the weighted average rate of interbank trading as the central rate for retail trading on the next business day and set limits on daily fluctuation in the interbank rate. Under the new trading system, only the fluctuation of small retail transactions up to U.S. $30,000 are limited.

9. The central bank reopened the forward market on November 1, 1993 (the 225th observation). Meanwhile, the bank raised foreign liability ceilings on banks and adopted the accrual basis in calculating a bank's foreign exchange positions, which consisted of spot and forward foreign exchange positions.

EXHIBIT 12-4

Smoothed Probability of State 2—One Futures

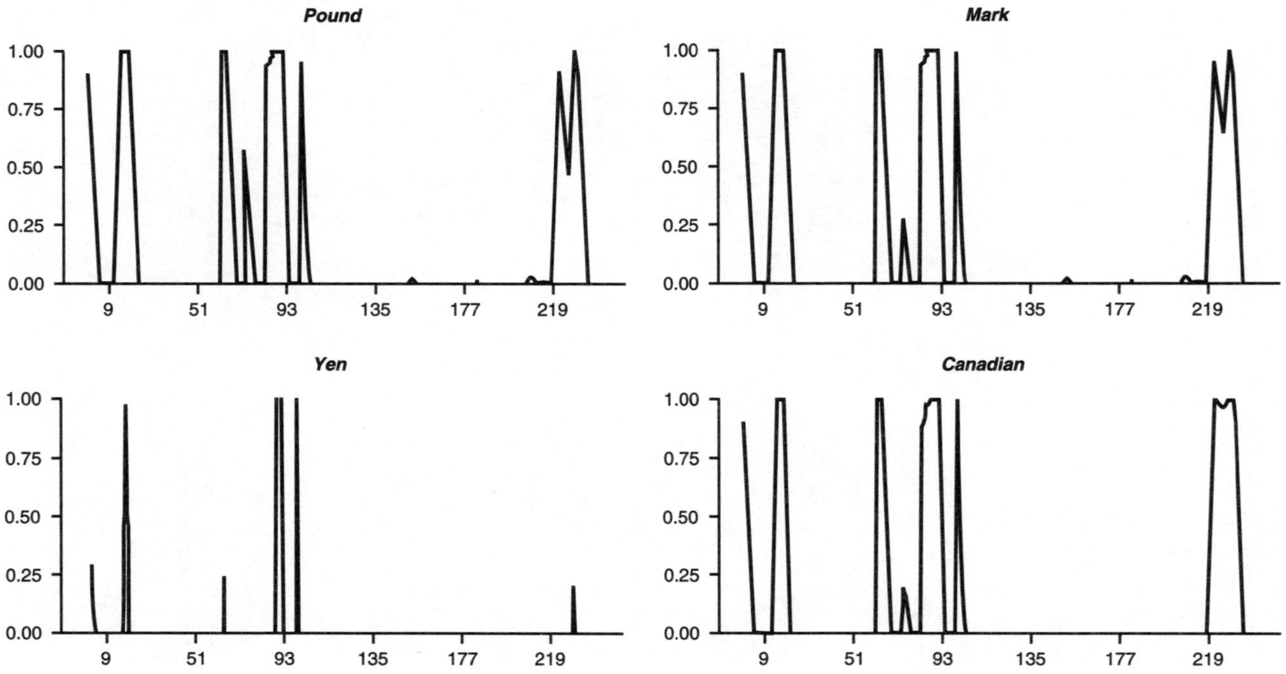

E X H I B I T   12–5

Mixture Distribution Model: Markov Switching Method
Multiple Cross Hedging—Two Futures
$$y_t = \alpha_s + \beta(1)f_t^1 + \beta(2)f_t^2 + \epsilon_t$$

		$\beta(1)$	$\beta(2)$	p_{ii}	R^2
BP JY	State 1	0.003	0.969*	0.980	0.140
		(0.37)	(3.93)		
	State 2	0.531*	− 2.276*	0.610	0.940
		(9.32)	(14.03)		
	χ^2-test	[66.92*]	[209.1*]	[15.01*]	
BP DM	State 1	0.021	− 0.002	0.963	0.047
		(0.19)	(0.06)		
	State 2	− 0.096	0.139	0.811	0.750
		(0.85)	(0.39)		
	χ^2-test	[1.09]	[0.17]	[67.69*]	
BP CD	State 1	0.016*	0.138*	0.971	0.080
		(2.08)	(2.78)		
	State 2	− 0.056*	0.433*	0.841	0.803
		(2.49)	(3.05)		
	χ^2-test	[9.68*]	[4.04*]	[23.15*]	
JY DM	State 1	0.135*	− 0.024	0.981	0.182
		(5.75)	(0.92)		
	State 2	− 1.376*	1.341*	0.703	0.831
		(12.03)	(7.53)		
	χ^2-test	[170.3*]	[57.05*]	[27.29*]	
JY CD	State 1	0.117*	0.008	0.986	0.166
		(6.55)	(0.19)		
	State 2	− 0.703*	2.341*	0.702	0.935
		(9.86)	(9.10)		
	χ^2-test	[123.9*]	[79.9*]	[23.15*]	
DM CD	State 1	0.153*	0.027	0.971	0.065
		(3.14)	(1.22)		
	State 2	0.445*	− 0.163*	0.839	0.814
		(3.02)	(2.62)		
	χ^2-test	[3.72**]	[8.83*]	[144.2*]	

Notes: Absolute *t*-values in parentheses.
*: Significance at the 5 % level.
**: Significance at the 10 % level.
$p_{ii} = Pr(s_t = i \mid s_{t-1} = i)$.
χ^2-test: Chi-squared statistics of $H_0^{(2)}$ and $H_0^{(3)}$.
U.S./JY is multiplied by 100; U.S./NT is multiplied by 20.

EXHIBIT 12-6

Mixture Distribution Model: Markov Switching Method
Multiple Cross-Hedging—Three Futures
$y_t = \alpha_s + \beta(1)f_t^1 + \beta(2)f_t^2 + \beta(3)f_t^3 + \epsilon_t$

		$\beta(1)$	$\beta(2)$	$\beta(3)$	p_{ii}	R^2
BP JY DM	State 1	0.019	0.125*	− 0.058**	0.984	0.206
		(1.55)	(4.32)	(1.69)		
	State 2	− 0.264*	− 0.691*	0.943*	0.821	0.766
		(2.09)	(3.70)	(4.16)		
	χ^2-test	[4.93*]	[18.68*]	[18.91*]	[77.21*]	
BP JY CD	State 1	0.006	0.106	0.004	0.986	0.168
		(0.61)	(0.43)	(.011)		
	State 2	0.099	− 1.915*	2.110*	0.693	0.945
		(1.05)	(4.33)	(6.43)		
	χ^2-test	[0.97]	[24.09*]	[40.42*]	[21.99*]	
BP DM CD	State 1	0.019**	− 0.012	0.138*	0.971	0.080
		(1.78)	(0.04)	(2.76)		
	State 2	0.006	− 0.178	0.452*	0.836	0.819
		(0.07)	(0.71)	(3.00)		
	χ^2-test	[0.02]	[0.44]	[4.15*]	[134.6*]	
JY DM CD	State 1	0.133*	− 0.029	0.008	0.986	0.171
		(5.95)	(1.19)	(0.19)		
	State 2	− 0.823*	0.237	2.071*	0.691	0.943
		(4.76)	(0.74)	(4.79)		
	χ^2-test	[30.17*]	[0.42]	[22.71*]	[21.59*]	

Notes: Absolute *t*-values in parentheses.
*: Significance at the 5 percent level.
**: Significance at the 10 percent level.
$p_{ii} = Pr(s_t = i \mid s_{t-1} = i)$.
χ^2-test: Chi-squared statistics of $H_0^{(2)}$ and $H_0^{(3)}$.
U.S./JY is multiplied by 100; U.S./NT is multiplied by 20.

First, low and high R^2s are found in states 1 and 2, respectively. Second, more hedge ratios are significant in state 2 than in state 1. Third, except for the case of multiple cross-hedgings (BP, DM) in Exhibit 12–5, all multiple cross-hedgings reject $H_0^{(2)}$. Finally, the null of $H_0^{(3)}$ is rejected at the 5 percent level for all cases; that is, the assumption of a finite mixture of two normal distributions also holds for multiple cross-hedgings.

E X H I B I T   12–7

Mixture Distribution Model: Markov Switching Method
Multiple Cross-Hedging—Four Futures

$$y_t = \alpha_s + \beta(1)f_t^1 + \beta(2)f_t^2 + \beta(3)f_t^3 + \beta(4)f_t^4 + \epsilon_t$$

		$\beta(1)$	$\beta(2)$	$\beta(3)$	$\beta(4)$	p_{ii}	R^2
BP JY	State 1	0.032*	0.063*	− 0.050*	− 0.008	0.966	0.173
DM CD		(2.83)	(2.24)	(1.68)	(0.19)		
	State 2	0.531*	− 0.111	1.253*	1.269*	0.777	0.839
		(8.48)	(1.52)	(9.32)	(6.49)		
	χ^2-test	[77.87*]	[5.06*]	[89.19*]	[41.34*]	[82.03*]	

Notes: Absolute *t*-value in parentheses.
*: Significance at the 5 percent level.
**: Significance at the 10 percent level.
$p_{ii} = Pr(s_t = i | s_{t-1} = i)$.
χ^2-test: Chi-squared statistics of $H_0^{(2)}$ and $H_0^{(3)}$.
U.S./JY is multiplied by 100; U.S./NT is multiplied by 20.

Next we consider the ideal hedging instrument to mitigate the NT dollar exchange rate risk. As investors can effectively reduce exchange rate risk only in state 2, the R^2 of state 2 is examined. In the single cross-hedging case (Exhibit 12–3), the yen futures yield the highest R^2 (= 0.958) of the four futures. In the case of two-futures hedging (Exhibit 12–5), the R^2s of using two futures—(BP, JY) and (JY, CD)—are 0.940 and 0.935, respectively, which are the highest among all two-futures hedgings. In the case of three futures hedgings (Exhibit 12–6), the combination of three futures (BP, JY, CD) produces the highest R^2 (= 0.945), and the combination of (JY, DM, CD) follows. One notable feature of the above results is that the yen futures always appear in the case with the best performance. This frequency suggests that yen futures are the ideal hedging instrument to reduce NT dollar exchange risk. Eaker and Grant (1987) found that trade ranks and hedging effectiveness are correlated with each other. Therefore, the yen futures may plausibly account for a large amount of the NT dollar exchange rate risk since Japan is the largest importing and the third largest exporting partner of Taiwan. A hedger desiring to reduce the NT dollar exchange risk can thus first predict the smoothed probability of state 2 of the next period. If the probability is more then 50 percent, the exchange risk can be reduced by employing the yen futures. If the probability is less than 50 percent, the market is more likely in state 1, indicating little opportunity to hedge.[10]

Exhibits 12–5–12–7 exhibit the smoothed probabilities of state 2 of multiple cross-hedgings. Similar patterns as those in Exhibit 12–4 are displayed. Most smoothed probabilities are quite close to unity during the above-mentioned two periods. The move of the central bank toward further foreign exchange liberalization has raised the probability of the occurrence of the effective hedging state.

CONCLUSION

Historically, less developed countries deal with foreign exchange risk by pegging. The recent tide of financial deregulation has allowed these countries' exchange rates to compete directly in the "dirty float" system. A means of reducing foreign exchange risk for these currencies, however, is not straightforward. A specific minor currency is employed here to illustrate a new estimation method for cross-hedging. However, this method can be applied to other minor currencies immediately.

Empirical evidence on the effectiveness of cross-hedging of NT dollar exchange rate risk is presented in this chapter. The Markov switching model demonstrates that the cross-hedgings exhibit effective risk reduction during certain periods. As the probabilities of these effective hedging periods are predictable, investors are capable of utilizing this information successfully to hedge the risk. These findings are different from those previously obtained by the OLS method, which infers that NT dollar exchange rate risk cannot be reduced at any time via the usage of cross-hedgings.

---

10. It is worth noting that no forecasting comparison on the basis of the objection function (1) is conducted in the present study. The reason for not doing so is that most OLS hedge ratios, which have been found to be insignificantly different from zero, offer little help in cross-hedging NT exchange risk. The MS model, on the other hand, argues that the cross-hedge is still possible if the smoothed probability of state 2 is high. Thus, employing the MS model can at least improve the chance of reducing NT exchange risk.

The following steps are recommended for hedgers seeking to avoid NT dollar exchange rate risk. First, apply the Markov model to forecast the smoothed probability of state 2. There will be little chance of hedging the risk if the predicted smoothed probability tends to be low (e.g., less than 50 percent) in the next period. On the other hand, if the predicted probability is high (e.g., more than 50 percent), investors can then consider yen futures to avoid exchange rate risk.

EXHIBIT 12–8

Smoothed Probability of State 2—Two Futures

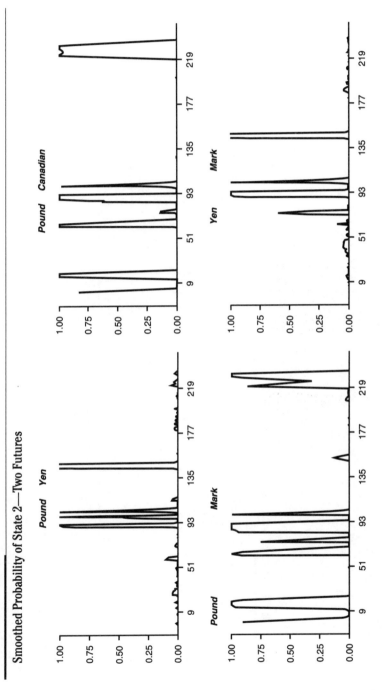

EXHIBIT 12-8 *Continued*

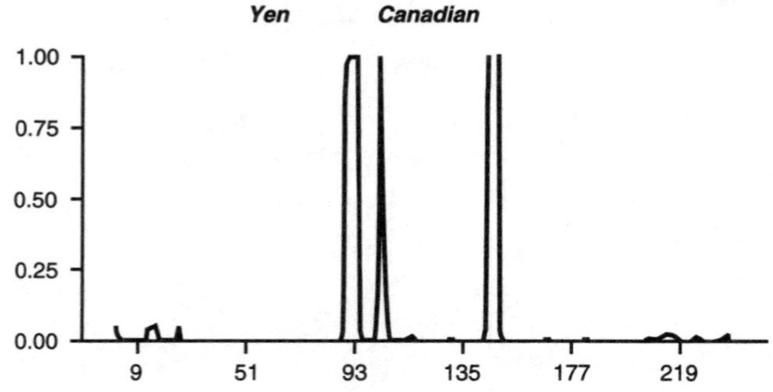

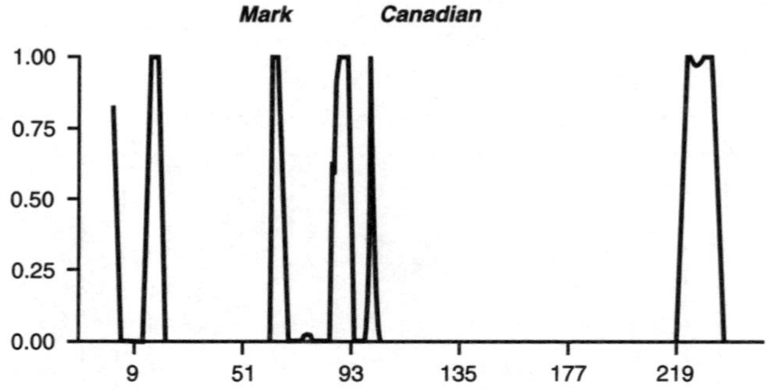

EXHIBIT 12-9

Smoothed Probability of State 2—Three Futures

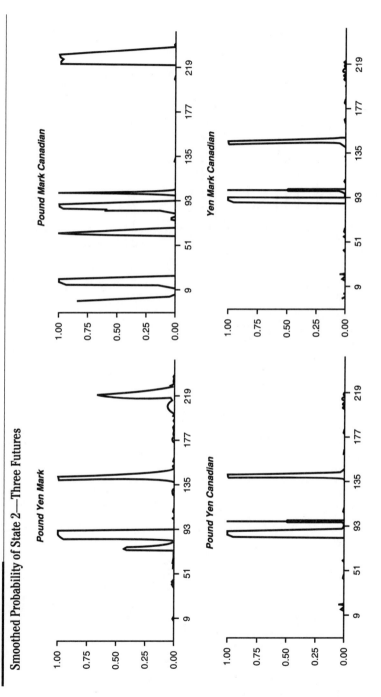

EXHIBIT 12–10

Smoothed Probability of State 2—Four Futures

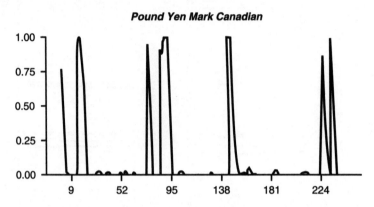

REFERENCES

Anderson, R. W.; and J. P. Danthine. "Cross Hedging." *The Journal of Political Economics* 89, no. 6(1981), pp. 1182–1196.

Benet, B. A. "Commodity Futures Cross Hedging of Foreign Exchange Exposure." *The Journal of Futures Markets* 10(1990), pp. 287–306.

Benet, B. A. "Hedge Period Length and Ex-Ante Futures Hedging Effectiveness: The Case of Foreign-Exchange Risk Cross Hedges." *The Journal of Futures Markets* 12(1992), pp. 163–175.

Eaker, M. R.; and D. Grant. "Cross-Hedging Foreign Currency Risk." *Journal of International Money and Finance* 6(March 1987), pp. 85–106.

Ederington, L. H. "The Hedging Performance of the New Futures Markets." *Journal of Finance* 34(1979), pp. 156–170.

Engle, C.; and J. D. Hamilton. "Long Swings in the Dollar: Are They in the Data and Do Markets Know It?" *American Economic Review* 80(1990), pp. 689–713.

Figlewski, S. "Hedging Performance and Basis Risk in Stock Index Futures." *Journal of Finance* 39(1984), pp. 657–669.

Figlewski, S. "Hedging with Stock Index Futures: Theory and Application in a New Market." *The Journal of Futures Markets* 5(1985), pp. 183–199.

Franckle, C. T. "The Hedging Performance of the New Futures Market: Comment." *Journal of Finance* 35(December 1980), pp. 1272–1279.

Gon, S. C.; and C. L. Chen. "Cross-Hedging Performance of Foreign Currency Futures—Varying Parameter Model." In *Proceedings of the Conference on the Theories and Practices of Security and Financial Markets,* pp. 630–655, Kung Shung, ROC, 1992.

Grammatikos, T. "Intervalling Effects and the Hedging Performance of Foreign Currency Futures." *Financial Review* 21(1986), pp. 21–36.

Grammatikos, T.; and A. Saunders. "Stability and the Hedging Performance of Foreign Currency Futures." *The Journal of Futures Markets* 3(1983), pp. 296–305.

Hamilton, J. D. "Rational Expectations Econometric Analysis of Changes in Regime." *Journal of Economic Dynamics and Control* 12(1988), pp. 385–423.

Hamilton, J. D. "A New Approach to the Economic Analysis of Nonstationary Time Series and the Business Cycle." *Econometrica* 57(1989), pp. 357–384.

Hamilton, J. D. "Analysis of Time Series Subject to Changes in Regime." *Journal of Econometrics* 45(1990), pp. 39–70.

Harris, L. "Price and Volume Effects Associated with Changes in the S&P 500 List: New Evidence for the Existence of Price Pressures." *Journal of Finance* 41(1986), pp. 815–829.

Hill, J.; Joseph Liro; and T. Schneeweis. "Hedging Performance of GNMA Futures Under Rising and Falling Interest Rates." *The Journal of Futures Markets* 3(1983), pp. 403–413.

Hill, J.; T. Schneeweis. "A Note on the Hedging Effectiveness of Foreign Currency Futures." *The Journal of Futures Markets* 1(1981), pp. 660–663.

Hill, J.; and T. Schneeweis. "Risk Reduction Potential of Financial Futures for Corporate Bond Positions." In *Interest Rate Futures,* eds. G. D. Gay and K. W. Kolb. Richmond, VA: Robert F. Dame, 1982.

Hill, J.; and T. Schneeweis. "Reducing Volatility with Financial Futures." *Financial Analysts Journal* 30(1984), pp. 34–40.

Howard, C.; and L. D'Antonio. "A Risk-Return Measure of Hedging Effectiveness." *Journal of Financial and Quantitative Analysis* 19(1984), pp. 101–112.

Johnson, L. L. "The Theory of Hedging and Speculation in Commodity Futures." *Review of Economic Studies* 27(1960), pp. 139–151.

Junkus, J. C.; and C. F. Lees. "Use of Three Stock Index Futures in Hedging Decisions." *The Journal of Futures Markets* 5(1985), pp. 201–222.

Malliaris, A. G.; and J. L. Urrutia. "Tests of Random Walk of Hedge Ratios and Measures of Hedging Effectiveness for Stock Indexes and Foreign Currencies," *The Journal of Futures Markets*, 11(1), February 1991, pp. 55–68.

Overdahl, J. A.; and D. R. Starleaf. "The Hedging Performance of the CD Futures Markets." *The Journal of Futures Markets* 6(1986), pp. 71–81.

Shen, C. H. "Estimating Efficiency of Taiwan–U.S. Exchange Rate Markets—A Markov Switching Model." *Asian Economic Journal,* forthcoming, 1994.

Stein, J. L. "The Simultaneous Determination of Spot and Futures Prices." *American Economic Review* 51(Autumn 1961), pp. 1012–1025.

Tauchen, G.; and M. Pitts. "The Price Variability–Volume Relationship on Speculative Markets." *Econometrica* 51(1983), pp. 485–505.

13

THE AVAILABILITY OF HEDGING INSTRUMENTS IN EMERGING MARKETS

George P. Tsetsekos, *Drexel University*

DERIVATIVE MARKETS IN EMERGING COUNTRY ECONOMIES

There are several active markets for derivatives in developing countries. Using data from the Futures Institute, we have counted 21 countries that already have established organized exchanges. Outside the G–7 countries, organized exchanges have been established in several other countries as well, including Argentina, Brazil, Denmark, the Philippines, Finland, Hong Kong, Hungary, Israel, Malaysia, Singapore, South Africa, Spain, Sweden, and Switzerland.

In Exhibit 13–1 we provide a tabulation of the exchanges. This exhibit reports the name of the exchange, the country where the exchange has been established, the contract classification, and the contract(s) description for each exchange. We have classified the exchange-traded derivative contracts into seven categories:

1. Agricultural instruments, including grains, food and fiber.
2. Index derivative instruments.

3. Financial instruments, including interest rate products.
4. Precious metals.
5. Swap contracts.
6. Equities derivative contracts.
7. Energy derivative contracts.

The country with the largest number of derivative contracts traded is Brazil, followed by Singapore, Hong Kong, and Spain. It appears that Brazil also trades the largest diversity of contracts in its exchange. In all of the developing countries, there is just one exchange where contracts are traded. The exception is Spain, where there are two exchanges with active derivative contracts: the MEFF Renta Fija (RF) and the MEFF Renta Variable (RV).

DERIVATIVE INSTRUMENTS IN EMERGING COUNTRY ECONOMIES

A closer examination of the exchange-traded instruments reveals that financial contracts are the most popular traded derivatives. There are over 44 interest rate derivative products traded in 21 developing country exchanges. Another class of derivative products that appears to be popular is the index on equities. We counted 39 contracts on equity indexes traded in the exchanges.

To determine the "aging" of exchange-traded derivatives, we developed Exhibit 13–2. This exhibit reports the contract classification, the country, the exchange, and the contract description, followed by the first date on which trading on the contract began. The Rosario Futures Exchange (ROFEX) is the oldest established exchange, with a contract traded on commodities in 1910! The majority of the contracts, however, initiated trading at the end of the 1980s, with a large portion of them establishing a presence in the exchange by the beginning of 1989–1990. Almost 25 percent of the contracts have been introduced in the local exchanges only recently, that is, after 1993. The evidence also suggests that the most recent derivative instruments are based on foreign exchange rates. Commodity derivative products constitute the oldest class of products introduced in these exchanges.

Taken together, these exhibits provide empirical evidence for the availability of exchange-traded derivative contracts in well-established exchanges in emerging country economies.

Emerging Markets Derivate Exchanges

Exchange	Country	Contract Classification	Contract Description
The Rosario Futures Exchange (ROFEX) (Mercado a Termino de Rosario, S.A.)	Argentina	Agriculture: Grains, food, and fiber	Corn, futures
The Rosario Futures Exchange (ROFEX) (Mercado a Termino de Rosario, S.A.)	Argentina	Agriculture: Grains, food and fiber	Rosafe soybean index futures
The Rosario Futures Exchange (ROFEX) (Mercado a Termino de Rosario, S.A.)	Argentina	Agriculture: Grains, food and fiber	Wheat futures
The Rosario Futures Exchange (ROFEX) (Mercado a Termino de Rosario, S.A.)	Argentina	Agriculture: Grains, food, and fiber	Options on rosafe soybean futures
Austrian Futures and Options Exchange (OTOB)	Austria	Equities 7	Equity options (7 listed)
Austrian Futures and Options Exchange (OTOB)	Austria	Index	Austrian-traded index (ATX) futures
Austrian Futures and Options Exchange (OTOB)	Austria	Index	Austrian-traded index (ATX) options
Austrian Futures and Options Exchange (OTOB)	Austria	Interest rate	Austrian government bond futures
BELFOX c.v./s.c.	Belgium	Currencies	Options on the USD/BEF exchange rate
BELFOX c.v./s.c.	Belgium	Equities 8	Equity options (8 listed)
BELFOX c.v./s.c.	Belgium	Index	BEL 20 index futures
BELFOX c.v./s.c.	Belgium	Index	Options on the BEL 20 index
BELFOX c.v./s.c.	Belgium	Index	B-Gold index options
BELFOX c.v./s.c.	Belgium	Interest rate	Belgian government bond futures

Continued

259

EXHIBIT 13-1 *Continued*

Exchange	Country	Contract Classification	Contract Description
BELFOX c.v./s.c.	Belgium	Interest rate	Options on the Belgian government bond futures
BELFOX s.c./c.v.	Belgium	Index	BIBOR three-month futures
Bolsa de Mercadorias & Futuros	Brazil	Agriculture: Grains, food, and fiber	Arabica coffee (U.S. dollar-denominated) futures
Bolsa de Mercadorias & Futuros	Brazil	Agriculture: Grains, food, and fiber	Robusta coffee (U.S. dollar-denominated) futures
Bolsa de Mercadorias & Futuros	Brazil	Agriculture: Grains, food, and fiber	Cotton futures (U.S. dollar-denominated)
Bolsa de Mercadorias & Futuros	Brazil	Agriculture: Grains, food, and fiber	Soybeans (U.S. dollar-denominated) futures
Bolsa de Mercadorias & Futuros	Brazil	Agriculture: Grains, food, and fiber	Crystal sugar (U.S. dollar-denominated) futures
Bolsa de Mercadorias & Futuros	Brazil	Agriculture: Grains, food, and fiber	Options on arabica coffee futures
Bolsa de Mercadorias & Futuros	Brazil	Agriculture: Meat and livestock	Feeder cattle (U.S. dollar-denominated) futures
Bolsa de Mercadorias & Futuros	Brazil	Agriculture: Meat and livestock	Live cattle (U.S. dollar-denominated) futures
Bolsa de Mercadorias & Futuros	Brazil	Agriculture: Meat and livestock	Options on live cattle futures
Bolsa de Mercadorias & Futuros	Brazil	Currencies	U.S. dollar (commercial) futures
Bolsa de Mercadorias & Futuros	Brazil	Currencies	U.S. dollar (floating) futures
Bolsa de Mercadorias & Futuros	Brazil	Currencies	U.S. dollar (commercial) options on actuals
Bolsa de Mercadorias & Futuros	Brazil	Currencies	U.S. dollar (flexible U.S. dollar options)
Bolsa de Mercadorias & Futuros	Brazil	Currencies	(Floating) options on actuals
Bolsa de Mercadorias & Futuros	Brazil	Currencies	Exchange rate swap
Bolsa de Mercadorias & Futuros	Brazil	Index	BOVESPA index futures
Bolsa de Mercadorias & Futuros	Brazil	Index	Options on BOVESPA stock index futures
Bolsa de Mercadorias & Futuros	Brazil	Interest rate	One-day interbank deposit futures
Bolsa de Mercadorias & Futuros	Brazil	Interest rate	Thirty-day interbank deposit futures
Bolsa de Mercadorias & Futuros	Brazil	Interest rate	Options on one-day interbank deposit futures

Exchange	Country	Contract Classification	Contract Description
Bolsa de Mercadorias & Futuros	Brazil	Interest rate	Interest rate swap
Bolsa de Mercadorias & Futuros	Brazil	Precious metals	Gold futures
Bolsa de Mercadorias & Futuros	Brazil	Precious metals	U.S. dollar-denominated gold futures
Bolsa de Mercadorias & Futuros	Brazil	Precious metals	Gold spot
Bolsa de Mercadorias & Futuros	Brazil	Precious metals	Gold options on actuals
Bolsa de Mercadorias & Futuros	Brazil	Swap	Basic financial rate × exchange rate swap
Bolsa de Mercadorias & Futuros	Brazil	Swap	Basic financial rate × gold price variation swap
Bolsa de Mercadorias & Futuros	Brazil	Swap	Basic financial rate × inflation index swap
Bolsa de Mercadorias & Futuros	Brazil	Swap	Basic financial rate × reference rate swap
Bolsa de Mercadorias & Futuros	Brazil	Swap	Exchange rate × gold price variation swap
Bolsa de Mercadorias & Futuros	Brazil	Swap	Inflation rate × exchange rate swap
Bolsa de Mercadorias & Futuros	Brazil	Swap	Inflation index × gold price variation swap
Bolsa de Mercadorias & Futuros	Brazil	Swap	Interest rate × basic financial rate swap
Bolsa de Mercadorias & Futuros	Brazil	Swap	Interest rate × exchange rate swap
Bolsa de Mercadorias & Futuros	Brazil	Swap	Interest rate × gold price swap
Bolsa de Mercadorias & Futuros	Brazil	Swap	Interest rate × inflation index swap
Bolsa de Mercadorias & Futuros	Brazil	Swap	Interest rate × reference rate swap
Bolsa de Mercadorias & Futuros	Brazil	Swap	Reference rate × exchange rate swap
Bolsa de Mercadorias & Futuros	Brazil	Swap	Reference rate × gold price variation swap
Bolsa de Mercadorias & Futuros	Brazil	Swap	Reference rate × inflation index swap
Rio de Janeiro Stock Exchange	Brazil	Equities 1	Options on equities
Rio de Janeiro Stock Exchange	Brazil	Index	ISENN stock index futures

Continued

EXHIBIT 13–1 *Continued*

Exchange	Country	Contract Classification	Contract Description
Rio de Janeiro Stock Exchange	Brazil	Index	ISENN stock index options
Copenhagen Stock Exchange	Denmark	Equities 9	Options on Danish equities (9 listed)
Copenhagen Stock Exchange	Denmark	Index	KFX, stock index futures
Copenhagen Stock Exchange	Denmark	Index	Options on KFX futures
Copenhagen Stock Exchange	Denmark	Interest rate	Futures on three-month CIBOR
Copenhagen Stock Exchange	Denmark	Interest rate	Long-term Danish government bond futures
Copenhagen Stock Exchange	Denmark	Interest rate	Medium-term Danish government bond futures
Copenhagen Stock Exchange	Denmark	Interest rate	Six percent 2026 mortgage credit bond futures
Copenhagen Stock Exchange	Denmark	Interest rate	Options on long-term Danish government bond futures
Manila International Futures Exchange, Inc.	Philippines	Agriculture: Grains, food, and fiber	Dry cocoon futures
Manila International Futures Exchange, Inc.	Philippines	Agriculture: Grains, food, and fiber	Coffee futures
Manila International Futures Exchange, Inc.	Philippines	Agriculture: Grains, food, and fiber	COPRA futures
Manila International Futures Exchange, Inc.	Philippines	Agriculture: Grains, food, and fiber	Soybean futures
Manila International Futures Exchange, Inc.	Philippines	Agriculture: Grains, food, and fiber	Sugar futures
Manila International Futures Exchange, Inc.	Philippines	Currencies	U.S. dollar–British pound futures
Manila International Futures Exchange, Inc.	Philippines	Currencies	U.S. dollar–Deutsche mark futures
Manila International Futures Exchange, Inc.	Philippines	Currencies	U.S.dollar–peso futures
Manila International Futures Exchange, Inc.	Philippines	Currencies	U.S. dollar–Swiss franc futures
Manila International Futures Exchange, Inc.	Philippines	Currencies	U.S. dollar–yen futures
Manila International Futures Exchange, Inc.	Philippines	Interest rate	Imterest rate futures
Finnish Options Market (SOM)	Finland	Currencies	Currency futures

Exchange	Country	Contract Classification	Contract Description
Finnish Options Market (SOM)	Finland	Currencies	Options on currency futures
Finnish Options Market (SOM)	Finland	Equities 11	STOX equity options (11 Stocks)
Finnish Options Market (SOM)	Finland	Equities 19	Finnish equity futures (STOX) (19 Stocks)
Finnish Options Market (SOM)	Finland	Index	FOX index futures
Finnish Options Market (SOM)	Finland	Index	FOX index options
Finnish Options Market (SOM)	Finland	Interest rate	Finnish government bond futures
Finnish Options Market (SOM)	Finland	Interest rate	HELIBOR futures
Hong Kong Futures Exchange Ltd.	Hong Kong	Currencies	Rolling FOREX futures (deutsche mark)
Hong Kong Futures Exchange Ltd.	Hong Kong	Currencies	Rolling FOREX futures (yen)
Hong Kong Futures Exchange Ltd.	Hong Kong	Equities 1	Hong Kong telecommunications (stock) futures
Hong Kong Futures Exchange Ltd.	Hong Kong	Equities 1	HSBC holdings (stock) PLC futures
Hong Kong Futures Exchange Ltd.	Hong Kong	Index	Hang Seng index futures
Hong Kong Futures Exchange Ltd.	Hong Kong	Index	Hang Seng commerce and industry sub-index futures
Hong Kong Futures Exchange Ltd.	Hong Kong	Index	Hang Seng finance sub-index futures
Hong Kong Futures Exchange Ltd.	Hong Kong	Index	Hang Seng properties sub-index futures
Hong Kong Futures Exchange Ltd.	Hong Kong	Index	Hang Seng utilities sub-index futures
Hong Kong Futures Exchange Ltd.	Hong Kong	Index	Options on the Hang Seng index
Hong Kong Futures Exchange Ltd.	Hong Kong	Interest rate	Three-month HIBOR futures
Hong Kong Futures Exchange Ltd.	Hong Kong	Precious Metals	Gold futures
Budapest Commodity Exchange	Hungary	Agriculture: Grains, food, and fiber	Feed barley futures
Budapest Commodity Exchange	Hungary	Agriculture: Grains, food, and fiber	Black seed futures
Budapest Commodity Exchange	Hungary	Agriculture: Grains, food, and fiber	Corn futures

Continued

263

E X H I B I T 13-1 *Continued*

Exchange	Country	Contract Classification	Contract Description
Budapest Commodity Exchange	Hungary	Agriculture: Grains, food, and fiber	Feed wheat futures
Budapest Commodity Exchange	Hungary	Agriculture: Grains, food, and fiber	Milling wheat futures
Budapest Commodity Exchange	Hungary	Agriculture: Grains, food, and fiber	BL 52 wheat flour futures
Budapest Commodity Exchange	Hungary	Agriculture: Meat and livestock	Live hog No. 1 futures
Budapest Commodity Exchange	Hungary	Agriculture: Meat and livestock	Live hog No. 2 futures
Budapest Commodity Exchange	Hungary	Currencies	USA Dollar (USD) futures
Budapest Commodity Exchange	Hungary	Currencies	German mark (DEM) futures
Budapest Commodity Exchange	Hungary	Currencies	Yen futures
Budapest Commodity Exchange	Hungary	Interest rate	Interest rate futures
Budapest Stock Exchange	Hungary	Currencies	DEM/HUF currency futures
Budapest Stock Exchange	Hungary	Currencies	USD/HUF currency futures
Budapest Stock Exchange	Hungary	Index	Budapest stock index (BUX) futures
Budapest Stock Exchange	Hungary	Interest rate	3-month Hungarian Treasury bill futures
Irish Futures and Options Exchange	Ireland	Interest rate	3-month DIBOR futures (Dublin interbank offered rate)
Irish Futures and Options Exchange	Ireland	Interest rate	Long gilt futures (Irish government stock)
Irish Futures and Options Exchange	Ireland	Interest rate	Medium gilt futures (Irish government stock)
Irish Futures and Options Exchange	Ireland	Interest rate	Short gilt futures (Irish government stock)
The Tel-Aviv Stock Exchange	Israel	Currencies	Shekel/dollar option
The Tel-Aviv Stock Exchange	Israel	Index	MAOF–25 index option
Kuala Lumpur Commodity Exchange	Malaysia	Agriculture: Grains, food, and fiber	Cocoa futures
Kuala Lumpur Commodity Exchange	Malaysia	Agriculture: Grains, food, and fiber	Crude palm kernel oil futures
Kuala Lumpur Commodity Exchange	Malaysia	Agriculture: Grains, food, and fiber	Crude palm oil futures

Exchange	Country	Contract Classification	Contract Description
Kuala Lumpur Commodity Exchange	Malaysia	Agriculture: Grains, food, and fiber	Standard Malaysia rubber (SMR) 20 futures
Kuala Lumpur Commodity Exchange	Malaysia	Nonprecious metals	Tin futures
Agricultural Futures Market Amsterdam (ATA)	Netherlands	Agriculture: Grains, food, and fiber	Potato BINTJE 50MM upwards futures
Oslo Stock Exchange	Norway	Index	OBX index futures
Oslo Stock Exchange	Norway	Index	Options on the OBX index
Oslo Stock Exchange	Norway	Index	Long OBX index call options
Oslo Stock Exchange	Norway	Interest rate	7-year Norwegian bond futures
Oslo Stock Exchange	Norway	Interest rate	10-year Norwegian bond futures
Singapore International Monetary Exchange	Singapore	Currencies	British pound futures—delisted June 23, 1995
Singapore International Monetary Exchange	Singapore	Currencies	Deferred spot U.S. dollar/deutsche mark
Singapore International Monetary Exchange	Singapore	Currencies	Deferred spot U.S. dollar/Japanese yen
Singapore International Monetary Exchange	Singapore	Currencies	Deutsche mark futures—delisted June 23, 1995
Singapore International Monetary Exchange	Singapore	Currencies	Eurodollar futures
Singapore International Monetary Exchange	Singapore	Currencies	Euromark futures
Singapore International Monetary Exchange	Singapore	Currencies	Euroyen futures
Singapore International Monetary Exchange	Singapore	Currencies	Japanese yen futures—delisted June 23, 1995

Continued

EXHIBIT 13-1 *Continued*

Exchange	Country	Contract Classification	Contract Description
Singapore International Monetary Exchange	Singapore	Currencies	Options on Eurodollar futures
Singapore International Monetary Exchange	Singapore	Currencies	Options on Euroyen futures
Singapore International Monetary Exchange	Singapore	Energy	Brent crude oil futures
Singapore International Monetary Exchange	Singapore	Energy	High sulphur fuel oil futures
Singapore International Monetary Exchange	Singapore	Index	Nikkei 225 stock average futures
Singapore International Monetary Exchange	Singapore	Index	Nikkei 300 futures contract
Singapore International Monetary Exchange	Singapore	Index	SIMEX MSCI Hong Kong index futures
Singapore International Monetary Exchange	Singapore	Index	Options on Nikkei 225 futures
Singapore International Monetary Exchange	Singapore	Index	Options on Nikkei 300 futures
Singapore International Monetary Exchange	Singapore	Interest rate	Japanese government bond futures
Singapore International Monetary Exchange	Singapore	Interest rate	Options on Japanese government bond futures
Singapore International Monetary Exchange	Singapore	Precious metals	Gold futures
The South African Futures Exchange (SAFEX)	South Africa	Index	JSE actuaries all share index futures

Exchange	Country	Contract Classification	Contract Description
The South African Futures Exchange (SAFEX)	South Africa	Index	JSE all industrial index futures
The South African Futures Exchange (SAFEX)	South Africa	Index	Krugerrand futures
The South African Futures Exchange (SAFEX)	South Africa	Index	Options on JSE actuaries all gold index futures
The South African Futures Exchange (SAFEX)	South Africa	Index	Options on JSE actuaries all share index futures
The South African Futures Exchange (SAFEX)	South Africa	Index	Options on JSE all industrial index futures
The South African Futures Exchange (SAFEX)	South Africa	Index	Options on Krugerrand futures
The South African Futures Exchange (SAFEX)	South Africa	Interest rate	3-month bank bill futures
The South African Futures Exchange (SAFEX)	South Africa	Interest rate	Long bond (E168) futures
The South African Futures Exchange (SAFEX)	South Africa	Interest rate	Long bond (R150) futures
The South African Futures Exchange (SAFEX)	South Africa	Interest rate	Options on 3-month bank bill futures
The South African Futures Exchange (SAFEX)	South Africa	Interest rate	Options on long bond (E168) futures
The South African Futures Exchange (SAFEX)	South Africa	Interest rate	Options on long bond (R150) futures
The South African Futures Exchange (SAFEX)	South Africa	Precious metals	JSE actuaries all gold index futures
MEFF Renta Fija (RF), S.A.	Spain	Interest rate	MIBOR '90 plus futures (Madrid Interbank Offered Rate)

Continued

267

EXHIBIT 13–1 *Continued*

Exchange	Country	Contract Classification	Contract Description
MEFF Renta Fija (RF), S.A. Offered Rate)	Spain	Interest rate	MIBOR '360 plus futures (Madrid Interbank
MEFF Renta Fija (RF), S.A. Offered Rate)	Spain	Interest rate	MIBOR '90 plus options (Madrid Interbank
MEFF Renta Fija (RF), S.A.	Spain	Interest rate	Ten-year notional bond monthly options
MEFF Renta Fija (RF), S.A.	Spain	Interest rate	Ten-year notional bond options
MEFF Renta Fija (RF), S.A.	Spain	Interest rate	Three-year notional bond options
MEFF Renta Fija (RF), S.A.	Spain	Interest rate	Ten-year notional Spanish bond futures
MEFF Renta Fija (RF), S.A.	Spain	Interest rate	Three-year notional Spanish bond futures
MEFF Renta Variable (RV). S.A.	Spain	Equities 4	Equity options
MEFF Renta Variable (RV). S.A.	Spain	Index	IBEX 35 futures
MEFF Renta Variable (RV). S.A.	Spain	Index	IBEX 35 options
The Citrus Fruit and Commodity Futures Market of Valencia	Spain	Agriculture: Grains, food, and fiber	Navel/Navelina oranges futures
The Citrus Fruit and Commodity Futures Market of Valencia	Spain	Agriculture: Grains, food, and fiber	Valencia late oranges futures
OM Stockholm	Sweden	Equities 23	Futures on individual Swedish equities
OM Stockholm	Sweden	Equities 23	Options on individual Swedish equities
OM Stockholm	Sweden	Equities 23	Long-term options on individual Swedish equities
OM Stockholm	Sweden	Index	OMX stock index futures
OM Stockholm	Sweden	Index	OMX (index) options
OM Stockholm	Sweden	Index	Long-term OMX index options
OM Stockholm	Sweden	Interest rate	IMM forward rate agreement IMM-FRA

Exchange	Country	Contract Classification	Contract Description
OM Stockholm MBB2/MBB5	Sweden	Interest rate	Five-year notional mortgage bond futures
OM Stockholm	Sweden	Interest rate	2-year notional Swedish bond futures OMR 2
OM Stockholm	Sweden	Interest rate	5-year notional Swedish bond futures OMR 5
OM Stockholm OMR 10	Sweden	Interest rate	10-year notional Swedish bond futures
OM Stockholm	Sweden	Interest rate	Two-year notional urban mortgage bank of Sweden bond futures ST2
OM Stockholm	Sweden	Interest rate	Five-year notional urban mortgage bank of Sweden bond futures ST5
OM Stockholm	Sweden	Interest rate	Swedish Treasury bill futures OMVX 180
OM Stockholm	Sweden	Interest rate	5-year notional Swedish bond options OMR5
Swiss Options and Financial Futures Exchange, Ltd. (SOFFEX)	Switzerland	Interest rate	Options on Swiss government bond (CONF) futures
Swiss Options and Financial Futures Exchange, Ltd. (SOFFEX)	Switzerland	Equities 1	Low exercise price equity options
Swiss Options and Financial Futures Exchange, Ltd. (SOFFEX)	Switzerland	Equities 13	Equity options
Swiss Options and Financial Futures Exchange, Ltd. (SOFFEX)	Switzerland	Equities 5	Long-term equity options
Swiss Options and Financial Futures Exchange, Ltd. (SOFFEX)	Switzerland	Index	Swiss market index futures
Swiss Options and Financial Futures Exchange, Ltd. (SOFFEX)	Switzerland	Index	Options on Swiss market index
Swiss Options and Financial Futures Exchange, Ltd. (SOFFEX)	Switzerland	Index	Long-term options on Swiss market index
Swiss Options and Financial Futures Exchange, Ltd. (SOFFEX)	Switzerland	Interest rate	Swiss government (CONF) futures

EXHIBIT 13-2

Contract Classification in Emerging Derivative Markets

Contract Classification	Country	Market	Began Trading	Contract Description
Agriculture: Grains, food, and fiber	Argentina	The Rosario Futures Exchange (ROFEX) Mercado a Termino de Rosario, S.A.	1910	Corn futures
Agriculture: Grains, food, and fiber	Argentina	The Rosario Futures Exchange (ROFEX) Mercado a Termino de Rosario, S.A.	25-Nov-93	Rosafe soybean index futures
Agriculture: Grains, food, and fiber	Argentina	The Rosario Futures Exchange (ROFEX) Mercado a Termino de Rosario, S.A.	1910	Wheat futures
Agriculture: Grains, food, and fiber	Argentina	The Rosario Futures Exchange (ROFEX) Mercado a Termino de Rosario, S.A.	25-Nov-93	Options on rosafe soybean futures
Agriculture: Grains, food, and fiber	Brazil	Bolsa de Mercadorias & Futuros	3-Aug-89	Arabica coffee (U.S. dollar-denominated) futures
Agriculture: Grains, food, and fiber	Brazil	Bolsa de Mercadorias & Futuros	20-Mar-92	Robusta coffee (U.S. dollar-denominated) futures
Agriculture: Grains, food, and fiber	Brazil	Bolsa de Mercadorias & Futuros	27-Sep-91	Cotton futures (U.S. dollar-denominated)
Agriculture: Grains, food, and fiber	Brazil	Bolsa de Mercadorias & Futuros	16-Jul-93	Soybeans (U.S. dollar-denominated) futures
Agriculture: Grains, food, and fiber	Brazil	Bolsa de Mercadorias & Futuros	29-Sep-95	Crystal sugar (U.S. dollar-denominated) futures
Agriculture: Grains, food, and fiber	Brazil	Bolsa de Mercadorias & Futuros	September 20, 1991	Options on Arabica coffee futures
Agriculture: Grains, food, and fiber	Philippines	Manila International Futures Exchange, Inc.	8-Jul-92	Dry cocoon futures
Agriculture: Grains, food, and fiber	Philippines	Manila International Futures Exchange, Inc.	1-Feb-88	Coffee futures
Agriculture: Grains, food, and fiber	Philippines	Manila International Futures Exchange, Inc.	1-Feb-88	Copra futures

Contract Classification	Country	Market	Began Trading	Contract Description
Agriculture: Grains, food, and fiber	Philippines	Manila International Futures Exchange, Inc.	20-Oct-86	Soybean futures
Agriculture: Grains, food, and fiber	Philippines	Manila International Futures Exchange, Inc.	20-Oct-86	Sugar futures
Agriculture: Grains, food, and fiber	Hungary	Budapest Commodity Exchange	1991	Feed barley futures
Agriculture: Grains, food, and fiber	Hungary	Budapest Commodity Exchange	1992	Black seed futures
Agriculture: Grains, food, and fiber	Hungary	Budapest Commodity Exchange	1989	Corn futures
Agriculture: Grains, food, and fiber	Hungary	Budapest Commodity Exchange	1989	Feed wheat futures
Agriculture: Grains, food, and fiber	Hungary	Budapest Commodity Exchange	1989	Milling wheat futures
Agriculture: Grains, food, and fiber	Hungary	Budapest Commodity Exchange	1989	BL 52 wheat flour futures
Agriculture: Grains, food, and fiber	Malaysia	Kuala Lumpur Commodity Exchange	Aug-88	Cocoa futures
Agriculture: Grains, food, and fiber	Malaysia	Kuala Lumpur Commodity Exchange	Oct-92	Crude palm kernel oil futures
Agriculture: Grains, food, and fiber	Malaysia	Kuala Lumpur Commodity Exchange	Oct-80	Crude palm oil futures
Agriculture: Grains, food, and fiber	Malaysia	Kuala Lumpur Commodity Exchange	Mar-86	Standard Malaysia rubber (SMR) 20 futures
Agriculture: Grains, food, and fiber	New Zealand	New Zealand Futures & Options Exchange	May-91	New Zealand wool futures
Agriculture: Grains, food, and fiber	Spain	The Citrus Fruit and Commodity Futures	Sep-95	Navel/Navelina oranges futures
Agriculture: Grains, food, and fiber	Spain	The Citrus Fruit and Commodity Futures	To be launched January	Valencia late oranges futures
Agriculture: Meat and livestock	Brazil	Bolsa de Mercadorias & Futuros	12-Jun-92	Feeder cattle (U.S. dollar-denominated) futures
Agriculture: Meat and livestock	Brazil	Bolsa de Mercadorias & Futuros	7-Jun-91	Live cattle (U.S. dollar-denominated) futures
Agriculture: Meat and livestock	Brazil	Bolsa de Mercadorias & Futuros	July 22, 1994 (calls an)	Options on live cattle futures
Agriculture: Meat and livestock	Hungary	Budapest Commodity Exchange	1991	Live hog No. 1 futures

Continued

EXHIBIT 13–2 *Continued*

Contract Classification	Country	Market	Began Trading	Contract Description
Agriculture: Meat and livestock	Hungary	Budapest Commodity Exchange	1991	Live hog No. 2 futures
Currencies	Belgium	BELFOX c.v./s.c.	30-Sep-94	Options on the USD/BEF exchange rate
Currencies	Brazil	Bolsa de Mercadorias & Futuros	23-Apr-87	U.S. dollar (commercial) futures
Currencies	Brazil	Bolsa de Mercadorias & Futuros	16-Aug-91	U.S. dollar (floating) futures
Currencies	Brazil	Bolsa de Mercadorias & Futuros	August 16, 1991 (call and put)	U.S. dollar (commercial) options on actuals
Currencies	Brazil	Bolsa de Mercadorias & Futuros	2-Jun-95	U.S. dollor (flexible U.S. dollar options)
Currencies	Brazil	Bolsa de Mercadorias & Futuros	August 16, 1991 (call and put)	(Floating) options on actuals
Currencies	Brazil	Bolsa de Mercadorias & Futuros	3-Dec-93	Exchange rate swap
Currencies	Philippines	Manila International Futures Exchange, Inc.	1-Mar-91	U.S. dollar–British pound futures
Currencies	Philippines	Manila International Futures Exchange, Inc.	1-Mar-91	U.S. dollar–deutsche mark futures
Currencies	Philippines	Manila International Futures Exchange, Inc.	Nov. 3, 1992	U.S. dollar–peso futures
Currencies	Philippines	Manila International Futures Exchange, Inc.	November 11, 1991	U.S. dollar–Swiss franc futures
Currencies	Philippines	Manila International Futures Exchange, Inc.	1-Mar-91	U.S. dollar–yen futures
Currencies	Finland	Finnish Options Market (SOM)	Oct-92	Currency futures
Currencies	Finland	Finnish Options Market (SOM)	Oct-92	Options on currency futures

Contract Classification	Country	Market	Began Trading	Contract Description
Currencies	Hon Kong	Hong Kong Futures Exchange Ltd.	Last quarter of 1995	Rolling FOREX futures (deutsche mark)
Currencies	Hong Kong	Hong Kong Futures Exchange Ltd.	Last quarter of 1995	Rolling FOREX futures (yen)
Currencies	Hungary	Budapest Commodity Exchange	1993	USA dollar (USD) futures
Currencies	Hungary	Budapest Commodity Exchange	1993	German mark (DEM) futures
Currencies	Hungary	Budapest Commodity Exchange	1994	Yen futures
Currencies	Hungary	Budapest Stock Exchange	31-Mar-95	DEM/HUF currency futures
Currencies	Hungary	Budapest Stock Exchange	31-Mar-95	USD/HUF currency futures
Currencies	Israel	The Tel-Aviv Stock Excahnge	4-Oct-94	Shekel/dollar option
Currencies	New Zealand	New Zealand Futures & Options Exchange	Jan-85	U.S. dollar futures
Currencies	Singapore	Singapore International Monetary Exchange	1-Jul-86	British pound futures–delisted June 23, 1995
Currencies	Singapore	Singapore International Monetary Exchange	1-Nov-93	Deferred spot U.S. dollar/deutsche mark
Currencies	Singapore	Singapore International Monetary Exchange	1-Nov.-93	Deferred spot U.S. dollar/Japanese yen
Currencies	Singapore	Singapore International Monetary Exchange	7-Sep-84	Deutsche mark futures –delisted June 23, 1995
Currencies	Singapore	Singapore International Monetary Exchange	7-Sep-84	Eurodollar futures
Currencies	Singapore	Singapore International Monetary Exchange	20-Sep-90	Euromark futures
Currencies	Singapore	Singapore International Monetary Exchange	27-Oct-89	Euroyen futures

Continued

273

EXHIBIT 13–2 *Continued*

Contract Classification	Country	Market	Began Trading	Contract Description
Currencies	Singapore	Singapore International Monetary Exchange	7-Nov-84	Japanese yen futures—delisted June 23, 1995
Currencies	Singapore	Singapore International Monetary Exchange	25-Sep-87	Options on Eurodollar futures
Currencies	Singapore	Singapore International Monetary Exchange	19-Jun-90	Options on Euroyen futures
Energy	Singapore	Singapore International Monetary Exchange	9-Jun-95	Brent crude oil futures
Energy	Singapore	Singapore International Monetary Exchange	22-Feb-89	High sulphur fuel oil futures
Equities 1	Brazil	Rio de Janeiro Stock Exchange	Dec-82	Options on equities
Equities 1	Hong Kong	Hong Kong Futures Exchange Ltd.	31-Mar-95	Hong Kong telecommunications (stock) futures
Equities 1	Hong Kong	Hong Kong Futures Exchange Ltd.	31-Mar-95	HSBC holdings (stock) PLC futures
Equities 1	Switzerland	Swiss Options and Financial Futures Exchange	May 21, 1991	Low exercise price equity options
Equities 11	Finland	Finnish Options Market (SOM)	Oct-93	STOX equity options (11 stocks)
Equities 13	Switzerland	Swiss Options and Financial Futures Exchange	May 19, 1988	Equity options
Equities 19	Finland	Finnish Options Market (SOM)	1990	Finnish equity futures (STOX) (19 stocks)
Equities 23	Sweden	OM Stockholm	1990	Futures on individual Swedish equities
Equities 23	Sweden	OM Stockholm	1990	Options on individual Swedish equities

Contract Classification	Country	Market	Began Trading	Contract Description
Equities 23	Sweden	OM Stockholm	Apr-92	Long-term options on individual Swedish equities
Equities 4	Spain	MEFF Renta Variable (RV), S.A.		Equity options
Equities 5	Switzerland	Swiss Options and Financial Futures Exchange	2-May-94	Long-term equity options
Equities 7	Austria	Austrian Futures and Options Exchange (OTOB)		Equity options (7 listed)
Equities 7	New Zealand	New Zealand Futures & Options Exchange Limited		Equity options
Equities 8	Belgium	BELFOX c.v./s.c.		Equity options (8 listed)
Equities 9	Denmark	Copenhagen Stock Exchange	1990	Options on Danish equities (9 listed)
Index	Austria	Austrian Futures and Options Exchange	Aug-92	Austrian traded index (ATX) futures
Index	Austria	Austrian Futures and Options Exchange	Aug-92	Austrian traded index (ATX) options
Index	Belgium	BELFOX c.v./s.c.	October 29, 1993	BEL 20 index futures
Index	Belgium	BELFOX c.v./s.c.	April 2, 1993 (November 29, 1993)	Options on the BEL 20 index
Index	Belgium	BELFOX c.v./s.c.	31-Mar-95	B-gold index options
Index	Belgium	BELFOX s.c./c.v.	August 21, 1992 (June)	BIBOR three-month futures
Index	Brazil	Bolsa de Mercadorias & Futuros	14-Feb-86	BOVESPA index futures
Index	Brazil	Bolsa de Mercadorias & Futuros	October 21, 1994 (call and put)	Options on BOVESPA stock index futures
Index	Brazil	Rio de Janeiro Stock Exchange	Sep-93	ISENN stock index futures

Continued

E X H I B I T   13-2   *Continued*

Contract Classification	Country	Market	Began Trading	Contract Description
Index	Brazil	Rio de Janeiro Stock Exchange	Mar-92	ISENN stock index options
Index	Denmark	Copenhagen Stock Exchange	1989	KFX stock index futures
Index	Denmark	Copenhagen Stock Exchange	1990	Options on KFX futures
Index	Finland	Finnish Options Market (SOM)	May-88	FOX index futures
Index	Finland	Finnish Options Market (SOM)	May-88	FOX index options
Index	Hong Kong	Hong Kong Futures Exchange Ltd.	May-86	Hang Seng index futures
Index	Hong Kong	Hong Kong Futures Exchange Ltd.	1991	Hang Seng commerce and industry sub-index futures
Index	Hong Kong	Hong Kong Futures Exchange Ltd.	1991	Hang Seng finance sub-index futures
Index	Hong Kong	Hong Kong Futures Exchange Ltd.	1991	Hang Seng properties sub-index futures
Index	Hong Kong	Hong Kong Futures Exchange Ltd.	1991	Hang Seng utilities sub-index futures
Index	Hong Kong	Hong Kong Futures Exchange Ltd.	Mar-93	Options on the Hang Seng index
Index	Hungary	Budapest Stock Exchange	31-Mar-95	Budapest stock index (BUX) futures
Index	Israel	The Tel-Aviv Stock Exchange	1-Aug-93	MAOF–25 index option
Index	New Zealand	New Zealand Futures & Options Exchange	Aug-95	NZSE–10 index futures—this contract replaces the NZSE 40 index
Index	New Zealand	New Zealand Futures & Options Exchange	Aug-95	Options on NZSE–10 index futures
Index	Norway	Oslo Stock Exchange	4-Sep-92	OBX index futures

Contract Classification	Country	Market	Began Trading	Contract Description
Index	Norway	Oslo Stock Exchange	27-Jun-90	Options on the OBX index
Index	Norway	Oslo Stock Exchange	Aug-93	Long OBX index call options
Index	Singapore	Singapore International Monetary Exchange	3-Sep-86	Nikkei 225 stock average futures
Index	Singapore	Singapore International Monetary Exchange	3-Feb-95	Nikkei 300 futures contract
Index	Singapore	Singapore International Monetary Exchange	31-Mar-93	SIMEX MSCI Hong Kong index futures
Index	Singapore	Singapore International Monetary Exchange	19-Mar-92	Options on Nikkei 225 futures
Index	Singapore	Singapore International Monetary Exchange	3-Feb-95	Options on Nikkei 300 futures
Index	South Africa	The South African Futures Exchange (SAFEX)	May-90	JSE actuaries all share index futures
Index	South Africa	The South African Futures Exchange (SAFEX)	May-90	JSE all industrial index futures
Index	South Africa	The South African Futures Exchange (SAFEX)	Oct-94	Krugerrand futures
Index	South Africa	The South African Futures Exchange (SAFEX)	16-Oct-92	Options on JSE actuaries all gold index futures
Index	South Africa	The South African Futures Exchange (SAFEX)	16-Oct-92	Options on JSE actuaries all share index futures
Index	South Africa	The South African Futures Exchange (SAFEX)	16-Oct-92	Options on JSE all industrial index futures
Index	South Africa	The South African Futures Exchange (SAFEX)	Oct-94	Options on Krugerrand futures
Index	Spain	MEFF Renta Variable (RV), S.A.		IBEX 35 futures

Continued

EXHIBIT 13-2 *Continued*

Contract Classification	Country	Market	Began Trading	Contract Description
Index	Spain	MEFF Renta Variable (RV), S.A.		IBEX 35 options
Index	Sweden	OM Stockholm		OMX stock index futures
Index	Sweden	OM Stockholm		OMX (index) options
ndex	Sweden	OM Stockholm	Mar-92	Long-term OMX index options
Index	Switzerland	Swiss Options and Financial Futures Exchange, Ltd (SOFFEX)	9-Nov-90	Swiss market index futures
Index	Switzerland	Swiss Options and Financial Future Exchange, Ltd (SOFFEX)	7-Dec-88	Options on Swiss market index
Index	Switzerland	Swiss Options and Financial Futures Exchange, Ltd (SOFFEX)	2-May-94	Long term options on Swiss market index
Interest rate	Austria	Austrian Futures and Options Exchange	Jul-93	Austrian government bond futures
Interest rate	Belgium	BELFOX c.v./s.c.	6-Dec-91	Belgian government bond futures
Interest rate	Belgium	BELFOX c.v./s.c.	18-Apr-94	Options on the Belgian government bond futures
Interest rate	Brazil	Bolsa de Mercadorias & Futuros	5-Jun-91	One-day interbank deposits futures
Interest rate	Brazil	Bolsa de Mercadorias & Futuros	5-Jun-91	Thirty-day interbank deposit futures
Interest rate	Brazil	Bolsa de Mercadorias & Futuros	21-Oct-94	Options on one day interbank deposit futures
IInterest rate	Brazil	Bolsa de Mercadorias & Futuros	22-Mar-93	Interest rate swap
Interest rate	Denmark	Copenhagen Stock Exchange	1993	Futures on three-month CIBOR

Contract Classification	Country	Market	Began Trading	Contract Description
Interest rate	Denmark	Copenhagen Stock Exchange	1989	Long-term Danish government bond futures
Interest rate	Denmark	Copenhagen Stock Exchange	1992	Medium term Danish government bond futures
Interest rate	Denmark	Copenhagen Stock Exchange	1993	Six percent 2026 mortgage credit bond futures
Interest rate	Denmark	Copenhagen Stock Exchange	1989	Options on long-term Danish government bond futures
Interest rate	Philippines	Manila International Futures Exchange, Inc.	22-Oct-90	Interest rate futures
Interest rate	Finland	Finnish Options Market (SOM)	17-Jan-94	Finnish government bond futures
Interest rate	Finland	Finnish Options Market (SOM)	1993	HELIBOR futures
Interest rate	Hong Kong	Hong Kong Futures Exchange Ltd.	Feb-90	Three-month HIBOR futures
Interest rate	Hungary	Budapest Commodity Exchange	1994	Interest rate futures
Interest rate	Hungary	Budapest Stock Exchange	31-Mar-95	3-month Hungarian Treasury bill futures
Interest rate	Ireland	Irish Futures and Options Exchange	1989	3-month DIBOR futures (Dublin interbank offered rate)
Interest rate	Ireland	Irish Futures and Options Exchange	1989	Long gilt futures (Irish government stock)
Interest rate	Ireland	Irish Futures and Options Exchange	March 1995 proposed listing date	Medium gilt futures (Irish government stock)
Interest rate	Ireland	Irish Futures and Options Exchange	1990	Short gilt futures (Irish government stock)

Continued

E X H I B I T   13-2 *Continued*

Contract Classification	Country	Market	Began Trading	Contract Description
Interest rate	New Zealand	New Zealand Futures & Options Exchange	Dec-86	Bank accepted bill futures
Interest rate	New Zealand	New Zealand Futures & Options Exchange	1993	Three-year government stock futures
Interest rate	New Zealand	New Zealand Futures & Options Exchange	Jun-91	Ten-year government stock futures
Interest rate	New Zealand	New Zealand Futures & Options Exchange	Dec-88	Options on bank accepted bills futures
Interest rate	New Zealand	New Zealand Futures & Options Exchange	1993	Options on three-year government stock futures
Interest rate	New Zealand	New Zealand Futures & Options Exchange	Jun-91	Options on ten-year government stock futures
Interest rate	Norway	Oslo Stock Exchange	1994	7-year Norwegian bond futures
Interest rate	Norway	Oslo Stock Exchange	1993	10-year Norwegian bond futures
Interest rate	Singapore	Singapore International Monetary Exchange	1-Oct-93	Japanese government bond futures
Interest rate	Singapore	Singapore International Monetary Exchange	11-May-94	Options on Japanese government bond futures
Interest rate	South Africa	The South African Futures Exchange (SAFEX)	Apr-93	3-month bank bill futures
Interest rate	South Africa	The South African Futures Exchange (SAFEX)	May-90	Long bond (E168) futures
Interest rate	South Africa	The South African Futures Exchange (SAFEX)	31-Oct-94	Long bond (R150) futures

Contract Classification	Country	Market	Began Trading	Contract Description
Interest rate	South Africa	The South African Futures Exchange (SAFEX)	16-Oct-90	Options on 3-month bank bill futures
Interest rate	South Africa	The South African Futures Exchange (SAFEX)	16-Oct-90	Options on long bond (E168) futures
Interest rate	South Africa	The South African Futures Exchange (SAFEX)	31-Oct-94	Options on long bond (R150) futures
Interest rate	Spain	MEFF Renta Fija (RF), S.A.	12-Jun-95	MIBOR '90 plus futures (Madrid interbank offered rate)
Interest rate	Spain	MEFF Renta Fija (RF), S.A.	12-Jun-95	MIBOR '360 plus futures (Madrid interbank offered rate)
Interest rate	Spain	MEFF Renta Fija (RF), S.A.	1992 — MIBOR '90 199	MIBOR '90 plus options (Madrid interbank offered rate)
Interest rate	Spain	MEFF Renta Fija (RF), S.A.	1994	Ten-year notional bond monthly options
Interest rate	Spain	MEFF Renta Fija (RF), S.A.	1992	Ten-year notional bond options
Interest rate	Spain	MEFF Renta Fija (RF), S.A.	1992	Three-year notional bond options
Interest rate	Spain	MEFF Renta Fija (RF), S.A.	1992	Ten-year notional Spanish bond futures
Interest rate	Spain	MEFF Renta Fija (RF), S.A.	16-Mar-90	Three-year notional Spanish bond futures
Interest rate	Sweden	OM Stockholm		IMM forward rate agreement IMM-FRA
Interest rate	Sweden	OM Stockholm		Five-year notional Mortgage bond futures MBB2/MBB5
Interest rate	Sweden	OM Stockholm		2-year notional Swedish bond futures OMR 2

Continued

EXHIBIT 13-2 *Continued*

Contract Classification	Country	Market	Began Trading	Contract Description
Interest rate	Sweden	OM Stockholm		5-year notional Swedish bond futures OMR 5
Interest rate	Sweden	OM Stockholm		10-year notional Swedish bond futures OMR 10
Interest rate	Sweden	OM Stockholm		Two-year notional urban mortgage bank of Sweden bond futures ST2
Interest rate	Sweden	OM Stockholm		Five-year notional urban mortgage bank of Sweden bond futures ST5
Interest rate	Sweden	OM Stockholm		Swedish Treasury bill futures OMVX 180
Interest rate	Sweden	OM Stockholm		5-year notional Swedish bond options OMR 5
Interest rate	Switzerland	Swiss Options and Financial Futures Exchange	28-Jan-94	Options on Swiss government bond (CONF) futures
Interest rate	Switzerland	Swiss Options and Financial Futures Exchange	29-May-92	Swiss government bond (CONF) futures
Nonprecious metals	Malaysia	Kuala Lumpur Commodity Exchange	Oct-87	Tin futures
Precious metals	Brazil	Bolsa de Mercadorias & Futuros	14-Mar-86	Gold futures
Precious metals	Brazil	Bolsa de Mercadorias & Futuros	27-Aug-93	U.S. dollar-denominated gold futures
Precious metals	Brazil	Bolsa de Mercadorias & Futuros	31-Jan-86	Gold spot
Precious metals	Brazil	Bolsa de Mercadorias & Futuros	Call options began trading on January 31, 1986. Put options began trading on November 27, 1987.	Gold options on actuals

Contract Classification	Country	Market	Began Trading	Contract Description
Precious metals	Hong Kong	Hong Kong Futures Exchange Ltd.	Aug-80	Gold futures
Precious metals	Singapore	Singapore International Monetary Exchange	2-May-90	Gold futures
Precious metals	South Africa	The South African Futures Exchange (SAFEX)	May-90	JSE actuaries all gold index futures
Swap	Brazil	Bolsa de Mercadorias & Futuros	28-Jul-95	Basic financial rate × exchange rate swap
Swap	Brazil	Bolsa de Mercadorias & Futuros	28-Jul-95	Basic financial rate × gold price variation swap
Swap	Brazil	Bolsa de Mercadorias & Futuros	28-Jul-95	Basic financial rate × inflation index swap
Swap	Brazil	Bolsa de Mercadorias & Futuros	28-Jul-95	Basic financial rate × reference rate swap
Swap	Brazil	Bolsa de Mercadorias & Futuros	17-Feb-95	Exchange rate × gold price variation swap
Swap	Brazil	Bolsa de Mercadorias & Futuros	17-Feb-95	Inflation rate × exchange rate swap
Swap	Brazil	Bolsa de Mercadorias & Futuros	17-Feb-95	Inflation index × gold price variation swap
Swap	Brazil	Bolsa de Mercadorias & Futuros	28-Jul-95	Interest rate × Basic financial rate swap
Swap	Brazil	Bolsa de Mercadorias & Futuros	3-Dec-93	Interest rate × exchange rate swap
Swap	Brazil	Bolsa de Mercadorias & Futuros	17-Jun-94	Interest rate × gold price swap
Swap	Brazil	Bolsa de Mercadorias & Futuros	17-Feb-95	Interest rate × inflation index swap

Continued

283

Contract Classification	Country	Market	Began Trading	Contract Description
Swap	Brazil	Bolsa de Mercadorias & Futuros	17-Jun-94	Interest rate × reference rate swap
Swap	Brazil	Bolsa de Mercadorias & Futuros	17-Feb-95	Reference rate × exchange rate swap
Swap	Brazil	Bolsa de Mercadorias & Futuros	17-Feb-95	Reference rate × gold price variation swap
Swap	Brazil	Bolsa de Mercadorias & Futuros	17-Feb-95	Reference rate × inflation index swap

Contract Classification	Country	Exchange		Contract Description
Agriculture: Grains, food, and fiber	Argentina	The Rosario Futures Exchange (ROFEX) (Mercado a Termino de Rosario, S.A.)		Corn futures
Agriculture: Grains, food, and fiber	Argentina	The Rosario Futures Exchange (ROFEX) (Mercado a Termino de Rosario, S.A.)		Rosafe soybean index futures
Agriculture: Grains, food, and fiber	Argentina	The Rosario Futures Exchange (ROFEX) (Mercado a Termino de Rosario, S.A.)		Wheat futures
Agriculture: Grains, food, and fiber	Argentina	The Rosario Futures Exchange (ROFEX) (Mercado a Termino de Rosario, S.A.)		Options on Rosafe soybean futures
Agriculture: Grains, food, and fiber	Australia	Sydney Futures Exchange		Wool futures
Agriculture: Grains, food, and fiber	Brazil	Bolsa de Mercadorias & Futuros		Arabica coffee (U.S. dollar-denominated) futures
Agriculture: Grains, food, and fiber	Brazil	Bolsa de Mercadorias & Futuros		Robusta coffee (U.S. dollar-denominated) futures
Agriculture: Grains, food, and fiber	Brazil	Bolsa de Mercadorias & Futuros		Cotton (U.S. dollar-denominated) futures
Agriculture: Grains, food, and fiber	Brazil	Bolsa de Mercadorias & Futuros		Soybeans (U.S. dollar-denominated) futures
Agriculture: Grains, food, and fiber	Brazil	Bolsa de Mercadorias & Futuros		Crystal sugar (U.S. dollar-denominated) futures

Contract Classification	Country	Exchange	Contract Description
Agriculture: Grains, food, and fiber	Brazil	Bolsa de Mercadorias & Futuros	Options on Arabica coffee futures
Agriculture: Grains, food, and fiber	Canada	The Winnipeg Commodity Exchange	Canadian domestic feed barley futures
Agriculture: Grains, food, and fiber	Canada	The Winnipeg Commodity Exchange	Western domestic feed barley futures
Agriculture: Grains, food, and fiber	Canada	The Winnipeg Commodity Exchange	Canola futures (Specifications applicable up to the August
Agriculture: Grains, food, and fiber	Canada	The Winnipeg Commodity Exchange	Flaxseed futures
Agriculture: Grains, food, and fiber	Canada	The Winnipeg Commodity Exchange	Oat futures
Agriculture: Grains, food, and fiber	Canada	The Winnipeg Commodity Exchange	Feed pea futures
Agriculture: Grains, food, and fiber	Canada	The Winnipeg Commodity Exchange	Rye futures—delisted September 1995
Agriculture: Grains, food, and fiber	Canada	The Winnipeg Commodity Exchange	Domestic feed wheat futures
Agriculture: Grains, food, and fiber	Canada	The Winnipeg Commodity Exchange	Canadian domestic feed barley options
Agriculture: Grains, food, and fiber	Canada	The Winnipeg Commodity Exchange	Western domestic feed barley options
Agriculture: Grains, food, and fiber	Canada	The Winnipeg Commodity Exchange	Options on canola futures
Agriculture: Grains, food, and fiber	Canada	The Winnipeg Commodity Exchange	Flaxseed options
Agriculture: Grains, food, and fiber	Canada	The Winnipeg Commodity Exchange	Domestic feed wheat options
Agriculture: Grains, food, and fiber	England	London Cocoa Futures Market (London Commodity Exchange)	No '7 cocoa futures
Agriculture: Grains, food, and fiber	England	London Cocoa Futures Market (London Commodity Exchange)	No '7 cocoa traded options
Agriculture: Grains, food, and fiber	England	London Coffee Futures Market (London Commodity Exchange)	Robusta coffee futures
Agriculture: Grains, food, and fiber	England	London Coffee Futures Market (London Commodity Exchange)	Robusta coffee traded options
Agriculture: Grains, food, and fiber	England	London Grain Futures Market (London Commodity Exchange)	EC barley futures

Continued

E X H I B I T   13-2 *Continued*

Contract Classification	Country	Exchange	Contract Description
Agriculture: Grains, food, and fiber	England	London Grain Futures Market (London Commodity Exchange)	EC wheat futures
Agriculture: Grains, food, and fiber	England	London Grain Futures Market (London Commodity Exchange)	Barley traded options
Agriculture: Grains, food, and fiber	England	London Grain Futures Market (London Commodity Exchange)	EC wheat traded options
Agriculture: Grains, food, and fiber	England	London Potato Futures Market (London Commodity Exchange)	Potato futures
Agriculture: Grains, food, and fiber	England	London Potato Futures Market (London Commodity Exchange)	Potato traded options
Agriculture: Grains, food, and fiber	England	London Sugar Futures Market (London Commodity Exchange)	No. 7 premium raw sugar futures
Agriculture: Grains, food, and fiber	England	London Sugar Futures Market (London Commodity Exchange)	No. 5 White sugar futures
Agriculture: Grains, food, and fiber	England	London Sugar Futures Market (London Commodity Exchange)	No. 5 White sugar traded options
Agriculture: Grains, food, and fiber	Philippines	Manila International Futures Exchange, Inc.	Dry cocoon futures
Agriculture: Grains, food, and fiber	Philippines	Manila International Futures Exchange, Inc.	Coffee futures
Agriculture: Grains, food, and fiber	Philippines	Manila International Futures Exchange, Inc.	COPRA futures
Agriculture: Grains, food, and fiber	Philippines	Manila International Futures Exchange, Inc.	Soybean futures
Agriculture: Grains, food, and fiber	Philippines	Manila International Futures Exchange, Inc.	Sugar futures
Agriculture: Grains, food, and fiber	France	MATIF, S.A.	Potato futures
Agriculture: Grains, food, and fiber	France	MATIF, S.A.	European rapeseed futures
Agriculture: Grains, food, and fiber	France	MATIF, S.A.	White sugar futures

Contract Classification	Country	Exchange	Contract Description
Agriculture: Grains, food, and fiber	Hungary	Budapest Commodity Exchange	Feed barley futures
Agriculture: Grains, food, and fiber	Hungary	Budapest Commodity Exchange	Black seed futures
Agriculture: Grains, food, and fiber	Hungary	Budapest Commodity Exchange	Corn futures
Agriculture: Grains, food, and fiber	Hungary	Budapest Commodity Exchange	Feed wheat futures
Agriculture: Grains, food, and fiber	Hungary	Budapest Commodity Exchange	Milling wheat futures
Agriculture: Grains, food, and fiber	Hungary	Budapest Commodity Exchange	BL 52 wheat flour futures
Agriculture: Grains, food, and fiber	Japan	Kanmon Commodity Exchange	Red bean futures
Agriculture: Grains, food, and fiber	Japan	Kanmon Commodity Exchange	White bean futures
Agriculture: Grains, food, and fiber	Japan	Kanmon Commodity Exchange	Yellow corn futures
Agriculture: Grains, food, and fiber	Japan	Kanmon Commodity Exchange	Potato starch futures
Agriculture: Grains, food, and fiber	Japan	Kanmon Commodity Exchange	Soybean (imported) futures
Agriculture: Grains, food, and fiber	Japan	Kanmon Commodity Exchange	Raw sugar futures
Agriculture: Grains, food, and fiber	Japan	Kanmon Commodity Exchange	Refined white soft sugar futures
Agriculture: Grains, food, and fiber	Japan	Kansai Agricultural Commodities Exchange	Azuki beans futures
Agriculture: Grains, food, and fiber	Japan	Kansai Agricultural Commodities Exchange	Imported soybean futures
Agriculture: Grains, food, and fiber	Japan	Kansai Agricultural Commodities Exchange	Raw sugar futures
Agriculture: Grains, food, and fiber	Japan	Kansai Agricultural Commodities Exchange	Options on raw sugar futures
Agriculture: Grains, food, and fiber	Japan	Maebashi Dried Cocoon Exchange	Dried cocoon futures
Agriculture: Grains, food, and fiber	Japan	Nagoya Textile Exchange	Cotton yarn futures
Agriculture: Grains, food, and fiber	Japan	Nagoya Textile Exchange	Staple fiber yarn futures
Agriculture: Grains, food, and fiber	Japan	Nagoya Textile Exchange	Woolen yarn futures
Agriculture: Grains, food, and fiber	Japan	Osaka Textile Exchange	Cotton yarn futures
Agriculture: Grains, food, and fiber	Japan	Osaka Textile Exchange	Staple fiber yarn futures
Agriculture: Grains, food, and fiber	Japan	Osaka Textile Exchange	Woolen yarn futures

Continued

EXHIBIT 13-2 *Continued*

Contract Classification	Country	Exchange	Contract Description
Agriculture: Grains, food, and fiber	Japan	The Kobe Raw Silk Exchange	Raw silk futures
Agriculture: Grains, food, and fiber	Japan	The Kobe Rubber Exchange	Natural rubber futures
Agriculture: Grains, food, and fiber	Japan	The Tokyo Commodity Exchange	Cotton yarn futures
Agriculture: Grains, food, and fiber	Japan	The Tokyo Commodity Exchange	Rubber futures
Agriculture: Grains, food, and fiber	Japan	The Tokyo Commodity Exchange	Wool futures
Agriculture: Grains, food, and fiber	Japan	The Tokyo Grain Exchange	Azuki (red beans) futures
Agriculture: Grains, food, and fiber	Japan	The Tokyo Grain Exchange	Corn futures
Agriculture: Grains, food, and fiber	Japan	The Tokyo Grain Exchange	Raw sugar futures (prior to March 1996 contract)
Agriculture: Grains, food, and fiber	Japan	The Tokyo Grain Exchange	Raw sugar futures (effective from March 1996 contract)
Agriculture: Grains, food, and fiber	Japan	The Tokyo Grain Exchange	Refined white soft sugar futures
Agriculture: Grains, food, and fiber	Japan	The Tokyo Grain Exchange	U.S. soybean futures
Agriculture: Grains, food, and fiber	Japan	The Tokyo Grain Exchange	Options on raw sugar futures (prior to March 1996 contract)
Agriculture: Grains, food, and fiber	Japan	The Tokyo Grain Exchange	Options on raw sugar futures (effective from March 1996 contract)
Agriculture: Grains, food, and fiber	Japan	The Tokyo Grain Exchange	Options on U.S. soybean futures
Agriculture: Grains, food, and fiber	Japan	Toyohashi Dried Cocoon	Dried cocoon futures
Agriculture: Grains, food, and fiber	Malaysia	Kuala Lumpur Commodity Exchange	Cocoa futures
Agriculture: Grains, food, and fiber	Malaysia	Kuala Lumpur Commodity Exchange	Crude palm kernel oil futures
Agriculture: Grains, food, and fiber	Malaysia	Kuala Lumpur Commodity Exchange	Crude palm oil futures
Agriculture: Grains, food, and fiber	Malaysia	Kuala Lumpur Commodity Exchange	Standard Malaysia rubber (SMR) 20 futures

Contract Classification	Country	Exchange	Contract Description
Agriculture: Grains, food, and fiber	Netherlands	Agricultural Futures Market Amsterdam (ATA)	Potato BINT JE 50MM upwards futures
Agriculture: Grains, food, and fiber	New Zealand	New Zealand Futures & Options Exchange Limited	New Zealand wool futures
Agriculture: Grains, food, and fiber	Spain	The Citrus Fruit and Commodity Futures Market of Valencia	Navel/Navelina oranges futures
Agriculture: Grains, food, and fiber	Spain	The Citrus Fruit and Commodity Futures Market of Valencia	Valencia late oranges futures
Agriculture: Grains, food, and fiber	U.S.	Chicago Board of Trade	Anhydrous ammonia (NH3) futures
Agriculture: Grains, food, and fiber	U.S.	Chicago Board of Trade	Corn futures
Agriculture: Grains, food, and fiber	U.S.	Chicago Board of Trade	Diammonium phosphate (DAP) futures
Agriculture: Grains, food, and fiber	U.S.	Chicago Board of Trade	Iowa corn yield insurance futures
Agriculture: Grains, food, and fiber	U.S.	Chicago Board of Trade	Oat futures
Agriculture: Grains, food, and fiber	U.S.	Chicago Board of Trade	Rough rice futures
Agriculture: Grains, food, and fiber	U.S.	Chicago Board of Trade	Soybean futures
Agriculture: Grains, food, and fiber	U.S.	Chicago Board of Trade	Soybean meal futures
Agriculture: Grains, food, and fiber	U.S.	Chicago Board of Trade	Soybean oil futures
Agriculture: Grains, food, and fiber	U.S.	Chicago Board of Trade	Wheat futures
Agriculture: Grains, food, and fiber	U.S.	Chicago Board of Trade	Options on corn futures
Agriculture: Grains, food, and fiber	U.S.	Chicago Board of Trade	Options on Iowa corn yield insurance futures
Agriculture: Grains, food, and fiber	U.S.	Chicago Board of Trade	Options on oat futures
Agriculture: Grains, food, and fiber	U.S.	Chicago Board of Trade	Options on rough rice futures
Agriculture: Grains, food, and fiber	U.S.	Chicago Board of Trade	Options on soybean futures
Agriculture: Grains, food, and fiber	U.S.	Chicago Board of Trade	Options on soybean meal futures
Agriculture: Grains, food, and fiber	U.S.	Chicago Board of Trade	Options on soybean oil futures
Agriculture: Grains, food, and fiber	U.S.	Chicago Board of Trade	Options on wheat futures
Agriculture: Grains, food, and fiber	U.S.	Chicago Mercantile Exchange	Random length lumber futures

Continued

EXHIBIT 13-2 *Continued*

Contract Classification	Country	Exchange	Contract Description
Agriculture: Grains, food, and fiber	U.S.	Chicago Mercantile Exchange	Options on random length lumber futures
Agriculture: Grains, food, and fiber	U.S.	Citrus Associates of the New York Cotton Exchange, Inc.	Frozen concentrated orange juice (FCOJ) futures
Agriculture: Grains, food, and fiber	U.S.	Citrus Associates of the New York Cotton Exchange, Inc.	Options on FCOJ futures
Agriculture: Grains, food, and fiber	U.S.	Coffee, Sugar & Cocoa Exchange, Inc.	Brazil differential (coffee) futures
Agriculture: Grains, food, and fiber	U.S.	Coffee, Sugar & Cocoa Exchange, Inc.	Cheddar cheese futures
Agriculture: Grains, food, and fiber	U.S.	Coffee, Sugar & Cocoa Exchange, Inc.	Cocoa futures
Agriculture: Grains, food, and fiber	U.S.	Coffee, Sugar & Cocoa Exchange, Inc.	Coffee 'C' futures
Agriculture: Grains, food, and fiber	U.S.	Coffee, Sugar & Cocoa Exchange, Inc.	Nonfat dry milk futures
Agriculture: Grains, food, and fiber	U.S.	Coffee, Sugar & Cocoa Exchange, Inc.	Domestic sugar No. 14 futures
Agriculture: Grains, food, and fiber	U.S.	Coffee, Sugar & Cocoa Exchange, Inc.	White sugar futures
Agriculture: Grains, food, and fiber	U.S.	Coffee, Sugar & Cocoa Exchange, Inc.	World sugar No. 11 futures
Agriculture: Grains, food, and fiber	U.S.	Coffee, Sugar & Cocoa Exchange, Inc.	Options on cheddar cheese futures
Agriculture: Grains, food, and fiber	U.S.	Coffee, Sugar & Cocoa Exchange, Inc.	Options on cocoa futures
Agriculture: Grains, food, and fiber	U.S.	Coffee, Sugar & Cocoa Exchange, Inc.	Options on coffee 'C' futures
Agriculture: Grains, food, and fiber	U.S.	Coffee, Sugar & Cocoa Exchange, Inc.	Options on nonfat dry milk futures
Agriculture: Grains, food, and fiber	U.S.	Coffee, Sugar & Cocoa Exchange, Inc.	Options on world sugar No. 11 futures
Agriculture: Grains, food, and fiber	U.S.	Kansas City Board of Trade	Hard red winter wheat futures
Agriculture: Grains, food, and fiber	U.S.	Kansas City Board of Trade	Options on hard red winter wheat futures
Agriculture: Grains, food, and fiber	U.S.	MidAmerica Commodity Exchange	Corn futures
Agriculture: Grains, food, and fiber	U.S.	MidAmerica Commodity Exchange	Oat futures
Agriculture: Grains, food, and fiber	U.S.	MidAmerica Commodity Exchange	Soybean futures

Contract Classification	Country	Exchange	Contract Description
Agriculture: Grains, food, and fiber	U.S.	MidAmerica Commodity Exchange	Soybean meal futures
Agriculture: Grains, food, and fiber	U.S.	MidAmerica Commodity Exchange	Soybean oil futures
Agriculture: Grains, food, and fiber	U.S.	MidAmerica Commodity Exchange	Wheat futures
Agriculture: Grains, food, and fiber	U.S.	MidAmerica Commodity Exchange	Options on corn futures
Agriculture: Grains, food, and fiber	U.S.	MidAmerica Commodity Exchange	Options on soybean futures
Agriculture: Grains, food, and fiber	U.S.	MidAmerica Commodity Exchange	Options on soybean oil futures
Agriculture: Grains, food, and fiber	U.S.	MidAmerica Commodity Exchange	Options on wheat futures
Agriculture: Grains, food, and fiber	U.S	Minneapolis Grain Exchange	Hard red spring wheat futures
Agriculture: Grains, food, and fiber	U.S	Minneapolis Grain Exchange	White wheat futures
Agriculture: Grains, food, and fiber	U.S	Minneapolis Grain Exchange	Options on hard red spring wheat futures—American
Agriculture: Grains, food, and fiber	U.S	Minneapolis Grain Exchange	Options on hard red spring wheat futures—European
Agriculture: Grains, food, and fiber	U.S	Minneapolis Grain Exchange	Options on white wheat futures
Agriculture: Grains, food, and fiber	U.S	New York Cotton Exchange	Cotton futures
Agriculture: Grains, food, and fiber	U.S	New York Cotton Exchange	Options on cotton futures
Agriculture: Grains, food, and fiber	U.S	Philadelphia Stock Exchange	Forest & paper products sector index options
Agriculture: Meat and livestock	Brazil	Bolsa de Mercadorias & Futuros	Feeder cattle (U.S. dollar-denominated)
Agriculture: Meat and livestock	Brazil	Bolsa de Mercadorias & Futuros	Live cattle (U.S. dollar-denominated) futures
Agriculture: Meat and livestock	Brazil	Bolsa de Mercadorias & Futuros	Options on live cattle futures
Agriculture: Meat and livestock	Hungary	Budapest Commodity Exchange	Live hog No. 1 futures
Agriculture: Meat and livestock	Hungary	Budapest Commodity Exchange	Live hog No. 2 futures

Continued

EXHIBIT 13-2 *Continued*

Contract Classification	Country	Exchange	Contract Description
Agriculture: Meat and livestock	Netherlands	Agricultural Futures Market Amsterdam (ATA)	Piglet futures
Agriculture: Meat and livestock	Netherlands	Agricultural Futures Market Amsterdam (ATA)	Live hog futures
Agriculture: Meat and livestock	U.S.	Chicago Mercantile Exchange	Broiler chicken futures
Agriculture: Meat and livestock	U.S.	Chicago Mercantile Exchange	Feeder cattle futures
Agriculture: Meat and livestock	U.S.	Chicago Mercantile Exchange	Frozen pork belly futures
Agriculture: Meat and livestock	U.S.	Chicago Mercantile Exchange	Live cattle futures
Agriculture: Meat and livestock	U.S.	Chicago Mercantile Exchange	Live hog futures
Agriculture: Meat and livestock	U.S.	Chicago Mercantile Exchange	Options on broiler chicken futures
Agriculture: Meat and livestock	U.S.	Chicago Mercantile Exchange	Options on feeder cattle futures
Agriculture: Meat and livestock	U.S.	Chicago Mercantile Exchange	Options on frozen pork belly futures
Agriculture: Meat and livestock	U.S.	Chicago Mercantile Exchange	Options on live cattle futures
Agriculture: Meat and livestock	U.S.	Chicago Mercantile Exchange	Options on live hog futures
Agriculture: Meat and livestock	U.S.	MidAmerica Commodity Exchange	Live cattle futures
Agriculture: Meat and livestock	U.S.	MidAmerica Commodity Exchange	Live hog futures
Agriculture: Meat and livestock	U.S.	Minneapolis Grain Exchange	Black tiger shrimp futures
Agriculture: Meat and livestock	U.S.	Minneapolis Grain Exchange	White shrimp futures
Agriculture: Meat and livestock	U.S.	Minneapolis Grain Exchange	Options on black tiger shrimp futures
Agriculture: Meat and livestock	U.S.	Minneapolis Grain Exchange	Options on white shrimp futures
Currencies	Belgium	BELFOX c.v./s.c.	Options on the USD/BEF exchange rate
Currencies	Brazil	Bolsa de Mercadorias & Futuros	U.S. dollar (commercial) futures
Currencies	Brazil	Bolsa de Mercadorias & Futuros	U.S. dollar (floating) futures

Contract Classification	Country	Exchange	Contract Description
Currencies	Brazil	Bolsa de Mercadorias & Futuros	U.S. dollar (commercial) options on actuals
Currencies	Brazil	Bolsa de Mercadorias & Futuros	U.S. dollar (flexible U.S. dollar options)
Currencies	Brazil	Bolsa de Mercadorias & Futuros	(Floating) options on actuals
Currencies	Brazil	Bolsa de Mercadorias & Futuros	Exchange rate swap
Currencies	England	OMLX, The London Securities and Derivatives Exchange	Futures on Swedish equities
Currencies	Philippines	Manila International Futures Exchange, Inc.	U.S. dollar–British pound futures
Currencies	Philippines	Manila International Futures Exchange, Inc.	U.S. dollar–deutsche mark futures
Currencies	Philippines	Manila International Futures Exchange, Inc.	U.S. dollar–peso futures
Currencies	Philippines	Manila International Futures Exchange, Inc.	U.S. dollar–Swiss franc futures
Currencies	Philippines	Manila International Futures Exchange, Inc.	U.S. dollar–yen futures
Currencies	Finland	Finnish Options Market (SOM)	Currency futures
Currencies	Finland	Finnish Options Market (SOM)	Options on currency futures
Currencies	France	MATIF, S.A.	Options on deutsche mark/French franc
Currencies	France	MATIF, S.A.	Options on deutsche mark/Italian lira
Currencies	France	MATIF, S.A.	Options on sterling/deutsche mark
Currencies	France	MATIF, S.A.	Options on U.S. dollar/deutsche mark
Currencies	France	MATIF, S.A.	Options U.S. dollar/French franc
Currencies	Hong Kong	Hong Kong Futures Exchange Ltd.	Rolling FOREX futures (deutsche mark)
Currencies	Hong Kong	Hong Kong Futures Exchange Ltd.	Rolling FOREX futures (yen)
Currencies	Hungary	Budapest Commodity Exchange	USA dollar (USD) futures
Currencies	Hungary	Budapest Commodity Exchange	German mark (DEM) futures
Currencies	Hungary	Budapest Commodity Exchange	Yen futures

Continued

EXHIBIT 13–2 *Continued*

Contract Classification	Country	Exchange	Contract Description
Currencies	U.S.	Chicago Mercantile Exchange (International Monetary Market)	Japanese yen rolling spot futures
Currencies	U.S.	Chicago Mercantile Exchange (International Monetary Market)	Mexican peso futures
Currencies	U.S.	Chicago Mercantile Exchange (International Monetary Market)	Swiss franc futures
Currencies	U.S.	Chicago Mercantile Exchange (International Monetary Market)	Options on Brazilian real futures
Currencies	U.S.	Chicago Mercantile Exchange (International Monetary Market)	Options on currency cross rate futures deutsche mark
Currencies	U.S.	FINEX	Deutsche mark–lira cross-rate currency futures
Currencies	U.S.	FINEX	Deutsche mark–French franc cross-rate currency futures
Currencies	U.S.	FINEX	Deutsche mark–Swiss franc cross-rate currency futures
Currencies	U.S.	FINEX	Deutsche mark–yen cross-rate currency futures
Currencies	U.S.	FINEX currency futures	Sterling–deutsche mark cross-rate
Currencies	U.S.	FINEX dollar based)	U.S. dollar/British pound futures (U.S.
Currencies	U.S.	FINEX	U.S. dollar/deutsche mark futures (U.S. dollar based)
Currencies	U.S.	FINEX	U.S. dollar/Japanese yen futures (U.S. dollar based)
Currencies dollar	U.S.	FINEX	U.S. dollar/Swiss franc futures (U.S. based)
Currencies	U.S.	FINEX	U.S. dollar index (USDX) futures

Contract Classification	Country	Exchange	Contract Description
Currencies	U.S.	FINEX	Options on the deutsche mark–French franc cross-rate currency
Currencies	U.S.	FINEX	Options on deutsche mark–Japanese yen cross-rate currency
Currencies	U.S.	FINEX	Options on deutsche mark–lira cross-rate currency
Currencies	U.S.	FINEX	Options on deutsche mark–Swiss franc cross-rate currency
Currencies	U.S.	FINEX	Options on the sterling–deutsche mark cross-rate C
Currencies	U.S.	MidAmerica Commodity Exchange	Australian dollar futures
Currencies	U.S.	MidAmerica Commodity Exchange	British pound futures
Currencies	U.S.	MidAmerica Commodity Exchange	Canadian dollar futures
Currencies	U.S.	MidAmerica Commodity Exchange	Deutsche mark futures
Currencies	U.S.	MidAmerica Commodity Exchange	Japanese yen futures
Currencies	U.S.	MidAmerica Commodity Exchange	Swiss franc futures
Currencies	U.S.	Philadelphia Board of Trade	Australian dollar futures
Currencies	U.S.	Philadelphia Board of Trade	British pound futures
Currencies	U.S.	Philadelphia Board of Trade	Canadian dollar futures
Currencies	U.S.	Philadelphia Board of Trade	Deutsche mark futures
Currencies	U.S.	Philadelphia Board of Trade	European currency unit futures
Currencies	U.S.	Philadelphia Board of Trade	French franc futures
Currencies	U.S.	Philadelphia Board of Trade	Japanese yen futures
Currencies	U.S.	Philadelphia Board of Trade	Swiss franc futures

Continued

E X H I B I T   13–2   *Continued*

Contract Classification	Country	Exchange	Contract Description
Currencies	U.S.	The United Currency Options Market of the Philadelphia Exchange	Australian dollar standardized options
Currencies	U.S.	The United Currency Options Market of the Philadelphia Exchange	British pound standardized options
Currencies	U.S.	The United Currency Options Market of the Philadelphia Exchange	British pound/deutsche mark standardized options
Currencies	U.S.	The United Currency Options Market of the Philadelphia Exchange	Canadian dollar standardized options
Currencies	U.S.	The United Currency Options Market of the Philadelphia Exchange	Customized currency options
Currencies	U.S.	The United Currency Options Market of the Philadelphia Exchange	Deutsche mark standardized options
Currencies	U.S.	The United Currency Options Market of the Philadelphia Exchange	3-D (dollar-denominated delivery) deutsche mark options
Currencies	U.S.	The United Currency Options Market of the Philadelphia Exchange	Deutsche mark/Japanese yen standardized options
Currencies	U.S.	The United Currency Options Market of the Philadelphia Exchange	European currency unit standardized options
Currencies	U.S.	The United Currency Options Market of the Philadelphia Exchange	French franc standardized options
Currencies	U.S.	The United Currency Options Market of the Philadelphia Exchange	Japanese yen standardized options
Currencies	U.S.	The United Currency Options Market of the Philadelphia Exchange	Swiss franc standardized options
Energy	England	International Petroleum Exchange	Brent crude oil futures
Energy	England	International Petroleum Exchange	Gas oil futures
Energy	England	International Petroleum Exchange	Unleaded gasoline futures

Contract Classification	Country	Exchange	Contract Description
Energy	England	International Petroleum Exchange	Options on brent crude oil futures
Energy	England	International Petroleum Exchange	Option on gas oil futures
Energy	Singapore	Singapore International Monetary Exchange	Brent crude oil futures
Energy	Singapore	Singapore International Monetary Exchange	High sulphur fuel oil futures
Energy	U.S.	Chicago Board of Trade	FOSFA international edible oils index futures—
Energy	U.S.	Kansas City Board of Trade	Western natural gas futures
Energy	U.S.	Kansas City Board of Trade	Options on western natural gas futures
Energy	U.S.	NYMEX Division, New York Mercantile Exchange	Light, sweet crude oil futures
Energy	U.S.	NYMEX Division, New York Mercantile Exchange	Sour crude oil futures
Energy	U.S.	NYMEX Division, New York Mercantile Exchange	Gulf Coast unleaded gasoline futures
Energy	U.S.	NYMEX Division, New York Mercantile Exchange	New York Harbor unleaded gasoline futures
Energy	U.S.	NYMEX Division, New York Mercantile Exchange	Heating oil futures
Energy	U.S.	NYMEX Division, New York Mercantile Exchange	Natural gas futures
Energy	U.S.	NYMEX Division, New York Mercantile Exchange	Propane futures
Energy	U.S.	NYMEX Division, New York Mercantile Exchange	Options on light, sweet crude oil futures
Energy	U.S.	NYMEX Division, New York Mercantile Exchange	Options on NY Harbor unleaded gasoline futures
Energy	U.S.	NYMEX Division, New York Mercantile Exchange	Options on gasoline/crude oil crack spread
Energy	U.S.	NYMEX Division, New York Mercantile Exchange	Options on heating oil futures
Energy	U.S.	NYMEX Division, New York Mercantile Exchange	Options on heating oil/crude oil crack spread
Energy	U.S.	NYMEX Division, New York Mercantile Exchange	Options on natural gas futures

Continued

E X H I B I T 13-2 *Continued*

Contract Classification	Country	Exchange	Contract Description
Equities 1	Brazil	Rio De Janeiro Stock Exchange	Options on equities
Equities 1	Hong Kong	Hong Kong Futures Exchange Ltd.	Hong Kong telecommunications (stock) futures
Equities 1	Hong Kong	Hong Kong Futures Exchange Ltd.	HSBC holdings (stock) PLC futures
Equities 1	Switzerland	Swiss Options and Financial Futures Exchange, Ltd. (SOFFEX)	Low exercise price equity options
Enquities 10	Australia	Sydeny Futures Exchange	Equity futures (10 contracts listed)
Enquities 10	Canada	Montreal Exchange	Long term stock options (leap(r) options) (10 listed)
Equities 11	Finland	Finnish Options Market (SOM)	STOX equity options (11 Stocks)
Equities 13	Switzerland	Swiss Options and Financial Futures Exchange, Ltd. (SOFFEX)	Equity options
Equities 16	Canada	Vancouver Stock Exchange	Eqity options (16 listed)
Equities 19	Finland	Finnish Options Market (SOM)	Finnish equity futures (STOX) (19 stocks)
Equities 20	Germany	DTB Deutsche Terminborse	Equity options (20 listed)
Equities 23	Sweden	OM Stockholm	Futures on individual Swedish equities
Equities 23	Sweden	OM Stockholm	Options on individual Swedish equities
Equities 23	Sweden	OM Stockholm	Long-term options on individual Swedish equities
Equities 26	Canada	Montreal Exchange	Equity options (26 listed)
Equities 26	England	OMLX, The London Securities and Derivatives Exchange	Options on Swedish equities
Equities 26	England	OMLX, The London Securities and Derivatives Exchange	Long term options on Swedish equities

Contract Classification	Country	Exchange	Contract Description
Equities 4	Spain	MEFF Renta Variable (RV), S.A.	Equity options
Equities 42	Netherlands	European Options Exchange	Equity options (42 Listed)
Equities 49	France	The MONEP	Equity options (49 listed)
Equities 5	Switzerland	Swiss Options and Financial Futures Exchange, Ltd. (SOFFEX)	Long-term equity options
Equities 60	U.S.	American Stock Exchange	Long-term equity anticipation securities (r)(LEAPS(r)) Equity
Equities 600	U.S.	Chicago Board Options Exchange	Equity options (600 listed)
Equities 7	Austria	Austrian Futures and Options Exchange (OTOB)	Equity options (7 listed)
Equities 7	New Zealand	New Zealand Futures & Options Exchange Limited	Equity options
Equities 71	England	LIFFE	Equity options (71 individual stocks)
Equities 8	Belgium	BELFOX c.v./s.c.	Equity options (8 listed)
Equities 83	U.S.	Chicago Board Options Exchange	Long term equity anticipation securities (r)(LEAPS (r)) Equity
Equities 9	Denmark	Copenhagen Stock Exchange	Options on Danish equities (9 listed)
Index	Australia	Sydney Futures Exchange	All ordinaries share price index futures (SPI)
Index	Australia	Sydney Futures Exchange	Options on all ordinaries share price index futures
Index	Australia	Sydney Futures Exchange	All ordinaries share price index (SPI) overnight option
Index	Austria	Austrian Futures and Options Exchange (OTOB)	Austrian traded index (ATX) futures
Index	Austria	Austrian Futures and Options Exchange (OTOB)	Austrian trade index (ATX) options
Index	Belgium	BELFOX c.v./s.c.	BEL 20 index futures
Index	Belgium	BELFOX c.v./s.c.	Options on the BEL 20 index

Continued

EXHIBIT 13–2 *Continued*

Contract Classification	Country	Exchange	Contract Description
Index	Belgium	BELFOX c.v./s.c.	B-Gold index options
Index	Belgium	BELFOX s.c./c.v.	BIBOR three-month futures
Index	Brazil	Bolsa de Mercadorias & Futuros	BOVESPA index futures
Index	Brazil	Bolsa de Mercadorias & Futuros	Options on BOVESPA stock index futures
Index	Brazil	Rio de Janeiro Stock Exchange	ISENN stock index futures
Index	Brazil	Rio de Janeiro Stock Exchange	ISENN stock index options
Index	Canada	Toronto Futures Exchange	Toronto 35 index futures
Index	Canada	Toronto Futures Exchange	TSE 100 index futures
Index	Canada	Toronto Futures Exchange	Toronto 35 index options
Index	Canada	Toronto Futures Exchange	TSE 100 index options
Index	Denmark	Copenhagen Stock Exchange	KFX stock index futures
Index	Denmark	Copenhagen Stock Exchange	Options on KFX futures
Index	England	LIFFE	FT-SE 100 index futures
Index	England	LIFFE	FT-SE 250 index futures
Index	England	LIFFE	Options on FT-SE IOO (American and European Types
Index	England	LIFFE	FLEX(r) options on FT-SE 100 index
Index	England	OMLX, The London Securities and Derivatives Exchange	FLEX(tm)FT-SE UK SERIES index futures flexible futures contracts
Index	England	OMLX, The London Securities and Derivatives Exchange	FT-SE mid 250 index futures——delisted as of February 1995
Index	England	OMLX, The London Securities and Derivatives Exchange	OMX index futures

Contract Classification	Country	Exchange	Contract Description
Index	England	OMLX, The London Securities and Derivatives Exchange	Options on FLEX(tm) FT-SE UK series indexes/flexible options
Index	England	OMLX, The London Securities and Derivatives Exchange	Option ON FT-SE mid 250 index
Index	England	OMLX, The London Securities and Derivatives Exchange	OMX index options
Index	England	OMLX, The London Securities and Derivatives Exchange	Long-term OMX index options
Index	England	The Baltic International Freight Futures Market (London)	BIFFEX futures
Index	England	The Baltic International Freight Futures Market (London)	BIFFEX traded options
Index	Finland	Finnish Options Market (SOM)	FOX index futures
Index	Finland	Finnish Options Market (SOM)	FOX index options
Index	France	MATIF, S.A.	CAC 40 stock index futures
Index	France	The MONEP	CAC 40 stock index long-term options
Index	France	The MONEP	CAC 40 stock index short-term options
Index	Germany	DTB Deutsche Terminborse	DAX (German stock index) futures
Index	Germany	DTB Deutsche Terminborse	Options on DAX futures
Index	Germany	DTB Deutsche Terminborse	Options on the DAX index
Index	Germany	DTB Deutsche Terminborse	Options on the BOBL future
Index	Hong Kong	Hong Kong Futures Exchange Ltd.	Hang Seng index futures
Index	Hong Kong	Hong Kong Futures Exchange Ltd.	Hang Seng commerce and industry sub-index futures
Index	Hong Kong	Hong Kong Futures Exchange Ltd.	Hang Seng finance sub-index futures
Index	Hong Kong	Hong Kong Futures Exchange Ltd.	Hang Seng properties sub-index futures
Index	Hong Kong	Hong Kong Futures Exchange Ltd.	Hang Seng utilities sub-index futures

Continued

EXHIBIT 13-2 *Continued*

Contract Classification	Country	Exchange	Contract Description
Index	Hong Kong	Hong Kong Futures Exchange Ltd.	Options on the Hang Seng index
Index	Hungary	Budapest Stock Exchange	Budapest stock index (BUX) futures
Index	Israel	The Tel-Aviv Stock Exchange	MAOF–25 index option
Index	Italy	Italian Derivatives Market (IDEM) of the Italian Stock Exchange	MIB 30 futures
Index	Japan	Osaka Securities Exchange	Nikkei 225 futures
Index	Japan	Osaka Securities Exchange	Nikkei 300 futures
Index	Japan	Osaka Securities Exchange	Nikkei 225 options
Index	Japan	Osaka Securities Exchange	Nikkei 300 options
Index	Japan	Tokyo Stock Exchange	TOPIX stock index futures
Index	Japan	Tokyo Stock Exchange	TOPIX stock index options
Index	Netherlands	European Options Exchange	Amsterdam EOE-index futures
Index	Netherlands	European Options Exchange	Dutch top 5 index futures
Index	Netherlands	European Options Exchange	Eurotop 100 index futures
Index	Netherlands	European Options Exchange	Dutch top 5 stock index options
Index	Netherlands	European Options Exchange	EOE Dutch stock index options
Index	Netherlands	European Options Exchange	Eurotop 100 index options
Index	Netherlands	European Options Exchange	Major market (XMI) index options
Index	Netherlands	European Options Exchange	Major market (XMI) index LEAPS options
Index	New Zealand	New Zealand Futures & Options Exchange Limited	NZSE–10 index futures—This contract replace
Index	New Zealand	New Zealand Futures & Options Exchange Limited	Options on NZSE–10 index futures
Index	Norway	Oslo Stock Exchange	Options on the OBX index

Contract Classification	Country	Exchange	Contract Description
Index	Norway	Oslo Stock Exchange	Long OBX index call options
Index	Singapore	Singapore International Monetary Exchange	Nikkei 225 stock average futures
Index	Singapore	Singapore International Monetary Exchange	Nikkei 300 futures contract
Index	Singapore	Singapore International Monetary Exchange	SIMEX MSCI Hong Kong index futures
Index	Singapore	Singapore International Monetary Exchange	Options on Nikkei 225 futures
Index	Singapore	Singapore International Monetary Exchange	Options on Nikkei 300 futures
Index	South Africa	The South African Futures Exchange (SAFEX)	JSE actuaries all share index futures
Index	South Africa	The South African Futures Exchange (SAFEX)	JSE all industrial index futures
Index	South Africa	The South African Futures Exchange (SAFEX)	Krugerrand futures
Index	South Africa	The South African Futures Exchange (SAFEX)	Options on JSE actuaries all gold index futures
Index	South Africa	The South African Futures Exchange (SAFEX)	Options on JSE actuaries all share index futures
Index	South Africa	The South African Futures Exchange (SAFEX)	Options on JSE all industrial index futures
Index	South Africa	The South African Futures Exchange (SAFEX)	Options on Krugerrand futures
Index	Spain	MEFF Renta Variable (RV), S.A.	IBEX 35 futures
Index	Spain	MEFF Renta Variable (RV), S.A.	IBEX 35 options
Index	Sweden	OM Stockholm	OMX stock index futures
Index	Sweden	OM Stockholm	OMX (index) options
Index	Sweden	OM Stockholm	Long-term OMX index options
Index	Switzerland	Swiss Options and Financial Futures Exchange, Ltd (SOFFEX)	Swiss market index futures
Index	Switzerland	Swiss Options and Financial Futures Exchange, Ltd (SOFFEX)	Options on Swiss market index

Continued

EXHIBIT 13-2 *Continued*

Contract Classification	Country	Exchange	Contract Description
Index	Switzerland	Swiss Options and Financial Futures Exchange, Ltd (SOFFEX)	Long-term options on Swiss market index
Index	U.S.	American Stock Exchange	Options on the airline index
Index	U.S.	American Stock Exchange	Options on the AMEX/OSCAR Gruss Israel index
Index	U.S.	American Stock Exchange	Options and LEAPS(r) on the biotechnology index
Index	U.S.	American Stock Exchange	Options on the computer technology index
Index	U.S.	American Stock Exchange	Options on the Eurotop 100 index
Index	U.S.	American Stock Exchange	Options and LEAPS(r) on the Hong Kong index
Index	U.S.	American Stock Exchange	Options and LEAPS(r) on the institutional index
Index	U.S.	American Stock Exchange	Options and LEAPS(r) on the Japan index
Index	U.S.	American Stock Exchange	Options and LEAPS(r) on the major market index
Index	U.S.	American Stock Exchange	Options and LEAPS(r) on the Mexico index
Index	U.S.	American Stock Exchange	Options on the Morgan Stanley Consumer Index
Index	U.S.	American Stock Exchange	Options on the Morgan Stanley Cyclical Index
Index	U.S.	American Stock Exchange	Options on the natural gas index
Index	U.S.	American Stock Exchange	Options on the North American telecommunications

Contract Classification	Country	Exchange	Contract Description
Index	U.S.	American Stock Exchange	Options on the oil index
Index	U.S.	American Stock Exchange	Options and LEAPS(r) on the pharmaceutical index
Index	U.S.	American Stock Exchange	Options on the securities broker/dealer index
Index	U.S.	American Stock Exchange	Options and LEAPS(r) on the S&P midcap 400 index
Index	U.S.	Chicago Board of Trade	Structural panel index futures
Index	U.S.	Chicago Board of Options Exchange	CBOE biotech index
Index	U.S.	Chicago Board of Options Exchange	CBOE biotech index (reduced value) LEAPS
Index	U.S.	Chicago Board of Options Exchange	CBOE computer software index
Index	U.S.	Chicago Board of Options Exchange	CBOE environmental index
Index	U.S.	Chicago Board of Options Exchange	CBOE global telecommunications index options
Index	U.S.	Chicago Board of Options Exchange	CBOE gaming index options
Index	U.S.	Chicago Board of Options Exchange	CBOE Israel index options
Index	U.S.	Chicago Board of Options Exchange	CBOE Latin 15 index (tm) options
Index	U.S.	Chicago Board of Options Exchange	CBOE Mexico index options
Index	U.S.	Chicago Board of Options Exchange	CBOE REIT index options
Index	U.S.	Chicago Board of Options Exchange	CBOE technology index options
Index	U.S.	Chicago Board of Options Exchange	CBOE telecommunications index options
Index	U.S.	Chicago Board of Options Exchange	FLEX (tm) options
Index	U.S.	Chicago Board of Options Exchange	FT-SE 100 index (reduced-value) options
Index	U.S.	Chicago Board of Options Exchange	NASDAQ–100 index options

Continued

305

E X H I B I T   13–2 *Continued*

Contract Classification	Country	Exchange	Contract Description
Index	U.S.	Chicago Board of Options Exchange	Nikkei 300 index options
Index	U.S.	Chicago Board of Options Exchange	Nikkei 300 index (reduced value) LEAPS(r)
Index	U.S.	Chicago Board of Options Exchange	OEX(r) and SPX(tm) index caps
Index	U.S.	Chicago Board of Options Exchange	Long-term equity anticipation securities (LEPS(r)) OEX
Index	U.S.	Chicago Board of Options Exchange	Russell 2000(r) index
Index	U.S.	Chicago Board of Options Exchange	Russell 2000(r) index (reduced-value) LEAPS(r)
Index	U.S.	Chicago Board of Options Exchange	S&P 100 index options
Index	U.S.	Chicago Board of Options Exchange	S&P 500 index options
Index	U.S.	Chicago Board of Options Exchange	S&P banks index options
Index	U.S.	Chicago Board of Options Exchange	S&P chemical index options
Index	U.S.	Chicago Board of Options Exchange	S&P health care index options
Index	U.S.	Chicago Board of Options Exchange	S&P insurance index options
Index	U.S.	Chicago Board of Options Exchange	S&P retail index options
Index	U.S.	Chicago Board of Options Exchange	S&P smallcap 600 index options
Index	U.S.	Chicago Board of Options Exchange	S&P transportation index options
Index	U.S.	Chicago Mercantile Exchange (Index and Option Markets)	FT-SE 100 share index futures
Index	U.S.	Chicago Mercantile Exchange (Index and Option Markets)	Goldman Sachs commodity index futures
Index	U.S.	Chicago Mercantile Exchange (Index and Option Markets)	Major market index futures
Index	U.S.	Chicago Mercantile Exchange (Index and Option Markets)	Nikkei stock index average futures*
Index	U.S.	Chicago Mercantile Exchange (Index and Option Marekts)	Russell 2000 stock price index futures

Contract Classification	Country	Exchange	Contract Description
Index	U.S.	Chicago Mercantile Exchange (Index and Option Markets)	Standard and Poor's midcap 400 stock price index futures
Index	U.S.	Chicago Mercantile Exchange (Index and Option Markets)	S&P 500/BARRA growth index futures
Index	U.S.	Chicago Mercantile Exchange (Index and Option Markets)	S&P 500/BARRA value index futures
Index	U.S.	Chicago Mercantile Exchange (Index and Option Markets)	Standard & Poor's 500 stock price index futures
Index	U.S.	Chicago Mercantile Exchange (Index and Option Markets)	Options on the FT-SE 100 share index futures
Index	U.S.	Chicago Mercantile Exchange (Index and Option Markets)	Options on the Goldman Sachs commodity index futures
Index	U.S.	Chicago Mercantile Exchange (Index and Option Markets)	Options on Nikkei stock index average futures
Index	U.S.	Chicago Mercantile Exchange (Index and Option Markets)	Options on the Russell 2000 stock price index futures
Index	U.S.	Chicago Mercantile Exchange (Index and Option Markets)	Options on the Standard and Poor's midcap 400 stocks
Index	U.S.	Chicago Mercantile Exchange (Index and Option Markets)	Options on S&P 500/BARRA growth index futures
Index	U.S.	Chicago Mercantile Exchange (Index and Option Markets)	Options on S&P 500/BARRA value index futures
Index	U.S.	Chicago Mercantile Exchange (Index and Option Markets)	Options on Standard & Poor's 500 stock price index
Index	U.S.	Chicago Mercantile Exchange (Index and Option Markets)	Options on major market index futures
Index	U.S.	COMEX Division, New York Mercantile Exchange	Eurotop 100 futures
Index	U.S.	COMEX Division, New York Mercantile Exchange	Options on Eurotop 100 index futures
Index	U.S.	FINEX	Options on U.S. dollar index (USDX) futures

Continued

EXHIBIT 13–2 *Continued*

Contract Classification	Country	Exchange	Contract Description
Index	U.S.	Kansas City Board of Trade	Mini Value Line stock index futures
Index	U.S.	Kansas City Board of Trade	Value Line stock index futures
Index	U.S.	Kansas City Board of Trade	Options on mini Value Line futures
Index	U.S.	New York Futures Exchange	KR-CRB index futures
Index	U.S.	New York Futures Exchange	NYSE composite index(r) futures
Index	U.S.	New York Futures Exchange	Options on KR-CRB index futures
Index	U.S.	New York Futures Exchange	Options on NYSE composite index(r) futures
Index	U.S.	Philadelphia Stock Exchange	Airline sector index options
Index	U.S.	Philadelphia Stock Exchange	Big cap sector index options
Index	U.S.	Philadelphia Stock Exchange	National over-the-counter sector index options
Index	U.S.	Philadelphia Stock Exchange	PHLX/KBW bank sector index options
Index	U.S.	Philadelphia Stock Exchange	Phone sector index options
Index	U.S.	Philadelphia Stock Exchange	Semiconductor sector index options
Index	U.S.	Philadelphia Stock Exchange	Super cap sector index options
Index	U.S.	Philadelphia Stock Exchange	U.S. top 100 index options
Index	U.S.	Philadelphia Stock Exchange	Utility sector index option
Index	U.S.	Philadelphia Stock Exchange	Value Line index options
Interest rate	Australia	Sydney Futures Exchange	Three-year Australian Treasury bond futures
Interest rate	Australia	Sydney Futures Exchange	Ten-year Australian Treasury bond futures
Interest rate	Australia	Sydney Futures Exchange	90-day bank accepted bill futures

Contract Classification	Country	Exchange	Contract Description
Interest rate	Australia	Sydney Futures Exchange	Options on three-year Australian Treasury bond futures
Interest rate	Australia	Sydney Futures Exchange	Overnight options on three-year Australian Treasury bond futures
Interest rate	Australia	Sydney Futures Exchange	Options on ten-year Australian Treasury bond futures
Interest rate	Australia	Sydney Futures Exchange	Overnight options on Australian 10-year Treasury bond futures
Interest rate	Australia	Sydney Futures Exchange	Options on bank accepted bill futures
Interest rate	Austria	Austrian Futures and Options Exchange (OTOB)	Austrian government bond futures
Interest rate	Belgium	BELFOX c.v./s.c.	Belgian govenment bond futures
Interest rate	Belgium	BELFOX c.v./s.c.	Options on the Belgian government bond futures
Interest rate	Brazil	Bolsa de Mercadorias & Futuros	One-day interbank deposits futures
Interest rate	Brazil	Bolsa de Mercadorias & Futuros	Thirty-day interbank deposit futures
Interest rate	Brazil	Bolsa de Mercadorias & Futuros	Options on one-day interbank deposit futures
Interest rate	Brazil	Bolsa de Mercadorias & Futuros	Interest rate swap
Interest rate	Canada	Montreal Exchange	One-month Canadian bankers' acceptance futures
Interest rate	Canada	Montreal Exchange	Three-month Canadian bankers' acceptance futures
Interest rate	Canada	Montreal Exchange	Five-year Government of Canada bond futures
Interest rate	Canada	Montreal Exchange	Ten-year Govenment of Canada bond futures

Continued

EXHIBIT 13-2 *Continued*

Contract Classification	Country	Exchange	Contract Description
Interest rate	Canada	Montreal Exchange	Options on three-month Canadian bankers' acceptances
Interest rate	Canada	Montreal Exchange	Government of Canada bond options
Interest rate	Canada	Montreal Exchange	Options on ten-year Government of Canada bond futures
Interest rate	Denmark	Copenhagen Stock Exchange	Futures on three-month CIBOR
Interest rate	Denmark	Copenhagen Stock Exchange	Long-term Danish government bond futures
Interest rate	Denmark	Copenhagen Stock Exchange	Medium-term Danish government bond futures
Interest rate	Denmark	Copenhagen Stock Exchange	Six percent 2026 Mortgage credit bond futures
Interest rate	Denmark	Copenhagen Stock Exchange	Options on long-term Danish government bond futures
Interest rate	England	LIFFE	Three-month ECU interest rate futures
Interest rate	England	LIFFE	Three-month Eurodollar interest rate futures
Interest rate	England	LIFFE	Three-month Eurolira interest rate futures
Interest rate	England	LIFFE	Three-month Eurodeutschmark (Euromark) interest rate futures
Interest rate	England	LIFFE	Three-month Euroswiss franc (Euroswiss) interest rate futures
Interest rate	England	LIFFE	Long-term German government bond (bund) futures
Interest rate	England	LIFFE	Italian government bond (BTP) futures

Contract Classification	Country	Exchange	Contract Description
Interest rate	England	LIFFE	Japanese government bond futures
Interest rate	England	LIFFE	Long gilt futures
Interest rate	England	LIFFE	Three-month sterling (short sterling) interest rate futures
Interest rate	England	LIFFE	Options on three-month Eurolira futures
Interest rate	England	LIFFE	Options on three-month Eurodeutschmark (Euromark) futures
Interest rate	England	LIFFE	Options on three-month/Euroswiss franc (Euroswiss) futures
Interest rate	England	LIFFE	Options on German government bond (BUND) futures
Interest rate	England	LIFFE	Options on Italian government bond (BTP) futures
Interest rate	England	LIFFE	Options on long gilt futures
Interest rate	England	LIFFE	Options on three-month sterling (short sterling) interest rate futures
Interest rate	Philippines	Manila International Futures Exchange, Inc.	Interest rate futures
Interest rate	Finland	Finnish Options Market (SOM)	Finnish government bond futures
Interest rate	Finland	Finnish Options Market (SOM)	HELIBOR futures
Interest rate	France	MATIF, S.A.	ECU bond futures
Interest rate	France	MATIF, S.A.	French notional bond futures
Interest rate	France	MATIF, S.A.	Three-month PIBOR futures
Interest rate	France	MATIF, S.A.	Options on ECU bond futures
Interest rate	France	MATIF, S.A.	Options on notional bond futures
Interest rate	France	MATIF, S.A.	Options on three-month PIBOR futures

Continued

311

EXHIBIT 13-2 *Continued*

Contract Classification	Country	Exchange	Contract Description
Interest rate	Germany	DTB Deutsche Terminborse	Three-month FIBOR future
Interest rate	Germany	DTB Deutsche Terminborse	BOBL (medium-term notional bond) futures
Interest rate	Germany	DTB Deutsche Terminborse	BUND (notional German government bond) futures
Interest rate	Germany	DTB Deutsche Terminborse	BUXL (notional German government long-term debt)
Interest rate	Germany	DTB Deutsche Terminborse	Options on the BUND fugure
Interest rate	Hong Kong	Hong Kong Futures Exchange Ltd.	Three-month HIBOR futures
Interest rate	Hungary	Budapest Commodity Exchange	Interest rate futures
Interest rate	Hungary	Budapest Stock Exchange	3-month Hungarian Treasury bill futures
Interest rate	Ireland	Irish Futures and Options Exchange	3-month DIBOR futures (Dublin interbank offered rate)
Interest rate	Ireland	Irish Futures and Options Exchange	Long gilt futures (Irish government stock)
Interest rate	Ireland	Irish Futures and Options Exchange	Medium gilt futures (Irish government stock)
Interest rate	Ireland	Irish Futures and Options Exchange	Short gilt futures (Irish government stock)
Interest rate	Italy	Mercato Italiano Futures	Options on 10-year BTP futures
Interest rate	Italy	Mercato Italiano Futures (Comitato di Gestione MF)	Ten-year Italian (BTP) futures
Interest rate	Italy	Mercato Italiano Futures (Comitato di Gestione MIF)	Five-year Italian (BTP) futures
Interest rate	Japan	Tokyo International Financial Futures Exchange	Options on three-month Euroyen futures
Interest rate	Japan	Tokyo Stock Exchange	10-year Japanese government bond futures

Contract Classification	Country	Exchange	Contract Description
Interest rate	Japan	Tokyo Stock Exchange	20-year Japanese government bond futures
Interest rate	Japan	Tokyo Stock Exchange	U.S. T-bond futures
Interest rate	Japan	Tokyo Stock Exchange	Options on 10-year Japanese government bond futures
Interest rate	Netherlands	European Options Exchange	Guilder bond futures
Interest rate	Netherlands	European Options Exchange	Dutch bond options
Interest rate	Netherlands	European Options Exchange	Flexible options on Dutch bonds
Interest rate	Netherlands	European Options Exchange	Notional bond options on futures
Interest rate	New Zealand	New Zealand Futures & Options Exchange Limited	Bank accepted bill futures
Interest rate	New Zealand	New Zealand Futures & Options Exchange Limited	Three-year government stock futures
Interest rate	New Zealand	New Zealand Futures & Options Exchange Limited	Ten-year government stock futures
Interest rate	New Zealand	New Zealand Futures & Options Exchange Limited	Options on bank accepted bills futures
Interest rate	New Zealand	New Zealand Futures & Options Exchange Limited	Options on three-year government stock futures
Interest rate	New Zealand	New Zealnad Futures & Options Exchange Limited	Options on ten-year government stock futures
Interest rate	Norway	Oslo Stock Exchange	7-year Norwegian bond futures
Interest rate	Norway	Oslo Stock Exchange	10-year Norwegian bond futures
Interest rate	Singapore	Singapore International Monetary Exchange	Japanese government bond futures
Interest rate	Singapore	Singapore International Monetary Exchange	Options on Japanese govrnment bond futures
Interest rate	South Africa	The South African Futures Exchange (SAFEX)	3-month bank bill futures
Interest rate	South Africa	The South African Futures Exchange (SAFEX)	Long bond (E168) futures

Continued

EXHIBIT 13-2 *Continued*

Contract Classification	Country	Exchange	Contract Description
Interest rate	South Africa	The South African Futures Exchange (SAFEX)	Long bond (R150) futures
Interest rate	South Africa	The South African Futures Exchange (SAFEX)	Options on 3-month bank bill futures
Interest rate	South Africa	The South African Futures Exchange (SAFEX)	Options on long bond (E168) futures
Interest rate	South Africa	The South African Futures Exchange (SAFEX)	Options on long bond (R150) futures
Interest rate	Spain	MEFF Renta Fija (RF), S.A.	MIBOR '90 plus futures (Madrid interbank offered rate)
Interest rate	Spain	MEFF Renta Fija (RF), S.A.	MIBOR '360 plus futures (Madrid interbank offered rate)
Interest rate	Spain	MEFF Renta Fija (RF), S.A.	MIBOR '90 plus options (Madrid interbank offered rate)
Interest rate	Spain	MEFF Renta Fija (RF), S.A.	Ten-year notional bond monthly options
Interest rate	Spain	MEFF Renta Fija (RF), S.A.	Ten-year notional bond options
Interest rate	Spain	MEFF Renta Fija (RF), S.A.	Three-year notional bond options
Interest rate	Spain	MEFF Renta Fija (RF), S.A.	Ten-year notional Spanish bond futures
Interest rate	Spain	MEFF Renta Fija (RF), S.A.	Three-year notional Spanish bond futures
Interest rate	Sweden	OM Stockholm	IMM forward rate agreement IMM-FRA
Interest rate	Sweden	OM Stockholm	Five-year notional mortgage bond futures MBB2/MBB
Interest rate	Sweden	OM Stockholm	2-year notional Swedish bond futures OMR 2
Interest rate	Sweden	OM Stockholm	5-year notional Swedish bond futures OMR 5
Interest rate	Sweden	OM Stockholm	10-year notional Swedish bond futures OMR 10

Contract Classification	Country	Exchange	Contract Description
Interest rate	Sweden	OM Stockholm	Two-year notional urban mortgage bank of Sweden
Interest rate	Sweden	OM Stockholm	Five-year notional urban mortgage bank of Sweden
Interest rate	Sweden	OM Stockholm	Swedish Treasury bill futures OMVX 180
Interest rate	Sweden	OM Stockholm	5-year notional Swedish bond options OMR 5
Interest rate	Switzerland	Swiss Options and Financial Futures Exchange, Ltd. (SOFFEX)	Options on Swiss government bond (CONF) futures
Interest rate	Switzerland	Swiss Options and Financial Futures Exchange, Ltd. (SOFFEX)	Swiss government bond (CONF) futures
Interest rate	U.S.	Chicago Board of Trade	Ten-year Canadian government bond futures
Interest rate	U.S.	Chicago Board of Trade	Catastrophe insurance (eastern) futures
Interest rate	U.S.	Chicago Board of Trade	Catastrophe insurance (midwestern) futures
Interest rate	U.S.	Chicago Board of Trade	Catastrophe insurance (national) futures
Interest rate	U.S.	Chicago Board of Trade	Catastrophe insurance (quarterly and annual western)
Interest rate	U.S.	Chicago Board of Trade	Municipal bond index futures
Interest rate	U.S.	Chicago Board of Trade	30-day Fed funds futures (formerly 30-day interest rate futures)
Interest rate	U.S.	Chicago Board of Trade	U.S. Treasury bond futures
Interest rate	U.S.	Chicago Board of Trade	Two-year U.S. Treasury note futures
Interest rate	U.S.	Chicago Board of Trade	Five-year U.S. Treasury note futures
Interest rate	U.S.	Chicago Board of Trade	Ten-year U.S. Treasury note futures

Continued

EXHIBIT 13–2 *Continued*

Contract Classification	Country	Exchange	Contract Description
Interest rate	U.S.	Chicago Board of Trade	Options on ten-year Canadian government bond futures
Interest rate	U.S.	Chicago Board of Trade	Options on catastrophe insurance (eastern) futures
Interest rate	U.S.	Chicago Board of Trade	Options on catastrophe insurance (midwestern) futures
Interest rate	U.S.	Chicago Board of Trade	Options on catastrophe insurance (national) futures
Interest rate	U.S.	Chicago Board of Trade	Annual property claim services (PCS) catastrophe insurance options
Interest rate	U.S.	Chicago Board of Trade	Quarterly property claim services (PCS) catastrophe insurance options
Interest rate	U.S.	Chicago Board of Trade	Options on catastrophe insurance (quarterly and annual western) futures
Interest rate	U.S.	Chicago Board of Trade	Options on municipal bond index futures
Interest rate	U.S.	Chicago Board of Trade	Options on U.S. Treasury bond futures
Interest rate	U.S.	Chicago Board of Trade	Flexible options on U.S. Treasury bond futures
Interest rate	U.S.	Chicago Board of Trade	Options on U.S. Treasury note futures (two-year)
Interest rate	U.S.	Chicago Board of Trade	Flexible options on U.S. Treasury note futures (two-year)
Interest rate	U.S.	Chicago Board of Trade	Options on U.S. Treasury note futures (five-year)
Interest rate	U.S.	Chicago Board of Trade	Flexible options on U.S. Treasury note futures (five-year)

Contract Classification	Country	Exchange	Contract Description
Interest rate	U.S.	Chicago Board of Trade	Options on U.S. Treasury note futures (ten-year)
Interest rate	U.S.	Chicago Board of Trade	Flexible options on U.S. Treasury note futures (ten-year)
Interest rate	U.S.	Chicago Board Options Exchange	Interest rate options
Interest rate	U.S.	Chicago Mercantile Exchange (Index and Option Mart)	Options on three-month U.S. Treasury bill futures
Interest rate	U.S.	Chicago Mercantile Exchange (Index and Option Mart)	Options on one-year U.S. Treasury bill futures
Interest rate	U.S.	Chicago Mercantile Exchange (International Monetary)	One-month LIBOR futures
Interest rate	U.S.	Chicago Mercantile Exchange (International Monetary)	Three-month U.S. Treasury bill futures
Interest rate	U.S.	Chicago Mercantile Exchange (International Monetary)	One-year U.S. Treasury bill futures
Interest rate	U.S.	Chicago Mercantile Exchange (International Monetary)	Options on Federal funds rate futures
Interest rate	U.S.	Chicago Mercantile Exchange (International Monetary)	Options on one-month LIBOR futures
Interest rate	U.S.	FINEX	Treasury auction two-year U.S. Treasury note futures
Interest rate	U.S.	FINEX	Treasury auction five-year U.S. Treasury note futures
Interest rate	U.S.	MidAmerica Commodity Exchange	Eurodollar futures
Interest rate	U.S.	MidAmerica Commodity Exchange	U.S. Treasury bill futures
Interest rate	U.S.	MidAmerica Commodity Exchange	U.S. Treasury bond futures
Interest rate	U.S.	MidAmerica Commodity Exchange	Five-year U.S. Treasury note futures
Interest rate	U.S.	MidAmerica Commodity Exchange	Ten-year U.S. Treasury note futures
Interest rate	U.S.	MidAmerica Commodity Exchange	Options on U.S. Treasury bond futures

Continued

EXHIBIT 13–2 *Continued*

Contract Classification	Country	Exchange	Contract Description
Nonprecious metals	England	The London Metal Exchange Limited	Aluminum alloy futures
Nonprecious metals	England	The London Metal Exchange Limited	High grade primary aluminum futures
Nonprecious metals	England	The London Metal Exchange Limited	Copper Grade A futures
Nonprecious metals	England	The London Metal Exchange Limited	Refined standard lead futures
Nonprecious metals	England	The London Metal Exchange Limited	Primary nickel futures
Nonprecious metals	England	The London Metal Exchange Limited	Refined tin futures
Nonprecious metals	England	The London Metal Exchange Limited	Special high grade zinc futures
Nonprecious metals	England	The London Metal Exchange Limited	Options on aluminum alloy futures
Nonprecious metals	England	The London Metal Exchange Limited	Options on primary aluminum futures
Nonprecious metals	England	The London Metal Exchange Limited	Options on copper futures
Nonprecious metals	England	The London Metal Exchange Limited	Options on lead futures
Nonprecious metals	England	The London Metal Exchange Limited	Options on nickel futures
Nonprecious metals	England	The London Metal Exchange Limited	Options on tin futures
Nonprecious metals	England	The London Metal Exchange Limited	Options on zinc futures
Nonprecious metals	Malaysia	Kaula Lumpur Commodity Exchange	Tin futures
Nonprecious metals	U.S.	COMEX Division, New York Mercantile Exchange	Copper futures
Nonprecious metals	U.S.	COMEX Division, New York Mercantile Exchange	Options on copper futures
Nonprecious metals	U.S.	COMEX Division, New York Mercantile Exchange	Five-day copper options
Precious metals	Brazil	Bolsa de Mercadorias & Futuros	Gold futures
Precious metals	Brazil	Bolsa de Mercadorias & Futuros	U.S. dollar-denominated gold futures
Precious metals	Brazil	Bolsa de Mercadorias & Futuros	Gold spot
Precious metals	Brazil	Bolsa de Mercadorias & Futuros	Gold options on actuals

Contract Classification	Country	Exchange	Contract Description
Precious metals	Canada	Toronto Futures Exchange	Silver options—delisted September 15, 1995
Precious metals	Canada	Vancouver Stock Exchange	Gold options
Precious metals	Hong Kong	Hong Kong Futures Exchange Ltd.	Gold futures
Precious metals	Japan	The Tokyo Commodity Exchange	Gold futures
Precious metals	Japan	The Tokyo Commodity Exchange	Palladium futures
Precious metals	Japan	The Tokyo Commodity Exchange	Platinum futures
Precious metals	Japan	The Tokyo Commodity Exchange	Silver futures
Precious metals	Japan	The Tokyo Commodity Exchange	Physical gold
Precious metals	Netherlands	EOE – Opliebeurs	Silver options
Precious metals	Netherlands	European Options Exchange	Gold options
Precious metals	Singapore	Singapore International Monetary Exchange	Gold futures
Precious metals	South Africa	The South African Futures Exchange (SAFEX)	JSE actuaries all gold index futures
Precious metals	U.S.	Chicago Board of Trade	Gold (kilo) futures
Precious metals	U.S.	Chicago Board of Trade	Gold (100 ounce) futures
Precious metals	U.S.	Chicago Board of Trade	Silver (5,000 ounce) futures
Precious metals	U.S.	Chicago Board of Trade	Silver (1,000-ounce) futures
Precious metals	U.S.	Chicago Board of Trade	Options on silver (1,000 ounce) futures
Precious metals	U.S.	COMEX Division, New York Mercantile Exchange	Gold futures
Precious metals	U.S.	COMEX Division, New York Mercantile Exchange	Silver futures
Precious metals	U.S.	COMEX Division, New York Mercantile Exchange	Options on gold futures
Precious metals	U.S.	COMEX Division, New York Mercantile Exchange	Five-day gold options

Continued

319

E X H I B I T 13–2 *Continued*

Contract Classification	Country	Exchange	Contract Description
Precious metals	U.S.	COMEX Division, New York Mercantile Exchange	Options on silver futures
Precious metals	U.S.	COMEX Division, New York Mercantile Exchange	Five-day silver options
Precious metals	U.S.	MidAmerica Commodity Exchange	New York gold futures
Precious metals	U.S.	MidAmerica Commodity Exchange	New York silver futures
Precious metals	U.S.	MidAmerica Commodity Exchange	Platinum futures
Precious metals	U.S.	NYMEX Division, New York Mercantile Exchange	Options on New York gold futures
Precious metals	U.S.	NYMEX Division, New York Mercantile Exchange	Palladium futures
Precious metals	U.S.	NYMEX Division, New York Mercantile Exchange	Platinum futures
Precious metals	U.S.	Philadelphia Stock Exchange	Options on Platinum futures
Precious metals	U.S.		Gold/silver sector index options
Swap	Brazil	Bolsa de Mercadorias & Futuros	Basic financial rate × exchange rate swap
Swap	Brazil	Bolsa de Mercadorias & Futuros	Basic financial rate × gold price variation swap
Swap	Brazil	Bolsa de Mercadorias & Futuros	Basic financial rate × inflation index swap
Swap	Brazil	Bolsa de Mercadorias & Futuros	Basic financial rate × reference rate swap
Swap	Brazil	Bolsa de Mercadorias & Futuros	Exchange rate × gold price variation swap
Swap	Brazil	Bolsa de Mercadorias & Futuros	Inflation rate × exchange rate swap
Swap	Brazil	Bolsa de Mercadorias & Futuros	Inflation index × gold price variation swap
Swap	Brazil	Bolsa de Mercadorias & Futuros	Interest rate × basic financial rate swap
Swap	Brazil	Bolsa de Mercadorias & Futuros	Interest rate × exchange rate swap
Swap	Brazil	Bolsa de Mercadorias & Futuros	Interest rate × gold price swap

Contract Classification	Country	Exchange	Contract Description
Swap	Brazil	Bolsa de Mercadorias & Futuros	Interest rate × inflation index swap
Swap	Brazil	Bolsa de Mercadorias & Futuros	Interest rate × reference rate swap
Swap	Brazil	Bolsa de Mercadorias & Futuros	Reference rate × exchange rate swap
Swap	Brazil	Bolsa de Mercadorias & Futuros	Reference rate × gold price variation swap
Swap	Brazil	Bolsa de Mercadorias & Futuros	Reference rate × inflation index swap
	Netherlands		–Financial futures market Amsterdam (FTA)
			—MERFOX–Mercado de futuros Opcic

14

THE INFLUENCE OF DERIVATIVES ON MONETARY POLICY IN AN EMERGING COUNTRY ECONOMY

Michael Papaioannou, *International Monetary Fund*
George P. Tsetsekos, *Drexel University*

INTRODUCTION

The development of derivatives has been the result of a demand for instruments that facilitate hedging and position-taking. The need for derivative instruments dealing with the currencies and securities markets of emerging economies is greater since such markets tend to fluctuate more than those in developed economies. Risks inherent in the derivatives business, including credit, market, liquidity, and legal risks, are apparently no different from those encountered and managed by financial institutions in connection with their traditional business. Derivatives allow end-users to diversify or hedge risks they already carry, thus reducing in principle their overall risk exposure. However, risk exposure may in general increase for firms that act as intermediaries and market makers or use derivatives to take positions. Nonetheless, in some of these firms, the consolidated position of derivative port-folios can lead to reduced risk exposure due to the possible ex-ploitation of position offsetting (netting) in closely related instruments, which tends to reduce capital and hedging costs. In theory, the risk characteristics of derivatives and other off-balance-sheet transactions should necessitate some capital adequacy requirements on behalf of the financial institutions involved. Such capital adequacy provisions should ensure the reduction of overall systemic risks and the efficiency of the financial sector.

In this chapter we discuss the ways in which the introduction and use of derivative financial instruments in an emerging market economy could alter the channels of influence in regard to monetary policy. In general, it is argued that the use of derivatives makes the following regulatory conditions imperative: the closer monitoring of monetary developments; the increased scrutiny of traditional measurement methods of monetary aggregates; the acute and swift use of existing monetary policy measures—or even the adoption or few supplementary measures—to attain monetary policy targets; and the development of a regulatory and supervisory framework to enforce smooth functioning of the derivatives industry and avoid systemic disruptions in the overall financial system. In summary, the use of derivatives implies an increased loss of control and makes the conduct of monetary policy more complicated, which in turn results in the significant undercutting of monetary policy makers' ability to achieve broad macroeconomic goals.

The chapter is organized as follows. In the next section, we briefly examine the main features and functions of derivative markets in emerging economies. Then we analyze certain channels of influence on monetary policy from the introduction and use of derivative financial instruments. In the last section, we provide concluding remarks.

MAIN FEATURES AND FUNCTIONS OF DERIVATIVE MARKETS

Derivative instruments are mainly used for hedging, arbitrage, and speculation purposes. The extent of each of these functions in the operations of each derivative market is difficult to estimate. However, some indication of the degree of participation of hedgers, arbitrageurs, and speculators in derivative markets may be gained from an evaluation of the relative liquidity of each market, in the sense that high relative liquidity indicates a market dominated by speculative activity. Another indication of a high proportion of speculators in the markets may be the daily difference between turnover and the change in the open interest positions of a market, in the sense that a positive difference may indicate offsetting positions. That is, such a difference may be to a large extent attributed to speculative operations opened and offset the same day, since hedge transactions usually are taken for more than one day.[1] Finally, an indication of arbitrageurs' participation in derivative markets may be the proximity to equilibrium of price relationship among forward, futures, and options markets, in the sense that extensive arbitrage opportunities prevent prices from remaining out of equilibrium.

The major players of derivative financial instruments on the end-user side—investors, corporate treasurers, pension funds, banks, and government agencies—mainly use them for hedging their respective interest rate and foreign exchange exposures. However, the same players can use the derivative markets for position taking and, therefore, for speculative reasons. Even if derivatives are used exclusively for hedging purposes, risks may not equal zero. A hedger should always have a view on the trend of the market. A wrong reading of the market trend may result in a loss from both the underlying physical position and the futures or options position. On the supply side, the major players are banks and other financial institutions, which primarily underwrite the risk contracts for the end-users and thus act as the risk absorbers of the financial system.

For an emerging-market economy, the following six preconditions are required for well-functioning derivatives: (1) a relatively stable macroeconomic policy environment is in place, with inflation under control, so that government paper can be issued for sufficiently long maturities and, therefore, a yield curve can be constructed; (2) primary and secondary markets for government securities function efficiently and the necessary institutional framework, particularly that of dematerialization of government

---

1. If positions only are opened, turnover is equal to the positive change in the open interest. The difference between turnover and the change indicates the amount for which positions are offset. If such a change is zero, the amount for which positions are opened is equal to the amount for which they are offset.

securities, is in effect; (3) trade and investment transactions are sufficiently developed and, therefore, a good deal of demand for hedging, arbitrage, and speculative operations exists and adequate liquidity in derivative markets is guaranteed; (4) financial institutions are willing to undertake derivative transactions, qualified professionals exist, and associated risks are well understood; (5) an appropriate regulatory and supervisory framework governing the workings of the derivatives industry has been developed according to the particular economic and financial conditions of the country; and (6) a sequential framework of development for derivative markets, starting with long-term government securities and proceeding with foreign exchange and commodities, is thoroughly worked out.

CHANNELS OF INFLUENCE ON MONETARY POLICY

There are at least four ways through which the conduct of monetary policy at the national level can be influenced by the introduction and use of derivative instruments in an emerging market economy. First, derivative financial instruments may distort the traditional measurement of monetary aggregates, and thus they may conceal information from decision makers who depend on that measurement. Second, the increased use of derivative instruments makes monetary management tougher since monetary policy changes have to become swifter and more sizable in order to be effective. Third, derivatives in principle reduce the transparency of the end-users' exposure, especially in emerging countries where accounting standards and disclosure procedures are relaxed, and thus they increase the risk undertaken by underwriters of such instruments. Such repercussions increase the fragility of the financial institutions involved and therefore monetary authorities should be particularly careful in planning and implementing their policies. Fourth, credit and market exposures and risks induced by derivative transactions may increase the systemic risks of the financial system. Thus, authorities should appropriately regulate derivative markets and be ready to act promptly to eliminate the potential spreading of financial disruptions stemming from mishaps and/or illiquidity in the derivative-instruments markets to other segments of the financial system.

Derivatives and Monetary Aggregates

The availability and use of financial derivative instruments may distort the level of emerging-market economies' monetary aggregates; therefore, the traditional measurement of monetary aggregates may not send the appropriate signals to monetary policy authorities.

Derivatives as off-balance-sheet items tend often to disguise actual exposure for underwriters and thus alter their risks (of all types, including market, credit and liquidity). In addition, they may affect cash flow availability for end-users. More specifically, derivative instruments acting as high-risk liabilities for underwriting financial institutions may alter the "true" level of their available reserves. Since the monetary transmission process operates through the impact of monetary operations on financial intermediaries, particularly banks, attention should be given to the impact of derivatives on banks' reserves by trying to assess the risks involved and the capital required to be set aside to cover such risks. It is then logical to infer that the greater the use of derivatives in an emerging economy, the greater the potential distortion in that economy's monetary aggregates.

It is imperative that derivatives be consistently and accurately represented in bank statements and appropriately registered in the accounts of other financial institutions so that possible distortions in financial statistics are traceable. Attempts to approximate the extent of such distortions have involved calculating on-balance-sheet *equivalent* exposures for most of these instruments (Canning, Pitman, and Williams, 1988). Such conversions also could provide estimates of the needed official capital cost of running derivative positions.

Moreover, data on many areas of emerging economies' derivative markets may not be available, especially due to the off-balance-sheet nature of derivative instruments. In addition, data may not be representative of the derivative markets' activity, as the respective market practices, including documentation, often are not standardized and the markets for new derivative instruments may be shallow and volatile. The lack of statistical information and timely disclosure of derivatives activity in the accounts of the entities involved (as well as the general lack of mark-to-market accounting) both hinders the regulatory process and poses a problem in assessing credit risk exposure. This in turn makes it difficult to appropriately evaluate the overall liquidity of the financial institutions engaged in derivative transactions.

One approach that could be used to contain credit risk exposure involves imposing limits on the overall exposure of banking institutions trading derivatives and also curtailing the spread of the unregulated over-the-counter (OTC) market by introducing regulated exchange-traded derivatives markets. In particular, regulations could limit retail derivative operations for banking institutions and retail brokerage could take place only by specialized registered derivatives brokers with minimum capitalization. On the other hand, the development of organized exchanges for derivative instruments will lead transaction volume to be divided between the organized and the OTC markets and risk to be minimized due to the existence of the clearinghouse. In OTC markets, the role of the clearinghouse is played by the institution that underwrites the instruments. Also, banks' balance sheets and cash flows may be adversely affected by sudden or unexpected changes in mark-to-market valuations of banks' derivative operations—especially of market and credit exposures. Such considerations not only make financial markets less tractable and thus less stable but also instill uncertainties in banks' statements and impreciseness in the measurement of monetary aggregates.

We maintain that monetary aggregates are indirectly affected by the introduction and use of derivative financial instruments traded in organized exchanges or over-the-counter, as well as by other types of financial innovation, deregulation, and institutional change. In general, the use of derivatives by end-users for hedging or arbitrage purposes does not appear to materially change in either direction the liquidity and monetary aggregates of an economy; rather, these operations tend to balance the opposite positions of the parties involved and thus work in a zero-sum-game sense. However, when derivative instruments are used for position taking and other speculative activities, they tend to directly affect the liquidity of speculators, as their operations create fresh funds or absorb available reserves from them depending on the outcome of their expectations. In cases where speculative anticipations are fulfilled, the liquidity of investors, and that of the economy as a whole, increases. The reverse holds true in the case that speculators are wrong. In particular, for exchange-trade derivative instruments where margin calls are required, the effects of derivative activities on monetary aggregates are more tractable at least for the part representing the transferring of funds for margins from end-users' and speculators' accounts to intermediaries. Such effects may be exacerbated if leveraged speculative positions prevail. This is the case because, by buying futures or options contracts usually for a fraction of what it would cost to purchase the underlying asset outright, speculators are allowed to obtain exposure to a given market with far less cash that they would need if they were buying the market directly.

For monetary authorities to ameliorate such potential sharp changes in monetary aggregates, they may intervene by changing margin payments or imposing some type of collateral agreement. Or they may choose to more directly affect derivative markets by imposing other forms of capital controls. Since derivatives also may amplify price movements in the underlying assets, the time in which monetary authorities of an emerging economy have to react is reduced significantly. To be able to act promptly and to decrease credit risk exposures decisively, monetary authorities should precautiously require that banks dealing in derivatives maintain higher capital levels that meet certain enhanced capital adequacy standards.

The extensive and growing use of derivatives in international markets, which has led to an explosive growth of banks' off-balance-sheet business, has necessitated the development of accounting schemes and standards for such financial instruments. A lack of accounting rules concerning derivative operations decreases the transparency of published balance sheets with respect to a financial or nonfinancial firm's derivatives activity and, in turn, increases the possibility of inaccurate measurement of bank reserves, capital requirements, and liquidity. Moreover, extensive use may alter the degree and nature of risk of the end-users of such products. To the extent that derivatives are used more for speculative purposes and trading gains than to hedge risk, derivatives may become new sources of risk and thus may not improve the transfer of risk from more risk-averse investors to those willing to take on risk—as they were originally intended to. As discussed above, high levels of open interest in the futures markets and the fact that swap transactions between traders outweigh agreements involving end-users seem to indicate large speculative trades. These alterations of risk may cause systemic disruptions.

Derivatives and Monetary Instruments

The way in which derivatives change banks' liquidity and interest rate risk management practices and how such changes affect the transmission process itself are particularly interesting questions for policymakers. Undoubtedly, the use of derivatives to hedge financial risk and to take positions makes monetary management much more difficult to conduct.

In the case of wide use of hedging instruments to reduce interest rate exposure, changes in monetary policy have to be much more swift and pronounced than when such instruments are not available or are minimally used. Derivatives that are intended to cover end-users from changes in interest rates up to a certain level act as buffer zones for users' portfolio choices or trade transactions; therefore, attainment of a certain restrictive or expansionary monetary policy would need to at least exceed such interest-rate hedged levels and possibly would require much greater changes in monetary measures. In other words, for a certain monetary policy to be effective, or targeted interest rate levels to be attained, money supply changes will in general be greater and, thus, changes in the levels of instruments will have to be much more drastic than in the absence of derivatives. This applies particularly to emerging economies, where monetary instruments to a large extent are fewer than in developing countries. Furthermore, the introduction of derivatives and therefore the greater availability of financial instruments in the system make the control of monetary targets much more difficult to attain.

Transactions in financial derivative instruments can constitute substitutes for bank deposits and new sources of credit. For example, hedge funds, which consist of private money—often drawn from bank deposits—invested in speculative portfolios concentrating in the futures and options markets, usually maintain large leveraged positions using the initial capital as collateral. As hedge funds are borrowing from banks in order to increase, or leverage, the positions they take on particular markets, they create bank exposures from the standpoint of counter-party risk and credit risk. In addition, commercial banks' lending to hedge funds may increase liquidity tremendously. This is so because a hedge fund can get a credit line at bank A and leverage its capital, say, 10 times, while at the same time it can get a line at bank B, borrowing the same amount of money and thus leveraging 20 times.

These scenarios suggest that financial innovations may diminish the role and relative importance of traditional financial institutions (in particular commercial banks) and, in turn, their effectiveness in the monetary transmission process as well as in containing and diffusing potential financial crises. Moreover, derivative products with complex provisions may carry a new systemic risk. Since monetary policy, by its nature, functions through the banking system and its links with other financial institutions and markets, it is widely believed that if the banking system is systemically vulnerable and financial markets susceptible to excess variability, then the conduct of monetary policy becomes ineffectively and the stability of the economic system is at risk.

As was mentioned above, the introduction of derivative instruments indirectly affects the available level of bank reserves and therefore may diminish the effectiveness of monetary policy instruments. The extent of such effects depends on the capital required to be set aside and/or the collateral requested from financial institutions dealing in derivatives. Let us first discuss briefly the traditional quantitative tools of monetary policy in an emerging country economy: changes in the discount rate, changes in the reserve requirements, and open market operations. Usually, the least implemented tool in emerging markets to control the reserves (and thus loans and deposits) of the banking system involves purchasing and selling government securities on the open market. The discount rate is the rate of interest charged when a bank borrows from its central bank. Depository institutions may borrow from the central bank for the purpose of obtaining the reserves needed to meet the reserve requirements. Also, banks may arrange in advance to borrow for seasonal needs and/or to borrow for longer than usual periods.

Borrowing from the central bank depends on the relationship of the discount rate to other short-term rates rather than to the level of the discount rate. In cases where collaterization is required for certain transactions with the central bank, borrowing may impact the financial institutions' balance sheets and cash flows; this might become destabilizing if demands for collateral arise at a time when a financial institution is already short of liquidity.

Total loans from the central bank, and therefore bank reserves, increase in periods of expansion because changes in the discount rate tend to lag behind changes in other short-term rates, especially in the case of emerging-market economies. During periods of recession, discount rate decreases tend to lag behind the decline in other short-term interest rates. The availability of discounting at the central bank probably reduces financial instability by increasing the liquidity of banks. Further, the greater the ability of the commercial bank to borrow (including borrowing from the central bank) in relation to holding liquid assets (i.e., in relation to the loan/deposit ratio), the greater the bank's liquidity. Higher margin requirements for interbank and other derivative transactions may hurt a bank's liquidity at the time when it is needed most.

The third major instrument of control is the central bank's ability to make changes in the legal reserve requirements of banks (i.e., on their net transaction accounts and on all nonpersonal time deposits). These reserve requirements establish an upper limit to the expansion of the loans, investments, and deposits of banks. Lowering the legal reserve ratios of depository institutions has the same effect on the supply of bank deposits and credit as open market purchases; this is so even though open market purchases increase bank reserves, whereas lower reserve requirements permit banks to make more loans and hold a larger volume of deposits with the same quantity of reserves. However, an advantage of using this last instrument of monetary control is that it immediately affects a very large number of banks. In contrast, the effects of open market operations are felt immediately by only a few banks, although eventually the effects spread throughout the system. Provisions for enhanced capital adequacy requirements for banks engaged in derivatives dealings work in tandem with increases in reserve requirements.

To guide the use of their instruments of control, the central bank authorities have targets of monetary policy, such as the rate of expansion of money supply, the level of market interest rates, and, to a lesser extent, the level of free reserves (i.e., the excess reserves held by commercial banks less their borrowing from the central bank) and the rate of growth of nonborrowed reserves. The authorities watch the targets in order to tell whether the actions that they have taken are expansionary or contractionary. In order to stimulate the economy, the monetary authorities may raise the level of free reserves, and, in order to restrain the economy, they may lower the level of free reserves. If collateral is required as part of the transaction or as a form of reducing credit exposures arising from financial derivative activities, the bank's liquidity is obviously adversely affected. Thus, the effect of a certain monetary policy in regard to a specific target might be less or completely unpredictable. The extent of the possible breakdown of the transmission process depends critically on the level of the restricted bank reserves due to the imposition of capital (collateral) requirements.

The introduction of derivative instruments may necessitate a selective rise in legal reserve ratios to provide for the increased risk undertaking, which could in turn embarrass banks that are not sufficiently liquid to meet the higher reserve requirements with ease. Therefore, for depository institutions engaged in derivative business, their available reserves are affected by the mandatory percentage of the risk-weighted assets to be maintained as a capital base and, in this sense, by the adopted methods of measuring risky assets. The capital requirements for risk exposures may include interest rate risk (or market risk), foreign exchange risk, credit risk, settlement/delivery risk, and counterparty risk. The interest rate risk is also known as "general risk" and is distinguished from credit risk, which is referred to as "specific risk." Capital charges for general risk are intended to capture the risk of loss arising from unanticipated changes in interest rates. Capital requirements for specific risk are intended to protect against an adverse price movement of a specific debt-type security (Gatzonas, 1994).

Finally, the established instruments and approaches of central banks may become ineffective because of the ambiguous impact of derivatives on commercial bank profits, capital, and liquidity,[2] if not in market share. If such an impact renders the

---

2. A way that has been proposed to increase banks' liquidity in on-balance-sheet foreign exchange operations is through the use of netting.

competitive position of banks ineffective over time and diminishes the critical mass of banking assets and transactions, then central banks will not have the essentials they need for an effective transmission of monetary policy.

It has been argued that the relative size of an economy's reserve base shrinks, and the velocity of turnover may be multiplied, following the introduction of derivative instruments. However, there is no conclusive evidence that monetary policy instruments have impacted the economy in a decisive manner. The capacity of monetary instruments to broadly and predictably influence interest rates, financial conditions, and ultimately the price level has not altered substantially; however, the lag effects and the size of changes in monetary instruments have been affected. This may be evident from the need to institute larger changes in interest rates today and wait longer in order to achieve a certain degree of economic restraint or stimulation in most developed countries.

Derivatives and Monetary Policy

Monetary authorities should be cautious in setting their policies because changes in interest rate policy may be detrimental to financial entities engaged in the derivatives business. It should be added here that the effect of monetary policy on financial markets in general, and derivative markets in particular, differs among countries. Changes in official interest rates might adversely affect a financial institution's condition through their effect on all interest-sensitive assets and liabilities. In particular, banks in several emerging-market economies that tend to be undercapitalized are more vulnerable to interest rate changes. Therefore, monetary authorities should consider more than on-balance-sheet items when they plan their policies, as their actions pertain to the overall interest rate risk run by financial institutions. Since monetary-policy moves affect the total portfolio of financial institutions, competent authorities also should have ways to estimate the implications of their policy changes on the off-balance-sheet items of financial institutions that are heavily involved in derivative instruments. This last suggestion might be very difficult to implement, however, due to the wide use of OTC transactions.

For financial institutions engaged in derivatives, the interest/ currency rate risk caused by unfavorable interest/currency rate developments may sometimes be enough to lead to failures. Depending on the extent of interest rate exposure and the interest sensitivity of the off-balance-sheet items, interest rate changes may prove crucial to a financial institution's existence in the marked-to-market "net asset" sense. That is, the economic value of a financial institution, or the difference between the marked-to-market assets and liabilities, may decrease drastically when interest rates increase unexpectedly.

The ability to absorb losses and avoid bankruptcy may be limited significantly for those institutions with an inadequate capital base. Thus, measurement of the interest rate risk exposure of the off-balance-sheet items, through methods of converting them to on-balance-sheet equivalent exposures, is particularly important especially when interest rates tend to be excessively volatile. However, dealing in derivatives may sometimes be utilized by depository institutions in such a way that such positions could offer a counterbalance to interest rate risk exposures from traditional interest sensitive on-balance-sheet items when adverse interest rate movements occur.

Therefore, depository institutions of emerging-market economies may have an incentive to adjust their portfolios by decreasing the share of off-balance-sheet assets, since such assets are considered riskier and, in turn, institutions are obliged for higher capital charges. The capital cost of running derivative positions (swaps, futures, and options) would be higher depending on the extent of the calculated on-balance-sheet equivalent exposures. The determination of the market value of derivative portfolios would not only allow the calculation of the respective equivalent on-balance-sheet positions, but it would also permit analysis of their relevant interest and exchange rate exposures. The Group of Thirty report (1993) suggests valuing derivative portfolios at mid-market value, less specific adjustments—which should capture expected future costs such as unearned credit spreads, close-out costs, administrative costs, and investing and funding costs. Often, all of these costs are implicitly assumed in the bid-offer method.

The growth of OTC interbank trading in longer maturities contracts could make credit risk exposures a substantial by-product of market risk trading activities. The lack of transparency of balance sheets (and especially what is omitted from them) is widely recognized as having greatly complicated the assessment and management of credit risk. There are also basic operational risks, in that firms may mistakenly believe risk to be hedged when it is not, or participants may simply overestimate the liquidity of their own position owing to a false perception of their own share of transactions or positions in various markets. Participants may find it difficult to manage the cash requirements connected with large derivative portfolios. Such cash requirements can arise suddenly and in large amounts, particularly when changes in market conditions or in perceptions of credit standing due to policy changes necessitate margin payments or the adjustment of hedges and positions. That is why authorities of emerging-market economies should pay particular attention to their conduct of monetary policy so that market conditions or perceptions of participants' credit standing do not change abruptly and substantially.

In the event of a sharp market movement or other surprises, a firm/bank active in the market may have to take the precaution of temporarily withdrawing from trading and refraining from extending credit to counterparties that have come under suspicion, thus disrupting the orderly functioning of financial markets. However, if such an event were to happen in an already unsettled market environment, the systemic implications of the withdrawal or the sudden failure of one or more market participants and the corresponding disruptions would not only reach the financial system but would also extend to the real sector of the economy (i.e., credit allocations, investment decisions, trade transactions, and so on). Note that such systemic risks and market failures are assumed not to be the result of fraudulent activities or market manipulations but only the potential result of miscalculations of risk and/or inappropriate or untimely monetary policy actions.

The most commonly experienced consequence of financial disruptions of a systemic nature is the dry-up of liquidity in the particular market that has failed. As financial markets are nowadays relatively closely linked, the likelihood is that the effects of such disruptions or shocks will be quickly transmitted to other markets, on which other participants rely to adjust or close positions at a certain time. This might apply above all to options, which, in the absence of a fully offsetting back-to-back option hedge, require dynamic hedging of underlying price exposure and hedging of volatility exposure. Such an event would primarily affect options writers, who depend heavily on liquid and orderly cash, both in exchange-traded and OTC options markets. Sometimes, however, monetary authorities of emerging-country economies may not be able to accurately estimate short-term interest rate and exchange rate volatility changes in the system, or market participants may not even be able to assess such volatilities in order to build them into hedging programs. In addition, volatility in the system may reflect changes in the desired monetary conditions; thus, monetary actions always should take both domestic and international implications into consideration. The important unsettled question is, of course, whether and how derivatives trading affects volatility in underlying markets.

Derivatives and Systemic Risks

Systemic risks may be thought of as potential disruptions of an emerging-market economy's financial system in the sense that if one firm or financial institution engaging in the OTC derivatives business becomes bankrupt, it might trigger a ripple-effect that could result in other firms' or financial institutions' collapsing as the commitments made by the first entity are not honored. One way of handling this risk involves the creation of a detailed internal control system.

Controls should include a permanent system for measuring the risk of each position, possibly using the on-balance-sheet equivalent exposures method, in a way that allows a derivative's transaction to be recorded immediately and the financial institution's overall exposure to be evaluated constantly. Such risks appear to be significantly diminished or even eliminated for exchange-traded derivative contracts, as the clearing-house is the guarantor of all transactions.

In many instances, the source of a firm's or a bank's failure is excess speculation. For example, imprudent speculation using derivatives could lead corporations to bankruptcies that might eventually cause serious problems to the financial system. Because futures and options contracts usually can be bought for a fraction of what it would cost to purchase the underlying asset outright, they allow speculators to obtain exposure to a given market (e.g., the foreign exchange market) with far less cash than they would need if they were buying the market directly. That creates a more leveraged position, giving rise to the potential for greater gains and, alternatively, larger losses, if expectations/forecasts for changes in the respective market do not materialize or, even worse, if they move sharply in the opposite direction. Such an event will not only jeopardize the financial soundness of the corporation engaged in such activities but also may affect other corporations and particularly financial institutions dealing with that corporation. The worse case scenario is the potential bankruptcy of corporations with heavy losses in derivative activities (e.g., losses caused by unfavorable interest and/or exchange rate developments), which could result in defaults on their loan payments and therefore the possible write-off of the respective assets by the financial institutions servicing them.

It has been argued that systemic risks of a country's financial system have not been appreciably aggravated by the introduction of derivatives, as they do not introduce risks of a fundamentally different kind and greater scale than those already present.[3] Undoubtedly, though, systemic risks associated with derivatives exist and include various disruptions originating in the derivative activities at the individual firm level or at the country level.

Concerns always should be raised about the possible underpricing of credit, market, liquidity, and other risks that can lead to large losses on derivative positions of individual firms. Especially, position-taking entails market exposure. Moreover, the decreased transparency of financial entities' exposures can contribute to liquidity problems and the develoment of a financial crisis. This last possibility may be exaggerated due to the increased market linkages and the corresponding feedback effects. In particular, options have the potential to exacerbate a sharp price move, as written options tend to be dyamically hedged and hence require selling into a falling market. This problem becomes acute for

---

3. These views are expressed in the forward to the Group of Thirty report (1993).

emerging-market economies, where financial markets tend to be less liquid. Monetary authorities may be required to impose margins or other collateral arrangements to manage such credit risks in derivative transactions.

Systemic risks for an emerging-market country's financial system also may arise from the threat that some OTC-derivatives contracts could be deemed unenforceable off-exchange forward contracts. Such a development could exacerbate a market downturn and put creditor financial institutions at risk. Moreover, for OTC options writers, and for some kinds of swaps as well, the risk position cannot always be managed and an open position may not always be able to be covered before it goes wrong. This may be the case when there is some probability of trading halts or the abandonment of market-making by a leading dealer. When that happens, normal market access shrinks and new hedges cannot be constructed; essentially, everybody in the market is trying to do the same thing at the same time. As a result, volatility can increase by orders of magnitudes, defeating even the best-planned options-hedging strategy.

Therefore, monetary authorities should monitor and be alert to any adverse developments in derivative markets; they must be ready to act swiftly and not only in extreme crisis situations. Only when problems with derivative-market users are detected before they become public knowledge, and possibly have been exaggerated, will authorities be able to intervene effectively and preclude any spreading to the rest of the financial system and thus eliminate any negative repercussion to the economy.

For the monetary authorities to be in constant command of derivative market developments, they should have in place capital standards that reflect the risk associated with derivative products. In addition, because derivatives play an important role in the management of interest rate and exchange rate risks at many banks, monetary authorities should utilize risk-based capital measurement schemes that encompass derivative products.

Containing systemic risks and therefore maintaining the stability of financial markets and payment and settlement systems presupposes the prudent management of risk and effective oversight policies within firms and banks and within the financial system itself. Such a multilevel approach would create an appropriate derivative-markets infrastructure that in turn would strengthen systemic benefits considerably.

With the continued growth of the swaps markets, concerns about the concentration of counterparty credit risks, especially in the interdealer markets, should be addressed because otherwise, they may become an important factor limiting market liquidity. For example, a clearinghouse for interest rate swaps always functions as an instrument for reducing counterparty risk exposures and related capital charges in the interdealer market. Furthermore, since derivative products (especially those in emerging-market economies) are constantly evolving, monetary authorities always should be ready to apply the appropriate regulatory regime that will ensure the competitive advantage of firms that are developing new derivative financial products and, at the same time, contain the possibility of exacerbating systemic problems.

Finally, it should be mentioned that the absence or significant reduction of systemic risks also has real effects for the economy. A well-functioning derivatives market increases the confidence of end-users of derivative products and encourages them to hedge interest rate and exchange rate risks. The improved ability to hedge reduces the sensitivity of corporations' investment decisions to interest rate and exchange rate movements; therefore, those corporations are more prompt in undertaking investment projects. In addition, containing market volatility through derivative markets might positively affect credit creation and investment and, ultimately, the transmission process of monetary policy.

Overall, monetary policies and/or the regulatory environment should be planned and exercised in a way that will preclude adverse developments in the derivative markets and eliminate the risk of financial disruptions so that investors' confidence in trade and financial transactions is warranted.

CONCLUDING REMARKS

The development of new derivative financial instruments and markets has originated from the effort of individual businesses and financial institutions to control risk exposures and achieve greater efficiency. The proliferation of new derivative instruments and new approaches for transferring and repackaging risks in emerging economies' financial markets is difficult to measure and trace. Much of it takes place outside the banking system and virtually all of it is reported off the balance sheet. It has been suggested that financial markets are more efficient and fluid after the introduction of derivative instruments. Nonetheless, there are uncertainties about the broader implications, both for the transmission of monetary policy and for the risk to the financial system.

The analysis presented in this chapter has examined some of the possible effects of the introduction of derivative instruments on the conduct of the monetary policy of emerging market economies at the national level. In principle, derivatives have uncertain effects on the traditional measurement of monetary aggregates, complicate the transmission process between changes in monetary policy measures and targets, necessitate swifter and more pronounced policy moves, and call for increased calculation of policy actions that ought to take into primary consideration off-balance-sheet activities and the systemic risks of the banking sector. Although such instruments lead to some loss of control of monetary policy to attain its macroeconomic goals, we cannot overlook the fact that derivatives have positive effects on both the end-users and the underwriters of these products if they are prudently used and sufficiently regulated and monitored.

The real benefits of derivatives take the form of more efficient allocation and management of risks. By lowering the costs of risk intermediation and providing more custom-made hedges, derivatives enable investors, corporate treasurers, and financial institutions to achieve exposures in their financial transactions that are more consistent with their overall business strategies. It is apparent that underwriters, as well as end-users, of deriviatives should use sound practices in dealing with these instruments to avoid uncontrolled risk exposures and thus reduce the chance that a major financial disruption will occur. For the containment of systemic risks and the endurance of the well- functioning of the financial system, the regulatory and supervisory role of emerging economies' monetary authorities is of great importance. However, the integration of world capital markets has multiplied the challenges facing policymakers; thus, there is an increased need for international cooperation and regulatory harmonization.

The general responsibilities of domestic monetary authorities include, first, understanding the role and behavior of firms operating in derivative financial markets and, second, understanding how their own policy actions affect the environment in which these markets operate. In general, organized exchanges for derivative instruments should pose less of a concern to authorities because of the associated clearinghouse guarantees, while OTC derivatives markets should be faced with greater reservations due to the lack of an institutional mandate to monitor the risks involved.

One basic aspect is to ensure that banks and other financial institutions engaging in derivatives are adequately capitalized. Recently proposed capital requirements for market risk at banks will ensure that risks are better covered and priced. Nonbanking entities raise bigger difficulties to regulatory and supervisory authorities than do banks in terms of the accounting and prudent measures that should be applied to them regarding derivatives. Above all, policymakers should be aware that derivatives are always relatively easy to introduce but are often difficult to control.

REFERENCES

Bank of England. "Local Authority Swaps." *Quarterly Bulletin*, May 1991, pp. 250–255.

—. *Derivatives: Report of an Internal Working Group*, April 1993.

Bank for Internal Settlements. *Derivative Financial Instruments and Banks' Involvement in Selected Off-Balance-Sheet Business*, April 1993.

Board of Governors of the Federal Reserve System. Federal Deposit Insurance Coporation, Office of the Comptroller of the Currency. *Derivative Product Activities of Commercial Banks—A Joint Study Conducted in Response to Questions Posed by Senator Riegle on Derivative Products*, January 27, 1993.

Canning, Andrew; Trevor Pitman; and Richard Williams. "Capital Adequacy: The BIS Framework and its Portfolio Implications." *The Journal of International Securities Markets*, Autumn 1988, pp. 292–315.

Economist. "Derivatives: Profit of Doom." *Economist,* October 23, 1993, pp. 93–94.

Financial Times. "Derivatives." *Financial Times Survey*, October 20, 1993, pp. 2–12.

Gatzonas, E.K. "Interest Rate Risk: From Theory to Directive 93/6 of the European Economic Community." Bank of Greece, mimeographed, December 1994.

Group of Ten. *International Capital Movements and Foreign Exchange Markets.* A Report to the Ministers and Governors by the Group of Deputies, April 1993.

Group of Thirty. *Derivatives: Practices and Principles—Global Derivatives Study.* Washington D.C., July 1993.

—. *Derivatives: Practices and Principles—Appendix I: Working Papers—Global Derivatives Study Group.* Washington D.C., July 1993.

Hull, John. *Options, Futures and Other Derivative Securities.* Prentice Hall International, Inc., 1989.

International Monetary Fund. *World Economic and Financial Surveys—International Capital Markets—Part II. Systemic Issues in International Finance.* Team led by Morris Goldstein and David Folkerts-Landau, August 1993.

McDonough, William J. "Comments on the Study by the Group of Thirty on Derivative Financial Instruments." *BIS Review*, no. 186.

Morris, Charles S.; and H. Sellon Jr. "Market Value Accounting for Banks: Pros and Cons." *Federal Reserve Bank of Kansas City Economic Review*, March/April 1991, pp. 5–19.

Organization for Economic Cooperation and Development. *Financial Market Trends—Special Features—World Securities Markets: Looking Ahead.* June 1993.

Remolona, Eli M. "The Recent Growth of Financial Derivative Markets." *Federal Reserve Bank of New York Quarterly Review*, Winter 1992–93, pp. 28–43.

Simons, Katherine. "Interest Rate Structure and the Credit Risk of Swaps." *New England Economic Review*, July/August 1993, pp. 23–34.

Wipperfurth, Heike. "The World's Fastest-Growing Exchanges."*Global Finance*, January 1994, pp. 60–62.

A Bibliography of Research in Emerging Capital Markets

Aggarwal, Raj. "The Nature of Currency Black Markets: Empirical Test of Weak and Semistrong Form Efficiency." *International Trade Journal* 5 (Fall 1990), pp. 1–24.

Aggarwal, Reena; and Pietra Rivoli. "Seasonal And Day-Of-The-Week Effects In Four Emerging Stock Markets," *Financial Review*, 1989, v24(4), 541–550.

Agtmael, Antoine van. *Emerging Securities Markets*. London: Euromoney Publications, 1984.

Aguilar, Linda M.; and Mike A. Singer. "Big Emerging Markets And U.S. Trade," *FRB Chicago—Economic Perspectives*, 1995, v19(4), 2–14.

Ajayi, Richard A.; and Seyed M. Mehdian. "Tests Of Investors' Reactions To Major Surprises: The Case Of Emerging Markets," *Journal of International Financial Management, Institutions and Markets*, 1994, v4(1/2), 115–128.

Ajayi, Richard; Jongmoo Jay Choi; and Seyed M. Mehdian. "The United States, Japan, And The Emerging Stock Markets Of the Pacific Basin: A Test Of Intertemporal Stability And Bloc Effect," *Advances in Pacific Basin Business, Economics and Finance*, 1995, v1(1), 321–335.

Amershi, Amin H.; and Sailesh B. Ramamurtie. "Rational Expectations Equilibrium in an Economy with Segmented Capital Asset Markets." Georgia State University, Department of Finance, College of Business Administration. Working Paper Series No. 91–01. November 1991.

Anckonie, Alex; and Chi Chang-hyun. "Internationalization of the Korean Stock Market." Paper presented at the Korea Economic Institute of America Meeting, November 5, 1986.

Ang, James S.; and Minje Jung. "An Alternative Test of Myers' Pecking Order Theory of Capital Structure: The Case of South Korean Firms." *Pacific-Basin Finance Journal* 1, no. 1 (March 1993), pp. 31–46.

Anwar, M. N., M. Ariff; and M. Shamsher. "Is Kuala Lumpur's Emerging Share Market Efficient?," *Journal of International Financial Management, Institutions and Markets*, 1994, v4(1/2), 89–100.

Association for Investment Management and Research, ICFA Continuing Education. *Managing Emerging Markets*. Association for Investment Management and Research, February 1994.

Awyni, Andrew. "Stock Exchange: A Potential Growth Area." *Africa Economic Digest* (U.K.) 5 (September 1991), pp. 9–22.

Aylen, Jonathan. "Privatization in Developing Countries." *Lloyds Bank Review*, January 1987, pp. 15–30.

Bailey, Warren. "U.S. Money Supply Announcements and Pacific Rim Stock Markets: Evidence and Implications." *Journal of International Money and Finance* 9 (September 1990), pp. 344–56.

Bailey Warren; and Joseph Lim. "Initial Public Offerings of Country Funds: Evidence and Implications." *Pacific Basin Capital Markets Research* 2 (1991), pp. 365–378.

Bailey, Warren; and Joseph Lim. "Evaluating the Diversification Benefits of the New Country Funds." *Jounal of Portfolio Management* 19 (Spring 1992), pp. 74–8.

Bailey, Warren; and Julapa Jagtiani. "Foreign Ownership Restrictions and Stock Prices in the Thai Capital Market." *Journal of Financial Economics* 36 (1994), pp. 57–87.

Bailey, Warren; and René M. Stultz. "Benefits of International Diversification: The Case of Pacific Basin Stock Markets." *Journal of Portfolio Management* 17 (1990), pp. 57–61.

Bailey, Warren; and René M. Stultz. "Measuring the Benefits of International Diversification with Daily Data: The Case of Pacific Basin Stock Markets." *Journal of Portfolio Management* 16 (Summer 1990), pp. 57–61.

Bailey, Warren; and Y. Peter Chung. "Exchange Rate Fluctuations, Political Risk, And Stock Returns: Some Evidence From An Emerging Market," *Journal of Financial and Quantitative Analysis*, 1995, v30(4), 541–561.

Balban, Ercan. "Day Of The Week Effects: New Evidence From An Emerging Stock Market," *Applied Economics Letters*, 1995, v2(5), 139–143.

Balino, Tomas J. T., Juhi Dhawan; and V. Sundararajan. "Payments Systems Reforms And Monetary Policy In Emerging Market Economies In Central And Eastern Europe," *International Monetary Fund Staff Papers*, 1994, v41(3), 383–410.

Bark, Hee-Kyung K. "Risk, Return, And Equilibrium In The Emerging Markets: Evidence From The Korean Stock Market," *Journal of Economics and Business*, 1991, v43(4), 353–362.

Barry, Christopher B.; Gonzalo Castañeda; and Joesph B. Lipscomb. "The Structure of Mortgage Markets in Mexico and Prospects for their Securitization." *Journal of Housing Research* 5 (Fall 1994), forthcoming.

Barry, Christopher B.; Gonzalo Castañeda; and Joseph B. Lipscomb. "Esquemas de Mercado para la Bursatilización de la Cartera Hipotecaria en México." *Inversión y Finanzas* 2 (January–June 1994), pp. 31–40.

Bauman, W. Scott. "Investment Research Analysis In An Emerging Market: Singapore and Malaysia," *Financial Analyst Journal*, 1989, v45(6), 60–67.

Bei, Duoguang, Arden Koontz; and Lewis Xiangqian Lu. "Emerging Securities Market In The PRC," *China Economic Review*, 1993, v3(2), 149–172.

Bekaert, Geert. "Market Integration and Investment Barriers in Emerging Equity Markets." *World Bank Economic Review*, forthcoming, 1984.

Bekaert, Geert; and Campbell R. Harvey. "Time-Varying World Market Integration." Working paper, Stanford University and Duke University, 1994.

Bekaert, Geert; and Campbell R. Harvey. "Emerging Equity Market Volatility." Working paper, Stanford University and Duke University, 1994.

Bekaert, Geert; and Michael S. Urias. "Diversification, Integration, and Emerging Market, Closed-End Funds." Working paper, Stanford University, 1994.

Bergstrom, Gary L. "A New Route to Higher Returns and Lower Risks." *The Journal of Portfolio Management*, Autumn 1975, pp. 30–38.

Bicksler, James L. "Gains from Portfolio Diversification in Less Developed Countries' Securities: A Comment." *Journal of International Business Studies,* Spring–Summer 1978.

Bonser-Neal, C.; Greggory Brauer; R. Neal; and S. Wheatley. "Closed-End Country Fund Prices and International Investment Restrictions." *Journal of Finance* 45 (June 1990), pp. 323–348.

Brainard, Lawrence J. "Reform in Eastern Europe: Creating a Capital Market." *Federal Reserve Bank of Kansas City Economic Review* 49 (January/February 1991).

Brown, Rob. "Risk and Return in the Emerging Markets." *Investing,* Spring 1991.

Brown, Stephen J.; and Toshiyuki Otsuki. "Risk Premia in Pacific-Basin Capital Markets." *Pacific-Basin Finance Journal* 1, no. 3 (September 1993), pp. 235–261.

Buckberg, Elaine. "Emerging Stock Markets and International Asset Pricing." Working paper, MIT, November 1992.

Calamanti, Andrea. "The Securities Market and Underdevelopment: The Stock Exchange in the Ivory Coast, Morocco and Tunisia." Milan: Giuffra, 1983.

Cambridge Associates, Inc. *Investing in Emerging Stock Markets.* Cambridge Associates, Inc., 1993.

—. *Investing in Emerging Stock Markets Executive Summary.* Cambridge Associates, Inc., 1993.

Caprio, Gerard; David Folkerts-Landau; and Timothy D. Lane, Editors. *Building Sound Finance in Emerging Market Economies.* Washington, D.C.: International Monetary Fund, 1994.

Castelin, Mark; and Douglas Stone. "Fundamental Factors Affecting Investing in the Emerging Markets." Working paper, Frank Russell Co., March 1990.

Chambers, Fred; and David Hyland. "Building a Banking System from Scratch— Advice for the Emerging Market Economies." *Banking World* 10 (March 1992), pp. 22–24.

Chan, Kalok; and Yue-cheong Chang. "Price Volatility in the Hong Kong Stock Market: A Test of the Information and Trading Noise Hypothesis." *Pacific-Basin Finance Journal* 1, no. 2 (May 1993), pp. 189–201.

Chang, Rosita P.; Toru Fukuda; S. Ghon Rhee; and Makoto Takano. "Intraday and Interday Behavior of the TOPIX." *Pacific-Basin Finance Journal* 1, no. 1 (March 1993), pp. 67–95.

Chaudhuri, Swapan Kanti. "Emerging Stock Markets: Return, Risk and Diversification." *MDI Management Journal* (India) 4 (July 1991), pp. 39–47.

Chen, Yea-Mow. "Price Limits and Stock Market Volatility in Taiwan." *Pacific-Basin Finance Journal* 1, no. 2 (May 1993), pp. 139–153.

Cheung, C. Sherman; and Jason Lee. "Integration vs. Segmentation in the Korean Stock Market." *Journal of Business Finance & Accounting* 20, no. 2 (January 1993), pp. 267–273.

Cheung, Yan-Leun; and Yan-Ki Ho. "The Intertemporal Stability of the Relationship Between the Asian Emerging Equity Markets and the Developed Equity Markets." *Journal of Business Finance and Accounting* (U.K.) 18 (January 1991), pp. 235–254.

Cheung, Yan-Leung; Kie-Ann Wong; and Yan-Ki Ho. "The Pricing Of Risky Assets In Two Emerging Asian Markets—Korea And Taiwan," *Applied Financial Economics*, 1993, v3(4), 315–324.

Cho, Yoon Je. "Inefficiencies from Financial Liberalization in the Absence of Well-functioning Equity Markets." *Journal of Money, Credit and Banking*, May 1986.

Choe, H.; R. W. Masulis; and V. Nanda. "Common Stock Offerings Across the Business Cycle: Theory and Evidence." *Journal of Empirical Finance* 1, no. 1 (June 1993), pp. 3–31.

Choe, Hyuk; and Hung Sik Shin. "An Analysis of Interday and Intraday Return Volatility—Evidence from the Korea Stock Exchange." *Pacific-Basin Finance Journal* 1, no. 2 (May 1993), pp. 175–188.

Chowdhry, Bhagwan; and Sheridan Titman. "Why Real Interest Rates, Cost of Capital & Price/Earnings Ratios Vary Across Countries." Working paper, December 1993.

Chuhan, Punam; Stijn Claessens; and Nlandu Mamingi. "Equity and Bond Flows to Asia and Latin America." The Policy Research Working Paper Series, WPS1160. International Economics Department, The World Bank, July 1993.

Chuppe, Terry M.; and Michael Atkin. "Regulation of Securities Markets: Some Recent Trends and Their Implications for Emerging Markets." Working paper, International Finance Corporation, 1992.

Claessens, Stijn; Susmita Dasgupta; and Jack Glen. "Stock Price Behavior in Emerging Markets," in Stijn CLAESSENS and Sudashan GOOPTU, eds., *Portfolio Investment in Developing Countries*, World Bank Discussion Papers No. 228, 1993, pp. 323–350.

Clark, Robert A. "African Security Markets: A Study in the Development of Africa's Emerging Security Markets." Working paper, University of Vermont, October 1993.

Conroy, Robert; Robert S. Harris; and Young S. Park. "Published Analysts' Earnings Forecasts in Japan: How Accurate Are They?" *Pacific-Basin Finance Journal* 1, no. 2 (May 1993), pp. 127–137.

Corbo, Vittorio; and Leonardo Hernandez. "Macroeconomic Adjustment to Portfolio Capital Inflows: Rationale and Some Recent Experiences." Working paper, World Bank, September 1993.

Cornelius, Peter K. "Monetary Policy and the Price Behavior in Emerging Stock Markets." Washington, D.C.: International Monetary Fund, Exchange and Trade Relations, March 1991.

Cornford, Andrew J. "Inside An Emerging Financial Market: System Design And Regulation For A Roller-Coaster," *Journal of Economic Issues*, 1995, v29(3), 929–938.

Corrigan, E. Gerald. "The Role Of Central Banks And The Financial System In Emerging Market Economies," *FRB New York—Quarterly Review*, 1990, v15(2), 1–7.

Dailami, M.; and E. H. Kim. "The Effects of Debt Subsidies on Corporate Investment Behavior." *Pacific-Basin Finance Journal* 2 (March 1994), pp. 1–22.

Darby, Rose. "Custody's Conundrum in the Emerging Markets." *Global Finance* 6 (October 1992), pp. 103–110.

Davis, Lyle H. "Portfolio Composition For Emerging Markets Equities," *Journal of Investing*, 1994, v3(4), 7–11.

de Caires, Brian; and Debbie Fletter. "Investing in Emerging Securities Markets." *Euromoney Publications*, 1990.

DeFusio, Richard A.; J. Geppart; and George P. Tsetsekos. "Long-Run Diversification Potential in Emerging Capital Markets," *Financial Review*, Vol. 31, No. 2, May 1996, pp. 343–363.

Demirguc-Kunt Asli; and Harry Huizinga. "Barriers to Portfolio Investments in Emerging Stock Markets." *Journal of Deveopment Economics*, 1995, 47(2), pp. 355–74.

Dickie, Robert. "Development of Third World Securities Markets: An Analysis of General Principles and Case Study of the Indonesian Market." *Law and Policy in International Business* 13 (1981), pp. 177–222.

Divecha, Arjun B.; Jaime Drach; and Dan Stefek. "Emerging Markets: A Quantitative Perspective," *Journal of Portfolio Management*, 1992, v19(1), 41–50.

Donaldson, Brent. "Liquidity Potential In The Emerging Secondary Market," *Real Estate Finance*, 1995, v12(3), 84–87.

Duke, Lawrence K.; and Michael G. Papaioannou. "Accessing Emerging Stock Markets: Prerequisites for International Investors," *The Journal of Investing*, Vol. 2, No. 2, 1993, pp. 18–26.

El-Erian, Mohamed A.; and Manmohan S. Kumar. "Emerging Equity Markets In Middle Eastern Countris," *International Monetary Fund Staff Papers*, 1995, v42(2), 313–343.

Errunza, Vihang R. "Emerging Markets: A New Opportunity For Improving Global Portfolio Performance," *Financial Analyst Journal*, 1983, v39(5), 51–58.

Errunza, Vihang R. "Emerging Markets: Some New Concepts," *Journal of Portfolio Management*, 1994, v20(3), 82–87.

Errunza, Vihang R.; and Prasad Padmanabhan. "Further Evidence on the Benefits of Portfolio Investments in Emerging Markets." *Financial Analysts Journal* 44 (1988), pp. 76–78.

Errunza, Vihang R.; and Barr Rosenberg. "Investment Risk in Developed and Less Developed Countries." *Journal of Financial and Quantitative Analysis* 17 (1982), pp. 741–762.

Errunza, Vihang; and Etienne Losq. "How Risky Are Emerging Markets," *Journal of Portfolio Management*, 1987, v14(1), 62–67.

Espana, Juan R. "The Mexican Peso Crisis: Impact on NAFTA And Emerging Markets," *Business Economics*, 1995, v30(3), 45–49.

Faber, Marc. "Life Cycles of Emerging Markets: There's a Time to Buy and a Time to Sell." *Barron's* 72 (July 13, 1992), pp. 20–22, 64.

Fager, Gregory B. "Financial Flows To The Major Emerging Markets In Asia," *Business Economics*, 1994, v29(2), 21–27.

Ferris, Stephen P.; G. Rodney Thompson; and Calin Valsan. "Foreign Direct Investment In An Emerging Market Economy," *Eastern European Economics*, 1994, v32(4), 81–95.

Ferson, Wayne E.; and Campbell R. Harvey. "The Risk and Predictability of International Equity Returns." *The Review of Financial Studies* 6, no. 3 (1993), pp. 527–566.

Ferson, Wayne E.; and Campbell R. Harvey. "Sources of Risk and Expected Returns in Global Equity Markets." *Journal of Banking and Finance* 18 (1994), forthcoming.

Fraga, Javier Gonzalez. "The Impact of Inflation on Securities Markets." *Capital Markets Under Inflation*, ed. Nicholas Bruck. Buenos Aires: Stock Exchange of Buenos Aires, Argentina, 1982.

Fraser, K. Michael. "A Market-by-Market Guide." *Global Finance* 6 (April 1992), pp. 50–63.

French, Kenneth R.; and James M. Poterba. "Investor Diversification and International Equity Markets." *American Economic Review* 31, no. 2 (May 1991), pp. 222–226.

Fritz, R. G. "Time Series Evidence of the Causal Relationship Between Financial Deepening and Economic Development." *Journal of Economic Development*, July 1984, pp. 91–111.

Gatzonas, E. K.; and Michael G. Papaioannou. "Premium/Discount Determinants of Emerging Market Closed-End Funds," *The Journal of Investing*, forthcoming.

Genesis Investment Management Ltd. *How to Develop a Stock Market: Preconditions for Portfolio Investment in Eastern Europe*. London: Genesis Investment Management Ltd., October 1991.

Giarraputo, Joseph. "Cavallo on Argentina: A Model for Emerging Markets." *Global Finance* 6 (July 1992), pp. 61–62.

Gill, David; and Peter Tropper. "Emerging Stock Markets in Developing Countries." *Finance and Development*, December 1988.

Glaessner, Thomas; and Daniel Oks. "NAFTA, Capital Mobility and Mexico's Financial System." Unpublished working paper, World Bank, January 1994.

Goldsbrough, David; and Ranjit Teja. *Globalization of Financial Markets and Implications for Pacific Basin Developing Countries*. Washington, D.C.: International Monetary Fund, 1991.

Gooptu, Sudarshan. "Portfolio Investment Flows to Emerging Markets." Working paper, World Bank, 1992.

Harvey, Campbell R. "Conditional Asset Allocation in Emerging Markets." NBER Working Paper #4623, January 1994.

—. "Predictable Risk and Returns in Emerging Markets." *Review of Financial Studies*, 1995, 8(3), 773–816.

—. "Portfolio Enhancement Using Emerging Markets and Conditioning Information." In *Portfolio Investment in Developing Countries*, Stijn, CLAESSENS and Sudarshan GOOPTU, eds., World Bank Discussion Papers No. 228, 1993, pp. 110–144.

—. "The Risk Exposure of Emerging Equity Markets." *World Bank Economic Review*, 1994, forthcoming.

—. "The World Price of Covariance Risk." *Journal of Finance* 46 (March 1991), pp. 111–157.

Harvey, C. R.; and G. Zhou. "International Asset Pricing With Alternative Distributional Specifications." *Journal of Empirical Finance* 1, no. 1 (June 1993), pp. 107–131.

Hauser, Shmuel; Matityahu Marcus; and Uzi Yaari. "Investing In Emerging Stock markets: Is It Worthwhile Hedging Foreign Exchange Risk?," *Journal of Portfolio Management*, 1994, v20(3), 76–81.

Heston, Steven; and K. Geert Rouwenhorst. "Does Industrial Structure Explain the Benefits of International Diversification?" *Journal of Financial Economics* 36 (1994), pp. 3–27.

Ho, Joseph M. L. "Investment Flows: The Third Wave in Asia." *Benefits and Compensation International* (U.K.), July/August 1990, pp. 23–28.

Ho, Y. K.; Y. L. Cheung; P. Draper; and P. Pope. "Return Volatilities And Trading Activities On An Emerging Asian Market," *Economics Letters*, 1992, v39(1), 91–94.

Ho, Yan-Ki; and Yan-Leung Cheung. "Behavior Of Intra-Daily Stock Return On An Asian Emerging Market—Hong Kong," *Applied Economics*, 1991, v23(5), 957–966.

Ho, Richard Yan-Ki; Yan-Leung Cheung; and Daniel W. W. Cheung. "Intraday Prices and Trading Volume Relationship in an Emerging Asian Market—Hong Kong." *Pacific-Basin Finance Journal* 1, no. 2 (May 1993), pp. 203–214.

Holland, Kelly; and William Glasgall. "Whiplash in Emerging Markets." *Business Week*, May 2, 1994, pp. 116–117.

Hossain, Mahmud; Lin Mei Tan; and Mike Adams. "Voluntary Disclosure In An Emerging Capital Market: Some Emperical Evidence From Companies listed On The Kuala Lumpur Stock Exchange," *International Journal of Accounting*, 1994, v29(4), 334–351.

How, Janice C. Y.; and Joy G. Low. "Fractional Ownership and Underpricing: Signals of IPO Firm Value?" *Pacific-Basin Finance Journal* 1, no. 1 (March 1993), pp. 47–65.

How, Janice C. Y.; and Joy G. Low. "International Portfolio Diversification: A Multivariate Analysis for a Group of Latin American Countries." *Journal of Finance*, June 1973, pp. 619–633.

How, Janice C. Y.; and Joy G. Low. "World, Country and Industry Relationships and Equity Returns: Implications for Risk Reduction Through International Diversifications." *Financial Analysts Journal*, January/February 1976, pp. 2–8.

Hung, Bill Wan-Sing; and Yan-Leung Cheung. "Interdependence Of Asian Emerging Equity Markets," *Journal of Business Finance And Accounting*, 1995, v22(2), 281–288.

Kodrzycki, Yolanda K. "Tax Reform In Newly Emerging Market Economies," *FRB New England—Economic Review*, 1993, v1993(6), 3–17.

Khambata, Farida; and Dara Khambata. "Emerging Capital markets: A Case Study Of Equity Markets In India," *Journal of Developing Areas*, 1989, v23(3), 425–438.

Kaurz, Leslie B.; Howard D. Perlaw; and George Sands. "Emerging Markets: A Framework For Institutional Investment," *Journal of Investing*, 1993, v1(3), 41–50.

Lessard, Donald R. "International Portfolio Diversification: A Multivariate Analysis for a Group of Latin American Countries." *Journal of Finance*, 1973, pp. 619–633.

Loudon, G. F. "Foreign Exchange Exposure and the Pricing of Currency Risk in Equity Returns: Some Australian Evidence." *Pacific-Basin Finance Journal* 1, no. 4 (December 1993), pp. 335–354.

Loughran, Tim; Jay R. Ritter; and Kristian Rydqvist. "Initial Public Offerings: International Insights." *Pacific-Basin Finance Journal* 2 (1994), pp. 165–199.

MacDonald, Scott B. "Quiet Revolution Explodes: Latin America's Stock Markets." *North South: The Magazine of the Americas* (U.S.), August–September 1991, pp. 42–47.

Maisonneuve, Virginia. "China: The New International Equities Market." *The Journal of Investing* 3, no. 3 (Fall 1994), pp. 95–8.

Malhotra, R. N. "Capital Market Development." *Reserve Bank of India Bulletin* 44 (December 1990), pp. 977–981.

Marcuse, Robert. "Access of Latin American Countries to the International Capital Markets." *World of Banking* (U.S.) 1 (March 1991), pp. 11–20.

Meier, John. "A Comparison of Emerging Markets Benchmarks." *The Journal of Investing*, Summer 1994, pp. 58–62.

Melvin, M.; and B. Peiers. "On the Possibility of a Yen Currency Bloc for Pacific-Basin Countries: A Stochastic Dominance Approach." *Pacific-Basin Finance Journal* 1, no. 4 (December 1993), pp. 309–333.

Miller, Gregory P.; and Robert Y. K. Cheung. "Asian Investment Guide 1991." *Asian Business* (H.K.) 27 (January 1991), pp. 49–94.

Miller, Merton. "The Economics and Politics of Index Arbitrage in the U.S. and Japan." *Pacific-Basin Finance Journal* 1, no. 1 (March 1993), pp. 3–11.

Modigliani, Franco. "Long-Term Financing in an Inflationary Environment." *Pacific-Basin Finance Journal* 1, no. 2 (May 1993), pp. 99–104.

Montagu-Pollock, Matthey. "Investment Trusts: Low Cost, High Gain; The Country Fund Gamble." *Asian Business* 28 (January 1992), pp. 94–99.

Mookerjee, R. "An Empirical Investigation Of Corporate Dividend Pay-Out Behaviour In An Emerging market," *Applied Financial Economics*, 1992, v2(4), 243–246.

Mullin, John. "Emerging Equity Markets in the Global Economy." *FRBNY Quarterly Review*, Summer 1993, pp. 54–83.

Morgan Stanley Capital International. *Perspective.* New York: Morgan Stanley, monthly and quarterly.

Mougoue, Mbodja. "Common Stochastic Trends In Exchange Rate Systems: Empirical Evidence From Four Emerging Markets," *Journal of International Financial Management, Institutions and Markets*, 1992, v2(2), 27–50.

Nayar, N. "Asymmetric Information, Voluntary Ratings and the Rating Agency of Malaysia." *Pacific-Basin Finance Journal* 1, no. 4 (December 1993), pp. 369–380.

Neofutistos, George; and Michael G. Papaioannou. "Modeling the Volatility of Prices of Shares Traded at the Athens Stock Exchange," mimeographed, Bank of Greece, October 1994.

O'Connor, Selina; and David Smith. *The GT Guide to World Equity Markets.* London: Euromoney Publications, 1991.

Oppong, Andrews. "Price-Earnings Research And The Emerging Capital Markets: The Case of Zimbabwe," *International Journal of Accounting,* 1993, v28(1), 71–77.

Oyhenart, Marta. "Equity Market Privatization: Sustained Growth in Developing Countries." *Privatization Review* 6 (Spring 1991), pp. 34–44.

Papaioannou, Michael G.; and Lawrence K. Duke. "The Internationalization of Emerging Equity Markets," *Finance and Development,* Vol. 30, No. 3, September 1993, pp. 36–39.

Papaioannou, Michael G.; and E. K. Gatzonas. "Financial Innovations Involving the Greek Drackma," mimeographed, Bank of Greece, 1995.

Papaioannou, Michael G.; and George Neofotistos. "Aspects of Derivatives Pricing: Forwards, Futures, and Options," mimeographed, Bank of Greece, January 1995.

Pardy, Robert. "Institutional Reform in Emerging Securities Markets." Working paper, World Bank, Washington, D.C, May 1992.

Park, K. H; and Antoine van Agtmael. *The World's Emerging Stock Markets.* Probus Publishing Company.

Parry, Robert, "Liberalization and Development of Asia's Financial Markets." *Journal of Asian Economics* (U.S.) 2 (Spring 1991), pp. 1–7.

Pearson, Peter. "Foreign Investment Funds from an International Investor's Viewpoint: Commentator Remarks." *Capital Market Development in the Asia-Pacific Region.* Philippines: Asian Development Bank, 1986.

Peavy, John W., ed. *Managing Emerging Markets Portfolios.* Association for Investment Management and Research, 1994.

Pilling, David. "Chile's Markets Come of Age." *Euromoney,* September 1993, pp. 323–328.

Pyo, Hak K. "Export-led Growth, Domestic Distortions, and Trade Liberalization: The Korean Experience during the 1980's." *Journal of Asian Economics* (U.S.) 1 (Fall 1990), pp. 225–47.

Reiss, Frank. "To Be, or Not to Be, an Emerging Market." *Trade Finance* (U.K.) 113 (September 1992), pp. 58–59.

Ribnikar, Ivan. "The Financial System Of A Small, Emerging Market Economy," *International Review of Financial Analysis,* 1994, v3(2), 137–148.

Ring, Trudy; and Marlene Givant Star. "Emerging Markets: Smorgasbord of Countries Tempts Investors." *Pensions & Investments* 19 (March 4, 1991), pp. 21–22, 25.

Rogers, John H. "Entry Barriers And Price Movements Between Major And Emerging Stock Markets," *Journal of Macroeconomics,* 1994, v16(2), 221–241.

Rosenburg, Sharon Harvey. "Mining Emerging Markets." *Institutional Investor* 26 (June 1992), pp. 133–134.

Rudd, Andrew. "International Investing: The Case for Emerging Markets." In *Global Portfolios: Quantitative Strategies for Maximum Performance,* eds. Robert Z. Aliber and Brian R. Bruce. Homewood, IL: Business One Irwin, 1991.

Rybczynski, T. M. "The Internationalization of Finance and Business." *Business Economics*, July 1988.

—. *The Internationalization of the Financial System and the Developing Countries: The Evolving Relationship*. World Bank Staff Working Paper 788. Washington, D.C.: World Bank, 1986.

Sametz, Arnold W. *Financial Development and Economic Growth: The Consequences of Underdeveloped Capital Markets*. New York: New York University Press, 1972.

Samuels, J. M.; and N. Yacout. "Stock Exchanges in Developing Countries." *Savings and Development* 4 (1981), pp. 217–230.

Sewell, Susan P.; Stanley R. Stansell; Insup Lee; and Ming-Shiun Pan. "Nonlinearities In Emerging Foreign Capital Markets," *Journal of Business Finance and Accounting*, 1993, v20(2), 237–248.

Shaw, Edward S. *Financial Deepening in Economic Development*. New York: Oxford University Press, 1973.

Solnik, R. "The Advantages of Domestic and International Diversification." In *International Capital Markets*, eds. E. J. Elton and M. J. Gruber, pp. 165–76. Amsterdam: North-Holland, 1975.

—. "The Performance of International Asset Allocation Strategies Using Conditioning Information." *Journal of Empirical Finance* 1, no. 1 (June 1993), pp. 33–55.

Sollinger, Andrew. "The Emerging-Markets Morass." *Institutional Investor* 26 (January 1992), pp. 215–216.

Speidell, Lawrence S. "The Frontier of Emerging Markets: Russia and China." *Journal of Investing* 1 (Summer 1992), pp. 7–12.

Speidell, Lawrence S.; and Ross Sappenfield. "Global Diversification in a Shrinking World." *Journal of Portfolio Management* 19 (Fall 1992), pp. 57–67.

Stone, Douglas. "The Emerging Markets and Strategic Asset Allocation." *Journal of Investing* 1 (Summer 1992), pp. 40–45.

Stulz, R. "On the Effects of Barriers to International Investment." *Journal of Finance* 36 (September 1981), pp. 923–934.

Stulz, René M. "International Portfolio Choice and Asset Pricing: An Integrative Survey." NBER Working Paper #4645, February 1994.

Subrahmanyam, Marti G. "On the Optimality of International Capital Market Integration." *Journal of Financial Economics* 2 (March 1975), pp. 3–28.

Sudweeks, Bryan L. "The Emerging Importance of Asset Allocation." *Capital Horizons*, November 1991, pp. 8–9.

Sudweeks, Bryan L.; and Alex Anckonie. "Portfolio Implications of Investing in Developing Countries." Paper presented to the Academy of International Business Conference, Chicago, November 1986.

Sudweeks, Bryan L.; and Alex Anckonie. *Equity Market Development in Developing Countries*. New York: Greenwood Press, 1989.

Sudweeks, Bryan L.; and Phillip Grub. "Securities Markets and the People's Republic of China." *Journal of Economic Development* 13 (June 1988), pp. 51–69.

Tam, On Kit. "Capital Market Development in China." *World Development* (U.K.) 19 (May 1991), pp. 511–32.

Tandon, Pankaj. "Mexico: Background, Telmex, Aeromexico, Mexicana." mimoeographed, World Bank, June 1992.

Tarumizu, Kimimasa. "Fostering Investor Confidence in the Asian and Pacific Capital Markets." *Pacific-Basin Finance Journal* 1, no. 2 (May 1993), pp. 105–110.

Terpstra, Robert H.; and Dennis K. K. Fan. "Dispersion of Financial Analysts' Forecasts of Earnings per Share and Trading Volume: The Hong Kong Experience." *Pacific-Basin Finance Journal* 1, no. 3 (September 1993), pp. 277–285.

Torres, Craig. "Latin American Firms Break With Past, Scramble to be Listed on U.S. Exchanges." *The Wall Street Journal*, September 28, 1993, p. C1.

Urrutia, Jorge L. "Tests Of Random Walk And Market Efficiency For Latin American Emerging Equity Markets," *Journal of Financial Research*, 1995, v18(3), 299–309.

Vittas, Dimitri. "Contractual Savings and Emerging Securities Markets." Washington, D.C.: World Bank, February 1992.

Waddell, S. J. "Emerging Social-Economic Institutions In The Venture Capital Industry," *American Journal Of Economics and Sociology*, 1995, v54(3), 323–338.

Walter, Ingo. "Emerging Equity Markets: Tapping into Global Investment Flows." New York University Stem School of Business Finance Department. Working Paper Series FD-/93–58, 1993.

Westlake, Melvyn. "Emerging Equity Markets: Who's Next for the Big League? Guide to Developing Markets." *Euromoney*, December 1990, pp. 42–51.

Wheatley, Simon. "Some Tests of International Equity Integration." *Journal of Financial Economics* 21 (1988), pp. 177–212.

Wilcox, Jarrod W. "Global Investing in Emerging Markets." *Financial Analysts Journal* 48 (January/February 1992), pp. 5–19.

—. "Taming Frontier Markets." *Journal of Portfolio Management* 19 (Fall 1992), pp. 51–55.

Wong, Kie Ann; Tak Kee Hui; and Choy Yin Chen. "Day-of-the-Week Effects: Evidence from Developing Stock Markets." *Applied Financial Economics* (U.K.) 2 (March 1992), pp. 49–56.

World Bank, Country Economics Department. *Privatization: The Lessons of Experience.*

World Bank, Debt and International Finance Division. *Financial Flows to Developing Countries*, Quarterly Review, July 1993.

World Bank, Economic Development Institute, EDI Seminar Series. *Financial Sector Reforms in Asian and Latin American Countries*, July 1993.

Yau, J. "The Performance of the Hong Kong Hang Seng Index Futures Contract in Risk-Return Management." *Pacific-Basin Finance Journal* 1, no. 4 (December 1993), pp. 381–406.

INDEX